ENGLISH WAYFARING LIFE
IN THE MIDDLE AGES

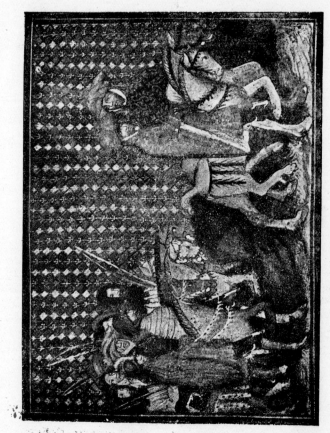

ENGLISH KNIGHTS TRAVELLING, AUGUST, 1399.

(From the MS. Harleian, 1319, painted circa A.D. 1400.)

ENGLISH
WAYFARING LIFE
IN THE MIDDLE AGES
(XIVth CENTURY)

BY

J. J. JUSSERAND

TRANSLATED FROM THE FRENCH BY

LUCY TOULMIN SMITH

A new Edition revised and enlarged by the Author

T. FISHER UNWIN LTD
LONDON : ADELPHI TERRACE

First Edition *1889*
Second Impression *1889*
Third Impression *1889*
Fourth Impresssion *1891*
Fifth Impression *1895*
Sixth Impression *1899*
Seventh Impression *1901*
Eighth Impression *1902*
Ninth Impression. *1909*
Second Edition (*Tenth Impression*) . *1920*
Eleventh Impression *1921*
Third Edition (*Twelfth Impression*) *1925*

WE know Egypt, thanks to her tombs, and we know Rome, thanks to Pompeii, in these modern days, better than we know the Middle Ages of Europe and the life of an ordinary man during that period. We cannot hope to find in any corner of France or England a Pompeii, catacombs, or pyramids. In our countries the human torrent has never ceased flowing; rapid and tumultuous in its course, it has at no time ensured the preservation of the past by deposits of quiet ooze.

Yet, this common life of our ancestors, is it indiscernible, impossible to reconstruct? is that of kings and princes alone accessible to our view through the remoteness of ages, like those huge monuments which men see from afar when they cannot distinguish the houses in a distant city? Surely not. But to reach the heart of the nation, to get into touch with the greater number, a patient and extended inquiry is necessary. To make this usefully, one must break more or less completely with the old habit of taking the ideas of every-day life in the Middle Ages only from the descriptions, the satires, or the eulogies of poets. Literature is no doubt of valuable help in these restorations, but it is not the only, nor even the principal source of information. Poets embellish, imagine, colour, or transform; we must not accept their statements without checking them.

To check them is what we can do. We may have no such

7

burial grounds to explore as in Egypt, nor a whole town to bring to light as at Pompeii, but we have what is worth almost as much : the incomparable depositories of the Records of old England. Immense strides have been made, especially within the last hundred years, to render their contents public. Thousands of documents have been printed or analysed, and the work is still continuing ; indeed, looking at the progress made of late, a feeling of wonder cannot be repressed at the premature alarm of historians like Robertson, who wrote in 1769 : " The universal progress of science during the two last centuries, the art of printing, and other obvious causes, have filled Europe with such a multiplicity of histories, and with such a vast collection of historical materials, that the term of human life is too short for the study or even the perusal of them." The field of research has never ceased to widen, while the boundaries of human life scarcely recede at all ; but students comprehend that the best means of rendering service is to impose limits on themselves and to study by preference separate points or periods of the immense problem to the best of their power. The work of unearthing is so far advanced that it is possible usefully to sift the riches drawn from these new catacombs.

At first sight all these petitions, these year-books full of reports of lawsuits, these long rows of statutes and ordinances seem the coldest things in the world, the most devoid of life. They are not even mummies or skeletons, they look as if they were but the dust of old bones. Yet to judge of them thus were to judge in a superficial manner ; no doubt it might seem pleasanter to keep to the descriptions of tale-tellers ; but how many chances of error do they not present ! With the year-books, and the petitions followed by inquiries, we are on distinctly more solid ground ; we soon grow accustomed to their language, and, under the apparently cold dust, sparks of life appear, we can then with little effort restore scenes, understand existences, perceive the distant echo of imprecations or shouts of triumph.

It was with this thought that the present work was under-

taken a good many years ago. In it there is a little less
mention of Chaucer and a little more of the "Rolls of Parliament" than is sometimes found in the works devoted to
the same period; this does not arise from want of admiration for the great man, far from it, but from the need of a
test and of means of control, which may perhaps be deemed
legitimate, and only increase, in the end, our sentiment for
him. The present writer has desired to confine himself in
this work within strict limits; one only of the many sides of
the common life in the fourteenth century is here studied, a
side little enough known and sometimes difficult to observe,
namely, the character and the quality of the chief kinds of
nomadic existence then carried on in England. And even in
that reduced compass he is very far from making claim to
completeness; so that this work is presented to the public
more as a sketch than a treatise.

In the remodelling of his text, which had appeared as
a French book in 1884 and as articles in English some years
earlier, the author has been assisted, he need hardly say, by
his learned translator, to whom he owes much for having
assumed the task of turning into English a work which she
herself would have been so well qualified to write. He has
been helped too by friends, all of whom he does not mean to
name here. But though feeling that in this also his incomplete-
ness will be very apparent, he cannot deprive himself of the
pleasure of inscribing on this page with gratitude and affection
the names of Gaston Paris, of the Institute of France; of
E. Maunde Thompson, Principal Librarian of the British
Museum; of F. J. Furnivall, Director of the Chaucer and many
other Societies; lastly, he ought, perhaps, to have said firstly,
of the poet and critic, Edmund Gosse, to whose kind initiative
and suggestion he owes it that his book is published under its
present form.

J.

Albert Gate,
    July 7th, 1889

*At the time of " les longs espoirs et les vastes pensées,"
so far back that I have but a hazy recollection of him, the young
author of these pages had formed so bold a plan that he kept
it to himself, which was to write, if a long life were granted
him, a complete description of the English people, during
it is true a single century, the fourteenth, that period,
of unique interest, when, after long years of probation, it
became certain that England would be English and nothing
else, when the language was formed, the first masterpieces
were written, the chief traits of the national character
became permanent, the principal institutions were founded,
and even a first attempt at Reformation was launched.*

*Old Barthélemy Saint Hilaire, the indefatigable trans-
lator of Aristotle, used to say to me when he was our
Foreign Minister : one must select, early in life, a vast
intellectual task, that will be like a literary companion, a
long-lived one, which you can never lose, because it is sure
to outlive you. The author of this study thought the ampler
work would be his literary companion.*

*But his official duties thereupon became more exacting,
and as they had a first claim, he had to part with his companion,
whom, as will happen in life's pilgrimage, others replaced
at later stages of the journey. He desired, however, that
some trace be left of an early comradeship : hence the present
essay, illustrated in part from his pen-and-ink sketches, also
a token of comradeship.*

*The need of this new issue has supplied the occasion for
a revision of the text, with numerous corrections and additions, written in a land unsuspected by the best-travelled
of the ever-moving heroes of these pages, written too at a time
when the Hundred years war of Chaucerian days has been
replaced by a Hundred years peace, and when great deeds
performed in common are, if we and our successors prove in
any way worthy of our dead, the harbingers of a friendship
not to be broken between France, England and America.*

WASHINGTON, 1920.   J.

CONTENTS

PART I

ENGLISH ROADS

PART II

LAY WAYFARERS

PART III

RELIGIOUS WAYFARERS

ILLUSTRATIONS

This MS. contains a chronicle of the last years of Richard II, written in his native tongue by a French gentleman called Créton, who accompanied the king in his last journey to Ireland. It is invaluable both for its text and its pictures ; in both the author seems to have been very careful to adhere to facts. He begins writing in verse, but afterwards takes to prose, stating that he is coming now to events of such importance that he prefers using prose, to make sure that he shall not allow himself to be led by fancy.

He must have himself superintended the painting with the greatest care. There can be no doubt that the figures are actual portraits ; of this there are two proofs : first, when the same person appears in several paintings he is always given the same features, and can be easily recognized ; second, the exact resemblance of one of the persons can be put beyond a doubt, which makes it likely that the others also resemble their originals. Richard II, the image of whom constantly recurs in the pictures, is easily recognizable as having the same features as in the bronze statue over his tomb at Westminster. And we know for certain that this tomb and statue were ordered by Richard himself during his lifetime ; the indenture with the seals attached, dated 18 Rich. II (1395), and binding two apparently English artists, viz., " Nicholas Broker et Godfrey Prest, citeins et copersmythes de Loundres," is still in existence at the Record Office.

The sitting of the parliament here represented is the famous one when Richard was deposed, and Henry of Lancaster came

forth to " chalenge yis Rewme of Yngland " (" Rolls of Parliament," iii. p. 422), Oct. 1399, and the throne was then, as
seen in the painting, left unoccupied, " sede regali cum pannis
auri solempniter preparata, tunc vacua," " Rolls," ibid.   On
the right of the throne are seated the spiritual lords ; on the
left the temporal lords, knights, &c.   The nearest to the throne
on the left is Henry of Lancaster (wearing a tall fur cap).   Says
Créton :

> " Entour le dit siége asez près
> Estoient les prélas assis . . .
> D'autre costé tous les seigneurs,
> Grans moyens petiz et meneurs (lesser ones) . . .
> Premiers seoit le duc Henry
> Et puis tout au plus près de ly
> Le duc Diore (York) son beau cousin," &c.   .   87

> " And he hadde ben somtyme in chivachie,
> In Flaundres, in Artoys, and in Picardie,
> And born him wel, as of so litel space,
> In hope to stonden in his lady grace.
> Embrowdid was he, as it were a mede
> Al ful of fressh floures, white and reede,
> Syngynge he was, or flowtynge al the day ;
> He was as fressh as is the moneth of May."

21–22. Ladies on horseback. Two drawings illustrative of both
ways of riding; sitting sideways : Chaucer's prioresse, and
riding astride : Chaucer's Wife of Bath. From the Ellesmere
MS. 105

23. A family dinner. From the MS. Addit. 28162, in the British
Museum, fol. 10 *b*, early fourteenth century ; French. Note
the carver, the cup-bearer, the musicians, the marshal of the
hall, whose mission it is to expel objectionable intruders,
whether men or dogs. In the present case, while this officer
is expelling a very objectionable lazar, come under pretence of
sprinkling the diners with holy water, a little further a dog
seizes his opportunity, and gets hold of a fish on the table. The
carver grasps the meat with his left hand ; forks then were
unknown, but good breeding was, nevertheless, not neglected,
and it consisted in the server's touching the meat only with
the *left* hand. Writing later than the time we speak of, John
Russell, marshal of the hall to Duke Humphrey of Gloucester
(fifteenth century), adds one refinement more, that is to use only
three fingers of the left hand. This was, in his mind, the acme
of fine breeding :

> " Sett never on fysche nor flesche, nor fowle trewly,
> Moore than ij fyngurs and a thombe, for that is curtesie.
> Touche never with youre right hande no maner mete surely."
>   " Boke of Nurture " (Furnivall, 1868, p. 137).

It may be seen from our picture that part of these niceties
was unknown yet to carvers in the first half of the fourteenth
century. The whole of the left hand is used to grasp the meat   109

24.

> " A cooke thei hadde . . .
> To boyle chiknes and the mary bones."

From the illumination in the Ellesmere MS. of the " Canterbury
Tales." The pot-hooks with three prongs, which he carries,
were the distinctive attribute of cooks and cookmaids, and appear
on all representations of such people : several are to be found
in the Louterell psalter ; see " Vetusta Monumenta," vol. vi.,
the Roy. MS. 10 E. IV., *passim*, &c. They used it to turn
the meat and take it out of the deep round-bellied pots, standing
on three legs over the fire, which were then in common use.   116

25. The new habits of luxury ; a gentleman, helped by two attend-
ants, dressing before the fire in his bedroom. From the MS.
2 B. vii., in the British Museum, fol. 72 *b*, English, early
fourteenth century   127
Of this luxury, of the spread of the use of chimneys, &c.,
Langland, as a satirist, complains ; and this, as a marshal of the
hall, John Russell a little later recommends as the proper method

of dressing for a gentleman. He then thus addresses the attendant :

"Than knele down on youre kne, and thus to youre soverayn ye say :
'Syr, what robe or govn pleseth it yow to were today?'" &c.
        "Boke of Nurture" (Furnivall, 1868, p. 178).

THE THREE-BRANCHED BRIDGE AT CROWLAND.

English Wayfaring Life in the Middle Ages (Fourteenth Century)

INTRODUCTION

> " O, dist Spadassin, voici un bon resveux,
> mais allons nous cacher au coin de la cheminée et
> là passons avec les dames nostre vie et nostre temps
> à enfiler des perles ou à filer comme Sardanapalus.
> Qui ne s'adventure n'a cheval ni mule, ce dist
> Salomon."
>
> VIE DE GARGANTUA.

AT the present day there are but few wayfarers.
The small trades plyed along the road, in
every chance village, are disappearing before our
newer methods of wholesale manufacture ; more and
more rarely do we see the pedlar unstrap his pack at the
farm door, the travelling cobbler mend by the wayside
the shoes which on Sunday will replace the wooden clogs,
or hear the wandering musician drone at the windows
his oft rehearsed tunes. Professional pilgrims exist no
longer, even quack doctors are losing their credit. It
was far otherwise in the Middle Ages ; many people
were bound to a wandering existence, and started even
from childhood on their life-long journey. Some trotted
their strange industries in the broad sunshine, through the
dust of the highroads ; others skulked in bye-lanes or

even in coppices, hiding their heads from the sheriff's officer—may be a criminal, may be a fugitive, " a wolf's head that any one may cut down," according to the terrible expression of an English jurist of the thirteenth century. Among these, many labourers who had broken the villeins bond, unhappy and oppressed in their hamlets, and who wandered through the country in quest of work, as though flight could enfranchise them : but " service est en le sank " (" service is in the blood "), the magistrate warned them.[1] Among them also, pedlars laden with petty wares ; pilgrims who from St. Thomas' to St. James' went begging along the roads, living by alms ; pardoners, those strange nomads, who sold to the common people the merits of the saints in paradise ; mendicant friars and preachers of all sorts who, according to the times, delivered ardently liberal harangues or contemptibly selfish discourses at the church doors. All these had one character in common, namely, that in the wide extent of country where they passed their lives, ever on the move, they served as links between the separated groups of other men who, attached to the soil by law or custom, spent the whole of their days, irremovable, under the same sky, on the same ground, at the same toil.

Pursuing their singular work, these wanderers, who had seen and experienced so much, served to give some idea of the great unknown world to the humble classes whom they met on their way. Together with many false beliefs and fables they put into the heads of the stay-at-homes certain notions of extent and of active life which these would hardly otherwise have acquired ; above all, they brought to the land-bound men news of their brethren in the neighbouring province, of their condition of misery or of happiness, and these were pitied

[1] " Year Books," 30, 31 Edward I. Edited by A. J. Horwood, for the Rolls Series, 1863.

or envied accordingly, and remembered as brothers or friends to call upon in the day of revolt.

At a period when, for the mass of mankind, ideas were transmitted orally and travelled with these wanderers along the roads, the nomads served as a link between the human groups of various districts. It would be therefore of great interest for the historian to know what were these channels of the popular thought, what life was led by those who filled such a function, what were their influence and manners. We shall try to study the chief types of this race, and shall choose them in England in the fourteenth century, in a country and at an epoch when their social importance was considerable. The interest which attaches to them is of course manifold ; the personality of these pardoners, professional pilgrims, and minstrels, extinct species, is in itself curious to scrutinize ; but not more so than their state of mind and the mode in which they carried on their businesses, both reacting on the social condition of a great people which had just been formed and was acquiring the features and the character still its own at the present day. It was the period when, thanks to the French wars and the incessant embarrassments of royalty, the subjects of Edward III and of Richard II gained a parliament similar to that which we now see ; the period when, in religious life, the independence of the English spirit asserted itself through the reforms of Wyclif, the statutes for the clergy, and the protests of the Good Parliament ; when, in literature, Chaucer inaugurated the series of England's great poets, and instead of one more commonplace dream, Langland, like Dante, gave to his compatriots *Visions* ; when, in short, from noble to villein was felt a stir which led without excessive revolution to that true liberty for which we, the French, had long to envy our neighbours. This epoch is decisive in the history of the country. It will be seen that in all the great questions debated in the cloister, in the castle, or on the market-place, the part played by the wayfarers, though scarcely visible at times, was not insignificant.

We must first examine the place of the scene, afterwards the events that happened there ; see what were the roads, then what were the beings who frequented them.

PART I

ENGLISH ROADS

OLD LONDON BRIDGE.
(*From MS. Roy.* 16 *F*2 *in the British Museum.*)

CHAPTER I

ROADS AND BRIDGES

THE maintenance of roads and bridges in England was in the fourteenth century one of those general charges which weighed, like military service, on the whole of the nation. All landed proprietors were obliged, in theory, to watch over the good condition of the highways ; their tenants had to execute the repairs for them. The religious houses themselves, owners of property given in *frank almoigne*, that is to say, with a purely charitable object, were dispensed from every service and rent towards their benefactor, no other charge being usually left but that of saying prayers or giving alms for the repose of the donor's soul. It remained, however, for them to satisfy for public weal the *trinoda necessitas*, or triple obligation, which among other duties consisted in the repairing of bridges.[1]

[1] And possibly, in early times, of roads also ; see McKechnie, " Magna

There existed in England a very considerable network
of roads, the principal of which dated as far back as the
Roman times. The province of Britain had been one of
those where the greatest care had been bestowed upon the
military and commercial ways by the Roman emperors.
" The network of roads in the island," says Mommsen,
" which was uncommonly developed, and for which in
particular Hadrian did much in connection with the
building of his wall, was of course primarily subservient
to military ends ; but alongside of, and in part taking
precedence over the legionary camps, Londinium occu-
pies in that respect a place which brings clearly into view
its leading position in traffic." [1] In many places are
yet to be found remnants of the Roman highways, the
more important of which were called in Anglo-Saxon
times, and since, Watling Street, Erming Street, the Fosse,
and Ikenild Street. " These Roman ways in Britain
have frequently been continued as the publick roads, so
that where a Roman military way is wanting, the pre-
sumption is in favour of the present highroad, if that
be nearly in the same direction." [2] There are two reasons
for that permanence : the first is that the roads were
built by the Romans to supply needs which have not
ceased to be felt ; being cut, for instance, from London
to the north through York ; towards Cornwall along
the sea coast ; towards the Welsh mines, &c. ; the
second reason is the way in which they were built. " A
portion of the Fosse Road which remains at Rad-
stock, about ten miles south-west of Bath, and was
opened in February, 1881, showed the following
construction :

Carta," Glasgow, 1905, p. 353. On the *Trinoda* or *Trimoda Necessitas*,
see W. H. Stevenson, in the " English Historical Review," Oct. 1914.
    [1] " History of Rome," translated by W. P. Dickson, London, 1886,
book viii. chap. v.
    [2] J. Horsley, " Britannia Romana," London, 1732, p. 391.

" 1. Pavimentum, or foundation, fine earth, hard beaten in.

" 2. Statumen, or bed of the road, composed of large stones, sometimes mixed with mortar.

" 3. Ruderatio, or small stones well mixed with mortar.

" 4. Nucleus, formed by mixing lime, chalk, pounded brick or tile ; or gravel, sand, and lime mixed with clay.

" 5. Upon this was laid the surface of the paved road, technically called the *summum dorsum*." [1]

All Roman roads were not built with so much care and in such an enduring fashion ; they were, however, all of them substantial enough to resist for centuries, and they remained in use during the Middle Ages. Other roads besides were opened during that epoch to provide for new fortified towns and castles, and to satisfy the needs of great landowners, religious or otherwise.

The keeping of roads and bridges in repair, the latter included in the *trinoda necessitas*, was not considered as worldly, but rather as pious and meritorious work before God, of the same sort as visiting the sick or caring for the poor ; [2] men saw in them a true charity for a certain category of sufferers, namely, travellers ; this is why the clergy submitted to it. The pious character of this kind of

[1] H. M. Scarth, " Roman Britain," S.P.C.K., London, 1883, p. 121. Cf. T. Codrington, "Roman Roads in Britain," S.P.C.K., 1903.

[2] When Henry VIII gave the lands of the dissolved monastery of Christ Church to Canterbury Cathedral, he declared that he made this donation " in order that charity to the poor, the reparation of roads and bridges, and other pious offices of all kinds should multiply and spread afar." Elton, " Tenures of Kent," London, 1867, p. 21. The gift is made " in liberam, puram et perpetuam eleemosynam." This pious character was long continued : " As late as the period of the Commonwealth land and money devoted to the maintenance of bridges and causeys were definitely included among the charitable uses which were to be unaffected by the sequestration of Bishops' land and other ecclesiastical revenues." C. T. Flower, " Public Works in Mediæval Law," Selden Society, 1905, i. p. xxi. Much valuable information also in vol. ii., 1925.

labour may suffice to prove that the roads were not so safe
or in such a good state as has been sometimes maintained.[1]
The noblest outcome of the religious spirit prevalent in
the Middle Ages was that disinterested enthusiasm
which, as soon as some distress of humanity became
flagrant, created societies for help and rendered self-
denial popular. One of these distresses was seen, for
example, in the power of the infidel, and the Crusades
were the consequence. The forsaken condition of the
lowest classes in the towns was noticed in the thirteenth
century, and St. Francis sent for the consolation of the
neglected, those mendicant friars at first so justly popular,
and who so promptly fell into disrepute. After the same
fashion travellers were considered as sufferers deserving
pity, and help was given to them to please God. A
religious order with this end in view had been founded
in the twelfth century, that of the *Pontiff* brothers, or
makers of bridges (*pons*, bridge), which spread into several
countries of the Continent.[2] In France they built over
the Rhône the celebrated bridge of Avignon, which
yet preserves four arches of their construction ; and the
one at Pont St. Esprit, which is still in use, nineteen out
of its twenty-five arches dating from the years 1265 to
1309 when it was erected. To break the force of such
a current as that of the Rhône they built, near together,
piers of oblong form, ending in a sharp angle at the
two extremities of their axis,[3] and their masonry was

---

[1] Thorold Rogers, " History of Agriculture and Prices in England,"
Oxford, 1866, vol. i. p. 138.

[2] See " Recherches historiques sur les congrégations hospitalières des
frères pontifes," by M. Grégoire, late Bishop of Blois. Paris, 1818.

[3] This practice was inherited from the Roman builders, whose formu-
laries continued to be transcribed throughout the middle ages. See Victor
Mortet : " Un Formulaire du VIIIe siécle pour les fondations d'édifices
et de ponts d'après des sources d'origine antique," in " Bulletin monumental . . . de la Société française d'Archéologie," vol. 71, 1907, p. 443.
The brief chapter in the " Mappæ Clavicula " (still copied in the twelfth

THE OLD BRIDGE AT AVIGNON.

(*Twelfth Century; present state.*)

3

so solid that in many places the waters have respected
it to the present day, that is, for eight centuries. They
also had establishments on the banks of rivers, and
helped to cross them by boat. Their most memorable
accomplishment was, however, the replacing of the same
ferries and of short-lived, often dangerous timber bridges
by stone ones, the normal progression for river crossing
being, throughout ages, the ford, the ferry, the timber
bridge, the stone bridge. Laymen learnt the secret
of their art and in the thirteenth century began to take
their place. Bridges multiplied in France ; many still
exist, such, for example, as the fine fourteenth-century
bridge at Orthez, the two at Limoges, of the thirteenth
century, one of them with its chapel, the beautiful bridge
at Cahors, where even the machicolated turrets which
formerly served to defend it are still preserved, restored,
it is true, by the clever but strong hand of Viollet
Le Duc.[1]

In England, as in France, wooden bridges had in most
cases preceded stone ones. The former were built of oak,
like the one over the river Lune, in the city of Lancaster,
for which we find John of Gaunt writing to " monsire
Adam de Hoghton, nostre chief forestier de Wyresdale,"
to hand to John Ermyte of Singleton, who had actually
paid for them, one hundred and twenty oak trees from
the said forest of Wyresdale, " selected among the properest
and aptest, such as the said John will designate. And

century), entitled " De fabrica in aqua," recommends that, " Si fabricam
in aqua necesse fuerit erigere, facis arcam triangulam," *arca* meaning *caisson*.
In this we see, Mr. Mortet writes, " la disposition venue de l'antiquité, trans-
mise et maintenue au moyen-âge, de la forme prismatique triangulaire des
avant-becs des ponts " (p. 461). This characteristic was conspicuous, *e.g.*
in the Avignon and London bridges (see the picture, p. 45) as well as in the
famous Roman Pont du Gard.

1 On French mediæval bridges still in existence, their dates, modes of
construction, crosses and chapels, see C. Enlart, " Manuel d'Archéologie
Française," Paris, 1902, ff. vol. ii. p. 264.

mind not to fail to act thus, nor cause that the
before mentioned work be thereby delayed in any
way." [1]

There is no trace in England of establishments founded
by the Bridge Friars, but it is certain that there, as elsewhere, the works for constructing bridges and highways
had a pious character. To encourage the faithful to take
part in them, Richard de Kellawe, Bishop of Durham from
1311 to 1316, remitted part of the penance for their sins.
The registry of his episcopal chancery contains frequent
entries such as the following : " Memorandum . . .
his lordship grants forty days indulgence to all who will
draw from the treasure that God has given them valuable
and charitable aid towards the building and repair of
Botyton bridge." Forty days are allowed on another
occasion for help towards the bridge and the highroad
between Billingham and Norton,[2] and forty days for the

[1] May 17, 1373, original in French. " John of Gaunt's Register,"
ed. S. Armitage Smith, London, 1911, vol. ii. p. 179. The work was
apparently in progress in 1374, since we find, on the 15th of September
of that year, an order to deliver to the same " trois cheisnes covenables "
from Okeden forest. *Ibid.*, p. 240.

[2] " Ubi frequens habetur populi transitus." " Registrum Palatinum
Dunelmense," ed. Hardy, Rolls Series, 1875, vol. i. pp. 615, 641, A.D. 1314.
This was a quite usual practice. The popes, who had every reason to
be interested in the welfare of the great bridge at Avignon, published
numerous bulls granting indulgences and other spiritual favours to the
benefactors of the edifice. See " Bullaire des indulgences concédées avant
1431 à l'œuvre du Pont d'Avignon," published by the Marquis de Ripert-
Monclar, Paris, 1912. The work contains the Latin text of papal bulls
of 1281, 1290, 1343, 1353, 1366, 1371, 1397, 1430, 1431. The bull
of 1343, issued by Pope Clement VI, at Avignon, grants to givers " tres
annos et tres quadragenas," and, under certain conditions, a plenary indulgence at the time of death : " Siquis vero catholicus dictis fratribus . . .
secundum quantitatem substancie et qualitatem . . . de bonis sibi a Deo
collatis dederit vel transmiserit quoquo modo ad reparacionem dicti pontis,
. . . si talis infra annum . . . vere penitens ac confessus ab hac luce deces-
serit, volumus et gratia speciali concedimus quod ab omnibus peccatis suis
remaneat absolutus." As for those who should be so bold as to hamper
in any way the collections made by the brothers for their bridge, their
punishment would be nothing less than excommunication (p. 6).

THE VALENTRÉ BRIDGE AT CAHORS.

(Thirteenth Century; photographed by Mr. Enlart, director of the Trocadero Museum.)

[p. 37.

great road from Brotherton to Ferrybridge. The wording of this last decree is characteristic :

" To all those, &c. Persuaded that the minds of the faithful are more ready to attach themselves to *pious works* when they have received the salutary encouragement of fuller indulgences, trusting in the mercy of God Almighty and the merits and prayers of the glorious Virgin his Mother, of St. Peter, St. Paul, and of the most holy confessor Cuthbert our patron, and all saints, we remit forty days of the penances imposed on all our parishioners and others . . . sincerely contrite and shriven of their sins, who shall help by their charitable gifts, *or by their bodily labour*, in the building or in the maintenance of the causeway between Brotherton and Ferrybridge on which *a great many people pass.*" [1]

Causeways, owing to the abundance of marshy ground, since drained, were scarcely less needed than bridges and were also considered a meritorious work. A passage in Leland well shows what they consisted of, how much wanted, and what a proper object they were, for generous minded, pious benefactors : " This cawsey by Skipbridge towards Yorke hathe a nineteen small bridges on it for avoydinge and overpassynge carres cuming out of the mores thereby. One Blackeburne, that was twys maior of Yorke, made this cawsey and a nothar without one of the suburbs of Yorke. This Blakeburn hathe a solemne *obiit* in the Minstar of Yorke and a cantuari at Richemond." [2]

Municipal bodies, as well as gilds, those lay brotherhoods imbued with the religious spirit, took care also in many cases of roads and bridges. The Gild of the Holy Cross in Birmingham, founded under Richard II, did this, and their intervention was most valuable, as the

[1] " Registrum Palatinum Dunelmense," ed. Hardy, Rolls Series, 1875, vol. i. p. 507.
[2] " Itinerary," ed. L. T. Smith, vol. v. p. 144.

Commissioners of Edward VI remarked two centuries later. The gild then "mainteigned . . , and kept in good reparaciouns two greate stone bridges, and divers foule and daungerous high wayes, the charge whereof the towne of hitsellfe ys not hable to mainteign. So that the lacke thereof wilbe a greate noysaunce to the kinges ma^{ties} subjectes passing to and from the marches of Wales and an vtter ruyne to the same towne, being one of the fayrest and most proffittuble townes to the kinges highnesse in all the shyre." [1]

An example of municipal action can be found in the Ordinances of Worcester, prescribing that "the Brugge (bridge) may be overseyn at alle tymes for the surete of the cite. And that the reparacion of the saide Brugge be overloked by the chamberleyns every quarter." [2]

Whether Queen Mathilda (twelfth century) got wetted or not, as is supposed, on passing the ford of the river at Stratford-atte-Bow—that same village where afterwards the French was spoken at which old Chaucer smiled—certain it is that she thought she was doing a meritorious work in constructing two bridges there.[3] Several times repaired, Bow Bridge was still standing in 1839. The queen endowed her foundation, granting land and a water-mill to the Abbess of Barking with a perpetual charge thereon for the maintenance of the bridge and the neighbouring roadway. When the queen died, an abbey for men was founded at the same Stratford, close to the bridges, and the abbess hastened to transfer to the new monastery the property in the mill and the charge of the reparations. The abbot had them done at first,

[1] Certificates of Chantries, quoted in " English Gilds, the Original Ordinances from MSS. of the Fourteenth and Fifteenth Centuries," ed. Toulmin Smith. E. E. T. S., 1870, p. 249. Gilds in Rochester, Bristol, Ludlow, &c., did the same.
[2] Text of the time of Edward IV, but " copied from laws still older." " English Gilds," as above, pp. 374, 411.
[3] " Archæologia," vols. xxvii. p. 77 ; xxix. p. 380.

then wearied of it, and delegated the care of them to
one Godfrey Pratt. He had built this man a house
on the causeway beside the bridge, and paid him an
annual grant. For a long time Pratt carried out the
contract, " getting assistance," says an inquiry of Edward I,
" from some passers-by, but without often having recourse
to their aid." He also received alms from travellers, and
his affairs prospered. They prospered so well that the
abbot thought he would withdraw his pension ; Pratt
indemnified himself the best way he could. He set up
iron bars across the bridge and made all pay who passed
over, except the rich, for he prudently made exception
" for nobility ; he feared them and let them pass without
molesting them." The dispute only ended in the time

BOW BRIDGE AS IT STOOD BEFORE ITS DEMOLITION IN 1839.
(*From a print dated* 1831.)

of Edward II ; the abbot acknowledged his fault ;
resumed the charge of the bridge, and suppressed the
iron bars, the toll, and Godfrey Pratt himself.

This bridge, over which no doubt Chaucer must have
passed, was of stone, the arches were narrow and the
piers thick ; strong angular buttresses strengthened them
and broke the force of the current ; these formed at the
upper part a triangle or siding which served as a refuge
for foot-passengers, for the way was so narrow that a
cart sufficed to fill it. When it was pulled down in
1839, it was found that the method of construction
had been very simple. To ground the piers in the bed
of the river the masons had simply thrown down stones
and mortar till the level of the water had been reached.

It was remarked also that the ill-will of Pratt or the abbot
or their successors must have rendered the bridge almost
as dangerous at certain moments as the primitive ford.
The wheels of the vehicles had hollowed such deep ruts
in the stone and the horses' shoes had so worn the pavement
that an arch had been at one time pierced through.

No less striking as a case where pious motives caused
the building of a bridge is the contract of the thirteenth
century, by which Reginald de Rosels allowed Peter, Abbot
of Whitby, to erect a permanent bridge on the river Esk,
between his own and the convent's lands. He pledged
himself in that act to permit to all comers free access to
the bridge through his own property. "For which
concession the aforesaid Abbot and convent have absolved
in chapter all the ancestors of the same Reginald of all
fault and transgression they may have committed against
the church of Whiteby and have made them participant of
all the good works, alms, and prayers of the church of
Whiteby." [1] Numerous other examples of the same sort
might be quoted ; but it will be enough to add, as being
perhaps more characteristic of the times than all the rest,
the recommendations which Truth in the "Vision concerning Piers the Plowman" makes to the wealthy English
merchants, the number of whom had so largely increased
during the fourteenth century. Truth bids them to do
several works of charity, which he considers of the highest
importance for their salvation ; they ought, among other
things, to "amenden mesondieux," that is, hospitals for
sick people and for travellers ; to repair "wikked wayes,"
that is to say, bad roads ; and also

> "... brygges to-broke · by the heye weyes
> Amende in som manere wise."

---

[1] "Cartularium Abbathiæ de Whiteby," edited by J. C. Atkinson,
Durham, Surtees Society, 1881, vol. ii. p. 401. The original of the Rosels
contract is in Latin.

For this and for helping prisoners, poor scholars, etc., they will have no little recompense. When they are about to die St. Michael himself will be sent to drive away devils that they be not tormented by evil spirits in their last moments :

" And ich shal sende yow my-selve · seynt Michel myn Angel
That no devel shal yow dere · ne despeir in youre deyinge,
And sende youre soules · ther ich my-self dwelle." [1]

The pious character of the bridges was also shown by the chapels that stood on them. Bow Bridge was thus placed under the protection of St. Catherine. London Bridge had a chapel dedicated to St. Thomas of Canterbury ; [2] a roomy Gothic building of apsidal form, with high windows and wrought pinnacles, almost a church. A miniature in a manuscript, of which a reproduction on a reduced scale is given at the beginning of this chapter, shows it fixed on the middle pier, whilst along the parapet are houses with gabled roofs, whose storeys project and overhang the Thames.

This was a famous bridge. No Englishman of the Middle Ages, and even of the Renaissance, ever spoke but with pride of London Bridge ; it was the great national wonder ; until the middle of the eighteenth century it remained (with the exception of some small ones which have disappeared as well as the narrow waters that they crossed) [3] the only bridge of the capital. It had been commenced in 1176, on the site of an old wooden

[1] Skeat's edition, Text C, pas. x. l. 29, *et seq.*
[2] Most of the French ones were dedicated to St. Nicholas, patron of travellers.
[3] Fleet bridge outside Ludgate, Oldbourne (Holborn) bridge, both of stone. Fleet bridge had been repaired by the mayor, John Wels, in 1431, " for," says Stow, " on the coping is engraven Wels imbraced by Angels." " Survey of London," ed. Kingsford, Oxford, 1908, 2 vols., vol. i. p. 26. The " Survey " had appeared in 1598, and been reprinted, with important additions in 1603.

structure, dating back to Saxon times,[1] by Peter Colechurch, "priest and chaplain," who had already once repaired the wooden bridge. The whole nation was stirred by this great and useful enterprise ; the King, the citizens of London, the dwellers in the shires endowed the building with lands and sent money to hasten its completion. The list of donors was still to be seen in the sixteenth century, on "a table fayre written for posterity," [2] in the bridge chapel.

A little while before his death in 1205 another had taken the place of Peter Colechurch, then very old, as director of the works. King John, who was in France, struck with the beauty of the bridges of that country, and having heard of the magnificent bridge of Saintes which lasted till the middle of the nineteenth century, and which was approached by a Roman triumphal arch, chose, as successor to Colechurch, a Frenchman, called Isembert, "master of the Saintes schools" (1202). Isembert, who had given proof of his capacity in the bridges of La Rochelle and of Saintes,[3] set out with his assistants, furnished with a royal patent addressed to the mayor and inhabitants of London. John Lackland therein vaunted the skill of the master, a man, he said, "of both knowledge and honesty," and declared that the revenue arising from the houses that he would build upon the bridge should be consecrated for ever to the maintenance of an edifice "so necessary for you and for all those passing thereby." [4]

[1] "The earliest proof [of the existence of a timber bridge] is in the record of the drowning of a witch at 'Lundene brigce' in King Edgar's time." Kingsford, Stow's "Survey," as above, vol. ii. p. 273.

[2] Stow's "Survey," i. p. 23. Stow, who examined the accounts of the bridge wardens for the year 1506 (22 Hen. VII), found that the bridge expenses were at that time £815 17s. 2d.

[3] King John became personally acquainted with those works only at a later date, viz. June 1206, when he landed at La Rochelle. He visited Saintes in July and August, and made again some stay at La Rochelle in October and November before sailing back to England. See his *Itinerary* in "A Description of the Patent Rolls in the Tower," by Thomas Duffus Hardy, London, 1835.   [4] See Appendix I. p 425.

PART OF LONDON BRIDGE WITH THE DRAWBRIDGE AND NONE-SUCH HOUSE. [*p.* 45.

(*As it stood about* A.D. 1600.)

The bridge was finished in 1209, when four " worthy marchants of London " had become " principall maisters of that work." [1]   It was furnished with houses, a chapel, and defensive towers. It immediately became celebrated, and was the admiration of all England. The Scot, Sir David Lindesay, Earl of Crawford, having fallen out with Lord Welles, ambassador at the Scottish Court, a duel was decided on, and Lindesay chose London Bridge as the place of combat (1390). He crossed the length of the kingdom, supplied with a safe-conduct from King Richard II, and the duel solemnly came off at the place fixed in the presence of an immense concourse. The first shock was so violent that the lances were shivered, but the Scotchman remained immovable in his saddle. The people, fearing for the success of the English diplomat, shouted that his adversary was tied to his horse against all rules. Hearing this Lindesay, by way of reply, leapt lightly to the ground, with one bound returned to the saddle and, charging his adversary anew, overthrew and grievously wounded him. [2]

The houses built on the bridge were several storeys high ; they had cellars in the thickness of the piers. When the inhabitants needed water they lowered their buckets by ropes out of the windows and filled them in the Thames. Sometimes they helped with their ropes poor fellows whose boat had capsized : the arches were narrow, and it was not uncommon in the dark for a boat to strike against the piers and be dashed to pieces. The Duke of Norfolk and several others were saved in this manner in 1428, but some of their companions were drowned. At other times the inhabitants themselves had need of help, for it happened occasionally that the houses, badly repaired, leaned forward and fell in one

---

[1] Stow's " Survey." ed. Kingsford, I. p. 23.
[2] Ibid., same edition, I. 25 ; II. 274. " Chronicles of London Bridge," by an Antiquary [Richard Thomson], London, 1827, pp. 187–193.

block into the river.   A catastrophe of this kind took
place in 1481.

One of the twenty arches of the bridge, the thirteenth
from the City side, formed a drawbridge to allow boats to
pass,[1] and also to close the approach to the town ; this was
the obstacle which in 1553 hindered the insurgents led
by Sir Thomas Wyatt from entering London.   Beside
the movable arch rose a tower on the summit of which
the executioner long placed the heads of decapitated
criminals.   That of the Lord Chancellor, Sir Thomas
More, bled for a time on the end of a pike on this tower
before it was redeemed by Margaret Roper, the daughter
of the thinker who had written—" Utopia."

Travellers wondered at the gruesome sight.   " In
London," wrote Joseph Justus Scaliger, who visited
the city in 1566, " there ever were many heads on the
bridge. . . . I have seen there, as it were [masts]
of ships and at the top of them quarters of men's
corpses." [2]

In 1576, this tower of sombre memories was splendidly
reconstructed ; the new one, containing fine rooms,
flooded with light by innumerable windows, was entirely
of wood, carved and gilt, in the " paper worke " style
popular in Elizabeth's time, censured by steady Harrison.
It was called " None-such House."   The heads of the
" traitors," sometimes traitors, sometimes saints, were no
more to pollute a building so cheerful in aspect ; they
were placed on the next tower on the Southwark side.
Four years after this change, fashionable Lyly the

[1] As to the toll collected there from certain foreign merchants A.D.
1334, see " Liber Albus," ed. Riley, Introduction, p. l.

[2] " Scaligerana," under the word " Londres."   The editions I have
seen give " mers de navires," the true reading being certainly " mâts."   An
enlarged portion of Visscher's panoramic view of London, 1616, showing
the " Bridge Gate " towards Southwark, with numerous mast-like poles
and heads on the top of them, serves as a frontispiece for vol. iii. of my
" Literary History of the English People."

Euphuist ended one of his books with a triumphal praise of England, its products, its universities, its capital, adding: "Among all the straunge and beautiful showes, mee thinketh there is none so notable as the Bridge which crosseth the Theames, which is in manner of a continuall streete, well replenyshed with large and stately houses on both sides, and situate upon twentie arches, whereof each one is made of excellent free stone squared, euerye one of them being three-score foote in height, and full twentie in distaunce one from an other." [1]

The same arrangement prevailed in the case of important bridges in many countries. In Paris the "Notre Dame" bridge had the appearance of a street with sixty-eight houses built on it.[2] The bridge at Poissy [3] and others were of the same sort, the most famous of those which remain being the "Ponte Vecchio" in Florence.

Even at the time when Lyly praised London Bridge as deserving a place among the "straunge and beautiful

---

[1] "Euphues and his England," 1st ed. 1580; Arber's reprint, 1868, p. 434. See besides the large coloured drawing of about the year 1600 (also the sketch above, p. 45), in the third part of Harrison's "Description of England," edited by F. J. Furnivall for the New Shakspere Society, 1877; and Mr. Wheatley's notes on Norden's Map of London, 1593, in vol. i. p. lxxxix of the same work. Visitors coming to London never failed to notice the bridge as one of the curiosities of the town. Dunbar, the Scottish poet, in his "London," written in the early years of the sixteenth century, compliments the city on its beauties, and especially its bridge :

"Upon thy lusty brigge of pylers white
Been merchauntis full royall to behold."

The Greek Nicander Nucius of Corcyra, who visited England in 1545-6 writes in his note-book : "A certain very large bridge is built, affording a passage to those in the city to the opposite inhabited bank, supported by stone cemented arches, and having also houses and turrets upon it." "Travels of Nicander Nucius," Camden Society, 1841, p. 7.

[2] F. de Belleforset, "L'ancienne et grande cité de Paris," ed. Dufour, 1882, p. 274.

[3] See woodcuts in "Le livre des Ordonnances de la ville de Paris," published by Vérard, 1500, reproduced by Claudin, "Histoire de l'Imprimerie," 1900, vol. ii. pp. 498, 499.

showes " of the city, and Stow described it as " a worke•
verie rare," the structure was giving more and more
frequent signs of decay. Ben Jonson describes a little
later his Pennyboy senior as minding

> "A curtesie no more then London-bridge
> What arch was mended last." [1]

Upon which that sour-mouthed reformer of poetry,
and of bridges, William Gifford, observed in his day :
" Two hundred years have nearly elapsed since this was
written, and the observation still holds. This pernicious
structure has wasted more money in perpetual repairs than
would have sufficed to build a dozen safe and commodious
bridges, and cost the lives, perhaps, of as many thousand
people. This may seem little to those whom it concerns—
but there is blood on the city, and a heavy account is before
them. Had an alderman or a turtle been lost there, the
nuisance would have been long removed." [2]

Without specifying whether it was out of fear of
Gifford, or interest in the aldermanic turtle, or perhaps
some higher motives too, the proper authorities took
radical measures as to the bridge in the first part of the
nineteenth century. An attempt was first made to preserve
it with the houses taken down, and broad, solid arches
replacing the old ones in the centre of the stream ; it
had finally to be removed altogether. The present
bridge, built near the site of the old one, replaced
the " straunge and beautiful showe " of Lylyan days,
the " pernicious structure " of Giffordian ones, and was
opened to circulation in 1831, the expense having been
£1,458,311. It must now live five centuries more to
equal the longevity of its predecessor.

This had been, all its life long, an exceptional bridge,

---

[1] " Staple of News," ii. 4 ; acted 1626, ed. De Winter, 1905, p. xviii.
[2] In " Works of Ben Jonson," London, 1816, v. 215.

TAKING DOWN THE HOUSES ON OLD LONDON BRIDGE.

(*From a water-colour painting by C. Pyne.*)

[p. 51.

with a biography of its own, worthy of a biographer, which it got ; [1] the others presented a less grandiose appearance. People were even very glad to find bridges like the one at Stratford-at-Bow, in spite of its want of width and its deep ruts ; or like the wooden bridge over the Dyke with arches so low and narrow that all water traffic was interrupted by any slight rising of the level of the water. The state of this last bridge, which, in truth, was more of a hindrance than a help to communications, at length excited the indignation of neighbouring counties. During the fifteenth century, it was granted, therefore, to the inhabitants upon their pressing request, that they might reconstruct the bridge, with a movable arch for boats.[2]

In the same way disappeared, also in the fifteenth century, a bridge described by Leland in his " Itinerary " as having been a " poore bridge of tymber and no causey to come to it," which crossed the Avon at Stratford. It was in such a state that " many poore folkys and othar refusyd to cum to Stratford when Avon was up, or cominge thithar stoode in jeoperdy of lyfe." The rich Sir Hugh of Clopton, sometime mayor of London, who was born at Clopton near Stratford, and died in 1497, moved by the danger of his compatriots, and " having never wife nor children, convertid a great peace of his substance in good workes in Stratford, first making a sumptuus new bridge and large of stone, wher in the middle be a vi great arches for the maine streame of Avon and at eche ende certen smaul arches to bere the causey, and so to passe commodiously at such tymes as the ryver risith." [3] This same bridge is still in use, and well deserves the praise bestowed upon it by Leland. But fine as it

[1] " Chronicles of London Bridge by an Antiquary " [Richard Thomson], London, 1827.

[2] See Appendix II. p. 426

[3] " The Itinerary of John Leland," edited by Miss Lucy Toulmin Smith, London, 1907, vol. ii. pp. 27, 49.

is, one would have less regretted its disappearance than the
destruction of a " praty house of bricke and tymbre,"
built by the same Hugh of Clopton with the purpose
of ending his days in it.   That house was purchased afterwards—also with the intent of ending his life in it—by
a certain countryman of Hugh, who has since become
famous enough, William Shakespeare, who repaired the
house, then called New Place, and died in it in the year
1616.

The calling in of the foreign cleric Isembert to superintend the works of London Bridge seems to have been
exceptional.   The building of ordinary bridges was
usually entrusted to local craftsmen or masons ; and it would
have been strange indeed if the people who could raise
such splendid cathedral naves all over England, had been
at a loss to span rivers with bridges.   One of the few
indentures for the building of a bridge which have come
down to us concerns the re-construction of Catterick
bridge, Yorkshire, in 1422, on the great Roman road, the
Erming Street, and the contractors seem to have been
English.   The document is curious in many respects.

The contract binds several authorities on the one
hand, and " Tho. Ampilforde, John Garette, and Robert
Maunselle, masons," on the other.   It is stated in it
" yat ye foresaides Tho., John, and Rob., schalle make
a brigge of stane oure (over) ye water of Swalle atte Catrik
be twix ye old stane brigge and ye new brigge of tree (of
wood), quilke forsaid brigge, with ye grace of God, salle
be made sufficiant [and war]kmanly in mason craft
accordand in substance to Barnacastelle brigge, aftir y^e
ground and ye watyr accordes, of twa pilers, twa land
stathes (abutments), and thre arches."   The deed goes
on to give a minute account of the way in which every part
of the work must be performed, of the material that
will be used, and of the time when the bridge must be
entirely finished and open to circulation :   " And y^e

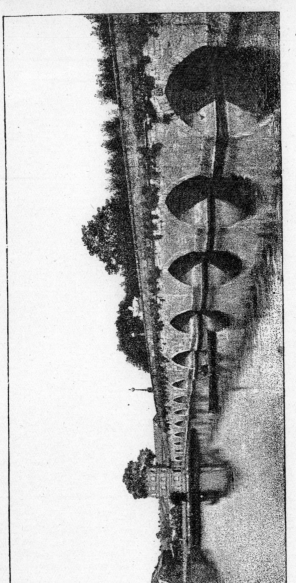

[p. 55.

HUGH OF CLOPTON'S BRIDGE AT STRATFORD-ON-AVON.

(*Fifteenth Century.*)

saides John, Tho., and Rob., schalle this forsaid brigge sufficiantly in masoncraft make and fully perfurnist in all partiez and holy endyd be ye Fest of Seint Michille ye Arcangelle quilk y^t shalle fall in ye yere of our Lorde Gode M^{le} ccccxxv." It is understood besides that they will receive in payment, at certain fixed dates, "gounes," and also sums of money, the total of which will be 260 marks sterling.[1]

The bridge built by the three masons, John, Thomas, and Robert, is still in existence, but it has undergone great and grievous alterations.

We have already seen some examples of the means employed at this period to secure the maintenance of these valuable constructions, when that maintenance had to be ensured by something more than the charges incident to the ownership of the neighbouring lands (*trinoda necessitas*) ; we know that it was sometimes provided through "indulgences" promised to benefactors, sometimes by the action of gilds, or municipalities, sometimes also by the endowments with which one of the great would enrich the bridge founded by him. But without speaking of occasional gifts,[2] several other methods were employed with success, even with profit, such as the lawful levying of those tolls which Godfrey Pratt had arbitrarily imposed on his fellow citizens, or the collection of pious offerings made at the chapel of the bridge and to its warden. The right of toll was called *brudtholl* (bridge-toll) or *pontagium*; the grantee, to whom the benefit went, bound himself in return to make all the necessary repairs. Sometimes the King accorded the right as a favour during a certain period, as appears, for example, from the fol-

---

[1] "The North Riding Record Society," edited by the Rev. J. C. Atkinson, London, vol. iii. part i. p. 33.

[2] Edward III gives the not insignificant sum of £15 for the reparation of the bridge at Newcastle-upon-Tyne. "Roll of Thomas de Brantingham," ed. Devon, p. 392, 44 Ed. III.

lowing petition, which is of the time of Edward I or Edward II :

"To our lord the king, prays his vassal William of Latymer lord of Yarm,[1] that he will grant him pontage for five years at the bridge of Yarm, which is broken down, where men were wont to pass with carts and with horses on the king's highway between the water of Tees towards Scotland. May it please him to do this for the soul of Madame his consort, who is to God commended, and for the common profit of the people who pass." The King's reply was favourable : " The King grants the pontage for the term." [2]

Some of the tariffs in force at certain bridges during the fourteenth century have come down to us and have been printed ; the most detailed of these is of the year 1306, and concerns London Bridge. It is annexed to a patent of Edward I, and enumerates not only passengers, carriages, and animals of every quality or description, but also every sort of " saleable " ware which may pass either on or under the bridge : though it may seem somewhat unfair to have drawn money from shipmen towards the expenses of a structure that was their most formidable competitor.[3] This list, which is a great help in forming an exact idea of the commodities brought

---

[1] Yarm on the Tees, 44 miles north-north-west of York. The " king's highway " in question is the highroad from Scotland, leading to the south, through York and London. The bridge was re-built in 1400 by Skirlaw, Bishop of Durham.

[2] " Rolls of Parliament," vol. i. p. 468. The right of pontage is frequently mentioned in the " Liber Custumarum," edited by Riley, Rolls Series.

[3] " Sciatis quod, in auxilium Pontis London, reparandi et sustentandi, concessimus vobis quod . . . capiatis ibidem de rebus venalibus ultra pontem predictum et subtus eundem transeuntibus consuetudines subscriptas, videlicet . . ." Then follows a very long list of dues. Text in Hearne's " Liber niger Scaccarii . . . Accedunt chartæ antiquæ," London, 1774, vol. i. p. 478*.

to London by land or by river, covers no less than four pages of printed matter : including coal, timber, beer, wines, horses, cattle, pigs, grain, sheep, butter and cheese, fish, furs and skins, metal pots and cups, millstones, silk and other cloths, etc. ; the place they come from is sometimes mentioned: Northampton, Flanders, Normandy.

Another very curious petition (1334) will show the use of the other mode, that is, the collection of voluntary offerings from charitable passers-by. The share of the clergy in the care of these buildings, the greediness with which the profitable right of collecting the gifts was disputed, and the embezzlements sometimes resulting therefrom are to be noticed :

" To our lord the king and his Council showeth their poor chaplain, Robert le Fenere, parson of the church of St. Clement, of Huntingdon, of the diocese of Lincoln, that there is a little chapel lately built in his parish on the bridge of Huntingdon, the keeping of which chapel our lord the king has granted and delivered during pleasure to one Sir Adam, warden of the house of St. John of Huntingdon, who receives and takes away all manner of offerings and alms without doing anything for the repair of the bridge or of the said chapel as he is bound to do. On the other hand, it seems hurtful to God and Holy Church that offerings should be appropriated to any one except to the parson within whose parish the chapel is founded. Wherefore the said Robert prays, for God and Holy Church and for the souls of our lord the king's father and his ancestors, that he may have the keeping of the said chapel annexed to his church, together with the charge of the bridge, and he will take heed with all care to maintain them well, with better will than any stranger, for the profit and honour of Holy Church, to please God and all people passing that way." [1]

[1] " Rolls of Parliament," vol. ii. p. 88.

This jumble of human and divine interests (from the birthplace, that was to be, of Oliver Cromwell) was submitted to the usual examination, and the request was set aside, with the following note : " Non est peticio parliamenti " ; it is not a petition for Parliament.

In many cases, the bridge was itself at once proprietor of real estate and beneficiary of the offerings made to its chapel, and sometimes also grantee of a right of toll ; it had income from both civil and religious sources. Such were notably the bridges of London, of Rochester,[1] of Bedford, and many others. John de Bodenho, chaplain, explains to Parliament that the inhabitants of Bedford hold their own town at farm from the king, and have undertaken to maintain their bridge. For this they " assigned certain tenements and rents in the said town to support it, and with their alms have newly built an oratory on the side of the water belonging to Lord Mowbray, by leave of the lord, adjoining the said bridge." The burgesses gave to the plaintiff the charge of the reparations, together with the whole revenues. But the priest, John of Derby, represented to the king that it was a royal chapel which he might dispose of, and the king has given it to him, which is very unjust, since the chapel is not the king's ; even those who founded it are still living. All these reasons were found good ; the judges were ordered to grant the plaintiff's plea, and

---

[1] See Hist. MSS. Commission, 9th Report, part i. p. 284. On the Rochester bridge, at first a wooden one, later rebuilt in stone, and on its upkeep, see " Rolls of Parliament," vol. iii. p. 254, 21 Ric. II, 1397. A view of the bridge appears on several seals, some reproduced in De Gray Birch, " Seals in . . . the British Museum," London, 1887, 2 vols., No. 5336. On this important bridge and its *biography*, see C. T. Flower, " Public Works in Mediæval Law," 1905, Selden Society, I., p. 203. Like many others, this very frequented bridge, on the road from London to Canterbury, and which existed long before the Conquest, was first of wood, then of stone, and is now (since 1856) of iron.

were reprimanded for not having done it sooner, as had already been prescribed to them.[1]

Enriched by so many offerings, protected by the *trinoda necessitas*, and by the common interest of the landed proprietors, these bridges should have been continually repaired, and have remained sound. But there was nothing of the sort, and the distance between legal theory and actual practice was great. When the taxes were regularly collected and honestly applied, they usually sufficed to support the building ; even the right of collecting them, being in itself profitable, was, as has been seen, strongly contested for ; but the example of Godfrey Pratt and of some others has already shown that all the wardens were not honest. Many, even in the highest positions, imitated Godfrey. London Bridge itself, so rich, so useful, so admired, was in constant need of repairs, never done until danger was imminent, or even a catastrophe had happened. Henry III granted the farm of the bridge revenues " to his beloved wife," who neglected to maintain it, and appropriated to herself without scruple the rents of the building ; none the less did the king renew his patent at the expiration of the term, that his said beloved might benefit " from a richer favour." The result was not long awaited ; it was soon found that the bridge was in ruins, and to restore it the ordinary resources were not enough ; it was necessary to send collectors throughout the country to gather offerings from those willing to give. Edward I, in January 1281, begged his subjects to hasten ; the bridge would give way if they did not send prompt assistance. He ordered the archbishops, bishops, all the clergy, to allow his collectors to address the people freely with " pious exhortations," that the subsidies should be craved without delay. But nevertheless the supplies arrived too late ; the catastrophe had already happened, a " sudden

[1] " Rolls of Parliament," vol. ii. p. 100, year 1338.

ruin " had befallen the bridge, and to repair this mis-•
fortune the king established a special tax upon the
passengers, merchandise and boats (February 4, 1282),
which tax was imposed again and the new tariff afore
mentioned was put into force on May 7, 1306. What
this sudden ruin was we learn from Stow's " Annales " ;
the winter had been very severe, the frost and snow
had caused great cracks in the floor of the bridge, so that
towards the Feast of the Purification (February 2), five
of the arches fell in. Many other bridges, too, in the
country had suffered damage, Rochester Bridge had even
entirely fallen.[1]

It may be imagined what fate awaited unendowed
country bridges. The alms from the passers-by proved
insufficient, so that little by little, nobody repairing them,
the arches wore through, the parapets were detached,
not a cart passed but fresh stones disappeared in the river,
and soon carriages and riders could not venture without
danger over the half demolished building. If moreover a flood should occur, all was over with the bridge
and often with the imprudent or hurried travellers who
might be crossing late in the evening. An accident
of this kind was brought up for his justification by
a chamberlain of North Wales, from whom Edward III
claimed a hundred marks. The chamberlain averred
that he had duly sent the money by his clerk, William
of Markeley ; but, alas, " the said William was drowned
in Severn, at Moneford bridge, by the rising flood of
water, and could not be found, so that he was devoured
by beasts ; thus the said hundred marks chanced to be

[1] " King Edward kept his feast of Christmas (1281) at Worcester.
From this Christmas till the purification of Our Lady, there was such a
frost and snow, as no man living could remember the like, wherethrough
five arches of London Bridge, and all Rochester Bridge were borne downe,
and carried away with the streame, and the like hapned to many bridges
in England." Stow's " Annales," London, 1631, p. 201. See Appendix III.

lost." [1] At that time there were still wolves in England, and the disappearance of the body, with the 100 marks, though even then wolves did not feed on marks, would appear less unlikely than at present.

In those days neglect attained a degree now impossible and which we can scarcely imagine. The Commons of the counties of Nottingham, Derby, and Lincoln, and of the town of Nottingham, declare to the Good Parliament of 1376, that there is near the town of Nottingham a great bridge over the Trent, called Heybethebridge, "to the making and repair of which nobody is bound and alms only are collected, by which bridge all the comers and goers between the north and the south parts should have their passage." This bridge is "ruinous," and "oftentimes have several persons been drowned, as well horsemen as carts, man, and harness." The complainants pray for power to appoint two bridge wardens, who shall administer the property that will be given in view of its maintenance, "for God and as a work of charity." But the king did not accede to their request. [2]

Or maybe it happened that the riverside proprietors let their obligation fall into oblivion, even when it was at the beginning formal and precise enough. The legislator had, however, taken some precautions ; he had inscribed bridges on the list of the articles for those inquiries periodically opened in England by the justices in Eyre, sheriffs and bailiffs, as we shall see further on [3] ; but those concerned found means to defraud the law. People had been so long used to see ruin menace the edifice, that when it actually did give way no one could say who ought to have repaired it. It then became neces-

---

[1] "Rolls of Parliament," vol. ii. p. 91 (9 Edward III), 1335.
[2] Ibid., p. 350.
[3] "De pontibus et calcetis fractis et communibus transitibus, quis ea reparare debeat et sustinere." "Fleta" (end of thirteenth century, below p. 111), I. ch. 20, § 41.

sary to apply to the king for a special inquiry, and to seek on whom lay the service. Parliament thus decides in 1339, on the demand of the prior of St. Neots : "*Item*, let there be good and true men assigned to survey the bridge and causeway of St. Neots, whether they be broken down and carried away by the rising of the waters, as the prior alleges, or not. And in case they are broken down and carried away, to inquire who ought and was used to have it repaired, and who is bound of right to do it ; and how the bridge and roadway may be re-made and repaired. And what they [1] find they shall return into the chancery."

In consequence of such inquests the persons charged with the maintenance being determined by the findings of a jury convened on the spot, a tax is levied upon them for the carrying out of the repairs. But they often protest and refuse to pay ; they are sued, they appeal to the king ; horse, cart, anything that may come to hand and which belongs to them is promptly seized to be sold for the benefit of the bridge ; the dispute drags on, and meanwhile the edifice gives way. Hamo de Morston, for example, in the eleventh year of Edward II, complains that his horse has been taken from him. Called to justify themselves, Simon Porter and two others who have made the seizure, explain that there is a bridge at Shoreham, called the Long bridge, which is half destroyed; now it has been found that the building ought to be restored at the expense of the tenants of the Archbishop of Canterbury. Hamo, who is one of them, having refused to pay his part of the contribution, Simon and the others took the horse. They acted by order of a bailiff, and their conduct is vindicated. Another case of the same period is that of the Abbot of Coggeshall who, after a similar inquest, refused to execute any

[1] *I.e.* the jury "of good and true men." "Rolls of Parliament," vol. ii. p. 111.

repairs to a bridge near his lands under pretext that within memory of man there had been no other bridge over the river " than a certain plank of board," and that at all times it had been found sufficient for horsemen and pedestrians. Innumerable are the examples of inquests of this sort and of the difficulties in executing the measures decided on.[1]

Owing to these several causes the chronicle-history of even the most important English bridges, when it is possible to trace it, is a long tale of crumblings into the river, rebuildings, and repairs, and ever-recurring catastrophes. Sometimes when the damage was great, and much money was needed and was not forthcoming, a ferry was established as a substitute for the late bridge, and remained in use for years and years together.

Such a series of events is offered by the history of the bridge on the Tweed at Berwick, which was one of the longest in England. The first time we hear of it is in the year 1199, and the news is that it gave way at that date, owing to a rise of the river. It was rebuilt and gave way again. Sometimes it was rebuilt of wood and sometimes of stone ; occasionally it fell altogether from end to end, and then a ferry was established, and was maintained for a long period. This was the case in 1294, when great harm was done by the inundations. " Where the bridge fell at this time," says the latest historian of Berwick, " there it lay for many years. The only method of crossing was by ferry boats, worked from both sides of the river ; while the ferry in times of danger was defended by soldiers. Thus, in Sir Robert Heron's (the controller) ' Book of Bills ' for 1310, there is allowed one half quarter of pease to each of six crossbowmen (one of them being John Sharp Arewe) guarding the ferry of the Tweed at Berwick." [2] The ferry

[1] Several instances will be found in Appendix IV. p. 429.
[2] John Scott, " Berwick-upon-Tweed," London, 1888, p. 408, *et seq.*

follows vicissitudes scarcely less numerous than the bridge
itself, and disputes arise as to the right of working it,
or rather of collecting its tolls. The revenues of the
bridge, now that there is no longer any bridge, are also
a matter of difficulty, and the king has to interfere to
settle the question of the rents of houses and of fisheries
belonging to the ruined monument.

In 1347 at last the citizens of the town began to think
seriously of rebuilding their bridge, and the king granted
them the right of collecting towards the expenses a toll
of sixpence on every ship entering their harbour. The
bridge was then rebuilt, but not in such a way as not
to fall again, which has since happened to it many times.

Not less doleful is the story of the bridge on the Dee
at Chester, of which we hear in the chronicles for the
first time in 1227 and 1297, on account of its being
carried away by the water,[1] and the same may be said
of many of the bridges of mediæval England, especially
the longer ones.

When rebuilding had to be done people generally
did not care to remove what remained of the old monument, for which reason, when a bridge has broken down
in our time, it has been often found that it was made
of an accumulation of superimposed bridges. Of this
the bridge over the Teign, between Newton Abbot and
Teignmouth, rebuilt in 1815, is an example. It became,
in this case, apparent that four successive bridges at least
had been at various times erected with or over the remains
of previous constructions. Mr. P. T. Taylor, who in-
vestigated the matter at that time, gave as his opinion
" that the last or upper work was done in the sixteenth
century, and that the red bridge had been built on the
salt marsh in the thirteenth century ; since which time
there has been an accumulation of soil to the depth of
ten feet. He supposes the wooden bridge to be as old

[1] Ormerod, " History of Chester," 1819, vol. i. p. 285.

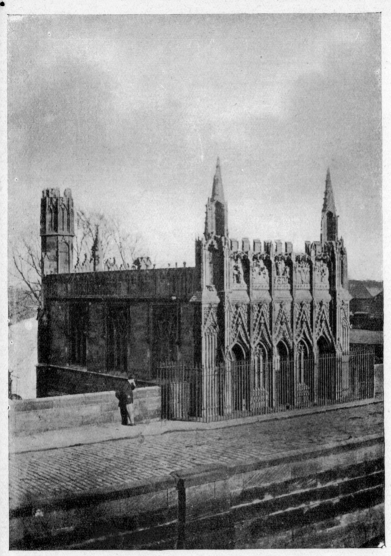

THE CHAPEL ON THE BRIDGE AT WAKEFIELD.

(Fourteenth Century ; present state.)

[p. 67.

as the Conquest, and the white stone bridge to have been a Roman work." [1]

Given these circumstances, it is rather a matter of surprise than otherwise to find that a good number of mediæval bridges still subsist in England ; the more so as the nineteenth century has been a great destroyer of bridges. The enormous increase of population and the proportionate want of means of communication during that period has proved fatal to many bridges, and especially to the more famous and important ones which had been built in the more largely populated districts. Owing to such necessities London Bridge itself has disappeared, and even the recollection of the long years, during which it had been, so to say, a factor in English history and associated with the life of the nation, could not save it.

Many others had the same fate, or were, at least, as at Norwich, Durham, Chester, Wakefield, Monmouth, and elsewhere, partly rebuilt or enlarged, not always in such a way as to retain much of their pristine appearance. For all that, however, enough of them remain to give an accurate idea of what they were, without having recourse merely to descriptions or drawings in contemporary manuscripts. None, it is true, can for elegance and completeness compete with such bridges as are still to be found in France ; for example, with the magnificent thirteenth-century bridge of *Valentré* at Cahors, of which a picture has been given above (p. 47). Those that remain are sufficient, nevertheless, to testify to the skill of old English architects in that branch of their art. As might have been expected, these bridges abound chiefly in those parts of the country where the increase of traffic and population has been the least conspicuous, on roads little more frequented to-day than in the Middle Ages, which then led to strong castles or flourishing monasteries, and only lead now to ivy-

[1] " Archæologia," t. xix. p. 310.

clad ruins. For this reason they are more numerous in
some parts of Wales than anywhere in England.

In several cases the chapels which placed them under
the protection of a saint and where offerings were collected
have escaped the hand of the restorer and are still extant.
There is one, of the fifteenth century, at Rotherham, Yorkshire, "a chapel of stone wel wrought," says Leland [1] ;
another, a fine small one, is to be seen on the bridge
at Bradford-on-Avon, Wiltshire ; a third, a very tall
structure, stands on the middle of the bridge at
St. Ives, Huntingdonshire ; but the finest example by
far is the chapel on the bridge at Wakefield, both
chapel and bridge dating from the fourteenth century.
Leland mentions them as " the faire bridge of stone of
nine arches, under which runnith the river of Calder,
and on the east side of this bridge is a right goodly chapel
of our lady and two cantuarie preestes founded in it."
This foundation was made about 1358 ; Edward III, by
a charter dated at Wakefield, settled " £10 per annum
on William Kaye and William Bull and their successors
for ever to perform divine service in a chapel of St. Mary
newly built on the bridge at Wakefield." [2]

In our century the bridge has been widened towards
the west, the arches being round on that side and having
been left Gothic on the other. The chapel, the founda-
tions of which rest on an island in the river, was
repaired in 1847, but its original style was carefully respected.[3] The greatest change is in the surroundings,
where nothing recalls either Dr. Primrose or the clear

---

[1] The date is shown by a will of the 24th of August, 1483, in which
a sum is left towards the building of the chapel to be erected on Rotherham
Bridge. See J. Guest, " Historic Notices of Rotherham," Worksop,
1879, fol., pp. 125–6. Two views of the bridge and chapel are given,
pp. 126 and 581.

[2] Camden's " Britannia," ed. Gough, vol. iii., Lond., 1789, pp. 38–9.

[3] T. Kilby, " Views in Wakefield," 1843, fol. ; J. C. and C. A. Buckler,
" Remarks upon Wayside Chapels," Oxford, 1843.

THE BRIDGE WITH A DEFENSIVE TOWER AT WARKWORTH, NORTHUMBERLAND.

(*Fourteenth Century : present state.*)

waters of Plantagenet times ; and the smoke and refuse of innumerable manufactures blacken the bridge, the chapel, the river, and even the sky itself.

Several specimens also remain of bridges with the triangular recesses we have mentioned, left on the top of the piers for the safety of foot passengers. Among many other examples may be quoted the beautiful fourteenth-century bridge at Warkworth, Northumberland,[1] which also deserves notice for another characteristic much more rarely to be met with, that is, the preservation of the tower built at one end for its defence. Most of the bridges of any importance were protected in this way, which, as the country became quieter, was found useless ; the consideration that they were ornamental rarely sufficed to prevent their being pulled down. Those at Chester were removed in 1782–1784 ; those at York were demolished with the bridge itself, of the thirteenth century, at the beginning of the nineteenth ; the Durham one, built on Framwellgate Bridge, in 1760 ; the beautiful fortified entrance to one of the two bridges at Shrewsbury disappeared in the same century, as well as the whole structure, with the picturesque old houses it bore. It must be conceded that those towers were sometimes very inconvenient. A witness of the fact told me that, quite recently, a gipsy's caravan was stopped at the tower on Warkworth Bridge, being unable to pass under it owing to the lowness of the arch. The pavement had to be hollowed out to allow of the caravan's proceeding on its way.

The best example of a defensive tower is the machicolated one at Monmouth, on the Monnow Bridge ; except for the opening of passages to be used by people on foot, the fortified gate looks as it did in the Middle

[1] " Twenty marks were left towards the rebuilding of this bridge, by John Cook, of Newcastle-upon-Tyne, 2 Rich. II, 1379." E. Mackenzie, " View of the County of Northumberland," 1825, vol. ii. p. 111.

Ages. The bridge itself, familiar to the Monmouth-
born " Prince Hal " of Shakespeare, and of England, has,
been, however, widened, as at Wakefield and elsewhere.
The ribs of the ancient arches are still visible within the
modern ones.

In Elizabethan times defensive towers for bridges
continued to be built, but in poetry only. Spenser raised,
in his lines, a beautiful structure, of Doric style, as befitted
the Renaissance days in which he lived, at the entrance
to the island of Venus :

> It was a bridge ybuilt in goodly wize,
> With curious corbes and pendants graven faire,
> And arched all with porches, did arize
> On stately pillours, fram'd after the Doricke guize.
>
> And for defence thereof, on th' other end
> There reared was a castle faire and strong,
> That warded all which in and out did wend,
> And flancked both the bridges sides along.[1]

But, except as castles in the air, such fortifications
were no longer in demand.

The rarest of all bridges are, nowadays in England,
those having houses on them, as was the fashion in the
Middle Ages. The picturesque High Bridge at Lincoln,
originally built in the 12th century, still preserves the
lodgings built over it [2] ; a solitary house remains on Elvet
Bridge at Durham, and the only bridge of some length,
with a complete row of houses is a comparatively recent
one, being the familiar Pulteney Bridge built at Bath by
William Pulteney in the eighteenth century.

[1] " Faerie Queene," Bk. iv. canto x.
[2] Mentioned by Leland : " High Bridge hath but one great arch, and
over a pece of it is a chapelle of St. George " ("Itinerary," ed. L. T.
Smith, i. 29), which chapel had been first dedicated to St. Thomas of Canterbury, but had apparently just been rebaptized, when Leland saw it,
Henry VIII having decided by a proclamation of November 16, 1538,
that other saints might be saints, but this one was not.

THE DEFENSIVE TOWER ON THE MONNOW BRIDGE, MONMOUTH. [p. 75.

The more numerous of the mediæval bridges still in existence are those of one arch ; there are many of them in Wales, some being most elegant and picturesque, such as the famous Devil's Bridge over the Mynach, near Aberystwith. In England the largest is the one over the moat of Norwich Castle ; and the most curious the three-branched one at Crowland, this last belonging in its

THE BRIDGE NEAR DANBY CASTLE, YORKSHIRE.

(*Fourteenth Century.*)

actual state to the fourteenth century. It is no longer used, as no road passes over it and no water under.[1] Another of the finest, and one of the least known, crosses the Esk, near Danby Castle, Yorkshire. Its date is about 1385 ; the arms of Neville, Lord Latimer, who had it built, are yet to be seen at the top of the parapet.

Lastly, a word may be said of the larger bridges, most

[1] See a sketch of it, above, p. 21.

of which have unfortunately undergone great alterations and repairs. Besides the Wakefield Bridge above mentioned, there is one over the Dee, at Chester, part of which is as old as the thirteenth century, thoroughly repaired since Ormerod disrespectfully described it as " a long fabric of red stone extremely dangerous and unsightly." [1]   At Durham there are the Framwellgate and Elvet bridges, both originally built in the twelfth century. A six-arched bridge, rebuilt in the fifteenth century, exists at Hereford ; another, repaired in 1449, with the help of indulgences, remains at Bidford.[2]   A four-arched one, built in the fourteenth century, over the Dee is to be seen at Llangollen, being " one of the *Tri Thlws Cymru*, or three beauties of Wales ; " [3] the arches are irregular in size, for the builder, in this and many other cases, minding more the solidity of the structure than its regularity, erected the piers at the places where the presence of rocks in the bed of the river made it most convenient. A very noteworthy one is the thirteenth-century bridge over the Nith, at Dumfries, in Scotland, which had formerly thirteen arches, seven of which only are now in use. It was long considered the finest after that of London.   Other mediæval bridges of several arches remain at Huntingdon,[4] at St. Ives, at Norwich (Bishop's Bridge), at Potter Heigham (a most picturesque one), at Tewkesbury, etc.[5]   The Tewkesbury one, with the middle arch enlarged in modern times, but the

[1] " History of Chester," London, 1819, vol. i. p. 285.

[2] Dugdale, " Warwickshire," 1730, ii. 724.

[3] J. G. Wood, " The Principal Rivers of Wales," London, 1813, vol. ii. p. 271.

[4] The Countess of Norfolk complains to Parliament that, contrary to their franchise, her tenants have been compelled to contribute towards the building of the bridge at Huntingdon. " Rolls of Parliament," 1 Ric. II, year 1377.

[5] See F. Stone, " Picturesque Views of the Bridges of Norfolk," Norwich, 1830. Rough sketches of more than thirty old English bridges appear in a curious engraving by Daniel King (seventeenth century),

triangular recesses for foot passengers still in use, dates
back to King John, *teste* Leland, whose biography of
the bridge shows that it went through the vicissitudes
usual in the life of such buildings : " King John beyng
Erle of Glocester by his wife caussid the bridge of Twekes-
byri to be made of stone. He that was put in truste to
do it first made a stone bridge over the gret poure of booth
the armes [of the Avon] by north and weste : and after,
to spede and spare mony, he made at the northe ende a
wodde bridge of a greate length for sodeyne land waters,
putting the residue of the mony to making of the castel
of Hanley . . .

" King John gave to the mayntenance of this bridge
the hole tolle of the Wensday and Saturday markets in
the towne, the which they yet possesse, turnyng it rather
holely to their owne profit then reparation of the
bridge." [1]

The maintenance of the roads much resembled that
of the bridges ; that is to say, it greatly depended upon
chance, opportunity, or the goodwill or piety of those to
whom the adjoining land belonged. In the case of roads,
as of bridges, petitions were sent to Parliament asking
that a tax be levied for the repair of the road upon
those who used it : an early attempt at the establishment
of that toll system which survived in England until
the highways were " disturnpiked " in the second half
of the nineteenth century. " Walter Godelak of Waling-
ford, prays for the establishment of a custom to be

bearing as a title : " An orthographical designe of severall viewes vpon ye
road in England and Wales," and as a subscription : " This designe is to
illustrate Cambden's Britannia, that where he mentions such places the
curious may see them, which is the indeavour, by Gods assistance, of
" Y. S. Daniell King."

A copy is bound in the MS. Harl. 2073, as fol. 126. Catterick Bridge
(*supra* p. 54) is among the bridges there represented.

[1] " The Itinerary of John Leland," ed. Lucy Toulmin Smith, London,
1907, 5 vols., iv. p. 137.

collected from every cart of merchandise using the road
between Jowermersh and Newenham, on account of the
depth and for the repair of the said way. *Reply* : The
King will do nothing therein." [1] Again, a lady arrogates
to herself the right to levy a tax on all comers : " To
our lord the King show the commonalty of the people of
Nottinghamshire passing between Kelm and Newur, that
whereas the King's highway between the said two towns
has been wont to be for all persons freely to pass, on horseback, in carts, and on foot from time immemorial, the
Lady of Egrum has got hold to herself of the said road
in severalty, taking from those passing along there grievous
ransoms and exactions, in disheritance of the King and his
crown and to the great hurt of the people." The king
orders an inquest. [2]

Even a bishop would occasionally set a bad example,
though bound more than any to set a good one. The
inhabitants of Huntingdonshire and "the Island of
Ely" remonstrate in 1314–15, because the men of those
parts, either on foot or on horseback, have always used
the Horketh causeway, "which causeway the bishop of
Ely is bound to repair and maintain, they say, for certain
rents which he gets ; and the causway is broken by the
fault of the bishop, and the same bishop does not allow
ships to pass there under the bridge without levying a
heavy water tax ("theolonium"), which tax ought to be
applied to the reparation and maintenance of the same
bridge and causeway, and they crave remedy." An
inquest is ordered. [3]

Sometimes the sheriffs in their turns ordered the levy
of taxes on those who did not repair the roads ; the law,
as we have seen, allowed it ; but those who were fined
protested before Parliament under the pretext that the

---

[1] " Rolls of Parliament," vol. i. p. 48, 18 Edward I, A.D. 1289.
[2] Ibid., vol. i. p. 424 ; 18 Edward II, 1324.
[3] Ibid., vol. i. p. 314 ; 8 Edward II.

roads and the bridges were " sufficient enough " :—
" *Item*, humbly pray the Commons of your realm, as well
spiritual as temporal, complaining that several sheriffs
of your kingdom feign and procure presentments in their
turns that divers roads, bridges, and causways are defective
from non-reparation, with purpose and intent to amerce
abbots, priors, and seculars, sometimes up to ten pounds,
sometimes more, sometimes less, and levy the said amercements by their officers called out-riders, without delay
or any reply of the parties, in places where the said roads,
bridges, and causeys are sufficient enough, or perhaps are
not in charge of the said amerced men." *Reply* : " Let
the common law be kept, and the amercements reasonable
in this case." [1]

Where negligence began, the ruts, or rather the quags,
began. Those numerous little subterranean arches, which
the foot-passenger now does not even notice, made to
carry off rivulets dry during a part of the year, did not
exist then, and the rivulet flowed through the road. In
the East at the present day, the caravaneers talk in the
bazaars of the town about the roads and pathways ; we
speak of them ourselves on returning home, as books of
travel show. There, however, a road is often nothing else
than a place along which men are accustomed to pass ; it
little resembles the dignified highways the idea of which the
word road evokes in European minds. During the rainy
season pools of water cut off the ordinary track of the
horsemen and camels ; they increase little by little, and at

[1] " Rolls of Parliament," vol. iii. p. 598 ; 7 and 8 Henry IV.
In the same way as for bridges, taxes were sometimes levied but misapplied.
See, in C. T. Flower, " Public Works in Mediæval Law," 1905, i. p. 25,
how William Caldecote of Aylesbury had been duly authorized to levy
a tax of one penny or one half-penny on carts of various sorts, and one farthing
on " every horse carrying goods for sale that should pass along Walton
street which leads from Walton to Aylesbury for the maintenance of the
said road, and that whereas the said William so received in 11 Rich. II
over and above the sum spent on the repair of the road 24s. which remain
in his hands, the road is flooded and dangerous by his default."

length overflow and form temporary rivers. At evening the
sun sets in the heavens and also in the empurpled road ;
the innumerable puddles along the way, dotting the ground,
reflect the red flaming clouds ; the wet horses and splashed
riders shiver in the midst of all these glimmerings, while
overhead and underfoot the two suns approach one another
to meet on the horizon. The roads of the Middle Ages
sometimes were like those of the modern East ; the sun-
sets were magnificent after showers, but to face long
journeys one had to be a robust horseman, inured to
fatigue, with unshakable health. The usual education and
training prepared people, it is true, for all these trials.

The roads in England would have been entirely impassable, and religious zeal would, no more than the
indulgences of the Bishop of Durham and his peers, have
been sufficient to keep them in condition, if the nobility
and the clergy, that is to say, the mass of the landed
proprietors, had not had an immediate and daily interest
in maintaining possible roads. The English kings had
had the prudence not to form great compact fiefs like
those which they themselves owned in France, and which
made of them such dangerous vassals. Their own example
had taught them, and, from the beginning, they are
found distributing to the shareholders in that great
undertaking, the Conquest, domains scattered in every
part of the island. This kind of chequered proprietorship,
still subsisting in the fourteenth century, was noticed by
Froissart : "And several times," he says, giving an
account of a talk with his friend and patron, Edward le
Despenser,[1] "it happened that when I rode about the
country with him, *for the lands and revenues of the
English barons are here and there and much scattered*, he
called me and said : 'Froissart, do you see that great
town with the high steeple ?'"

[1] Grandson and great-grandson of the two Despensers who had been
executed in 1326 by order of Queen Isabella, their estates being confiscated.

"'Yes, my lord,' I answered, 'Why do you say so?'"

"'I say so because it should be mine, but there was a bad queen in this country who took all from us.'

"And thus, on one occasion or another, did he show me, here and there in England, more than forty such places." [1]

The tragic fated Despensers were not alone in having the lands which they owed to the prince's favour sown haphazard in every county; all the great of their rank were in the same case. The king himself, with all his court, as well as the landed nobility, ceaselessly went from one country place to another,[2] partly from choice and partly because they could not do otherwise. In times of peace it was a semblance of activity that was not displeasing, but especially it was an economical necessity. All, however rich, were obliged, like land-owners of every age, to live upon the produce of their domains, first of one, then of the other, and as they went from place to place, it was very important for them to have passable roads, where their horses would not stumble and where their baggage wagons, which served for veritable removals, might have a chance of not being overturned.

Military necessity, Scottish wars, French wars, Welsh or Irish wars had a similar effect, and so had, to a degree, nowadays incredible, the kings' passion for hawking. They did not want to be stopped when following their birds by a broken bridge, and they would order the commonalty, whether or not it was bound to do so, to make prompt repairs in view of their coming. Hence Article 23 in the Great Charter, meant to check this

[1] Ed. Siméon Luce, vol. i. p. 257.

[2] Royal Itineraries show, for instance, that in the 28th year of his reign, Edward I changed seventy-five times his place of abode, that is about three times each fortnight. "Liber quotidianus Garderobæ," London, 1787, p. lxvii.

propensity : " Let no community or man be constrained
to make bridges on rivers except those who were legally
bound from old to do so." As late, however, as
October 6, 1373, we find that Edward III commanded
' the sheriff of Oxfordshire to declare that all bridges
should be repaired and all fords marked out with stakes
for the crossing of the King ' with his falcons' during
the approaching winter season." [1]

In the same way the monks, those vast-landed
husbandmen, were much interested in the proper
maintenance of the roads. Their agricultural undertakings were of considerable extent ; an abbey such as
that of Meaux, near Beverley, had in the middle of the
fourteenth century, 2,638 sheep, 515 oxen, and 98 horses,
with land in proportion.[2] Besides, as we have seen, the
care of watching over the good condition of the roads
was more incumbent on the clergy than on any other
class, because it was a pious and meritorious work.

All these motives combined were enough to provide
roads sufficient for the usual needs, but in those days people
were content with little. Carts and even carriages were
heavy, lumbering, solid machines, which stood the hardest
jolts. People of any worth journeyed on horseback, the use
of a carriage being exceptional. As to those who travelled
on foot, they were used to all sorts of misery. Little then
sufficed ; and if other proofs were wanting of the state
into which the roads were liable to fall, even in the most
frequented places, we should find them in a patent of
Edward III of November 20, 1353, which orders the
paving of the highroad, *alta via*, running from Temple
Bar to Westminster. This road, being almost a street,
had been paved, but, the king explains, it is " so full
of holes and bogs . . . and the pavement is so damaged

---

[1] McKechnie, " Magna Carta," 1905, p. 357.
[2] " Chronica monasterii de Melsa," ed. E. A. Bond ; Rolls Series,
1868, London, vol. iii. preface, p. xv.

and broken,ʻ that the traffic has become very dangerous
for men and carts. He orders, in consequence, each land-
owner on both sides of the road to remake, at his own
expense, a footway of seven feet up to the ditch, *usque
canellum*. The middle of the road—*inter canellos*—the
width of which is unfortunately not given, is to be
paved, and the expense covered by means of a tax laid on
all the merchandise going to the staple at Westminster.[1]

Three years later a general tax was laid by the City
of London on all carts and horses bringing merchandise
or materials of any kind to the town. The regulation
which imposed it, of the thirtieth year of Edward III,
first states that all the roads in the immediate environs
of London are in such bad condition that the carriers,
merchants, etc., " are oftentimes in peril of losing what
they bring." Henceforth, to help the reparations, a due
will be levied on all vehicles and all laden beasts coming
to or going from the city ; a penny per cart and a farthing
per horse each way ; reductions were granted in case of
constant traffic : a cart bringing sand, gravel, or clay,
paid only threepence a week. By an article the unfair-
ness of which had nothing exceptional, the richer were
made to pay less than the poorer : " But for the carts
and horses of great people and other folks that bring their
own victuals and other goods for the use and consumption
of their own hostels, nothing shall be taken." [2]

The environs of Paris about the same time presented
roads and bridges quite as badly kept as those in the neighbourhood of London. Charles VI, in one of his ordinances, states that the hedges and brambles have greatly
encroached on the roads, and that there are even some
in the midst of which trees have shot up :

[1] Patent Roll, 27 Edward III, in Rymer (ed. 1708), vol. v. p. 774.
See as to the repair of this same road in 1314, thirty-nine years earlier,
" Rolls of Parliament," vol. i. p. 302 *b*.
[2] Riley's " Memorials of London," London, 1868, p. 291.

" Outside the said town of Paris, in several parts of the suburbs, *prévosté* and *vicomté* of the same, there are many notable and ancient highways, bridges, lanes, and roads, which are much injured, damaged, or decayed and otherwise hindered, by ravines of water and great stones, by hedges, brambles, and many other trees which have grown there, and by many other supervening hindrances, because they have not been maintained and provided for in time past ; and they are in such a bad state that they cannot be securely used on foot or horseback, nor by vehicles, without great perils and inconveniences ; and some of them are entirely abandoned because men cannot resort there." The Provost of Paris is ordered to cause the repairs to be made by all to whom it pertained ; and, if necessary, to compel by force " all " the inhabitants of the towns in the neighbourhood of the bridges and highways to help in the work.[1]

But what makes us understand better than ordinances the difficulty of journeys in bad weather, and enables us to picture to ourselves flooded roads resembling those of the East in the rainy season, is the impossibility sometimes acknowledged in official documents of responding to the most important royal summons, owing to the inclemency of the elements. Thus, for example, it might happen that the bulk of the members called to Parliament from all parts of England would fail at the appointed day, for no other reason than bad weather having, as the event showed, caused the roads to be impassable. The record of the sittings of the second Parliament of the thirteenth year of Edward III (1339) show that it was necessary to declare to the few representatives of the Commons and of the nobility who had been able to reach Westminster, "that because the prelates, earls, barons, and

[1] Ordonance of March 1, 1388, " Recueil d'Isambert," vol. vi. p. 665. On the state of roads and bridges and on travelling in France, see d'Avenel, " L'Évolution des Moyens de Transport," Paris, 1919.

THE PARLIAMENT SITTING AT WESTMINSTER, OCT., 1399.

(From the Harl. MS. 1319, painted circa A.D. 1400.)

other lords and knights of the shires, citizens and burgesses of cities and boroughs were so troubled by the bad weather that they could not arrive that day, it would be proper to await their coming." [1]

Yet these members were not poor folks, they had good horses, good coats, thick cloaks covering their necks up to their hats, with large hanging sleeves falling over their knees ; [2] no matter : the snow or the rain, the floods or the frost, had been the stronger. Battling against the weather that hampered their journey, prelates, barons, or knights, halted their steeds at some roadside inn, and as they listened to the tap of the sleet on the wooden panels closing the window, with their feet at the fire in the smoky room while awaiting the subsidence of the waters, they must have thought on the royal displeasure which soon, no doubt, would show itself in the " painted chamber " at Westminster. In short, though there were roads, though land was burdened with service for their support, though laws from time to time recalled their obligations to the owners of the soil, though the private interest of lords and of monks, in addition to the interest of the public, gave occasion to reparation now and then, the fate of the traveller in a snowfall or in a thaw was very precarious. Well might the Church have pity on him, and include him, together with the sick and the captive, among the unfortunates whom she recommended to the daily prayers of pious souls.[3]

---

[1] " Rolls of Parliament," ii. p. 107.
[2] See frontispiece of this volume, and p. 14.
[3] To give shelter (" tego," I shelter, in the enumeration devised by St. Thomas Aquinas) was one of the seven " Works of Charity." In the evening prayers at home, in my childhood, part of which had been handed down from remote times, travellers were still remembered, as well as those who had been " bitten by venomous beasts."

A COMMON CART.

*(From the MS. 10 E. IV. in the British Museum. English ; Fourteenth
Century.)*

CHAPTER II

THE ORDINARY TRAVELLER AND THE
CASUAL PASSER-BY

I

THUS kept up, the roads stretched away from the
towns and plunged into the country, interrupted
by rivulets in winter and dotted with holes ;
the heavy carts slowly followed their devious course, and
the sound of creaking wood accompanied the vehicle.
These carts were numerous and in very common use.
Some were square-shaped timbrels, simple massive boxes
made of planks borne on two wheels ; others, somewhat
lighter, were formed of slatts latticed with a willow trellis.
To add to their solidity, the wheels were studded with
big-headed nails.[1] Both sorts were used for labour in the

---

[1] See representations of these carts in the manuscripts of the fourteenth
century, and especially in MS. Roy., 10 E. IV, in the British Museum,
fol. 63, 94, 110, &c., and in the Louterell psalter. We give above a fac-
simile of one of them, and further a representation of a reaper's cart from
the Louterell psalter. See also Bodl. MS. 264, fos. 42, 84, 103, 110.

country ; they were to be found everywhere, and as they abounded their hire was not expensive. Twopence for carrying a ton weight a distance of one mile was the average price ; for carrying corn, it was about a penny a mile per ton.[1] All this does not prove that the roads were excellent, but that these carts, indispensable to agriculture, were numerous. They did not cost much to the villagers, who usually were the makers thereof ; they were built solid and massive because they were easier to set up thus and resisted better the jolts of the roads ; a modest remuneration would suffice for their owners. The king always employed a number ; when he moved from one manor to another, the brilliant *cortège* of the lords was followed by an army of loud-creaking borrowed carts.

The official purveyors found the carts wherever they went and freely appropriated them ; they exercised their requisitions ten leagues on either side of the road followed by the royal convoy. They even took without scruple the carts of travellers who had come perhaps thirty or forty leagues distance, and whose journey was thus abruptly interrupted. There were indeed statutes against forced loans, which specifically provided that suitable payment should be made, that is to say, " ten pence a day for a cart with two horses, and fourteen pence for a cart with three horses." But often no payment came. The " poor Commons " renewed their protests, the parliament their statutes, and the purveyors their exactions.

Besides the carts they required corn, hay, oats, beer, meat ; it was a little army that had to be fed, and the requisitions caused the villagers painful apprehension. People did what they could to be exempted ; the simplest way was to bribe the purveyor, but the poor could not. Yet numberless regulations had successively promised

[1] Thorold Rogers, " History of Agriculture and Prices," i. pp. 650–661.

that there should never be any further abuse. The king
was powerless ; under an imperfect government, laws
created to last for ever rapidly lose their vitality, and those
made at that time died in a day.

Purveyors swarmed ; impostors gave themselves out
as king's officers who were not, and did not prove the
least greedy. All bought at inadequate prices and limited
themselves to fair promises of payment. The statute of 1330
shows how these payments never came ; how also when
twenty-five quarters of corn were taken only twenty were
reckoned because they were measured by " the heaped
bushel." [1] In the same way, for hay, straw, etc., the
purveyors found means to reckon at a halfpenny what
was worth two or three pence ; they ordered that supplies
of wine should be held in readiness for them, kept the
best for themselves in order to sell it again to their own
profit, and exacted payment for returning a part to
the original owners, which was a strange reversal of
things. The king acknowledged all these evils and
decreed reforms accordingly. A little later he did so
again, with no more result. In 1362 he declared that
henceforth the purveyors should pay ready money at
the current market price ; and he gravely added, as an
important guarantee, that the purveyors should lose their
detested name and should be called buyers: " that the
heinous name of purveyor be changed, and named
achatour." [2] A word reform, if any.[3]

The same abuses existed in France, and numerous
ordinances may be read in the pages of Isambert, con-
ceived in exactly the same spirit and corresponding to

[1] " Statutes of the Realm," 4 Edward III, ch. 3. Eight bushels make
a quarter. [The Act 25 Edward III, stat. 5, ch. 10, A.D. 1351, provided
that every measure of corn should be striken without heap, and that the
royal purveyors should use this measure. Hence the name *strike* for a
bushel. L. T. S.]

[2] Statute 36 Edward III, stat. 1, ch. 2.

[3] See several texts in Appendix V. p. 430

A REAPER'S CART GOING UP-HILL.

(*From the Louterell Psalter : Fourteenth Century : "Vetusta Monumenta," vol. vi.*)

the same complaints ; ordinances of Philip the Fair in 1308, of Louis X in 1342, of Philip VI, who willed that the " preneurs pour nous " (takers for us), should not take unless they had " new letters from us," which shows the existence of false purveyors as in England. John of France renews all the restrictions of his predecessors, December 25, 1355, and so on.

The king and his lords journeyed on horseback for the most part, but they had carriages too. Nothing gives a better idea of the awkward, cumbersome luxury which gave its splendour to civil life during this century, than the structure of these heavy machines. The best had four wheels, and were drawn by three or four horses, one behind the other, one of them mounted by a postilion provided with a short-handled whip of many thongs ; solid beams rested on the axles, and above this framework rose an archway rounded like a tunnel ; [1] an ungainly whole. But the details were extremely elegant, the wheels were carved and their spokes expanded near the hoop into ribs forming pointed arches ; the beams were painted and gilded, the inside was hung with those dazzling tapestries, the glory of the age ; the seats were furnished with embroidered cushions ; a lady might stretch out there, half sitting, half lying ; pillows were placed in the corners as if to invite sleep or meditation, square windows opened on the sides and were hung with silk curtains.[2]

[1] A shape in use from the remotest times. Carriages quite similar to those painted in our mediæval MSS. are to be seen on the alabaster funeral chests of Etruscan days, for example at the Guarnacei Museum, Volterra, in Italy, where there is an abundance of them, showing the dead, in their own round-topped, richly ornamented carriage, on their way to the other world.

[2] Representations of carriages of this kind are frequent in manuscripts. Many are to be found, with two wheels and an abundance of ornament- ation, in the romance of King Meliadus (MS. of the fourteenth century in the British Museum, Add. 12,228, fos. 198, 243). The celebrated four wheeled carriage of the Louterell psalter, also of fourteenth century, is here

Thus travelled the noble lady, slim in form, tightly clad in a dress which outlined every curve of the body, her long slender hands caressing the favourite dog or bird. The knight, equally tight in his *cote-hardie*, looked at her with a complacent eye, and, if he knew good manners, opened his heart to his nonchalant companion in long phrases imitated from romances, themselves supposed to imitate the language of his peers. The broad forehead of the lady, who has perhaps coquettishly plucked out some of her hair as well as her eyebrows, a process about which satirists were bitter,[1] brightens up occasionally, and her smile is like a ray of sunshine. Meanwhile the axles groan, the horse-shoes crunch the ground, the machine advances by fits and starts, descends into the hollows, bounds all of a piece at the ditches, and comes down with a heavy thud. The knight must speak pretty loud to make his dainty discourse, Round Table flavoured, heard by his companion. So trivial a necessity ever sufficed to break the charm of the most delicate thought ; too many shocks shake the flower, and when the knight presents it, it has lost its perfumed pollen.

The possession of such a carriage was a princely luxury. They were bequeathed by will from one to another, and the heirloom was valuable. On September 25, 1355, Elizabeth de Burgh, Lady Clare, wrote her last will and endowed her eldest daughter with " her great carriage

reproduced. It is drawn by five horses harnessed single file. On the second sits a postilion with a short whip of several thongs ; on the fifth, that is, the nearest to the carriage, sits another postilion with a long whip of the shape in use at the present day.

[1] La Tour-Landry relates a story of a holy hermit who saw in a dream his nephew's wife in purgatory. The demons were pushing burning needles into her eyebrows. An angel told him that it was because she had trimmed her eyebrows and temples, and increased her forehead, and plucked out her hair, thinking to beautify herself and to please the world. " Le livre du Chevalier de La Tour-Landry," ed. Montaiglon, Paris, 1854. An English translation of the fifteenth century was published by the Early English Text Society in 1868.

AN ENGLISH CARRIAGE OF THE FOURTEENTH CENTURY.

(*From the Louterell Psalter.*)

with the covertures, carpets, and cushions." In the twentieth year of Richard II Roger Rouland received £400 sterling " for making the Queen's chariot"; and John le Charer, in the sixth of Edward III, received £1,000 for the carriage of the Lady Eleanor.[1] These were enormous sums. In the fourteenth century the average price of an ox was thirteen shillings, one penny farthing ; of a sheep, one shilling and five pence ; of a cow, nine shillings and five pence ; and a penny for a fowl.[2] Lady Eleanor's carriage thus represented the value of a herd of sixteen hundred oxen.

Scarcely less ornamented were the horse-litters some-times used by people of rank, especially by ladies. They were of the same shape as the carriages, being covered with a sort of·rounded vault, in which were cut more or less large openings. Two horses carried them, one before, the other behind, each being placed between the shafts with which the contrivance was provided at both ends.[3]

Between these luxurious carriages and the peasants' carts there was nothing analogous to the multitude of middle-class conveyances to which we are now accus-tomed ; the middle class itself being as yet but imperfectly developed. True, there were some not so expensive as

[1] The king's sister. Devon's " Issues of the Exchequer," 1837, p. 142. As Englished by Devon, the Latin text referred to would mean that the receiver of the money and maker of the carriage was Master la Zousche, but la Zousche was the clerk of the wardrobe, who had the money from the Exchequer to give it to John le Charer, " per manus John le Charer." *Per* has here the meaning of *pro*, a use of the word of which several instances may be found in Du Cange. This indication of Devon's mistake is due to the late Mr. Bradshaw, of Cambridge.

[2] Thorold Rogers, " History of Agriculture and Prices," i. pp. 361–363.

[3] Curious representations of such litters are to be found in mediæval manuscripts ; for instance, the one here reproduced from the MS. 118 Français, in the Bibliothèque Nationale, Paris, fol. 285, where two persons are to be seen using the litter, a lady and a wounded knight (Romance of Lancelot, fourteenth century) ; or in the MS. Roy, 18 E. II, in the British Museum, fol. 7 (Chronicles of Froissart).

those belonging to the princesses of Edward's Court, but not many. Every one at this time knew how to ride on horseback, and it was much more practical to use one's mount than the heavy vehicles of the period. One went much faster, and was more certain to arrive. "The Paston Letters" show that matters had changed little in the fifteenth century. John Paston being ill

A YOUNG SQUIRE (CHAUCER'S SQUIRE) TRAVELLING ON HORSEBACK.
(*From the Ellesmere MS.*)

in London, his wife wrote asking him to return as soon as he could bear the horse-ride ; the idea of returning in a carriage did not even occur to them. Yet it was a serious case, " a grete dysese."

Margaret Paston writes on September 28, 1443, " If I might have had my will, I should have seen you ere this time ; I would ye were at home, if it were your ease, and your sore might be as well looked to here as it is where

tenoit en son guion. J. chenaillier naure de grans
desiures plaies quil auoit ou corps et en la teste
et entour la litiere cheuauchoient .iiij. escuiers
deux dune part. et deux daultre. De aj. jniam.

et la damoiselle faisoit mout grant
dueil pour le chenaillier dont elle estoit mout angoisseuse. car cestoit la
riens ou monde quelle plus amoit
et messe gauuain la damoiselle si
tost comme il vint pres delu. et celle respondi q̃
dieux le benesse. ne pour ce ne laissa mie son dueil

TRAVELLING IN A HORSE LITTER. [p. 101.

*(From the MS. 118 Français, in the Bibliothèque Nationale, late Fourteenth
Century.)*

ye be, now liefer than a gown though it were of scarlet.
I pray you if your sore be whole, and so that ye may endure
to ride, when my father comes to London, that ye will
ask leave, and come home, when the horse shall be sent
home again, for I hope ye should be kept as tenderly here
as ye be at London." [1]

Women were accustomed to riding almost as much
as men, and when they had to travel they usually did it
on horseback.   A peculiarity of their horsemanship, which
we have seen of late becoming again the fashion after a
lapse of five centuries, was that they habitually rode astride.
The custom of riding sideways did not spread in England
before the latter part of the fourteenth century, and even
then it was not general.   In the invaluable manuscript
of the Decretals in the British Museum,[2] ladies on horseback are constantly represented, always riding astride.
At one place [3] horses are shown being brought for a knight
and a lady ; both saddles are exactly the same ; each
have tall backs, so as to form a sort of comfortable chair.
The numerous ivories of the fourteenth century in the
Victoria and Albert Museum and in the British Museum
often represent a lady and her lover, both on horseback,
and hawking.   In almost all cases the lady unmistakably
rides astride.   Both ways of riding are shown in the
fifteenth-century illuminations in the Ellesmere manuscript of Chaucer's " Canterbury Tales."   The wife of
Bath rides astride, with large spurs ; the prioress sits
sideways.

II

There were few places in England where the sight
of the royal train was not familiar.   For the motives

---

[1] " Paston Letters," 1422–1509, edited by Jas. Gairdner, 1872,
vol. i. p. 49 ; spelling modernized.
[2] Roy. 10 E. IV.   [3] Fol. 310.

mentioned above, the Court's journeys were incessant.
The royal itineraries that have come down to us throw
a flood of light on this continual need of movement.   The
itinerary of King John shows that he rarely passed a month
in the same place, most frequently he did not even remain
there a week.   Within a fortnight he is often found at
five or six different towns or castles.[1]   The same with
Edward I, who, as we have seen, would change his
abode three times every fortnight.[2]

And when the king moved, not only was he preceded
by twenty-four archers in his pay, receiving threepence
a day,[3] but he was accompanied by all those officers whom
the author of " Fleta " enumerates with so much com-
placency.   The sovereign took with him his two marshals,
his outer marshal (*forinsecus*) who in time of war
disposed the armies for battle, selected the halting-places
on his journeys, and at all times arrested malefactors found
in the *virgata regia*, that is to say, within twelve leagues
around his dwelling ; [4] and his inner marshal (*intrinsecus*),
who guarded the palace and castles, and cleared them
as much as possible of courtesans.   He collected from
every common harlot (*meretrice communi*) four pence by
way of fine the first time that he arrested her ; if she
returned she was brought before the steward, who solemnly
forbid her ever to present herself at the dwelling of the
king, queen, or their children ; the third time she was
imprisoned and the tresses of her hair were shorn off ;

1 " A Description of the Patent Rolls . . . to which is added an
Itinerary of King John," by T. Duffus Hardy, London, 1835.

2 1299–1300.   " Liber quotidianus Garderobæ," Society of An-
tiquaries, London, 1787, p. 67.

3 " Archers.   And xxiiij archers on foote for garde of the kinge's body,
who shall goe before the kinge as he travaleth thorough the cuntry " (" King
Edward II's . . . Ordinances," 1323, ed. Furnivall, p. 46).

4 " Fleta, seu commentarius juris Anglicani, editio secunda," London
1685, lib. ii. cap. 2, 4.   This treatise is believed to have been composed
in the Fleet prison by a lawyer in the time of Edward I.   It is later than
1292, for mention is made in it of the submission of Scotland.

A WOMAN RIDING ASTRIDE (CHAUCER'S WIFE OF BATH).

(From the Ellesmere MS.)

A LADY RIDING SIDEWAYS (CHAUCER'S PRIORESS). [*p.* 105.

(From the Ellesmere MS.)

the fourth time one of those hideous punishments was resorted to which the Middle Ages in their brutality tolerated ; the upper lip of these women was cut off, " ne de cætero concupiscantur ad libidinem." [1] There was also the chamberlain, who took care that the interior of the house was comfortable : " He has to arrange decently for the king's bed, and to see that the rooms be furnished with carpets and benches ; " the treasurer of the wardrobe, who kept the accounts ; the marshal of the hall, whose mission it was to eject unworthy intruders and dogs,— " non enim permittat canes aulam ingredi,"—and a crowd of other officers.[2]

Overtopping all the rest, there was, moreover, the king's seneschal or steward, first officer of his household, and his great justiciary. Wherever the king went the apparatus of justice was transported with him ; when he was about to start the steward gave to the sheriff notice of the place where the Court would stop, in order that he might bring his prisoners to the town where the prince was to be stationed.[3] All the cases amenable to the jurisdiction of the justices in eyre were then determined by the steward, as the king's justiciary, who prescribed, if necessary, the judicial duel, pronounced sentences of outlawry, and judged in criminal and civil cases.[4] This

[1] Lib. ii. cap. 5.   The ordinance of Edward II mentioned further, p. 110, speaks only of the brand by a hot iron on the forehead.   " King Edward II's Household and Wardrobe Ordinances," A.D. 1323, Chaucer Society, ed. Furnivall, 1876.

[2] Lib. ii. cap. 14, 15.

[3] He sent a *mandatum* to this effect, and he withdrew it when the king changed his mind as to the place where he wished to go, which happened often enough.   " Debet autem senescallus nomine capitalis justitiarii cujus vices gerit mandare vicecomiti loci ubi dominus rex fuerit declinaturus, quod venire faciat ad certum diem, ubicumque tunc rex fuerit in ballivia sua, omnes assisas comitatus sui et omnes prisones cum suis atachiamentis." " Fleta," lib. ii. cap. 3, § 4.

[4] " Habet etiam ex virtute officii sui potestatem procedendi ad utlagationes et duella jungendi et singula faciendi quæ ad justitiarios itinerantes, prout supra dictum est pertinent faciendi." " Fleta," lib. ii. cap. 3, § 11.

right of criminal justice even accompanied the king abroad, but he only exercised it when the criminal had been arrested in his own royal place of abode. One such case happened in the fourteenth year of the reign of Edward I. This sovereign being at Paris, Ingelram de Nogent came into his house to steal, and was caught in the act. After some discussion it was acknowledged that Edward, by his royal privilege, should remain judge in the matter ; he delivered the robber over to Robert Fitz-John, his steward, who caused Ingelram to be hung from the gibbet of St. Germain-des-Prés.[1]

For a long time the chancellor himself, and the clerks who made out the writs, followed the king on his journeys, and Palgrave notes that frequently a strong horse was requisitioned from the nearest convent to carry the rolls ; [2] but this custom came to a close in the fourth year of Edward III, when the Chancery was permanently established at Westminster.

The tribunal moving on, a crowd of suitors moved with it. No matter though they were not inscribed on the rolls, they followed without losing patience, as gulls follow the ship, hoping that something may come their way. Parties with a lawsuit, petitioners of every kind, women " of ill life " (*de fole vie*), a whole herd of individuals with no one to vouch for them, persisted in escorting the prince and his courtiers. They quarrelled among each other, robbed by the way, sometimes committed murders, and, as may be imagined, did not contribute to render the news of the king's arrival welcome to his subjects.

In the ordinances of his household, Edward II enumerates and deplores all these abuses ; he orders that masterless men who follow the Court shall be put in irons for forty days on bread and water, and that the women of ill life shall be likewise imprisoned and branded with a

[1] " Fleta," lib. ii. cap. 3, § 9.
[2] " Original authority of the King's Council," p. 115.

A FAMILY DINNER AMONG THE GREAT, WITH DOGS, MUSICIANS, CARVER, CUPBEARER, MARSHAL OF
THE HALL (EXPELLING A LAZAR).

(*From the MS. Addit. 28162 in the British Museum. Fourteenth Century.*)

[*p.* 109.

hot iron ; he forbids his knights, clerks, squires, valets, grooms, in short, all who accompany him, to bring their wives with them, unless these have any post or employment at Court, this host of feminine beings increasing the chances of trouble. He also limits the number of persons who should accompany the marshal, which had, as will happen, increased little by little beyond all bounds. His ordinances, like so many others in the Middle Ages, were conspicuous for their wisdom, their minuteness, and their prompt decay.

Justice did not travel only in the king's suite. She was peripatetic in England, visiting the counties in the company of the royal itinerant judges and going from hundred to hundred with that governor, military chief, police magistrate, financial agent, the sheriff, a functionary of great local, and sometimes tyrannical, power, appointed and dismissed at will by the king during certain periods, elected at others.

Both kinds, at fixed times, were on the move and caused a considerable portion of the inhabitants to leave their work, take to the road and be on the move too, in order to come to the court that was to be held. Both kinds put before the jurors a number of questions which the twelve men had to answer under oath, some of those questions being obviously quite uncomfortable to reply to.

The sheriff goes about the hundreds [1] in his shire and holds the " view of frank pledge," chiefly established for the maintenance of that ancient system of enforced solidarity which obliged, theoretically at least, every male

[1] " The county is divided into hundreds or into wapentakes or into wards, the term wapentake appearing in Yorkshire, Lincolnshire, Derbyshire, Nottinghamshire, the term ward in the northernmost counties." (" History of English Law before Edward I," by Sir Frederick Pollock and F. W. Maitland, Cambridge, 2 vols., 1895, vol. i. p. 543.) At the head of the hundred was the bailiff, appointed by the sheriff, acting under him, and giving also rise to numerous complaints. See, e.g. " Rolls of Parliament," ii. 357, a petition of 1376.

to belong to a particular group of inhabitants of ten or
more (tithing), jointly responsible for the misdeeds of any
of their number in case the culprit cannot be found,
fined, jailed or hanged, according to the occasion.   By
degrees the old " articles of the view," greatly varying
from place to place,[1] had increased in number, and the
jurors had to answer as to a variety of smaller offences
often duplicating the justices' own interrogatories.[2]

The " turns " or " tourns " of the sheriffs might,
according to the Great Charter, only take place twice a
year, not oftener, because their coming occasioned loss
of time and money to the sworn men and others who had
to leave home and attend the court, and to the king's
subjects at whose houses these officers and their train went
to lodge.[3]   In spite of institutions which, as we shall
see, had made the very men placed under the jurisdiction of the sheriffs, bailiffs, etc. themselves the censors
of these same officials, abuses were numerous, the Commons
were ever complaining, and frequent statutes, one after
the other, denounced corrupt practices and stopped them
—for a time.[4]

[1] The lists which have reached us " leave us doubting whether any
of them had received a solemn sanction from the central power."   Same
" History of English Law," ii. 508.   On the origin, growth, decay, uses
and abuses of the institution, see W. A. Morris, " The Frankpledge System,"
London, 1910.

[2] In many places great people, lay or ecclesiastic, had somehow secured
for themselves the properly royal privilege of holding the " view " ; it
became attached to some manors and was conveyed with them.   See the
petition of an abbess who claims the view of frankpledge attached to the
manor of Shorwalle, Isle of Wight, which had been given her ; Isabella
de Forte disputes her this right, the real object of the quarrel between the
two ladies being the fines levied when the view was held.

Towards the end of the fourteenth century the frankpledge had fallen
into decay.

[3] " Magna Carta," cap. 42 of the second confirmation by Henry III
(1217) ; Stubbs' " Select Charters," p. 337. " Nec liceat alicui vicecomiti
vel ballivo tenere turnum suum per hundredum nisi bis per annum ; " " Fleta,"
Lib. ii. cap. 52.

[4] See Appendix VI, p. 431.

The itinerant justices' inquiry covered a much larger field ; their " Articles of the Eyre," or *Capitula Itineris*, included every imaginable misdeed from highest to lowest, from " crimen læsæ Majestatis," above which nothing could be imagined, to fishing by means of " kidels " (weirs) or the using of nets to capture pigeons without the owner's permit.

Coming four times a year in accordance with Art. 18 of the Great Charter, sitting in the full court of the county, growing in importance, while that of the sheriff as a judge went diminishing and the system of the frankpledge was falling into disuse, the itinerant justices submitted to the jury a ceaselessly increasing number of questions, a whole quire of them in the first half of the fourteenth century.[1] They asked what crimes, what misdemeanours, what infractions against the statutes had come to their know-ledge. And in these minute interrogatories at every moment came up the names of the sheriff, the coroner,[2] the bailiff, the constable, of all the royal functionaries, whose conduct was thus placed under popular control. Has any of these officers, says the judge, released some robber, or counterfeiter or a clipper of coin ? Has he for any consideration neglected the pursuit against a vaga-bond or an assassin ? Has he unjustly received fines ? Has he been paid by men who wished to avoid a public charge (for example, of being sworn as member of a jury) ? Has the sheriff claimed more than reasonable hospitality from those in his jurisdiction, in tourns held too oft ? Has he come with more than five or six horses ? And

[1] " The articles for the London eyre of 1244 are in ' Munimenta Gild-hallæ,' i. 79 ; those for the eyre of 1321 are in ' Munim. Gild.,' ii. 347. The latter are fully seven times as long as the former and fill fifteen octavo pages." Pollock and Maitland, " History of English Law," ii. 519 ; cf. " Fleta," i. cap. 19 and 20 : " De Processu coram Justiciariis itinerantibus— De capitulis Coronæ et Itineris." Cf. W. C. Bolland, " The General Eyre," 1922.

[2] Originally, *custos placitorum coronæ*, record keeper of the pleas of the Crown.

the juror was obliged in the same way to denounce,
under his oath, the great who had arbitrarily imprisoned
travellers passing through their lands, and all those who
had neglected to assist in arresting a thief and running with
the " hue and cry ; " [1] for in this society each man is
by turns peace officer, soldier, and judge, and even the
humbler ones, menaced by so many exactions, have their
share too in the administration of justice and the maintenance of public order.   Highly important were, therefore,
from a social point of view, these judicial tourns, which
periodically reminded the mere man that he was a citizen,
and that the affairs of the State were also his affairs.[2]

Juries could at times, like so many other picturesque
groups of inhabitants, become one of the sights of the road.
If they perjured themselves or accepted bribes, they would
be sent to London and be jailed in the Tower ; they were
to travel along, not by night, but " by clear day, in the
view of all, so that the country people might see the pain
and shame of those guilty men who will be thereby the
better punished." [3]

Or else, if that unanimity which became obligatory
in the latter part of the fourteenth century had not been
secured, the itinerant justices, in order to get it any way,

[1] In existence also in France and Germany from the earliest times,
thus defined in the " Grand Coutumier de Normandie," chap. 54 : " Il
ne doit être crié fors pour cause criminelle, si comme pour feu et pour larcin
ou pour homicide ou pour autre évident péril, si comme si aucun court
sus à un autre le couteau trait.   Car cil qui crie haro sans apert (obvious)
péril le doit amender au prince . . . A ce cri doivent isser tous ceux qui
l'ont oui."   This custom remained in use in Normandy until the French
Revolution.   Glasson, " Origines de la clameur de haro," Paris, 1882.
In England the statutes concerning the " hue and cry " were repealed only
in 1827.

[2] " Fleta," lib. i. cap. 19, 20. See also " Local Self-Government
and Centralization," by Toulmin Smith, 1848, pp. 220–232, 298.

[3] " Mais de cler jour, à la veue de toutz, issint qe gentz de pays puissent
veer la peine et la hounte que les ditz atteintz ount, et par tant en soient les
meuz chastiez."   Year, probably, 33 Ed. I ; Palgrave, " Original Authority
of the King's Council," p. 56.

were free to place the twelve men in carts and carry them about wherever they went, until the twelve chose to agree.[1]

When monks came out of the cloister and travelled, they wilfully modified their costume, and it became difficult to distinguish them from the great. I saw, writes Chaucer :

> " I saugh his sleves purfiled atte hond
> With grys, and that the fynest of a lond,
> And for to festne his hood undur his chyn
> He hadde of gold y-wrought a curious pyn,
> A love-knotte in the gretter end ther was." [2]

But the councils are still more explicit, and do more than justify the satire of the poet. Thus the Council of London in 1342, reproaches the religious with wearing clothing " fit rather for knights than for clerks, that is to say short, very tight, with excessively wide sleeves, not reaching the elbows, but hanging down very low, lined with fur or with silk." They made themselves conspicuous by their long beards, rings on their fingers, costly girdles, purses or bags whereon figures were embroidered in gold, knives resembling swords, boots red or party-coloured, or slashed long-pointed shoes (the Polish-born poulaine) ; in a word, all the luxury of the magnates of the land. Later, in 1367, the Council of York renewed the same criticisms ; the religious have " ridiculously short " clothing ; they dare publicly to wear those coats " which do not come down to the middle of the legs, and do not even cover the knees." Severe prohibitions were made for the future, though on a journey tunics shorter than the regulation gown were tolerated.[3]

A bishop did not start on a journey without a great train ; and the bishops, besides their episcopal visitations,

[1] Reeves, " History of English Law," ed. Finlason, ii. p. 408.
[2] Prologue to the " Canterbury Tales ; " The Monk.
[3] See Appendix VII, p. 432.

had, like the nobility, to travel to visit their lands and to
live on them.   On all these occasions they took with them
their servants of different kinds and their followers, as
the king did his court.   The accounts of the expenses
of Richard de Swinfield, Bishop of Hereford, give an idea
of the lordly life led by well-to-do prelates.   He was a
bishop of some importance, and rich in proportion ; many
manors belonged to his bishopric ; he could hold his

A COOK ON A JOURNEY (CHAUCER'S COOK).
(*From the Ellesmere MS.*)

rank as prelate and as lord, be hospitable, charitable to
the poor, and spend much on requests and suits at the
court of Rome and elsewhere.   He had constantly in
his pay about forty persons of different ranks, the greater
part of whom accompanied him in his numerous changes
of residence.   His squires (*armigeri*) had from a mark
(13s. 4d.) to a pound a year ; his *valleti*, that is, the clerks
of his chapel and others, his carters, porters, falconers,
grooms, messengers, etc., had from a crown to eight

shillings and eightpence. In the third category came the
kitchen servants, the baker, with two to four shillings a
year ; in the fourth, that of the boys or pages who helped
the other servants, and whose wages greatly varied, being
from one to six shillings a year.   All the household was
dressed alike, in striped cloth (*pannus stragulatus*), supplied
by the bishop, besides the fixed salary.   One of the most
peculiar retainers of the bishop belonged to a now extinct
race, and was his champion, Thomas de Bruges, who
received an annual payment to fight in the prelate's name
in case any lawsuit should have to be terminated by a
judicial duel.[1]

III

At eventide, monks, great men, and travellers of all
degree sought shelter for the night. When the king,
preceded by his twenty-four archers, and escorted by his
lords and the officers of his household, was expected in
a town, the marshal selected a certain number of the best
houses, which were marked with chalk. The chamberlain asked the inhabitants to make room, and the
Court settled as well as it could in the lodgings.
Even the capital was not exempt from the annoyance
of this burden ; the marshal had, however, to come

[1] " Household Expenses of Richard de Swinfield," ed. J. Webb, 1854,
Camden Society, vols. i. p. 125, ii. pp. xxx-xxxvi. The duels of Thomas
de Bruges were not those of the cases of felony and crime which resulted
in the death of the vanquished; it was merely the duel with staff and shield,
cum fuste et scuto, which required, as may be imagined, the replacement
of the champion much less frequently. In the twenty-ninth year of Edward
III, a duel took place by means of champions between the Bishop of Salisbury and the Earl of Salisbury. When the judges, conformably to the
laws, came to examine the dress of the combatants, they found that the
bishop's champion had several sheets of prayers and incantations sown in
his garments (" Year Books of Edward I," Rolls Series, 32–33d year, preface,
p. xvi, note). This examination of the clothing was always made with the
intention of discovering frauds of this kind, which were considered as the
most dangerous and disloyal of all.

there to an understanding with the mayor, sheriffs, and city officers for the selection of the habitations. Sometimes the royal agent chose to forget this wise proviso, and trouble followed. In the nineteenth year of Edward II, that prince having come to the Tower, the people of his household quartered themselves on the citizens without the mayor and aldermen having been consulted ; the very sheriff's house was marked with chalk. Great was the wrath of this officer when he found Richard de Ayremynne, the king's own secretary, established in his house, the stranger's horses in his stable, his servants in the kitchen. Undaunted by the thought of a royal secretary's importance, the sheriff, counting on the privilege of the city, drove out the secretary and his suite by force, rubbed off the marks of the chalk, and became once more master of his own abode. Cited to appear before the Court steward, and accused of having contemned the king's orders to the extent of at least £1,000, he stoutly defended himself, and appealed in defence to the mayor and citizens, who produced the charters of the city privileges. The charters were clear, their purport could not be denied ; the sheriff's boldness was excused ; Ayremynne consoled himself as best he could, and did not receive any indemnity.[1]

In the country, if the king did not happen to be within easy reach of one of his own or his lieges' castles, he often went to lodge at the neighbouring monastery, sure of being received there as master. The great on their journeys did their best to imitate the prince in this respect.[2]   In

[1] See Riley's " Liber Albus," p. 303, where the case is entered in full.
[2] One has only to peruse Froissart to notice the extreme frequency of this custom. Jean de Hainaut arrives at Denain : " There he lodged in the abbey that night " (lib. i. part i. ch. 14) ; the queen disembarks in England with the same Jean de Hainaut, " and then they found a great abbey of black monks which is called St. Aymon, and they were harboured there and refreshed for three days " (ch. 18) ; " there the king stopped and lodged in an abbey " (ch. 292) ; " King Philippe came to the good town of Amiens, and there lodged in the abbey of Gard " (ch. 296), etc.

the convents hospitality was a religious duty ; for the order of St. John of Jerusalem the first of duties. This order had establishments all over England, and it was a piece of good fortune for the poor traveller to come to one of them. No doubt he was treated there according to his rank, but it was much not to find the door closed. The accounts of the year 1338,[1] show that these knight-monks did not seek at all to avoid the heavy burden of hospitality ; in their lists of expenditure are always to be found charges occasioned by *supervenientibus* (strangers). When it was an affair of kings or princes, they outdid themselves ; thus the Prior of Clerkenwell mentions " much expenditure which cannot be given in detail, caused by the hospitality offered to strangers, members of the royal family, and to other grandees of the realm who stay at Clerkenwell and remain there at the cost of the house." In consequence, the account closes with this sad summing up : " Thus the expenditure exceeds the receipts by twenty-one pounds, eleven shillings and fourpence." The mere proximity of a great man was a source of expense, for, even if he did not go himself, he would send his suit to profit of the hospitality of the convent. In the accounts for Hampton, the list of people to whom beer and bread have been furnished ends by these words : " because the Duke of Cornwall is staying in the vicinity." [2]

It should be noted that most of these houses had been endowed by the nobles, and each one, recognizing his own land or that of a relative, a friend, or an ancestor,

[1] " The Knights Hospitallers in England," edited by Larking and Kemble, Camden Society, 1857. It is the text of a manuscript found at Malta entitled, " Extenta terrarum et tenementorum Hospitalis Sancti Johannis Jerusalem in Anglia, A.D. 1338."

[2] " Knights Hospitallers," pp. 99, 101, 127. The effect of the Scottish wars on the possessions of the Knights is strikingly set forth : " Omnes possessiones hospitalis in Scocia sunt destructa, combusta per fortem guerram ibidem per multos annos continuatam unde nil his diebus potest levari. Solebat tamen, tempore pacis, reddere per annum, cc marcas " (p. 129).

felt himself at home in the monastery. But these turbulent
lords, friends of good cheer, abused of the monks' gratitude, and their excesses caused complaints which came
to the ears of the king.[1]   Edward I forbade any one to
venture to eat or lodge in a religious house, unless the
superior had explicitly invited him, or he were the
founder of the establishment, and even then his consumption should be moderate. The poor only, who more than
any one lost by the excesses of the great, might continue
to be lodged for nothing : " The king intendeth not that
the grace of hospitality should be withdrawn from the
destitute." [2]   Edward II, in 1309, confirmed these rules,
which had apparently fallen into abeyance, and promised
again, six years later, that neither he nor his family would
make inordinate use of the hospitality of the monks.[3]

All in vain ; these abuses were already comprised
among those which the *Articles of the Eyre* had for their
object to discover, but failed to suppress. Periodically
the magistrate came to question the country folk on the
subject. Have " any lords or others gone to lodge in
religious houses without being invited by the superiors,
or gone at their own expense, against the will of the same ? "
Have any been so bold as to " send to the houses or mansions
belonging to the monks or others, men, horses, or dogs
to sojourn there at an expense not their own ? " The
application of these rules did not go without difficulty
or even danger, for the magistrate questioned also the
jury about " any who may have taken revenge for refusal
of food or lodging." [4]

The Commons in parliament, mindful as they were
in such matters of the fate of the poorest, were not unmindful of their own, and took steps to prevent, in a
general way and without reference to the impecunious,

---

[1] See Appendix VIII. p. 433.   [2] Statute 3 Edward I, cap. 1.
[3] Statute 9 Edward II, cap. 11, *Articuli Cleri*, A.D. 1315–1316.
[4] " Fleta," lib. i. cap. 20, § 68, 72.

the falling into disuse of monachal hospitality. The non-residence of the clergy, which was to be one of the causes of the Reformation two hundred years later, occasioned bitter protests during the fourteenth century. The Commons object especially because from this abuse there results a decay of the duties of hospitality. " And that all other persons advanced to the benefices of Holy Church," they request of the king, " should remain on their said benefices in order to keep hospitality there, on the same penalty, exception made for the king's clerks and the clerks of the great of the realm." [1] Parliament protests also against the bestowal by the pope of rich priories on foreigners who remain abroad. These foreigners " suffer the noble edifices built of old time when they were occupied by the English to fall quite to ruin," and neglect " to keep hospitality." [2]

Only people of high rank were admitted into the monastery proper. The mass of travellers, pilgrims and others, were housed and fed in the guest-house, a building made on purpose to receive passers-by ; it usually stood by itself, and was even, sometimes, erected outside the precincts of the monastery. Such, for instance, was the case in Battle Abbey, where the guest-house is still to be seen outside the large entrance gate. These edifices commonly consisted of a hall with doors opening on each side into sleeping rooms. People slept also in the hall ; old inventories, for instance the one concerning the Maison-Dieu or hospital at Dover, show that beds were set up in the hall and remained, it seems, permanently there.[3]

[1] " Rolls of Parliament," iii. p. 501, A.D. 1402.
[2] Ibid., iii. p. 82, A.D. 1379–80. The clergy, on the other hand, complain that the sheriffs sometimes come " with their wives and other excessive number of people on horseback as well as on foot," to stay in monasteries, under pretext of collecting monies for the king. Ibid. p. 26, A.D. 1377.
[3] " Inventories of St. Mary's Hospital, or Maison Dieu, Dover," by M. E. C. Walcott, " Archæologia Cantiana," London, 1869.

It is hardly necessary to recall that hospitality was also exercised in castles ; noblemen who were not at feud willingly received one another ; there were much stricter ties of brotherhood among them than now exist among people of the same class. We do not often now give lodging to unknown persons who knock at the door ; at the most, and but rarely, do we permit a poor man passing along in the country to sleep for a night in our hay-loft. In the Middle Ages, men received their equals, not by way of simple charity, but as a habit of courtesy and also for pleasure. Known or unknown, the travelling knight was rarely refused the door of a country manor. His coming in time of peace was a happy diversion from the monotony of the days. There was in every house the *hall*, or large room where the meals were taken in common ; the new-comer ate with the lord at a table placed on a raised platform called the *dais*, erected at one end of the room ; his followers were at the lower tables disposed along the side walls. Supper finished, all soon retired to rest, people went to bed and rose early in those days. The traveller withdrew sometimes into a special room for guests, if the house were large ; sometimes into that of the master himself, the *solar* (room on the first storey), and spent the night there with him. Meanwhile, in the hall, the lower tables were taken out, for in general these were not standing, but movable ; [1] mattresses were placed on the ground over the litter of rushes which day and night covered the pavement, and the people of the household, the suite of the traveller, the strangers of less im-

[1] " Mensæ de medio removentur," or, in the English version by S. Bateman, of 1582, fol. 81, " when they have eaten, boord, clothes, and reliefe bee borne awaye "—description of a dinner in England, by Bartholomew the Englishman (de Glanville), 13th century. " Bartholomi Anglici de proprietatibus rerum," Frankfort, 1609, lib. vi. cap. 32. Smollett, in the eighteenth century, notes the existence of similar customs in Scotland ; people dine, then sleep in the hall, where mattresses are stretched, replacing the tables (" Humphrey Clinker ").

portance, stretched themselves out there till morning. Such a litter of herbs or rushes was in constant use, and was to be found in the king's palace as well as in the houses of mere merchants in the city : it was spread in lieu of a carpet, to keep the room warm and to give a feeling of comfort. It is still to be met with, and this is, apparently, the last place where it has found refuge, in old-fashioned French provincial *diligences ;* the straw in English country omnibuses is also its lineal descendant. So it was at least when, in pre-automobile times, these lines were originally written.

Prices paid for the purchase of rushes constantly recur in the accounts of the royal expenses.[1] They were so largely used in towns as well as in the country, that people in cities did not know what to do with the soiled ones, and the local authorities had to interfere over and over again, especially in London, where the inhabitants were apt to throw them into the Thames, with the result of greatly damaging and polluting the water.

Through a window opened in the partition between his room and the hall, over the dais, the lord could see and even hear all that was done or said below. In the king's house itself the hall was used for sleeping as is shown by the ordinances of Edward IV ;[2] at a period much nearer our day (1514), Barclay still complains that at Court the same couch serves for two :

And never in the court shalt thou have bed alone,

and that the noise from the comers and goers, from brawlers,

---

[1] " Hall and chamber, for litter, 20d. ; hall and chamber, for rushes, 16d. ; hall, &c., for litter, 1d., &c." Extracts from the " Rotulus familiæ," 18 Ed. I, " Archæologia," vol. xv. p. 350. The king was then at Langley Castle, Buckinghamshire.

[2] Turner and Parker, " Domestic Architecture in England, from Edward I to Richard II," Oxford, 1853, p. 75. See also in " Archæologia," vi. p. 366, the illustrated description of the royal hall at Eltham.

coughers, and chatterers never ceases, and prevents sleep.[1]
At the first streak of dawn, sending through the white or
coloured panes of the high windows shafts of light on
the dark carved timber-work, which, high above the pavement, supported the roof, all stirred on their couches ;
soon they were out of doors, horses were saddled, and the
clatter of hoofs sounded anew on the highway.

Towards the latter part of the fourteenth century a
change became noticeable in the use of the hall. It was
first pointed out by that acute observer of manners, William
Langland, the author of the " Visions." Life was becoming, by degrees, less patriarchal and more private ;
people were less fond of dining almost publicly in their
halls. Well-to-do individuals began to prefer having their
meals by themselves in rooms with chimneys, which last
particular Langland is careful to note as a sign of the
growing luxuriousness of the times. " Elyng " (dull,
silent) " is the hall," he said, in a well-known passage :

> " There the lorde ne the lady · liketh noughte to sytte.
> Now hathe uche riche a reule · to eten bi hym-selve
> In a prive parloure · for pore mennes sake,
> Or in a chambre with a chymneye · and leve the chief halle,
> That was made for meles · men to eten inne." [2]

Less and less inhabited, the hall gradually became little
more than a sort of thoroughfare leading to the rooms
where people were living a life more private than before.
It decreased in size as well as in importance, until it was
nothing in ordinary houses but the vestibule which we
now see.

It must have been chiefly to the very poor, or the
very rich or powerful that the monastery served as a
hostelry. Monks received the former out of charity,

[1] Eclogue III in the edition of the " Cytezen and Vplondyshman,"
published by the Percy Society, 1847, p. li.

[2] " The Vision concerning Piers the Plowman," ed. Skeat, Text B,
passus x. line 96.

and the latter out of necessity, the common inns being at once too dear for the one and too miserable for the other. They were intended for the middle class : merchants, small landowners, itinerant packmen, etc. A certain number of beds were placed in one room, and a certain number of men in each bed, usually two, but sometimes three, the latter number being in any case frequent in Germany, according to Chaucer's friend, Eustache Des Champs, sent to those parts as " ambassador and messenger " by the French king : " No one lies apart, but two and two in a dark room, or oftener three and three, in the same bed as it chances." He regrets the better manners and more refined customs of his own country, " doux pays, terre très honorable." [1]

Travellers bought separately their food and drink, chiefly bread, a little meat, and beer. Complaints as to excessive prices were not less frequent than now. The innkeeper's extortions were supplemented by those of his assistants. Chaucer's good parson, branding those men who encourage the evil practices of their subordinates, does not forget " thilke that holden hostelries," and who " sustenen the theft of hir hostilers (ostlers)." [2] The people petitioned parliament and the king interfered accordingly with his wonted useless good will. Edward III promulgated, in the 23rd year of his reign, a statute to constrain " hostelers et herbergers " to sell food at reasonable prices ; and again, four years later, tried to put an end to the " great and outrageous cost of victuals kept up in all the realm by inn-keepers and other retailers of

---

[1] "Chascuns ne gist mie a part soy,
    Mais deux et deux en chambre obscure,
    Ou le plus souvent troy et troy,
    En un seul lit à l'aventure,"

with fleas as big as those of the monks of Citeaux. " Œuvres Complètes," ed. de Queux de St. Hilaire, vol vii. pp. 79, 117.
[2] " Works," Skeat, iv, 595.

victuals, to the great detriment of the people travelling
through the realm." [1]

To have an example of ordinary travelling, we may
follow the warden and two fellows of Merton College,
who went with four servants from Oxford to Durham
and Newcastle in 1331.[2] They travelled on horseback ;
it was in the dead of winter. Their food was very simple
and their lodging inexpensive, the same items constantly
recur ; they comprise, on account of the season, candles
and fire, sometimes a coal fire. One of their days may
give an idea of the rest : for a Sunday spent at Alreton
they write down :

Bread	.	.	.	.	.	4d.	Candles	.	.	.	.	.	¼d.
Beer	.	.	.	.	.	2d.	Fuel	.	.	.	.	.	2d.
Wine	.	.	.	.	.	1¼d.	Beds	.	.	.	.	.	2d.
Meat	.	.	.	.	.	5½d.	Fodder for Horses	.	.	10d.
Potage	.	.	.	.	.	¼d.						

Beds, we see, were not expensive ; our men did not
spend more for them than for their beer. Another time,
the servants alone are at the inn, and the sleeping of the
four comes to a penny for two nights. Generally, when
the party is complete, the whole of their beds cost twopence ; at London the price was a little higher, that is

[1] Statutes 23 Ed. III, ch. 6, and 27 Ed. III, st. 1, ch. 3. As to the
inns of the Middle Ages, see Francisque Michel and Ed. Fournier, " La
Grande Bohème, histoire de classes réprouvées," vol. i, " Hôtelleries et
cabarets," Paris, 1851 ; d'Avenel, " L'évolution des Moyens de Transport,"
Paris, 1919. There is in the " Vetusta monumenta," vol. iv, 1815, pl.
xxxv., a fine view of the George Inn at Glastonbury (fifteenth century).
The New Inn at Gloucester, Northgate-street, is a good specimen of an
English inn of the fifteenth century (below, p. 131). Charming sketches of
several by Herbert Railton adorn an article on " Coaching Days and Coaching
Ways," in the " English Illustrated Magazine," July, 1888. See also
Turner and Parker, who mention several, of the fifteenth century,
' Domestic Architecture," vol. iii. pp. 46 ff.

[2] The Latin text of their account of expenses was published by Thorold
Rogers in his " History of Agriculture and Prices," ii. p. 638.

THE NEW HABITS OF LUXURY. A GENTLEMAN DRESSING BEFORE THE FIRE. [p. 127.

(From the MS. 2 B. vii., in the British Museum. Fourteenth Century.)

a penny a head.[1]   Sometimes they have eggs or vegetables for a farthing, a chicken or a capon.   When they had sauce or condiments, they put them down separately, for example: fat, $\frac{1}{2}$d. ; gravy, $\frac{1}{2}$d. ; pickle, the same price ; sugar, 4d. ; pepper, saffron, mustard.   Fish recurs regularly every Friday.   Evening comes, the roads are dark ; the way is lost, they take a guide, to whom they give a penny : " In famulo ducenti nos de nocte, 1d."   On crossing the Humber they pay eightpence, which may appear much, compared with the other prices ; but we must remember that the river was wide and difficult to cross, especially

AN ENGLISH INN IN THE FOURTEENTH CENTURY.

(*From the Louterell Psalter.*)

in winter.   The annals of the Abbey of Meaux frequently tell of the ravages caused by the river's overflow, of farms and mills destroyed, of entire domains submerged, and of crops swept away.   The ferry owners benefited by these accidents, in continually augmenting their prices, and at last the king himself was obliged to intervene in order to re-establish the normal rate, which was a penny for a horseman ; this is what the warden and fellows

[1] " Liber Albus," ed. Riley, Introduction, p. lviii.   Cf. the journey from Cambridge to York of a party of twenty-six scholars, in 1319.   The beds, wherever they sleep, uniformly cost 8d. for the twenty-six.   W. W. Rouse Ball, " Cambridge Papers," London, 1918, ch. ix. " A Christmas Journey in 1319."

with their company paid.[1]   Sometimes our travellers furnished themselves beforehand with provisions to carry
with them ; a salmon was bought, " for the journey,"
eighteenpence, and for having it cooked, doubtless with
some complicated sauce, they pay eightpence.

Life-like specimens of dialogues on arrival, between
traveller and innkeeper, and discussion as to the price
of victuals, may be read in the Manual of French Conversation, composed at the end of the fourteenth century
by an Englishman, under the title of " La Manière de
Language que t'enseignera bien à droit parler et escrire
doulz François." [2]

Chapter iii is particularly interesting.   It shows " how
a man who is going far out of his own country, riding
or walking, should behave himself and talk upon the
way."   The servant sent forward to engage the room
utters the fond hope " ' that there are no fleas, nor
bugs, nor other vermin.'   ' No, sir, please God,' replies
the host, ' for I make bold that you shall be well and comfortably lodged here—save that there is a great peck of
rats and mice.' "

The provisions are passed in review, the fire lighted,
supper prepared : the traveller arrives, and it is curious
to note in what unceremonious fashion he assures himself before dismounting that he will find at the inn " good
supper, good lodging, and the rest." [3]

Further on (chap. xiii) another hostelry is described,
and the conversation between two travellers who have
just slept in the same bed shows what a trouble the
fleas were : " William, undress and wash your legs,
and then dry them with a cloth, and rub them well for
love of the fleas, that they may not leap on your legs, for

[1] See Appendix IX.
[2] Published by Prof. Paul Meyer in the *Revue Critique* (1870), vol. x.
p. 373.
[3] " Bon souper, bon gîte, et le reste " (La Fontaine).

THE NEW INN, GLOUCESTER.

(Built for Pilgrims, Fifteenth Century, still in use.)

[p. 131

there is a peck of them lying in the dust under the rushes.
. . . Hi ! the fleas bite me so ! and do me great harm,
for I have scratched my shoulders till the blood flows."

Beer was drunk along the way, and was found in
other places besides the inn where travellers slept at night.
At the cross-roads, in the more frequented parts of the
country, alehouses, with a long projecting pole above the
door and a bush at the end of it, invited the traveller to
have a rest and a drink. Chaucer's pilgrims, riding on
the way to Canterbury, dismounted at a house of this kind.

ON THE ROADSIDE. THE ALEHOUSE.
(*From the MS. 10 E. IV. ; English ; Fourteenth Century.*)

The pardoner, who had his habits, would not begin
his tale without a little comfort :

> " But first, quod he, her at this ale-stake
> I wil bothe drynke and byten on a cake."

A miniature of the fourteenth century, of which we give
a reproduction, represents the alehouse with its long
horizontal pole holding its bush well out in front above
the road. The house consists but of one storey, a woman
stands before the door with a large beer-jug, and a hermit
is drinking from a large cup. It was the fashion to have
extremely long poles, which offered no inconvenience in
the country, but in town they had to be regulated, and
a maximum length fixed. According to the wording of
the Act, poles so long were used, that they " did tend
to the great deterioration of the houses in which they

were placed," and they reached so far and had signs so
low, that they were in the way of the riders' heads.   The
Act of 1375 relating these grievances orders that in future
poles shall not extend more than seven feet over the public
way,[1] which was enough to give picturesqueness to streets
not so wide as ours.

There were taverns of ill-fame, especially in towns,
so bad some of them, that they might almost have gone
by another name.   In one of the Latin dramas of Hrots-
vitha,[2] tenth century, is shown the holy hermit Abraham,
who, learning that the girl Mary, whom he had reared in
virtue, lived as a courtesan in a hostelry, goes to her, pretending love, and converts her.   In most mediæval story
books telling of the prodigal son, he is usually represented sowing his very wild oats at the inn or tavern.
Musicians of the meanest order would entertain the sitters
at the table with their pipings, and then pass the hat.[3]
Having to answer before Archbishop Arundel for his dis-
paraging statements concerning pilgrimages, the Lollard
William Thorpe declares in 1407 that pilgrims are fre-
quenters of ill-famed hostelries, " spending their goods
upon vitious hostelars, which are oft uncleane women of
their bodies." [4]   In some such inn, the " Cheker of the
Hope " (hoop) in Canterbury, the continuator of Chaucer
leads his pilgrims, and shows how the pardoner's advances
to Kit the tapster had the edifying result of getting for him
many more blows than caresses.[5]

In London it was forbidden by the king to keep open

[1] Riley's " Memorials of London," p. 386.
[2] Ed. Barack, Nurenberg, 1858; Fr. translation by Magnin, Paris, 1845.
[3] F. Michel and E. Fournier, " La Grande Bohème" I, pp. 200 ff.
[4] Furnivall, " Tale of Beryn," Early English Text Society, 1887
p. viii., or Arber, " English Garner," vi. 84.
[5] " When all this ffreshe feleship were com to Cauntirbury . . .
    They toke hir In, and loggit hem at mydmorrowe, I trowe,
    Atte ' Cheker of the hope,' that many a man doith knowe."
Prologue to the " Tale of Beryn."   E.E.T.S., 1909, p. 1.

house after curfew, and for very sufficient reasons, " because such offenders as aforesaid, going about by night, do commonly resort and have their meetings and hold their evil talk in taverns more than elsewhere, and there do seek for shelter, lying in wait and watching their time to do mischief." [1]

It was for fear of such dangers that when the sheriffs and bailiffs held their Views of Frankpledge, they asked the juries of their hundreds to say upon oath what they knew " of such as continually haunt taverns, and no man knoweth whence they come ; of such as sleep by day and watch by night, eat well and drink well, and possess nothing." [2]

Langland's life-like picture of a tavern in the fourteenth century is well known. With a vivid realism worthy of Rabelais he makes us hear and see the tumultuous scenes at the alehouse, the discussions, the quarrels, the big bumpers, the drunkenness which ensues ; every face is plainly visible, coarse words, laughter and attitudes strike the on-looker in that strange assembly, where the hermit meets the cobbler and " the clerk of the churche," a band of cut-purses and bald-headed tooth-drawers :

> " Thomme the tynkere · and tweye of hus knaves,
> Hicke the hakeneyman · and Howe the neldere,[3]
> Claryce of Cockeslane · the clerk of the churche,
> Syre Peeres of Prydie · and Purnel of Flanders,
> An haywarde and an heremyte · the hangeman of Tyborne,
> Dauwe the dykere · with a dosen harlotes,
> Of portours and of pyke-porses · and pylede toth-drawers. . . .
> Ther was lauhyng and lakeryng and ' let go the coppe!'
> Bargeynes and bevereges · by-gunne to aryse,
> And seten so til evesong rang." [4]

---

[1] Statutes for the City of London, 13 Ed. I, " Statutes of the Realm," vol. i. p. 102, A.D. 1285.

[2] Articles of the View of Frankpledge, of probably 18 Ed. II, " Statutes," vol. i. p. 246 (French text).   [3] Hugh the needle-seller.

[4] " Piers the Plowman," Skeat's edition, Text C, passus vii. ll. 364–370, 394.

Peasants, too, are found there. Christine de Pisan, that poetess whose writings and character so often recall steady John Gower, shows them drinking, fighting, gambling ; they have to appear before the provost, and fines accrue to augment their losses:

"At these taverns each day will you find them established, and enjoying long potations. As soon as their work is over, many agree to go there and drink, and they spend, you may be sure, more than they have earned all day. Do not ask if they fight when they are tipsy, the provost has several pounds in fines from it during the year. . . . And there also are to be seen some of those idle gallants who haunt taverns, handsome and gay." [1]

Art, literature, the trend of thought were changed at the time of the Rennaissance, but taverns remained the same ; witness Skelton's description of an alehouse on the highroad, quite similar to those which Langland had known a century and a half earlier. The ale-wife, who brews, God knows how, her beer herself, is a withered old crony, not unlike the " weird sisters " who were to welcome

[1] "Par ces tavernes chacun jour,
Vous en trouveriez à séjour,
Beuvans là toute la journée
Aussi tost que ont fait leur journée.
Maint y aconvient aler boire :
Là despendent, c'est chose voire,
Plus que toute jour n'ont gaigné.

*   *   *   *   *

Là ne convient il demander
S'ilz s'entrebatent quand sont yvres ;
Le prévost en a plusieurs livres
D'amande tout au long de l'an.

*   *   *   *   *

Et y verriés de ces gallans
Oyseux qui tavernes poursuivent,
Gays et jolis."

" Le Livre de la mutacion de fortune," Bk. iii, MS. Fr. 603, Biblio-thèque Nationale, Paris. Christine de Pisan's " Œuvres poétiques," are being published by the " Société de Anciens textes Français," ed. Maurice Roy, 1886 ff.

Macbeth on the heath.   She keeps her tavern near Leather-
head, in Surrey, on a declivity by the highroad, and there
gathers as motley a crowd as that in the " Visions,"

> " Her nose somdele hoked,
> And camously croked . . .
> Her skynne lose and slacke,
> Grained like a sacke,
> With a croked backe. . . .
> She breweth noppy ale,
> And maketh therof port sale
> To travellars, to tynkers,
> To swetcrs, to swynkers,
> And all good ale drinkers."

Passers-by and dwellers in the neighbourhood flock
to her house :

> " Some go streyght thyder,
> Be it slaty or slyder ;
> They holde the hye waye,
> They care not what men say,
> Be that as be may ;
> Some, lothe to be espyde,
> Start in at the back syde,
> Over the hedge and pale,
> And all for the good ale."

The reputation of the houses with a long pole and
bush had not improved, and many of those who frequented them had, as we see, little wish to be " espyde."
As for paying the score, there was the rub ! Devotees of
drink whose purse was empty would not deprive themselves, however, and they paid in kind :

> " Instede of coyne and monny,
> Some brynge her a conny,
> And some a pot with honny,
> Some a salt, and some a spone,
> Some their hose, some theyr shone."

As to the women, one brings :

> " her weddynge-ryngc
> To pay for her scot,
> As cometh to her lot.
> Som bryngeth her husbandes hood,
> Because the ale is good." [1]

The worst-famed of these houses began a little later to receive the visits of the most illustrious of their customers, one who held his court under their smoky rafters and came there to his earthly end, " babbling of green fields," immortal Sir John Falstaff.

IV

Other isolated houses along the roads, by the fords or the bridges, on sacred spots, on the cliffs by the sea, had also much to do with travellers, those of the hermits. Such holy men would tell the way, help to cross a river, sometimes give shelter, sometimes absolution.[2] One shrives passers-by in that gem of mediæval French stories, " Le chevalier au barisel "; another, in the " Roman de Renard," being favoured with a visit from no less a person than the hero of the romance. Led by a peasant through the pathless wood, Master Reynard reaches the secluded spot ; the mallet was hanging before the door, and the peasant having given with it a loud knock the hermit hastened to draw the bolt :

[1] "Elynour Rummynge." "Poetical Works of John Skelton," ed. Dyce, 1843, vol. i. p. 95.

[2] Jurors find in 1375 that the bridge in the midst of the causey between Brant Broughton and Lincoln was primarily made " by a certain hermit after the first pestilence," and consisted " in a board placed above the ford " which had to be waded through : " Jurati dicunt supra sacramentum suum . . . quod pons predictus post primam pestilenciam ibidem primo per quendam heremitum factus fuit, ponendo tabulam ultra quoddam vadum in medio calceti predicti." Complete text in C. T. Flower, " Public Works in Mediæval Law," Selden Society, 1915, i. 263.

THE HERMITAGE CHAPEL OF ST. ROBERT.

(Hewn out of the rock, Knaresborough; the knight of a much later date.) [p. 139.

Tant ont erré par le bocage
Qu'ils sont venu à l'ermitage.
Le maillet trovèrent pendant
A la porte par de devant.
Li vileins hurte durement
Et l'ermite vint erraument (promptly),
Li fermal oste de la roille (bolt).[1]

Most holy in early times, living examples of renounce-
ment, teaching virtue and piety by their words and deeds,
hermits became, some of them, canonized saints, like
St. Robert of Knaresborough,[2] or devotional writers of
fame like Richard Rolle, the hermit of Hampole ; pilgrims
flocked to their cells in order to be sanctified by their
advice and presence. An " officium de Sancto Ricardo
eremita " was composed after Richard Rolle's death, in
the thought that he would surely be canonized some day :

Letetur felix Anglorum patria . . .
Pange lingua graciosi
Ricardi preconium,
Pii, puri, preciosi,
Fugientis vitium.[3]

These men fasted, had ecstasies, were tempted by the
devil, who in the case of Richard, instead of clumsily taking
some hideous shape (see further, p. 290) took the much
more enticing one of "a faire yonge womane, the
whilke," wrote the hermit, "I had sene be-fore and
the whilke luffed (loved) me noght a little in gude
lufe."[4]

The cave or hermitage in which Saint Robert spent

[1] " Roman de Renart," Branch viii. ed. Martin i. p. 267. On the
outcome of this confession, see further, Part iii. chap. iii.

[2] The son of a mayor of York; d. about 1235. Miracles are said
to have been worked at the Knaresborough hermitage, Yorkshire, where
he had lived and was buried.

[3] " English Prose Treaties," ed. Perry, E.E.T.S., 1866, pp. xv, xvi.
Rolle died in 1349.

[4] Ibid. p. 5.

most of his life still exists at Knaresborough, entirely hollowed out of the rock, with a later-date perpendicular window.[1]

Persuaded, rightly or wrongly, that they had much to atone for, the kings included among the redeeming good works to be performed by them aid to holy hermits. One of the pilgrims who visited St. Robert was King John, who came unheralded and who, according to the metrical life of the saint, had some trouble in making him notice his presence :

> Roberd he fand knelan prayand,
> Hys orysons contynuand,
> That for nai noyse that thai couth maike
> Nay mare he mowed than dose ane ake (oak).[2]

Edward III gives to " three hermits and eight anchorite recluse persons within the city of London and in the suburbs thereof, to wit to each of them, 13s. 4d. in aid of their support." [3] Welcomed on his landing, in 1399, by a seaside hermit called Matthew Danthorp, " in quodam loco called Ravenserespourne " (Ravenspur), Bolingbroke,

[1] Another example still in existence is the hermitage at Warkworth, Northumberland, partly of masonry and partly scooped out of the rock. It was apparently enlarged by its successive inhabitants, but seems from the style of the windows and carvings to belong mostly to the fourteenth century.

[2] " The Metrical Life of Saint Robert of Knaresborough," ed. Haslewood and Douce, Roxburghe Club, 1824, p. 36.   Cf. " Rotuli Chartarum in Turri Londinensi asservati," ed. T. D. Hardy, 1837, p. 158, where King John is seen bestowing on one Robert, in 1205, " locum in quo heremitorium sancte Wereburge sedet " (the famous St. Werburga, abbess of Ely, seventh century).   He does so " pro amore Dei et pro salute anime nostre."   He grants, " in puram et perpetuam elemosinam," the " heremitorium de Godeland " to the monks of Whitby, Oct. 26, 1205, ibid. p. 159.

[3] Both sorts generally lived by themselves, but the recluse never left his cell while the hermit could roam about.   " Issue Roll of Thomas de Brantingham," ed. Devon, p. 393, 44 Ed. III ; the same king gives also 20s. " in aid of her support " to " Alice de Latimer a recluse anchorite," ibid. p. xxxvi.

soon to be King Henry IV, grants him and all the hermits his successors a variety of favours, including the right to any waif or wreck cast by the sea on the sand for two leagues about his hermitage : " Cum wrecco maris, et wayfs et omnibus aliis proficuis et commoditatibus super sabulum per duas leucas circa eundem locum contingentibus imperpetuum," in spite of any statute to the contrary.[1]

Less brilliant fortunes and less holy a fame usually fell to the lot of English hermits of the fourteenth century. Those like Rolle of Hampole, doing ceaseless penance, consumed by divine love, were rare exceptions ; they lived by preference in cottages, built at the most frequented parts of the highway, or at the entrance to bridges.[2] They throve there, like Godfrey Pratt,[3] on the charity of the passers-by ; the bridge with its chapel was in itself almost a sacred building ; the presence of the hermit sanctified it still further. He attended to the keeping in order of the building, or was supposed to do so, and was willingly given a farthing.[4] A strange race of men, which in that century of disorganization and reform, when everything seemed either to die or undergo a new birth, multiplied in spite of rules and regulations. They swelled the number of parasites of the religious edifice, cloaking under a dignified habit a life that was less so. These evil growths

[1] " Teste Rege, apud Westmonasterium, 1° die Octobris [1399]." Rymer's " Fœdera."

[2] See, for an example of a hermit settled at the corner of a bridge, an Act of resumption which formally excepts a grant of 14s. yearly to the " Heremyte of the Brigge of Loyne and his successours," 4 Ed. IV, " Rolls of Parliament," v. p. 546. Another example is to be found in J. Britton, " On Ancient Gate-houses," " Memoirs illustrative of the History of Norfolk," London, Archæological Institute, 1851, p. 137, where hermits are mentioned who lived on Bishop's Bridge, Norwich, in the thirteenth century and after.

[3] See before, pp. 41 ff.

[4] See above as to the part taken by the clergy in the collection of offerings, and in the care and maintenance of bridges, chap. i.

clung, like moss in the damp of the cathedral, to the fissures
of the stones, and by the slow work of centuries threatened
the noble structure with ruin.   What remedy was there ?
To mow down the ever-growing weeds was scarcely
possible ; a patient hand, guided by a vigilant eye, was
needed to pluck them out one by one, and to fill up the
interstices : saints can do this, but saints are rare. Episcopal
prescriptions might often seem to do great work ; a mere
seeming. Though the heads were beaten down, the

A HERMIT TEMPTED BY THE DEVIL.

(*From the MS. 10 E. IV ; English ; Fourteenth Century.*)

roots remained, and the lively parasite struck yet deeper
into the heart of the wall.

Solemn interdictions and rigorous rules were not
wanting, bowing down heads which ever rose again.   To
become a hermit a man must be resolved on an exemplary
life of poverty and privations, and, that imposture should
be impossible, he must have episcopal sanction, that is,
possess " testimonial letters from the ordinary." [1]   These

---

[1] 12 Rich. II, chap. vii, " Statutes of the Realm."   A sample of a
hermit's vow, with an analysis of a fourteenth-century text describing the
ceremony for the consecration of a hermit, is in E. L. Cutts, " Scenes and

rules were broken, however, without scruple. Inside his
dwelling the not very devout creature in hermit's garb
could lead a quiet, easy life, and it was so hard elsewhere !
The charity of passers-by was enough for him to live
upon, especially if he was not harassed by an over-exact-
ing conscience and knew how to beg ; no labour, no
pressing obligation, the bishop was distant and the alehouse near.   All these reasons caused a never-ending
growth of the mischievous species of false hermits who
only took the habit to live by it, without asking any permit
from any one.   In the statutes they were bracketed with
beggars, wandering labourers, and vagabonds of all kinds,
pell mell, to be imprisoned awaiting judgment.   There
was exception only for " approved " hermits : " Except
men of religion and approved hermits having letters testimonial from the ordinary."   A statute like this is enough
to show that Langland did not exaggerate ; his verse is
but a commentary on the law.   The author of the
" Visions " is impartial and does justice to sincere anchor-
ites : true Christians resemble them.[1]   But what are these
false saints who have pitched their tent by the side of
the highroads or even in the towns, at the door of the
alehouse, who beg under the church porches, who eat
and drink plentifully, and leisurely pass the evenings
warming themselves ?

   " Ac eremites that en-habiten · by the heye weyes,
     And in borwes a-mong brewesters · and beggen in churches." [2]

What is that man who rests and roasts himself by
the hot coals, and when he has drunk his fill has nothing
to do but go to bed ?

Characters of the Middle Ages," 1872, pp. 98, 99.   A list is given, p. 111,
of the still subsisting English hermitages.
   [1] " Piers Plowman," Skeat's edition, Text C, passus i. l. 30 ; passus
x. l. 195.
   [2] Ibid., passus x. l. 188.

" lewede eremytes,
That loken ful louheliche · to lacchen [1] mennes almesse,
In hope to sitten at even · by the hote coles,
Unlouke hus legges abrod · other lygge at hus ese, ·
Reste hym and roste hym · and his ryg (back) turne,
Drynke drue and deepe · and drawe hym thanne to bedde ;
And when hym lyketh and lust · hus leve ys to aryse ;
When he ys rysen, rometh out · and ryght wel aspieth
Whar he may rathest have a repast · other a rounde of bacon,
Sulver other sode mete · and som tyme bothe,
A loof other half a loof · other a lompe of chese ;
And carieth it hom to hus cote · and cast hym to lyve
In ydelnesse and in ese." [2]

All these are unworthy of pity, and, adds Langland, with that aristocratic touch which now and then recurs in his lines, all these hermits were common artisans, " workmen, webbes and taillours, and carters' knaves " ; formerly they had " long labour and lyte wynnynge," but they noticed one day that these deceitful friars swarming everywhere, " hadde fatte chekus " (cheeks) ; they thereupon abandoned their labour and took lying garments, as though they were clerks :

. . . " Other of som ordre, other elles a prophete."

They are seldom seen at church, these false hermits, but they are found seated at great men's tables because of their cloth. Look at them eating and drinking of the best ! they who formerly were of the lowest rank, at the side tables, never tasting wine, never eating white bread, without a blanket for their bed :

" Ac while he wrought in thys worlde · and wan hus mete with treuthe,
He sat atte sydbenche · and secounde table ;
Cam no wyn in hus wombe · thorw the weke longe,
Nother blankett in hus bed · ne white bred by-fore hym.
The cause of al thys caitifte · cometh of meny bisshopes
That suffren suche sottes." [3]

---

[1] Look humbly to gain alms.
[2] " Piers Plowman," Skeat's edition, Text C, passus x. ll. 140–152.
[3] Text C, passus x. ll. 251–256.

These rascals escape the bishops, who ought to have their eyes wider open. " Alas ! " said, in charming language, a French poet of the thirteenth century, Rutebeuf, " the coat does not make the hermit ; if a man dwell in a hermitage and be clothed in hermit's dress, I don't care two straws for his habit nor his vesture if he does not lead a life as pure as his frock betokens. But many folk make a fine show and marvellous seeming of worth ; they resemble those over-blossoming trees that fail to bring forth fruit." [1]

Under the eyes of the placid hermit, comfortably established by the roadside, calmly preparing himself by a carefree life for a blissful eternity, moved the variegated flow of travellers, vagabonds, wayfarers, and wanderers. His benediction rewarded the generous passer-by ; the stern look of the austere man did not disturb his sanctimonious indifference. The life of others might rapidly consume itself, burnt by the sun, gnawed by care ; his own endured in the shade of the trees, and continued without hurt, lulled by the murmur of human passions—

> Et je dirai, songeant aux hommes, que font-ils ?
> Et le ressouvenir des amours et des haines
> Me bercera pareil au bruit des mers lointaines.
> (Sully Prudhomme.)

---

[1] " Li abis ne fet pas l'ermite ;
S'uns hom en hermitage abite
Et s'il en a les dras vestus,
Je ne pris mie deus festus
Son abit ne sa vesteure,
S'il ne maine vie aussi pure
Comme son abit nous démonstre ;
Mes maintes genz font bele monstre
Et merveilleux sanblant qu'il vaillent :
Il sanblent les arbres qui faillent
Qui furent trop bel au florir."

Le Dit de frère Denise. " Œuvres complètes de Rutebeuf," ed. Jubinal. Paris, 1874, vol. ii. p. 63.

Good or bad, the whole race (still surviving in the East) disappeared in England at the Reformation, leaving but a memory, and surviving only in poetry :

> It is the Hermit good !
> He singeth loud his godly hymns
> That he makes in the wood.
> He'll shrive my soul, he'll wash away
> The Albatross's blood.

AN ESCAPED PRISONER FLYING TO SANCTUARY.
(*From the MS.* 10 *E. IV.*)

CHAPTER III

SECURITY OF THE ROADS

THESE roads, thus followed in every direction by the king and the lords moving from one manor to another, by the merchants and peasants going to the fair, the market, or the staple, by sheriffs, monks and itinerant justices, by ladies in carriages and villains driving their carts, were they safe? The theorist studying the legal ordinances of the period, and the manner in which the county police and the town watch and ward were organized, might come to the conclusion that precautions were well taken for the prevention of misdeeds, and that travelling did not present more danger than it does at present. If we add, as Mr. Thorold Rogers has shown, that common carriers plied their trade between Oxford and London, Winchester, Newcastle, etc., and that the price of transport was not dear, we might be persuaded that the roads were quite safe, and we should be wrong ; wrong too, if on the faith of romantic tales, we pictured to ourselves brigands in every thicket, a hanged man on every branch, and robber barons at every cross-road. But *accident*, or the unexpected, must be taken into account.

Accident played a great part in the social life of the fourteenth century. It was the moment when modern life began, the outward brilliancy of a novel civilization had recently modified society from top to bottom, the need to be constantly on the watch had become less apparent ; the moated castle with its drawbridge, battlements and loop-holes, had begun to change into a villa or a mansion, while the hut was growing into a house. Confidence was greater, but not always justified : accidents are unexpected mishaps.

More means were taken than formerly to hinder ill-doing ; but numerous occurrences happened to destroy this incipient security. Society was in reality neither calm nor quite settled, and many of its members were still half savage. The term " half " may be taken literally. If a list were made of the characteristics of such or such an individual of the time, it would be found that some belonged to a refined, and some to a barbarous world. Hence these contrasts : on one side order, which it would perhaps be unjust not to consider as the normal condition ; and on the other, the frequent ebullitions of the untamed nature. Let us select an example of such accidents which could take at times remarkable proportions. Here are a knight and his men at the corner of a road, waiting for a troop of merchants. The text itself of the victims' petition gives all the details of the encounter.[1]

The facts happened in 1342. Some Lichfield merchants state to their lord, the Earl of Arundel, that on a certain Friday they sent two servants and two horses laden with " spicery and mercery," worth forty pounds, to Stafford for the next market day. When their men " came beneath Cannock Wood " they met Sir Robert de Rideware, Knight, waiting for them, together with

[1] Printed in the " Archæological Journal," vol. iv. p. 69.

two of his men, who seized on the servants, horses, and goods, and took them to the priory of Lappeley. Unfortunately for the knight, during the journey, one of the servants escaped.

At the priory the band found " Sir John de Oddyngesles, Esmon de Oddyngesles, and several others, knights as well as others." It was evidently a pre-arranged affair, carefully devised ; all was done according to rule ; they shared " among them the aforesaid mercery and spicery, each one a portion according to his degree." That done, the company left Lappeley and rode to the priory of Blythebury, a nuns' priory. Sir Robert declared that they were the king's men, quite exhausted, and begged for hospitality. But the company had obviously a suspicious appearance, and the abbess refused. Indignant at this unfriendly reception, the knights burst open the doors of the barns and lofts, gave hay and oats to their horses, and so passed the night.

But they were not the only people to have made a good use of their time. The escaped servant had followed them at a distance ; when he saw they had taken up their quarters at the priory he returned with all speed to Lichfield and warned the bailiff who hastened to collect his men for the pursuit of the robbers. The latter, men of the sword, as soon as they were met, stood their ground, and a real battle took place, in which they had at first the upper hand, and wounded several of their pursuers. At length, however, they were worsted and fled ; all the spices were recovered, and four of their company taken, who, without further ado, were beheaded on the spot.

Robert de Rideware was not one of the latter, and did not lose heart. He met his relative Walter de Rideware, lord of Hamstall Rideware, with some of his followers, while the bailiff was on his way back to Lichfield ; all together veered around in pursuit of the bailiff. A fresh fight. This time the king's officer was routed and fled, while the highway gentlemen once more captured the spices.

What resource remained for the unhappy William and Richard, authors of the petition? Resort to justice? This they wanted to do. But as they were going for this purpose to Stafford, chief town of the county, they found at the gates some retainers of their persecutors, who barred their passage and even attacked them so hotly that they had difficulty in escaping without grievous hurt. They returned to Lichfield, watched by their enemies, and led there a pitiable existence. " And, sir, the aforesaid William and Richard, and several people of the town of Lichfield, are menaced by the said robbers and their maintainers, so that they dare not go anywhere out of the said town." [1]

This legal document, the original of which has been preserved, is, in many ways, characteristic, and shows us local tyrants not unlike the latter day ones in the *Promessi Sposi* and their terrible *bravi*. One may, especially, notice the coolness and determination of the knights, not disconcerted by the death of four of their number ; the attack under cover of a wood ; the selection of the victims, " garsuns " belonging to rich merchants ; the request for hospitality in a priory under pretext of journeying in the king's service ; the expeditious justice of the bailiff, and the persistent surveillance to which the victims were subjected by their lordly robbers.

These, though remarkable, are not quite exceptional facts, and Robert of Rideware was not the only man on the look out in the copses along the roads. Other noblemen were, like him, supported by devoted retainers, ready for any enterprise. Capes and liveries of their masters' colours were given to them, and they went about as the

---

[1] " E, sire, les avant ditz William e Richart e plusours gentz de la ville de Lichfield sount menacé des ditz larons e lour maintenours qu'ils n'osent nule part aler hors de la dite ville."

uniformed soldiers of their chief ;   a lord well surrounded
with his partizans considered himself as above the common
law, and it was no easy matter for justice to make herself
respected by him.   The custom of having a number of
resolute followers wearing one's colours became universal
at the end of Edward III's reign and under Richard II ;
it survived in spite of statutes [1] during the whole of the
fifteenth century, and contributed to render even more
embittered and bloody the War of the Roses.

But even outside the periods of civil war, the misdeeds
of certain barons and their retainers, or of retainers acting
on their own account under cover of their lord's colours
—" notoirs meffesours et meintenours of meffesours," the
statute said of both,[2]—were at times so frequent and serious
that parts of the country seemed to be in a state of war.
Throughout the fourteenth century, the abuse called
maintenance, which word meant in old French *protection*,
was on the increase, in spite of all the efforts of king and
Parliament.   The great of the land, and some lesser people
too, had their own men, sworn to their service and ready
to do anything they were commanded, which consisted
sometimes in the most monstrous deeds, such as securing
property or other goods to which neither their masters,
nor any claimant paying their master in order to be thus
" protected," [3] had any title.   They terrorized the rightful

---

[1] Richard II had several times to renew and confirm them, but without
effect.   In his first statute upon this subject he condemns the super-
abundance of retainers which many men, though of indifferent means, delight
in ; he declares " that divers people of small revenue of land, rent, or other
possessions, do make great retinue of people, as well of esquires as of other,
in many parts of the realm " (1 Richard II, cap. 7, A.D. 1377).   The third
statute of 13 Richard II, that of his 16th year (cap. 4), that of his 20th
year (cap. 1 and 2), are likewise directed against the abuse of liveries and
the number of retainers of the " lords spiritual and temporal."   Henry VI
renewed these statutes, also without result.

[2] 10 Ed. III, year 1336.

[3] Those who divided among themselves the prospective profit of a lawsuit " maintained " in this way, were called " champertors," *campi participes*,

owners, the judges and the juries, ransoming, beating and maiming any opponent.[1]

Statutes were, as usual, numerous, well-meant, peremptory, and inefficient. The evil was so general that Edward III had to forbid the people nearest him, the chief officers of his court, his " dearest consort, the queen," his son the prince of Wales, the prelates of Holy Church,[2] to thus interfere with the regular course of the law. The will of the king is that " the poor should enjoy their right just as the rich."[3] But they do not ; great ladies practice maintenance, one among others even dearer to the king than his dear consort, namely his mistress, Alice Perers.[4]

A new reign begins ; maintenance flourishes better than ever before. The preamble of a statute of the second year of Richard II [5] gives a perhaps somewhat exaggerated picture of these disorders so as to better justify rigorous measures, but the description must have been at least partly true. We there see—and the king, it is stated, has learnt it both from the petitions addressed to parliament and by public rumour—that certain people in several parts of the kingdom claimed " to have right to divers lands, tenements and other possessions, and some espying women and damsels unmarried, and some desiring to make maintenance in their marches, do gather together to a great number of men of arms and archers, *to the manner of war*, and confederate themselves by oath and other confederacy." These people, having no " consideration to God, nor to the laws of Holy Church, nor of the land,

which was forbidden by numerous statutes. See e.g. the " Ordinacio de Conspiratoribus," 33 Ed. I, year 1305.

[1] 4 Ed. III, chap. 2, year 1330.

[2] 20 Ed. III, chap. 4, 5, 6, year 1346.

[3] " Le Roi désire que commun droit soit fait à toutz, auxibien à povres come à riches." 1 Ed. III, stat. ii, ch. 14.

[4] In the petition to the Good Parliament, 1376, she is included among " les femmes qui ont pursuys en les Courtz du Roi diverses busoignes et quereles par voie de maintenance et pur lower (gain) et part avoir."

[5] Statute 2 Richard II, stat. i. cap. 6, A.D. 1378.

nor to right, nor justice, but refusing and setting apart all process of the law, do ride in great routs in divers parts of England, and take possession and set them in divers manors, lands, and other possessions of their own authority, and hold the same long with such force, *doing many manner apparelments of war* ; and in some places do ravish women and damsels, and bring them into strange countries, where please them ; and in some places lying in await with such routs do beat and maim, murder and slay the people, for to have their wives and their goods, and the same women and goods retain to their own use ; and sometimes take the king's liege people in their houses, and bring and hold them as prisoners, and at the last put them to fine and ransom *as it were in a land of war* ; and sometimes come before the justices in their sessions in such guise with great force, whereby the justices be afraid and not hardy to do the law ; and do many other riots and horrible offences, whereby the realm in divers parts is put in great trouble, to the great mischief and grievance of the people." [1] Which shows how vainly the Good Parliament had worked, for, in 1376, the Commons had already made exactly similar complaints : " Now great riot begins anew by

[1] The picture in this statute is so complete that there is scarcely need to quote other texts ; they are, however, numerous. In the petitions to parliament will be found many complaints by private people for acts of violence of which they had been victims, for imprisonment by their enemies, robberies, arson, destruction of game or fish in the parks. Examples : petition of Agnes Atte Wode, she and her son beaten and robbed (ibid. i. p. 372) ; of Agnes of Aldenby, beaten by malefactors (" Rolls of Parliament," i. p. 375) ; of the inhabitants of several towns of the county of Hertford, who have been imprisoned and forced to pay ransom by the knight John of Patmer (i. p. 389) ; of John of Grey, who was attacked by fifteen malefactors so resolute as to set fire to a town and storm a castle (i. p. 397) ; of Robert Power, who is robbed and his mansion sacked, his people beaten, by " men all armed as men of war " (i. p. 410) ; of Ralph le Botiller, who has seen his mansion pillaged and burnt by eighty men, who came with arms and baggage, bringing ropes and hatchets on carts (ii. p. 88), etc. In France, it is well known, the misdeeds of this kind were still more numerous but then a continual state of war was raging there.

many people in different parts of England who ride with
a great number of armed men," etc.[1]

Besides these organized and quasi-scignorial bands,
there were ordinary robbers, numerous enough for chantries
to have been founded " for the safety of travellers who
were in danger from thieves." [2] Against those people
who impeded travelling much more grievously than
ever the floods and broken bridges, Edward I had taken,
in 1285, special measures in the Statute of Winchester.
These men were described there as accustomed to crouch
down in the ditches, coppice, or brushwoods near the
roads, especially those linking two market towns. This
was, of course, the passage-way of many easy victims,
richly laden. The king orders therefore that, for a space
of two hundred feet, the ground on each side of the road
should be cleared in such a manner that there remain
neither coppice nor brushwood, nor hollow nor ditch
which serve as shelter for malefactors : " où leur peut
tapir pur mal fere." Only large trees such as oaks might
be left. The owner of the soil had to do the work; if he
neglected it, he would be responsible for robberies and
murders, and have to pay a fine to the king.   If the road
went through a park, the same obligation lay on the lord,
unless he consented to close it by a wall or a hedge so
thick, or by a ditch so wide and deep, that robbers could
not cross them : " qe meffesurs ne pussent passer ne
returner pur mal fere." The king sets the example and
orders such clearings to be made at once on the lands
belonging to the crown.[3]

After which, things continued pretty much as before :
" Meanwhile," writes a chronicler for the years 1303-05,

[1] " Rolls of Parliament," ii. p. 351.
[2] One founded with that object by Matthew of Dunstable in 1295, and
" known as the chantry of Biddenham bridge in Bromham parish." " Victoria History of the Counties of England," Bedfordshire, vol. iii. p. 49,
[3] " Statutes of the Realm," year 1285.

"certain malefactors, bound together, four, six, ten or twenty went in company to fairs and markets, rifled the houses of honest people and were not ashamed to capture through their misdoings the goods of the faithful and rich people." [1]   Worse than that : we find as we progress in the fourteenth century, that these common thieves had improved their methods and increased their profits.   They allied themselves, sometimes secretly, sometimes openly, to the seignorial bands, and were not henceforward unticketed men for whom no one was responsible.   The Commons were aware of the fact, and complained accordingly : "Whereas it is notoriously known *throughout all the shires of England* that robbers, thieves, and other malefactors on foot and on horseback, go and ride on the highway through all the land in divers places, committing larcenies and robberies : may it please our lord the king to charge the nobility of the land that none such be maintained by them, privately nor openly ; but that they help to arrest and take such bad ones." [2]   In the preceding parliament the same complaints had been made, and the king had already promised that he would order "such remedy as should be pleasing to God and man." [3] But neither God nor man had had apparently cause to be pleased.

In addition to the support of the great, these evildoers enjoyed various privileges.   Some of them could be met along the roads, cross in hand ; both king and church forbade seizing them, they were men who had forsworn the realm.   When a robber, a murderer, or any felon found himself too hard pressed, he fled into a church and found safety.   In almost all societies having reached a certain stage of civilization the same privilege has existed or still exists.   It was known to the Romans,

[1] "Chronica Monasterii de Melsa," Rolls Series, ii. 275.
[2] "Rolls of Parliament," vol. ii. p. 201 (22 E. III, 1348).
[3] Ibid., vol. ii. p. 165.

was legislated about by Theodosius the Great, Justinian
and the early councils,[1] and is still in constant use in
many parts of the East. A church in the Middle Ages
was an inviolable place : whoever crossed its threshold
was under the protection of God, and many wonderful
miracles, the history of which was familiar to everybody,
attested with what particular favour the right of sanctuary
was regarded especially by the Holy Virgin. At Walsingham, one of the most famous British pilgrimages, people
never failed to go and see the " Gate of the Knight,"
a gate which had stretched itself so as to give miraculous

THE KNOCKER OF THE DURHAM SANCTUARY (NORMAN).

shelter to a man on horseback, hard pursued by his enemies,
and who found himself thus opportunely placed beyond
the reach of men as well as beyond the reach of law.

Several interesting relics of old English sanctuaries are
still in existence, such as stone sign-posts which helped
the fugitive to avoid either vengeance or justice : " Even
to-day, in various parts of England, curious stone crosses,

[1] Earliest reference in England: that in the laws of Ethelbert, King of
Kent, later part of the sixth century, where it is said that " the penalty for
violation of church *frith* is to be twice that exacted for an ordinary breach
of peace." Trenholme, " The Right of Sanctuary in England," University
o. Missouri Studies, 1903, p. 11.

inscribed with the word SANCTUARIUM, are to be met with. Such crosses probably marked the way to a sanctuary and served to guide fugitives." [1] At Durham is to be seen a beautiful bronze knocker, cast and chiselled in Norman times, still affixed to the cathedral door through which malefactors were admitted to the sanctuary.[2] As soon as they had knocked, the door was opened, the bell in the Galilee tower was rung, and after having confessed before witnesses their crime, which was at once put into writing, the culprits were allowed to enjoy the peace of St. Cuthbert. Several churches had a chair or stool called the *fridstool*, or peace chair (originally, in some cases, a presbyteral or episcopal seat) the reaching of which by the fugitive secured for him the maximum protection. Beverley has one of the oldest, in stone, perfectly plain, formerly accompanied with a Latin inscription, saying : " This stone seat is called *freedstoll*, that is, chair of peace, on reaching which a fugitive criminal enjoys complete safety." [3] The Beverley sanctuary was the most cele-brated and safest in England.[4] In this case, and in some others, at Hexham for example, the privilege extended not only to the church, but to one mile or more round it, the space being divided into several circles, usually marked by stone crosses, and it was more and more sinful to remove fugitives violently from the sanctuary the nearer

[1] Trenholme, as above, p. 48.

[2] R. W. Billings, " Architectural Illustrations . . . of the Church at Durham," London, 1843, p. 20.

[3] " Erant hujusmodi cathedrarum multæ in Anglia . . . Beverlaci autem celeberrima, quæ priscorum regum benignitate (puta Æthelstani vel alterius cujuspiam) asyli nacta privilegium, tali honestabatur inscriptione : ' Hæc sedes lapidea *Freedstoll* dicitur, i.e. pacis cathedra, ad quam reus fugiendo perveniens, omnimodam habet securitatem.' " H. Spelman, " Glossarium Archaiologicum," 3rd ed., London, 1687, p. 248.

[4] Though every consecrated place was a sanctuary, some of them afforded far more safety than others, the penalties for abductors being much greater. A list of the safest of the English sanctuaries is in S. Pegge, " A Sketch of the History of the Asylum or Sanctuary," in " Archæologia," 1787, vol. viii. p. 41.

they were to the inner circle. If they were dragged from
the altar or the fridstool, no money atonement was accepted
from the abductor, who thus apparently forfeited his life.
Describing the several circles around the Hexham sanctuary, Prior Richard, who wrote between 1154 and 1167,
says of the inner one : " If any one, moved by a spirit
of madness, ventured with diabolical boldness to seize
one in the stone chair near the altar which the English
call *fridstol*, that is a chair of quiet or peace, or at the shrine
of the holy relics, back of the altar, no compensation will
be determined for such a glaring sacrilege, no amount

THE FRIDSTOOL AT HEXHAM ABBEY, NORTHUMBERLAND (NORMAN).

of money will serve as an atonement, for it is what the
English call *botolos* (bootless), that is a thing for which
there can be no compensation." [1]

That same fridstool has been preserved, being not
improbably the original episcopal seat of the famous St.
Wilfrid, born about 634, the builder of the old church

[1] " Brevis annotatio Ricardi, prioris Hagustaldensis ecclesiæ de
antiquo et moderno statu ejusdem ecclesiæ," ed. Raine, " The priory of
Hexham," Surtees Society, 1864–5, 2 vols. illustrated, i. 62. The prior
has also a chapter v, " De pace inviolabili per unum milliare circumquaque
ipsius ecclesiæ," p. 19, and a chapter xiv on the privilege, granted by the
king, to the Hexham Sanctuary, p. 61.

THE FRIDSTOOL AT SPROTBOROUGH, YORKSHIRE.

Fourteenth Century.

11

at Hexham, a crypt of which, with some Roman stones used for the walls, is still in existence.

Near the fridstool was to be seen a queer, short, stone statue now moved to another place in the church, of a man, with brutal features, " wearing a long coat, buttoned in front from the neck to the waist, having three coils or clumsy ligatures . . . round his ankles ; and he holds erect with both hands a staff or club as tall as himself." A. B. Wright, author of an " Essay towards the history of Hexham," expresses the opinion that, " it was intended to represent an officer of justice, with his staff and plume, his feet bared and manacled, to show that within the bounds of sanctuary he dared not move towards his design and that there his authority availed him not." [1]

A confirmation of this opinion may be found in the figures carved on the little known but very curious frid-stool at Sprotborough, Yorkshire, apparently of the four-teenth century : the fugitive who could not be represented seated in the chair, since this would have made it impos-sible of use, is shown protected by it, while a grotesque not to say caricatural image of maybe some law official carrying his staff stands at one of the sides of the chair, but unable to move, being bound to it by a collar or *carcannum* [2] The whole is hard to interpret.

Among the most curious remembrances of the English sanctuaries figure the registers still preserved in some few places, in which were entered the confessions of the criminals at the moment they asked for admittance. The Beverley and the Durham ones have been printed ; both date from the fifteenth century ; that of Durham covers the years 1464 to 1524 ; it includes, besides other crimes, 195 murders and homicides, in which 283 persons

---

[1] Raine, as above, II, p. lxiv. Wright's " Essay " appeared in 1823.
[2] Usually worn by the accused, but the law officer's intrusion would have made him a guilty man. " Carcannum," says Du Cange, " collis-trigium, vinculum quo rei collum stringitur, nostris, *carcan*."

are concerned, and which are divided as follows, according
to the trades and avocations of the perpetrators :

" Husbandmen	.	.	.	.	8
Labourers	.	.	.	.	4
Yeomen .	.	.	.	.	4
Gentlemen .	.	.	.	.	4
Ecclesiastics .	.	.	.	.	3
Merchants .	.	.	.	.	2
Tailor	.	.	.	.	1
Plumber	.	.	.	.	1
Carpenter	.	.	.	.	1

Tanner .	.	.	.	.	1
Baxster .	.	.	.	.	1
Glover .	.	.	.	.	1
Sailor	.	.	.	.	1
Apprentice .	.	.	.	.	1
Under-Bailiff	.	.	.	.	1
Servant .	.	.	.	.	1
Knight (an accessory)	.	.	1

" The occupations of the remainder are not mentioned." [1]

The entries in the two registers are much alike ; the
formalities are of the same kind ; the Galilee bell is
tolled, the culprit confesses ; witnesses are called to hear
him, and the names of all concerned are given in full.
Here is an example translated from the Latin original :
" To be remembered that on the 6th day of October,
1477, William Rome and William Nicholson, of the parish
of Forsate, fled to the cathedral church of St. Cuthbert
in Durham, where on account, among other things, of
a felony committed and publicly confessed by them, consisting of the murder by them of William Aliand, they
asked from the venerable and religious men, Sir Thomas
Haughton, sacristan of the said church, and William
Cuthbert, master of the Galilee there, both brothers and
monks of the same church, to be admitted to the benefit
of the immunity of the church, according to the liberties
and privileges conceded in old time to the most glorious
confessor Cuthbert. And by the ringing of one bell
according to custom, they obtained this benefit. There
were present there, seeing and hearing, the discreet men
William Heyhyngton, Thomas Hudson, John Wrangham,

[1] J. Raine, " Sanctuarium Dunelmense et Sanctuarium Beverlacense,"
London, Surtees Society, 1827, p. xxv.

and Thomas Strynger, witnesses called in especially for the occasion." [1]

At Beverley there were no witnesses : the culprit swore, his hand on the Book. Besides stating the cause of his flying to sanctuary he took his oath to remain peaceful, to help in case of fire or strife, to be present at mass on the commemoration day of King Athelstan, benefactor of the church, etc. :

" Also ye shall bere no poynted wepen, dagger, knyfe, ne none other wapen, ayenst the kynges pece.

" Also ye shalbe redy at all your power, if ther be any debate or stryf, or oder sodan case of fyre within the towne, to help to surcess it.

" Also ye shalbe redy at the obite of Kyng Adelstan, at the dirige, and the messe, at such tyme as it is done, at the warnyng of the belman of the towne, and doe your dewte in ryngyng, and for to offer at the messe on the morne," [2] etc.

To drag men out of the sanctuary was a sacrilege punished with whipping, heavy fines, excommunication, or even death. Nicholas le Porter had helped to snatch from the church of the Carmelites of Newcastle some laymen who had taken refuge there " for the safety of their lives," and who, once delivered to the civil authority, had been executed. Only the Pope's nuncio could secure for him his pardon, and he had to submit to a public penance very little in accord with our present customs :

" We order," wrote Bishop Richard to the parson of St. Nicholas of Durham, " that on Monday, Tuesday, and Wednesday of the Whitsun-week just coming, he shall receive the whip from your hands publicly, before the chief door of your church, in his shirt, bare-headed,

---

[1] See Appendix X, p. 434.

[2] " Sanctuarium Dunelmense et Sanctuarium Beverlacense," p. 111.

and barefoot.[1]　He shall there proclaim in English the
reason for his penance and shall admit his fault ; and
when he has thus been whipped the said Nicholas will
go to the cathedral church of Durham, bareheaded, barefoot, and dressed as above, he will walk in front, you will
follow him ; and you will whip him in the same manner
before the door of the cathedral these three days, and he
will repeat there the confession of his sin." [2]

Excommunication was the punishment meted out
to Ralph de Ferrers, one of the retainers of the then all-
powerful John of Gaunt, for having dragged from the
Westminster sanctuary, at mass time, two prisoners escaped
from the Tower where his master had sent them, and
for having killed one in the process, 1378. The Duke
of Lancaster, in alliance then with Wyclif, caused the
reformer to write one of his most virulent treatises against
the right of sanctuary, asking for its abolition.

The right was, however, maintained ; the king himself
did not dare to infringe upon it, and, though unwilling, had
to let traitors escape, by such means, his revenge or justice.
In a case of this kind, one of the Henries wrote to the
Prior of Durham, and careful as he was to state that he
bound himself only " for the present occasion," there is
no doubt that his acknowledgment of the full immunities
enjoyed by St. Cuthbert's church had nothing excep-

[1] Penance of this kind was not applied only to men. Women of all
ranks were obliged to submit to it. In the same Register Palatine of Durham may be seen the case of Isabella of Murley, condemned for adultery
with her sister's husband, John d'Amundeville, to receive publicly " six
whippings around the market of Durham " (vol. ii. p. 695). The case
was not one of people of the lower sort ; the Amundeville family was
powerful and old-established in the county. Particulars about them from
the thirteenth century may be found in Surtees, " History and Antiquities
of the County Palatine of Durham," London, 1823, vol. iii. p. 270. Another
example is in the "Constitutiones . . . Walteri de Cantilupo " (Bishop
of Worcester), A.D. 1240 ; Wilkins' " Concilia Magnæ Britanniæ et Hiber-
niæ," London, 1757, vol. i. p. 668.

[2] " Registrum Palatinum Dunelmense," ed. Sir T. D. Hardy, London,
1875, vol. i. p. 315, A.D. 1313.

tional : "Trusty and welbeloved in God," says the king,[1] "we grete you well. And wheras we undirstand that Robert Marshall late comitted to prison for treason is now escapid and broken from the same into youre church of Duresme, we havyng tender zele and devocion to ye honour of God and St. Cuthbert, and for the tendir favour and affection that the right reverend father in God our right trusty and welbeloved the Bisshop of Duresme our chauncellor of England we have for his merits wol that for that occasion nothyng be attempted that shud be contrarie to the liberties and immunities of [your] church. We therefor wol and charge you that he be surely kept there as ye wol answere unto us for him." As there could be very little need for the king to declare such an obvious feeling as his respect for St. Cuthbert, the earnest recommendation by which he ends his epistle is most likely to have been the real cause of his writing to his wellbeloved the Prior of Durham. Another characteristic instance is the rebellion of Jack Cade in 1450, when one of his accomplices fled to St. Martin-le-Grand, the most famous of the London sanctuaries. The king in this case wrote to the Dean of St. Martin's ordering him to produce the traitor. This the Dean refused to do, and he exhibited his charters, which being found correct and explicit, the fugitive was allowed to remain in safety where he was.[2]

The right of sanctuary was most valuable, not only for political offenders, but also, and more frequently, for robbers. They escaped from prison, fled to the church, and saved their lives. "In this year," 1324, say the "Croniques de London,"[3] "ten persons escaped out of Newgate, of whom five were retaken, and four escaped

[1] Henry IV or Henry V. Raine, "Sanctuarium Dunelmense," p. xvii.

[2] "Historical Notices of the Collegiate Church or Royal free Chapel and Sanctuary of St. Martin le Grand, London," by A. J. Kempe, London, 1825, p. 136.

[3] "Croniques de London," edited by G. J. Aungier, Camden Society, 1844, p. 48 ; written by a contemporary of the events.

to the church of St. Sepulchre, and one to the church of
St. Bride, and afterwards all for-swore England." But
when the refugees were watched in the church by their
personal enemies, their situation, as evidenced by the
statute of 1315-1316, became perilous. The authors of
a petition [1] to the king set forth in that year that armed
men established themselves in the cemetery, and even
in the sanctuary, to watch the fugitive, and guarded him
so strictly that he could not even go out to satisfy his
natural wants. They hindered food from reaching him ;
if the felon decided to swear that he would quit the kingdom his enemies followed him on the road, and in spite
of the law's protection dragged him away and beheaded
him without judgment. The king reforms all these
abuses,[2] and re-enacts the old regulations as to abjuration,
which were as follows : " When a robber, murderer, or
other evil-doer shall fly unto any church upon his confession of felony, the coroner shall cause the abjuration
to be made thus : Let the felon be brought to the church
door, and there be assigned unto him a port, near or far
off, and a time appointed for him to go out of the realm,
so that in going towards that port he carry a cross in his
hand, and that he go not out of the king's highway, neither
on the right hand, nor on the left, but that he keep it
always until he shall be gone out of the land ; and that
he shall not return without special grace of our lord the
king."

The felon took oath in the following terms : " This
hear thou, sir coroner, that I, N., am a robber of sheep,
or of any other beast, or a murderer of one or of more,
and a felon to our lord the King of England, and because
I have done many such evils or robberies in this land, I

---

[1] " Articuli cleri," statute 9 E. II, cap. 10.
[2] He forbids those on guard to stay in the cemetery, unless there is
imminent danger of flight. The felon may have the " necessaries of life "
in the sanctuary.

do abjure the land of our lord Edward King of England,
and I shall haste me towards the port of such a place which
thou hast given me, and I shall not go out of the highway,
and if I do I will that I be taken as a robber and felon
to our lord the king ; and at such a place I will diligently
seek for passage, and that I will tarry there but one flood
and ebb, if I can have passage ; and unless I can have
it in such a place I will go every day into the sea up to my
knees assaying to pass over ; and unless I can do this
within forty days, I will put myself again into the church
as a robber and a felon to our lord the king. So God me
help and his holy judgment." [1]

Dover was the port oftenest assigned to abjurors.
The time limit varied, being on occasions so brief, that
it must have been almost impossible for people on foot
to fulfil the condition : which was most probably what
the coroner had in view, for he would assign sometimes
different delays to different refugees for the same distance. " The distance from York to Dover over London
Bridge was nearly 270 miles, and there are several entries
of eight days being the allotted time, thus maintaining
a rate of over 33 miles a day." [2]

[1] " Statutes of the Realm," i. p. 250, text of uncertain date, but probably of the reign of Edward II. All this was clasified as " Abuses" by
the not very trustworthy author of the " Mirror for Justices " (Andrew
Horne ?), early fourteenth century, ed. Whittaker and Maitland, Selden Soc ,
1895, p. 158. At all events it was the law. According to " Fleta," lib.
i. cap. xxix, at the end of forty days in sanctuary, if the malefactors have
not abjured the kingdom, food must be refused to them, and they will no
longer be allowed to emigrate. On the road to the port, according to
the same, the felon wore a garb which would cause him to be recognized,
being " ungirt, un-shod, bare-headed, in his bare shirt, as if he were to be
hanged on the gallows, having received a cross in his hands," " discinctus
et discalceatus, capite discooperto, in pura tunica, tanquam in patibulo
suspendendus, accepta cruce in manibus." " Fleta " stated that he must
try to cross, till he got into water, not up to the knees, but up to the neck.
On the " Abjuratio Regni," see the capital article, with a complete bibliography of the subject by André Réville, in the " Revue Historique,"
Sept. 1892.

[2] " The Sanctuaries and Sanctuary Seekers of Mediæval England," by

In the church robbers found themselves side by side
with insolvent debtors. These before seeking refuge
were usually careful to make a general donation of all
their property, and the creditors who cited them to justice
remained empty handed. In 1379,[1] Richard II enacted
remedial legislation. During five weeks, once a week, the
debtor is to be summoned, by proclamation made at the
door of the sanctuary, to appear in person or by attorney
before the king's judges. If he does not choose to appear
justice shall take its course ; sentence will be passed, and
the property that he had given away will be shared
among the creditors.

This, however, served, as usual, only for a time. In the
first years of the following reign the Commons are found
lamenting the same abuses. Apprentices who have plun-
dered their masters, tradesmen in debt, robbers, flee to
St. Martin-le-Grand and live there in quiet on the money
they have stolen. They employ the leisure which this
peaceful existence leaves them in patiently forging " obligations, indentures, acquitances," imitating the signatures
and seals of honest city merchants and of other people.
Felons, murderers and thieves avail themselves of this
restful seclusion for preparing new crimes ; they go out
at night to commit them, and safely return in the morning
to their inviolate retreat. The king, apparently puzzled
as to what to do, when the abuse is so great and the privilege

the Rev. J. Charles Cox, quoting a coroner's roll of the time of Edward III.
London, 1911, p. 28.

[1] Statute 2 Rich. II, stat. 2, chap. 3. These frauds had been already
complained of under Edward III. A petition of the Commons in the
parliament of 1376–77 (" Rolls of Parliament," ii. p. 369), declares that
certain people, after having received money or merchandise on loan, and
having made a pretended gift of all their property to friends, " flee to Westminster, St. Martin's, or other such privileged places, and lie there a long
time, . . . so long that the said creditors are only too pleased to take a
small part of their debt and release the rest." Then the debtors return
home, and their friends give them back their property.

so sacred, vaguely promises that " reasonable remedy shall be had." [1]

Some years later (A.D. 1447) the Goldsmiths' Company of London was startled on finding that a quantity of sham gold and silver plate and jewellery had been issued from the privileged precincts of St. Martin-le-Grand's sanctuary, to the great detriment of their own worshipful company. They brought the facts to the notice of the king, who wrote to the Dean recommending him to check this abuse if possible : " Trustie and welbeloved, we grete you wel, and let you to wote that we be informed that there be divers persons dwellinge within our seinctuarie of St. Martin's that forge and sell laton and coper, some gilt and some sylverd for gold and silver, unto the great deceipt of our lege people. . . . " [2] The tone of the king's letter is very moderate ; he seems to write only to please the Goldsmiths' Company, while realizing that he is powerless in the matter, and that his recommendations will come to nothing.

A priest who took refuge in a church was not obliged to quit England ; he swore that he was a priest, and " enjoyed ecclesiastic privilege, according to the praiseworthy custom of the kingdom." [3] But the church, who accorded to all comers the benefit of sanctuary, reserved to herself the power of removal from it. " In this year (1320), a woman who was named Isabel of Bury, killed the priest of the church of All Saints, near London Wall, and she remained in the same church five days, so that the Bishop of London issued his letter that the church would not save her, wherefore she was brought out of the church to Newgate and was hanged on the third day afterwards." [4]

[1] See Appendix X, p. 435.
[2] A. J. Kempe, " Historical Notices of . . . St. Martin le Grand," London, 1825, p. 135.
[3] Statute 9 Ed. II, cap. 15.
[4] " Croniques de London," Camden Society, 1884, p. 42.

In those days, when riots and rebellions were not uncommon, the right of sanctuary might be valuable for any one ; reformers like Wyclif vainly protested against this exorbitant but useful custom.[1]   A bishop even, however sacred his person, might have to spur his horse and fly towards a church to save his head. The Bishop of Exeter tried and failed when Isabella and her son came to overthrow Edward II : [2] " The same day came one Sir Walter de Stapleton, who was Bishop of Exeter, and the king's treasurer the previous year, riding to his house in Elde Deanes lane to his dinner, and there he was proclaimed traitor ; and he seeing that fled on his horse towards the church of St. Paul's, and was there met and quickly unhorsed, and brought to Cheap, and there he was stripped and his head cut off."

Under Richard III might be seen a queen and a king's son refuse to quit the sacred enclosure of Westminster, in which their lives were safe, thanks to the sanctity of the place. Sir Thomas More has left in his history of the usurper, the first real history in the national language, a moving picture of the plucky defence of Edward IV's widow and of the persistent efforts of Richard to snatch the second child of the late king from the abbey.   To reiterated demands the queen replied : " In what place coulde I recken him sure, if he be not sure in this the sentuarye whereof was there never tiraunt yet so develish, that durst presume to breake. . . . For soth he hath founden a goodly glose, by whiche that place that may defend a thefe, may not save an innocent." [3] The " goodly glose " of Richard III consisted simply in having the right of sanctuary abolished.   In a speech in favour of

[1] See Appendix X.

[2] " Croniques de London," Camden Society, 1844, p. 52.

[3] " The History of King Richard the Thirde (unfinished), writen by Master Thomas More, than one of the Under Sherriffs of London : about the yeare of our Lorde, 1513," " Workes," London, 1557. Reprinted by S. W. Singer, Chiswick, 1821, p. 55.

the measure, which was aimed especially at the places of refuge of St. Paul's and Westminster, the Duke of Buckingham is represented by More drawing a very lively as well as an exact picture of the disorders there : "What a rabble of theves, murtherers, and malicious heyghnous traitours, and that in twoo places specyallye. . . . Mens wyves runne thither with theyr housebandes plate, and saye, thei dare not abyde with theyr housebandes for beatinge. Theves bryng thyther theyr stolen goodes, and there lyve thereon. There devise thei newe roberies ; nightlye they steale out, they robbe and reve, and kyll, and come in again as though those places gave them not only a safe garde for the harme they have done, but a license also to doo more." [1]

This privilege endured, however, and even survived the Reformation ; but from that hour it was less respected. Lord Chancellor Bacon speaks of the sanctuary of Colnham, near Abingdon, as being considered "insufficient" for traitors, under Henry VII ; several political criminals who had taken refuge there, were seized, therefore, and one of them was executed.[2] Sanctuaries were suppressed, legally at least, in the twenty-first year of the reign of James I : "And be it alsoe enacted by the authoritie of this present parliament that no sanctuarie or priviledge

[1] "The History of King Richard the Thirde," pp. 44, 45. A list of the "contents" of the same Westminster sanctuary, in 1532, has been printed by the Rev. J. C. Cox, showing that "there were then fifty fugitives, including one woman under the protection of the abbey, as life prisoners, one of whom had been there for twenty years. Sixteen were there for felonies, probably all robberies, eleven for murder or homicide, eighteen for debt, and two for sacrilege," the church having particular merit in protecting the latter. One was a priest : "Sir James Whytakere, preste, for murdre" ; some were there for a matter so small as to inspire pity : "John ap Howell for felony ; a poore mane, for stellynge of herrings." "Sanctuaries," 1911, pp. 72 ff.

[2] "History of the reign of King Henry VII," Ellis and Spedding's edition of Bacon's Works, vol. vi. p. 43. Bacon says that Henry "was tender in the privilege of sanctuaries, though they wrought him much mischief" (p. 238).

of sanctuary shal be hereafter admitted or allowed in any case." [1] But they lingered on in England as well as on the continent. Cromwell complains, in one of his most famous speeches, of the difficulties his Government sometimes experience on that account when they have to ask from foreign potentates that justice be done. He alludes to the recent assassination of an English messenger, and says : " It is the pleasure of the Pope at any time to tell you that though the man is murdered, yet his murderer has got into the sanctuary." Another proof that, after the statute of James I, the right of sanctuary did not fall entirely into disuse in England is that it had to be re-abolished in 1697 ; sanctuaries are to be found even so late as the reign of George I, when the one at St. Peter's, Westminster, was demolished.

With all their penal severity, law and custom still gave other encouragements to malefactors. They often received charters of pardon which the royal chancery willingly granted because they must be paid for, while the Commons unweariedly renewed their complaints against this abuse. The priest, John Crochille, states to the king in parliament that while he was at the Court of Rome he has been outlawed, and was imprisoned on his return. The chancellor has granted him a charter of pardon, but he is " so impoverished that he has not wherewith to pay for the said charter." [2]

Charters were thus given to the innocent for money, and to " common felons and murderers " also, which had two results : the number of brigands increased by reason of their impunity, and men dared not bring the most formidable criminals to justice for fear of seeing them return pardoned and ready to wreak a terrible revenge.

Most unluckily, the interest that the great had in

---

[1] 21 James I, cap. 28, § 7 ; " Statutes," vol. iv. part ii. p. 1237.
[2] " Rolls of Parliament," 21 Ed. III, vol. ii. p. 178. See also the petition of the Commons in 1350–51, 25 Ed. III, vol. ii. p. 229.

the continuance of this abuse tended also to its maintenance. In league with their retainers, they wanted to defend them from justice as they themselves were defended by them in the street or on the road ; and the best means of saving these *bravi* from the consequences of some assassination was to obtain or buy for them a charter of pardon. The Commons knew it, and reminded the king that often the protectors of such criminals secured charters for them on the representation that these men were abroad, occupied in fighting for the prince. The charter once obtained, the malefactors returned and renewed their ill-deeds, without fear of being troubled by any one.[1]

For all these reasons the traveller would not have been prudent if he had not foreseen on starting the chance of some untoward meeting, and if he had not armed himself in consequence. This was such a recognized necessity that the Chancellor of the University of Oxford allowed the students, on the occasion of a journey, to carry arms, otherwise strictly forbidden.[2]

There was, then, at best, but moderate safety against robbers, and there was not always much against the sheriff's officers themselves. At a time when prowlers were so numerous, it was enough to be a stranger in the district, especially if it were night, to be sent to gaol on suspicion,

[1] " Our lord the king by untrue recommendations has several times granted his charter of pardon to notorious robbers and to common murderers, when it is given him to understand that they are staying for his wars beyond the sea, whence they suddenly return into their country to persevere in their misdeeds." The king orders that on the charter shall be written " the name of him who made the recommendation to the king ; " the judges before whom this charter shall be presented by the felon to have his liberty shall have the power to make inquiry, and if they find that the recommendation is not well founded, they shall hold the charter of non effect. " Rolls of Parliament," vol. ii. p. 253, A.D. 1353.

[2] Regulations of 1313. " Munimenta Academica ; or documents illustrative of academical life and studies at Oxford," edited by H. Anstey, London, 1868, Rolls Series, vol. i. p. 91. The penalty was prison and the loss of the weapons.

as shown by a statute of Edward III.[1] Nothing more general than the terms of this law ; the power to arrest is almost unlimited : " Whereas, in the statute made at Winchester in the time of King Edward, grandfather to the king that now is, it is contained, That if any stranger pass by the country in the night, of whom any have suspicion, he shall presently be arrested and delivered to the sheriff, and remain in ward till he be duly delivered ; and because there have been divers manslaughters, felonies, and robberies [2] done in times past, by people that be called roberdesmen, wastors, and draw-latches . . ." whoever suspects any to be one such, " be it by day or by night," shall cause him immediately to be arrested by the constables of the towns ; the man shall be kept in prison till the justices of gaol delivery come down, and meanwhile inquiry shall be made.

Think now of a stranger passing through the town by night ; some constable feels suspicious and wants to arrest him ; imagining himself already in prison " till the justices come down," the man runs away instead of allowing himself to be taken. The statute has provided for his case.[3] " If they will not obey the arrest, hue and cry shall be levied upon them, and such as keep the watch shall follow with hue and cry with all the town, and the towns near, and so hue and cry shall be made from town to town until that they be taken and delivered

---

[1] 5 Edward III, cap. 14.

[2] A characteristic example of thief-catching, the man being a vagabond, is in Thorold Rogers : William atte Lane had " feloniously bereft Richard [de Herbarton] of a striped gown, worth ten shillings."   Richard ran after him, " cum hutesio et clamore," and the man was caught " by the bailiff of the liberty of Holywell, Oxford."   William pleaded not guilty and asked for a jury, " ponit se super patriam."   The jury found him guilty, ordered that he restitute the gown to Richard, and as he had no goods to make atonement, and was " a vagabond belonging to no ward," he be hanged, " suspendatur," (Dec. 8, 1337) ; the marginal note " susp." shows that he was actually hanged.   " Hist. of Agriculture," ii. 665.

[3] Statute of Winchester, 13 Ed. I, cap. 4.

to the sheriff." [1] A singular picture : night wraps in its shadows the crooked lanes of the unlit city ; the stranger is perhaps a robber, perhaps an honest man, who has lost his way, not knowing the place ; his fault is not to be within doors by curfew ; he gropes his way as best he can ; the watch perceives and challenges him ; fearing the result he takes to his heels, and behold ! the hue and cry begins, the watch runs, the town wakes up, lights appear, and one after the other the more zealous join in the chase. If the town is fortified, the postern gates have long been closed, and he will be surely taken. Scarcely can he hope to cast himself into some unshut doorway at a turning of the street, behind which he will cower, listening with trembling hand and beating heart to the watch who pass heavily along at a charging pace, followed by a crowd of furious shouters. The number of steps lessen, and the shouts become fainter, then die away, lost in the depths of the city.

If the place is not important enough to be enclosed by walls, the first thought of the fugitive will be to gain the open, and then he must not fear marshes, ditches, hedges ; he must know how, at a bend of the ground, to leave the high-road and profit by any place where the Statute of Winchester has been negligently applied. But for that he is lost, the constables follow, the town follows, the " cry " continues, and at the next village the scene of the start will begin over again. The inhabitants, warned by the clamour, light their lanterns, and see, they are already in the chase. Before he reaches the end of the high-street some peasant will be found on the alert, ready to bar the passage of the road to him. All have an interest in it, all have been robbed, or their friends, or relatives ;

[1] " Clamor patriæ " in the Latin texts, " Fleta " for example ; " clameur de haro " in France, where the practice existed even before the time of Childebert, sixth century, and was still in use, in Normandy at least, until the Revolution. See above, p. 114, note 1.

someone of their kin may have been wounded or murdered on the road as he returned from market. Every
one has heard of such misfortunes, and feels himself
personally menaced. Hence this zeal in joining the chase
with the hue and cry, and the conviction that, running so
hard and making so many folk run, the fugitive must be
a famous brigand ready for the gibbet.[1]

[1] This power of running down the first comer was, like many practices
of the time, at once a guarantee for public safety and a dangerous
arm in the hands of felons. Robbers used it, and it happened sometimes
that they imprisoned by this means their own victims. Alisot, wife of
Henry of Upatherle, sets forth to the king that her husband was made
prisoner by the Scotch at the battle of Stirling, remained their captive more
than a year, then returned after having paid forty pounds ransom. In
his absence, Thomas of Upatherle and Robert of Prestbury seized on the
fields which he possessed at Upatherle, divided them, pulled down the
houses and acted as the owners, taking to their own homes all the goods they
could move. The prisoner's return surprised them ; as soon as they knew
that he had re-appeared on his lands, " the said Thomas, by false agreement
between him and the said Robert, raised hue and cry on the said Henry
and put upon him that he had robbed him (Thomas) of his chattels to
the value of £100." They were believed ; " the said Henry was taken
and imprisoned in Gloucester castle for a long time," waiting for the coming
of the justices, exactly as the statute said. Henry recovered his liberty
in the end, and obtained a writ against his enemies ; but they brought force
and came to meet their victim, " and beat the said Henry in the town of
Gloucester, that is they bruised his two arms, both his thighs, and both
his legs, and his head on both sides, and quite wrecked and vilely treated
his body, so that he barely escaped death." The king's reply is not satisfactory : " If the husband be alive, the plaint is his, if he be dead the wife's
plaint is nothing." " Rolls of Parliament," vol. ii. p. 35, A.D. 1330.

PART II

LAY WAYFARERS

AN ADVENTURE SEEKER.

(From the MS. 2 B. vii; English; early Fourteenth Century.)

INTRODUCTORY NOTE

> "*Qui ne s'adventure n'a cheval ni mule, ce dist Salomon.—Qui trop s'adventure perd cheval et mule, respondit Malcon.*"
>
> Vie de Gargantua.

WE have seen the aspect and usual condition of English roads ; we must now take separately the principal types of the wandering class and see what sort of a life the wayfarer led, and what was his importance in society or in the State.

Wayfarers belonging to civil life were, in the first place, quacks and drug-sellers, glee-men, tumblers, minstrels, and singers ; then messengers, pedlars, and itinerant chapmen ; lastly, outlaws, thieves of all kinds, peasants out of bond or perambulating workmen, and beggars. To ecclesiastic life belonged preachers, mendicant friars, and those strange dealers in indulgences called pardoners. Lastly there were palmers and pilgrims, whose journeyings had a religious object, but in whose ranks, as in Chaucer's book, clerk and lay were mingled.

Many of these individuals, the friars for instance, had, it is true, a resting-place, but their existence was spent, for the greater part, on the roads ; when they left their abode their purpose was not to reach this or that place, they had no fixed itinerary, but spent their time in ceaseless rambles about the country, begging as they went. They had, in the long run, caught the manners and the language of true nomadic wayfarers, and in common opinion were generally confounded with them ; they belonged to that caste or family of beings.

As for the strange race which we still see at the present day wandering from country to country, and which, later than any, will represent among us the caste of wanderers, it had not yet made its appearance in the British world, and are outside the limits of the present work. The Bohemians or Gipsies remained entirely unknown in England till the fifteenth century.

BLIND BEGGAR AND HIS DOG.
(*From the MS.* 10 *E. IV.*)

" THER WAS ALSO A DOCTOUR OF PHISIK " (CHAUCER'S DOCTOR).

(From the Ellesmere MS.)

CHAPTER I

HERBALISTS, CHARLATANS, MINSTRELS, JUGGLERS, AND TUMBLERS

THE most popular of all the wanderers were naturally the most cheerful, or those held to be the most beneficent. These latter were the folks with a universal panacea, very numerous in the Middle Ages ; they went about the world selling health. They established themselves in the village green, or the market place, on holidays, spreading a carpet or a piece of cloth on the ground ; they displayed their drugs, and began to harangue the people. Their numbers go diminishing nowadays, for the laws are more and more unkind to them, but they have not yet entirely disappeared, so natural to man are credulity and the longing for health. One may still hear at the present day discourses not very different from those they spoke in the fourteenth century in England, France, or Italy ; their profession is one that has changed less than any. In the thirteenth century the herbalist of Rutebeuf spoke like Ben Jonson's mountebank of the seventeenth, like the charlatan who yesterday a few steps from our door attracted the crowd to his trestle, limiting however his sales, on account of the churlish-ness of the legislator, to tonics, tooth pastes and the like. Big words, marvellous tales, praise of their noble and distant origin, enumeration of the extraordinary cures they have made, ostentatious display of an unbounded devotion to the public good, and of entire pecuniary dis-interestedness : all this is found, and always will be found, in the talk of these insinuating itinerants, as it is also found to-day in the advertisements, on walls or in newspapers, of wondrous cures discovered by a priest, by a convent, by a gentleman of worth and disinterestedness ; which adver-tisements have, to some extent, replaced the itinerant healer of olden times.

"Good people," said Rutebeuf's medicinal herb-seller six hundred years ago, "I am not one of those poor preachers, nor one of those poor herbalists who stand in front of churches with their miserable ill-sown cloak, who carry boxes and sachets and spread out a carpet. Know that I am not one of these ; but I belong to a lady whose name is Madame Trote de Salerno, who makes a kerchief of her ears, and whose eyebrows hang down as silver chains behind her shoulders : know that she is the wisest lady that is in all the four parts of the world. My lady sends us into different lands and countries, into Apulia, Calabria, Burgundy, into the forest of Ardennes to kill wild beasts in order to extract good ointments from them, and give medicine to those who are ill in body. . . . And because she made me swear by the saints when I parted from her, I will teach you the proper cure for worms, if you will listen.   Will you listen ?

". . . Take off your caps, give ear, look at my herbs which my lady sends into this land and country ; and because she wishes the poor as well as the rich to have access thereto, she told me that I should make penny-worths of them, for a man may have a penny in his purse who has not five pounds ; and she told and commanded that I might take pence of the current coin in the land and country wherever I should come. . . .

" These herbs, you will not eat them ; for there is no ox in this country, no charger, be he never so strong, who if he had a bit the size of a pea upon his tongue would not die a hard death, they are so strong and bitter. . . . You will put them three days to sleep in good white wine ; if you have no white take red, if you have no red take fine clear water, for one may have a well before his door who has not a cask of wine in his cellar. If you breakfast from it for thirteen mornings you will be cured of your various maladies. For if my father and mother were in danger of death and they were to ask of me the best herb I could give them, I should give them this. This is how I sell my herbs and my ointments ; if you want any, come and take them ; if you don't, let them alone." [1]

This herbalist was of those early maligned in France and England by royal ordinances for the illegal practice of medicine. Philip the Fair in 1311, John the Good in 1352, had issued severe decrees against them. They were berated with being " ignorant of men's temperament, of the time and mode of administering, of the virtues of medicines, above all, of laxative ones in which lies danger of death." These people " often come from abroad," go through town and suburbs, and venture to administer to the confiding sick, " clisteria multum laxativa et alia

[1] " Diz de l'Erberie." " Œuvres complètes de Rutebeuf," Jubinal's edition, 1874, vol. ii. p. 58.

eis illicita," [1] at which the royal authority was justly
indignant.

In England the itinerant drug-sellers had no better
reputation ; the popular songs, satires and farces always
show them associating in taverns with the meanest rabble,
and using—true to nature—the most ridiculous rant.
Master Brundyche's man, in a play of the fifteenth century,
thus prepares the minds of the hearers for the advent of
the " leech," his master, deriding both :

> What dysease or syknesse y[t] ever ye have,
> He wyl never leve yow tylle ye be in your grave.[2]

To have an idea of what their recipes might be, one
must recall what the medicine was that the statutes of
the kingdom protected. John of Gaddesden, court doctor
under Edward II, got rid of the marks of the small-pox
by wrapping the sick man in red cloths, and he thus cured
the heir to the throne himself.[3]   He had for a long time
been troubled how to cure stone : " At last," says he,
in his " Rosa Anglica," " I bethought myself of collecting

---

[1] Isambert, " Recueil Général des anciennes lois Françaises," vol. iii.
p. 16, and iv. p. 676.

[2] " The Play of the Sacrament," " Philological Society Transactions,"
ed. Whiteley Stokes, 1860, p. 127.

[3] " Let scarlet cloth be taken, and let him who is suffering small-pox
be entirely wrapped in it or in some other red cloth ; I did thus when the
son of the illustrious King of England suffered from small-pox ; I took
care that all about his bed should be red, and that cure succeeded very
well."   Original in Latin, " Joannis Anglici, Praxis Medica Rosa Anglica
dicta," Augsburg, 1595, lib. ii. p. 1050.

To which Gaddesden, I now make humble apologies : for since the
above lines were written years ago, modern discoveries, those especially of
Niels Finsen, of Copenhagen, a man of the truest worth, whom I saw
at work, have justified him.   Red light, it has been found, really has an
influence on the healing of the scars left by small-pox, and even of the
disease itself.   So, biding the time when his beetle remedy, mentioned
next, may prove operative too, I hold Gaddesden justified in turning, from
above, the laugh on his deriders : and I submit to the penance in the
same contrite spirit as Dr. Johnson once did at Uttoxeter.

a good number of those beetles which in summer are found
in the dung of oxen, also of the crickets which sing in the
fields. I cut off the heads and the wings of the crickets
and put them with the beetles and common oil into a pot ;
I covered it and left it afterwards for a day and night in
a bread oven. I drew out the pot and heated it at a
moderate fire, I pounded the whole and rubbed the sick
parts ; in three days the pain had disappeared " ; under
the influence of the beetles and the crickets the stone had
broken into bits.[1] It was almost always thus, by a sudden
illumination, bethinking himself of beetles or of something else, that the learned man discovered his most effi-
cacious remedies : Madame Trote de Salerno never
confided to her agents in the various parts of the
world the secret of more marvellous and unexpected
recipes.

The law, however, made a clear distinction between
a court physician and a quack of the cross-ways. Kings
and princes had their own healers, attached to their persons,
whom they trusted more than they did their ministers.
Securing by indentures of 1372 and 1373 the services
of " frere William de Appleton, phisicien et surgien,"
and of " Maistre Johan Bray," granting them forty marks
yearly pension with the " bouche en court," or right to be
fed at his tables, and other advantages, John of Gaunt,
" roy de Castille," was careful to bind those men of
learning to attend on him " in peace and in war, *so long
as they lived*," a pledge which his brother, King Edward,
never exacted from his chancellors. A Gaddesden had
the support of an established reputation to apply any
medicament to his patients, and he offered the warranty
of his high position. He had studied at Oxford, and he
was an authority ; a grave physician like Chaucer's
" doctour," who had grown rich during the plague, his
wealth increasing his repute—

[1] " Rosa Anglica," vol. i. p. 496.

"For gold in physik is a cordial,"

had not neglected to pore over the works of " Gatesden."

With lesser book-knowledge but an equal ingenuity, the wandering herbalist was not so advantageously known : *he* could not, like the royal physician, rely on his good reputation and his " bouche en court " to make his patients swallow glow-worms, rub them with beetles and crickets, or give them " seven heads of fat bats " [1] as remedies. The legislator kept his eye on him. In the country, like most of the other wayfarers, the man nearly always found means to escape the rigour of the laws ; but in towns the risk was greater. The unhappy Roger Clerk was sued in 1381 for the illegal practice of medicine in London, because he tried to cure a woman by making her wear a certain parchment on her bosom. Though such a nostrum could not possibly be more hurtful than the use of fat bats, he was carried to the pillory " through the middle of the city, with trumpets and pipes," on a horse without a saddle, his parchment and a whetstone round his neck, unseemly pottery hanging round his neck and down his back, in token that he had lied.[2]

Uneasy at the increase of these abuses, Henry V issued in 1421 an *Ordinance against the meddlers with physic and surgery*, " to get rid of the mischiefs and dangers which have long continued within the kingdom among the people by means of those who have used the art and practice of physic and surgery, pretending to be well and sufficiently taught in the same arts, when of truth they are not so." Henceforth there would be severe punishments for all practitioners who have not been approved in their speciality, " that is to say, those of physic by the universities, and the surgeons by the masters of that art." [3]   The mischief

---

[1] A remedy for diseases of the spleen (" Rosa Anglica ").

[2] " Memorials of London," documents relating to the thirteenth, fourteenth and fifteenth centuries, edited by H. Riley, London, 1868, p. 466.

[3] " L'ordinance encontre les entremettours de fisik et de surgerie," " Rolls of Parliament," 9 Hen. V, vol. iv. p. 130.

continued just as before ; which seeing, in order to give
more authority to the medicine approved by the State,
Edward IV, in the first year of his reign, erected the Company of Barbers of London using the faculty of surgery,
into a corporation.[1]

The Renaissance came and found barbers, quacks,
empirics, and sorcerers continuing to prosper on British
soil, and still the subject of song, satire and play.   John
Heywood's Pothecary is a lineal descendant of Rutebeuf's
herbalist ; he sells a wonderful *Syrapus de Byzansis*, and
advertises it in such a way that, anything that happens,
he is right :

> "These be the thynges that breke all stryfe
> Betweene mannes sycknes and his lyfe ;
> From all payne these shall you delever
> And set you even at reste for ever."[2]

Henry VIII deplored the hold those men kept on
the common people, and on some of their betters
too ;   he considered it his duty to enact new rules.
" The science and connyng of physyke and surgerie,"
said the king in his statute, " to the perfecte know-
lege wherof bee requisite bothe grete lernyng and ripe
experience, ys daily within this Royalme exercised by a
grete multitude of ignoraunt persones, of whom the grete
partie have no maner of insight in the same nor in any
other kynde of lernyng ;   some also can no lettres on the
boke, soofarfurth that common artificers, as smythes,
wevers, and women boldely and custumably take upon
theim grete curis and thyngys of great difficultie, in the
which they partely use sorcery and which-crafte, partely
applie such medicine unto the disease as be verey noyous
and nothyng metely therfore, to the high displeasoure

---

[1] Their charter of 1461 is given in Report and Appendix of the City
Liveries' Commission, 1884, vol. iii. p. 74.   [L. T. S.]

[2] " The Foure P." London, 1545.

of God . . . and destruccion of many of the kynge's liege people, most specially of them that cannot descerne the uncunnyng from the cunnyng." [1]   The examples above have shown how difficult it must often have been to "descerne" between them.

Consequently, the king continues, every one who may wish to practise in London or seven miles round, must previously submit to an examination before the bishop of that city, or before the Dean of St. Paul's, assisted by four "doctors of phisyk." In the country the examination will take place before the bishop of the diocese or his vicar-general. In 1540, the same prince united the corporation of the barbers and the college of surgeons, and granted each year to the new association the bodies of four condemned criminals "for anathomies."

Hardly were all these privileges conceded than doubts filled the mind of the legislator himself, and who, it may be wondered, did he regret ? precisely those old unregistered quacks, those possessors of infallible secrets, those village empirics so harshly treated in the statute of 1511. A new law was enacted, which is but one long enumeration of the guilty practices of qualified doctors ; they poison their clients as thoroughly as the quacks of old, the chief difference is that they take more for it, refusing even to interfere if the patient is poor :

"Mynding oonelie theyre owne lucres, and nothing the profite or ease of the diseased or patient, [they] have sued, troubled and vexed divers honest persones aswell men as woomen, whome God hathe endued with the knowledge of the nature, kinde, and operacion of certeyne herbes, rotes, and waters, . . . and yet the saide persones have not takin any thing for theyre peynes and cooning, but have mynistred the same to the poore people oonelie for neighbourhode and Goddes sake, and of pite and

1 Statute 3 Hen. VIII, cap. 11.

charytie ; and it is nowe well knowen that the surgeons admytted wooll doo no cure to any persone, but where they shall knowe to be rewarded with a greater soome or rewarde than the cure extendeth unto, for in cace they wolde mynistre theyre coonning to sore people unrewarded, there shoulde not so manye rotte and perishe to deathe for lacke of helpe of surgerye as dailie doo." Besides, in spite of the examinations by the Bishop of London, " the most parte of the persones of the said crafte of surgeons have small coonning." For which cause all the king's subjects who have, " by speculacion or practyse," knowledge of the virtues of plants, roots, and waters, may as before, notwithstanding enactments to the contrary, cure any malady apparent on the surface of the body, by means of plasters, poultices, and ointments " within any parte of the realme of Englande, or within any other the kinges dominions." [1]

A radical change, as we see ; the secrets and " speculacions " of country people were no longer those of sorcerers, but precious recipes which they had received from God by intuition ; the poor, subject to die without a doctor, rejoiced, the quacks breathed once more—but were led again onto the boards of the comic stage just as before. Ben Jonson, that bold pedestrian who walked all the way from London to Scotland, and who, in his long rambles through villages or cities, had become familiar with the variegated characters haunting their market places, painted, in his turn, the portrait of the " mountebank doctor," one of the best, not better however than Rutebeuf's, and very similar to it, for, as we said, the type passed on from century to century, unchanged.

Old Ben, as usual, paints from life, having seen and heard more than once at Bartholomew and other fairs the drug-seller pacing his scaffold and exclaiming, " O, health, health ! the blessing of the rich ! the riches of the

[1] Statutes 32 Hen. VIII, cap. 42 ; 34 and 35 Hen. VIII, cap. 8.

poor ! who can buy thee at too dear a rate, since there is no enjoying this world without thee." Upon which the man makes game of the despicable "asses" his rivals, boasts of his incomparable panacea, into which enters a little human fat, which is worth a thousand crowns, but which he will part with for eight crowns, no, for six, finally for sixpence. A thousand crowns is what the cardinals Montalto and Farnese and his friend the Grand Duke of Tuscany have paid him, but he despises money and he makes sacrifices for the people. Likewise he has a little of the powder which gave beauty to Venus and to Helen ; one of his friends, a great traveller, found it in the ruins of Troy and sent it him. This friend also sent a little of it to the French Court, but that portion had become "sophisticated," and the ladies who use it do not obtain from it such good results.[1]

Three years later, an English traveller, finding himself at Venice, was filled with wonder at the talk of the Italian mountebanks, and describing them, he too, from life, gave another copy of the same immutable original. "Truely," wrote Coryat, "I often wondered at many of these natural orators. For they would tell their tales with such admirable volubility and plausible grace, even *extempore*, and seasoned with that singular variety of elegant jests and witty conceits, that they did often strike great admiration into strangers that never heard them before." They sell "oyles, soueraigne waters, amorous songs printed, apothecary drugs, and a common-weale of other trifles. . . . I saw one of them holde a viper in his hand, and play with his sting a quarter of an houre together, and yet receive no hurt. . . . He made us all beleeve that the same viper was lineally descended from the generation of that viper that lept out of the fire upon St. Paul's hand, in the island of Melita, now called Malta." [2]

1 "The Fox," Act II, sc. 1 (1605).
2 "Coryat's Crudities," reprinted from the edition of 1611, London, 1776, vol. ii. pp. 50, 53. Coryat set out from Dover, 14 May, 1608.

No doubt the loquacity, the volubility, the momen-
tary conviction, the grace, the insinuating tone, the light,
winged gaiety of the southern charlatan were not found
so fully or so charmingly at the festivals of old England.
These festivals were, however, merry and boisterous,
attended by large crowds, among which moved many an
artful character so full of jest and guile that Shakespeare
thought them worthy of immortality ; he gave it them
indeed in creating, as a model of those men whose
" revenue is the silly cheat," his incomparable " Autolycus,
a rogue."

Country labourers went in numbers to these meetings,
to stand jests which, aimed at them, were an amusement
even to themselves, and to buy some drug which would do
them good : they are to be seen there still.   At the present
day they continue to collect before the vendors of cures
for the toothache and other troubles.   Certificates abound
round the booth ; it seems as though all the illustrious
people in the world must have been benefited by the discovery ; the man now addresses himself to the rest of
humanity. He talks, gesticulates, gets excited, leans
over with a grave tone and a deep voice. The peasants
press around, gaping with inquisitive eye, uncertain if
they ought to laugh or to be afraid, and in the end get
confident. The large hand fumbles in the new coat,
the purse is drawn forth with an awkward air, the piece
of money is held out and the medicine received, while
the shining eye and undecided physiognomy say plainly
that the cunning and the habitual practical sense are here
at fault ; that these good souls, clever and invincible in
their own domain when it is a question of a sheep or a
cow, are the victims of every one in an unknown land,
the land of medical lore. The vendor bestirs himself,
and now, as formerly, triumphs over indecision by means
of direct appeals.

In England the incomparable Goose Fair at Notting-

13

ham should be chosen as the place to see these spectacles, which shine there in all their infinite variety, with quacks as racy as those of pristine days, scenes reminding one of Rubens' great " Kermesse " at the Louvre, and at every turn and before every shop living confutations of St. Evremond and others' ideas of the temper of the English, ever lost in their thoughts, as if merry England were no more.[1]

Greater still was, in the Middle Ages, the popularity of those wayfarers, numerous too at the Goose Fair, who came not to cure, but to amuse, and who, if they did not offer remedies for diseases, at least brought forgetfulness of troubles ; the minstrels, tumblers, jugglers, and singers. Minstrels and *jongleurs*, under different names, exercised the same profession, that is, they chanted songs and romances to the accompaniment of their instruments, as is still done in the East, in Persia for instance, where poems are not told but chanted, in various keys according to the subject. At a time when books were rare, and the theatre, properly so called, did not exist, poetry and music travelled with the minstrels and gleemen along the roads ; such guests were always welcome. They were to be found at every feast, wherever there were rejoicings ; it was expected from them, as from wine or beer, that care would be lulled to sleep, and merriment would replace it. They had many ways to fulfil the expectation, some digni- fied, some not. Of the first sort was the singing and reciting, either in French or English, of the loves and deeds of ancient heroes.

This was a grand part to play, one held in much reverence ; the harpers and minstrels who arrived at the castle gates, their heads full of war stories, or sweet tales, or lively songs to excite laughter, " ad ridendum," were received with the highest favour. On their coming they announced themselves without by some " murie

[1] Visited in 1875, not since.

singing " overheard in the house ; soon came the order
to bring them in ; they were ranged at one end of the
hall, and every one gave ear to them.[1] They preluded
on their instruments, and then began to sing. On what
subject ?

> " Perhaps the plaintive numbers flow
>   For old unhappy far off things
>   And battles long ago :
>   Or is it some more humble lay
>   Familiar matter of to-day ?
>   Some natural sorrow, loss, or pain
>   That has been and may be again ? "[2]

Like Taillefer at Hastings, they told of the prowess of
Charlemagne and of Roland, or they spoke of Arthur,
or of the heroes of the wars of Troy, undoubted ancestors
of the Britons of England :

> " Men lykyn jestis for to here,
>   And romans rede in diuers manere
>   Of Alexandre the conqueroure,
>   Of Julius Cesar the emperoure,
>   Of Grece and Troy the strong stryf,
>   There many a man lost his lyf,

---

[1] Horn and his companions, in the romance of " King Horn," disguise
themselves as minstrels, and range themselves at the gate of Rymenhild's
castle :

> " Hi yeden bi the gravel
>   Toward the castel,
>   Hi gunne murie singe
>   And makede here gleowinge.
>   Rymenhild hit gan ihere
>   And axede what hi were:
>   Hi sede, hi weren harpurs,
>   And sume were gigours.
>   He dude Horn inn late
>   Right at halle gate,
>   He sette him on a benche
>   His harpe for to clenche."

" King Horn," ed. J. R. Lumby, Early English Text Society, 1866,
l. 1465.

[2] Wordsworth, " The Solitary Reaper."

Of Brute that baron bold of hond
The first conqueroure of Englond,
Of kyng Artour that was so riche,
Was non in his tyme him liche,

*   *   *   *   *

How kyng Charlis and Rowlond fawght
With Sarzyns nold they be cawght,
Of Tristrem and of Ysoude the swete
How they with love first gan mete,
Of kyng John and of Isombras,
Of Ydoyne and of Amadas,
Stories of diuerce thynggis
Of pryncis, prelatis, and of kynggis,
Many songgis of diuers ryme,
As english, frensh, and latyne." [1]

In the fourteenth century most of these old romances, heroic, forceful, or touching, had been re-cast and put into new language ; florid descriptions, complicated adventures, marvels and prodigies had been added to them ; many had been turned into prose, and instead of being sung they were read.[2] The lord listened with pleasure, and his taste, palled by surfeit, caused him to take delight in the strange entanglements with which every event was henceforth enveloped. He now lived a more complex life than formerly ; being more refined he had more wants, and grand, simple pictures in poems like the Song of Roland no longer satisfied his imagination : he preferred variety to grandeur. The heroes of romance

[1] "Cursor Mundi," a Northumbrian poem of the fourteenth century, edited by R. Morris for the Early English Text Society, vol. v. p. 1651 and vol. i. p. 8.

[2] It began to be customary to read aloud verses too, instead of singing them. Chaucer foresees that his poem of "Troilus" may be indifferently read or sung, and he writes, addressing his book :

"So preye I to God, that non myswrite the,
Ne the mys-metere, for defaute of tonge !
And red wher so thow be, or elles songe,
That thow be understonde, God I beseche!"
("Troilus," book v., l. 1809.)

found harder and harder tasks imposed on them, and were obliged to triumph over more and more marvellous enchantments. As the hand became more alert the modelling improved ; the softer-hearted heroes of amorous adventures were endowed by the poet with that charm, at once mystic and sensual, so characteristic of the sculptured figures of the fourteenth century. The author of " Sir Gawayne " takes a scarcely concealed pleasure in describing the visits which his knight receives, in painting his lady, so gentle, so pretty, with easy motions and gay smile ; he puts into his picture all his art, all his soul ; he finds words which seem caresses, and verses which shine as with a golden gleam.[1]

These pictures, not rare in the thirteenth century, greatly multiplied in the fourteenth, but toward the end thereof passed from the romance into the tale, or into poems, half tale, half romance, such as the " Troilus " of Chaucer. After many transformations the metrical romance was gradually giving way to new forms and styles which better suited the tastes of the hour. A hundred years earlier such a man as Chaucer would have taken up the Arthur legends in his turn, and would have written some splendid long-winded poetical romance for the minstrels ; but he left us tales and lyric poems because his own taste and that of the age were different, and he felt that people were still curious but not enthusiastic about old heroic stories, that few any longer followed them with passion to the end, and that they were rather made the ornament of libraries than the subject of daily thought.[2] Thenceforward men liked to find separately in

---

[1] " Sir Gawayne and the Green Knight," ed. R. Morris, Early English Text Society, 1864, pp. 38, ff.

[2] Brilliantly illuminated manuscripts of romances continued, however, to multiply ; they were very well paid for. Edward III bought, in 1331, of Isabella of Lancaster, nun of Aumbresbury, a book of romance for which he paid her £66 13s. 4d., which was an enormous sum. When the king had this book he kept it in his own room (Devon's " Issues of the

ballads and in tales the lyric breath and the spirit of observation formerly contained with all the rest in the great metrical romances, the poetical *summæ* of earlier days ; and these, abandoned to the less expert of the itinerant rhymers, became such wretched copies of the old originals that they were the laughing-stock of people of sense and taste.

Many of the grand French epics were thus abridged and put into skipping, barren English verse, the epics being out of fashion, their substitutes valueless. So, when Chaucer, surrounded by his fellow pilgrims, favoured them with a story of Sir Thopas, popular good sense, personated by the host, rebelled, and the performance was rudely interrupted. Yet from Sir Thopas to many of the romances which ran the streets or the roads the distance is small, and the laughable parody was hardly more than a close imitation. Robert Thornton, in the first half of the fifteenth century, copied from older texts a good number of these remodelled romances. In turning their pages one is struck by the excellence of Chaucer's jesting, his caricature being almost a portrait.

These poems are all cut after one and the same pattern, tripping and sprightly, with little thought and less senti- ment ; the cadenced stanzas march on, clear, easy, and empty ; no constraint, no effort ; one may open and close the book without a sigh, without regret, with no positive weariness nor really-felt pleasure. Were it not for the proper names, the reader might pass chancewise from one romance to another without noticing the change. Take no matter which, " Sir Isumbras " for example :

Exchequer," 1837, p. 144). Richard II (ibid. 213) bought a bible in French, a " Roman de la Rose," and a " Roman de Perceval " for £28. To give an idea of these prices we must recall, for example, that a few years before Edward bought his book of romance, the inhabitants of London entered in the City accounts £7 1cs. for ten oxen, £4 for twenty pigs, and £6 for twenty-four swans, which they had given to the king. Year 1328, Riley's " Memorials of London," 1868, p. 170.

after a prayer for form's sake, the rhymer vaunts the valour of the hero, then praises a quality of especial value, with which he was happily endowed, his fondness for minstrels and his generosity towards them :

> " He luffede glewmene well in haulle
> He gafe thame robis riche of palle (fine cloth)
> Bothe of golde and also fee ;
> Of curtasye was he kynge,
> Of mete and drynke no nythynge,
> On lyfe was none so fre."

Isumbras, his wife, and his son, are without peers ; he is the most valiant of knights, his wife the most lovely of women :

> " I wille yow telle of a knyghte
> That bothe was stalworthe and wyghte,
> And worthily undir wede ;
> His name was hattene syr Ysambrace."

So is also Sir Eglamour :

> " Y shalle telle yow of a knyght
> That was bothe hardy and wyght,
> And stronge in eche a stowre."

So is also Sir Degrevant :

> " And y schalle karppe off a knyght
> That was both hardy and wyght,
> Sire Degrevaunt that hend hyght,
> That dowghty was of dede." [1]

---

[1] The " Thornton Romances," edited by J. O. Halliwell for the Camden Society, pp. 88, 121, 177. The romances in this volume are, " Perceval," " Isumbras," " Eglamour," and " Degrevant " ; the longest scarcely reaches 3,000 lines, " Isumbras " not 1,000. The manuscript, which is in Lincoln Cathedral, is a collection containing many other romances, especially a " Life of Alexander," a " Mort d'Arthur," an " Octavian," and a " Diocletian," besides numerous prayers in verse, recipes for curing toothache, prophecies of the weather, etc.

So is also Chaucer's Sir Thopas :

> " . . . I wol telle verrayment
> Of myrthe and of solas,
> Al of a knyght was fair and gent
> In batail and in tornament,
> His name was Sir Thopas."

And though Sir Thopas almost comes within the
scope of the present work, being an adventure seeker,
" a knight auntrous," ever on his way, never sleeping in
a house—

> "And for he was a knight auntrous,
> He nolde slepen in non hous,
> But liggen in his hode ;
> His bright helm was his wonger (pillow),"

yet must we abide by the ruling of mine host and leave
him alone :

> "No more of this for Goddes dignitee."

But, even at a comparatively late date, the inmate of
an out of the way castle usually proved more lenient. He
welcomed the minstrel, his verse and his viol as he welcomed change ; he lent a complacent ear to his commonplace romances, his ballads on every subject, his praise
of flowers, women, wine, spring, heroes and saints, his
goliardic dispraise of women,[1] monks and friars, his
tales of love or laughter, his patriotic songs the rarest of
all, for the Hundred Years War was for the English chiefly
a royal and not a national war, and this alone can explain
the scant place occupied in the songs of the time by Crécy

---

[1] From Golias, the type of the debauched and gluttonous prelate, made
famous by Latin poems attributed to Walter Map, twelfth century, ed.
Th. Wright, Camden Society, 1841 ; cf. " The Cambridge Songs, a
Goliard's song book of the eleventh century," ed. Karl Breul, Cambridge,
1916.

and Poictiers, never mentioned by Chaucer, never mentioned by Langland (who disapproved of the war), celebrated only by one solitary songster known by name
and otherwise unknown, the unimitated and ungifted
Laurence Minot.[1] The noble listened ; he had few
intellectual diversions ; he gave little time if any to reading,
which was not for him then an unmixed pleasure, and
needed effort ; there was no theatre for him to go to.
At long intervals only, when the great yearly feasts came
round, the knight might go, in company with the crowd,
to see Pilate and Jesus on the boards. There he found
sometimes not only the crowd but the king too. Richard II,
for example, witnessed a religious play or mystery in the
fourteenth year of his reign, and had ten pounds distri-
buted among several clerks of London who had played
before him at Skinnerwell " the play of the Passion and of
the creation of the world." [2] A few years later he saw
the famous York plays, at the feast of Corpus Christi,
performed in the streets of that city.[3] In ordinary times
the knight was only too happy to receive in his home
men of vast memory, who knew more verse and more
music than could be heard in a day.

The king himself liked their coming. He had them
sometimes brought up to him in his very chamber, where
he was pleased to sit and hear their music. Edward II
received four minstrels in his chamber at Westminster
and heard their songs, and when they went he ordered
twenty ells of cloth to be given them for their reward.[4]
No one thought in those days of rejoicings without minstrels ; there were four hundred and twenty-six of them

[1] Help me God, my wit es then,

he says himself. " Poems," ed. T. Hall, Oxford, 1887, p. 21.
[2] " Issues of the Exchequer," p. 244.
[3] " Extracts from the Municipal Records of the City of York," by
Rob. Davies, London, 1843, p. 230.
[4] Wardrobe Accounts ; " Archæologia," vol. xxvi. p. 342.

at the marriage of the Princess Margaret, daughter of
Edward I.[1]　Edward III gave a hundred pounds to those
who were present at the marriage of his daughter Isabella,[2]
some figured also at his tournaments.[3]　When a bishop
went on his pastoral rounds he was occasionally greeted
by minstrels, hired on purpose to cheer him ; they were
of necessity chosen among local artists, who were apt
to fiddle cheap music to his lordship.　Bishop Swinfield,
in one of his rounds, gave a penny a piece to two minstrels
who had just played before him ; but on another occasion
he distributed twelve pence a piece.[4]

When men of importance were travelling they sometimes had the pleasure of hearing minstrels at the inn,
and in that manner whiled away the long empty evenings.
In the curious manual already quoted, called " La manière
de langage," composed in French by an Englishman of
the fourteenth century, the traveller of distinction is
represented listening to the musicians at the inn, and
mingling his voice at need with their music : " Then,"
says our author, " come forward into the lord's presence
the trumpeters and horn-blowers with their frestels (pipes)
and clarions, and begin to play and blow very loud, and
then the lord with his squires begin to move, to sway,
to dance, to utter and sing fine carols till midnight without
ceasing." [5]

In great houses minstrels' music was the usual season-
ing of meals.　At table there are only two amusements,

1 Thomas Wright, " Domestic Manners and Sentiments," 1862, p. 181.

2 40 Ed. III, Devon's " Issue Rolls of the Exchequer," p. 188.

3 See two examples of like cases in the introduction to the " Issue Roll
of Thomas de Brantingham," p. xxxix.

4 " Roll of Household Expenses of Richard de Swinfield, Bishop of
Hereford," ed. J. Webb, Camden Society, 1854–55, vol. i. pp. 152, 155.
On the condition of minstrels, jugglers, bear-wards, etc., in France, see e.g.
" Histoire économique de la Propriété, des Salaires . . . et de tous les
Prix," by Vicomte d'Avenel, Paris, 1914, vol. v. p. 264, and Bédier, " Les
Fabliaux," 1895, p. 389.

5 Ed. P. Meyer, in " Revue Critique," vol. x. (1870), p. 373.

says Langland, in his " Visions " : to listen to the minstrels, and, when they are silent, to talk religion and to
scoff at its mysteries.[1] The repasts which Sir Gawain takes
at the house of his host the Green Knight are enlivened
with songs and music. On the second day the amusement extends till after supper ; they listen during the
meal and after it to many noble songs, such as Christmas
carols and new songs, with all possible mirth :

> " Mony athel songez,
> As coundutes of kryst-masse, and carolez newe,
> With all the manerly merthe that mon may of telle."

On the third day,

> " With merthe and mynstralsye, with metez at hor wylle,
> Thay maden as mery as any men moghten." [2]

In Chaucer's " Squire's Tale," King Cambynskan
gives a

> " Feste so solempne and so riche
> That in this worlde ne was ther noon it liche."

And this prince is shown sitting after the third course
among his nobles, listening to the music :

> " . . . So bifelle after the thridde cours,
> Whil that the kyng sit thus in his nobleye,
> Herkyng his mynstrales her thinges pleye
> Byforn him atte boord deliciously. . . ."

During all these meals the sound of the viol, the voice
of the singers, the " delicious things " of the minstrels,
were interrupted, it is true, by the crunching of the bones

---

[1] " Piers Plowman," Text C, pass. xii. ll. 35–39.
[2] " Sir Gawayne and the Green Knight," ed. R. Morris, Early English
Text Society, 1864, ll. 484, 1652–1656, and 1952. In the same manner
Arthur, after an exploit by Gawain, sits down to table, " Wythe alle maner
of mete and mynstralcie bothe."

gnawed by the dogs under the tables, by the quarrels of the same, or by the sharp cry of some ill-bred falcon ; for many noblemen kept during dinner these favourite birds on a perch behind them. Their masters, enjoying their presence, were indulgent with the liberties they took.

The minstrels of Cambynskan are represented as attached to his person ; those belonging to the King of England also had permanent functions. The sovereign was seldom without them, and even when he went abroad was accompanied by them as well as by his hawks and hounds, a complete orchestra. Henry V engaged eighteen, who were to follow him to Guyenne and elsewhere.[1] Their chief is sometimes called *king* or *marshal* of the minstrels.[2] On May 2, 1387, Richard II gave a passport to John Caumz (? Camuz), "rex ministrallorum nostrorum," who was setting out for a journey beyond the sea.[3] On January 19, 1464, Edward IV grants a pension of ten marks " to our beloved Walter Haliday, marshall of our minstrels."[4] The Roll of Thomas Brantingham, treasurer to Edward III, bears frequent mention of royal minstrels, to whom a fixed salary of seven pence-halfpenny a day is paid.[5] King Richard II had in the same manner minstrels in his pay, and enjoyed their music

[1] " This indenture, made 5 June in the 3rd year of our sovereign lord King Henry the fifth since the Conquest, witnesseth that John Clyff, minstrel, and 17 other minstrels, have received from our said lord the king, through Thomas, Earl of Arundel and Surrey, treasurer of England, forty pounds as their wages, to each of them 12d. a day for a quarter of a year, for serving our said lord in the parts of Guyenne or elsewhere." Rymer's " Fœdera," ed. 1704–32, year 1415, vol. ix. p. 260.

[2] The chief of the minstrels of Beverley was called *alderman*. [L. T. S.]

[3] " Fœdera," year 1387, vol. vii. p. 555. In Sir John Hawkins' " History of Music," London, 1893, vol. i. p. 193, John of Gaunt's charter to the king of his minstrels in Tutbury, dated 4 Richard II, is given at length. [L. T. S.]

[4] " Fœdera," year 1464, vol. xi. p. 512.

[5] " Issue Roll of Thos. de Brantingham," ed. Devon, pp. 54–57 and 296–298. These pensions were granted for life.

when travelling. When he went for the last time to Ireland he had to wait for ten days at Milford on account of contrary winds. That French gentleman, Créton, who was with him, and wrote afterwards a most interesting account of what befell the unfortunate king during the last year of his reign, states in his chronicle that the time was merrily passed at Milford while expecting a change in the weather, and that day and night they had music and songs of minstrels.[1]

The richer nobles imitated, of course, the king, and had their own companies, whom they allowed to play at times in various parts of the country (as was the case later with regular actors), and whom they supplied with testimonial letters vouching for them and their artistic ability.[2] The accounts of Winchester College under Edward IV show that this college recompensed the services of minstrels belonging to the king, the Earl of Arundel, Lord de la Ware, the Duke of Gloucester, the [Earl] of Northumberland, and the Bishop of Winchester ; these last often recur. In the same accounts, time of Henry IV, mention is made of the expenses occasioned by the visit of the Countess of Westmoreland, accompanied by her suite. Her minstrels formed part of it, and a sum of money was given them.[3]

[1] " La feumes nous en joie et en depport
    Dix jours entiers, atendant le vent nort
        Pour nous partir.
    Mainte trompette y povoit on oir
    De jour, de nuit, menestrelz retentir."

MS. Harl. 1319, in the British Museum, printed in " Archæologia," vol. xx. p. 297.

[2] Of which letters, models have come down to us, " and judging by the lavish eulogy they employ, the minstrels themselves must have had a hand in drawing them up." E. K. Chambers, " The Mediæval Stage," Oxford, 1903, 2 vols., i. p. 53 ; three chapters on minstrels of great interest and importance, beginning with a bibliography of the subject, i. 23.

[3] Warton's " History of English Poetry," Hazlitt's edition, 1871 ii. p. 98. John of Gaunt orders £16 13s. 4d. to be paid to " various min-

When visiting towns and performing before the citizens, itinerant troups made a collection among the bystanders, having, however, themselves a fee to pay for the privilege. A curious example of this is recorded in John of Gaunt's register, where his seneschal of New-castle-under-Lyme is ordered to see to it that 4d. be paid to William de Brompton a burgess of that city and Margery his wife, " by every minstrel coming there to make his minstralcy against the feast of St. Giles the Abbot," and that a payment be also made to the same for every bear brought there to be baited, a regular inquest having shown that such fees had been paid to that couple and to Margery's ancestors from time immemorial.

Like lords and princes, from the early fifteenth century at least, cities themselves had their troups of minstrels : " London, Coventry, Bristol, Shrewsbury, Norwich, Chester, York, Beverley, Leicester, Lynn, Canterbury, had them, to name no others. They received fixed fees or dues, wore the town livery and badge of a silver scutcheon, played at all local celebrations and festivities and were commonly known as *waits*." [2]

Besides money and good meals, those musical wan-derers often received a variety of gifts, such as cloaks, furred robes, and the like. Langland alludes more than once to these largesses, which proves that they were considerable, and he regrets that all this was not distri-buted to the poor who go, they too, from door to door, and are the minstrels of God :

strels of his very dear cousin the count of Flanders," and £65 to various heralds, etc., of " our most redoubted lord and father, the king at Eltham." " John of Gaunt's Register," ed. S. A. Smith, 1911, vol, ii. p. 279. Lang-land notices the good reception given, when they were travelling, to the king's minstrels, in order to please their master, known to be sensible of these marks of good will.

¹ November 26, 1372. " John of Gaunt's Register," ed. S. A. Smith, 1911, ii. 98.

² Chambers, ibid. i. 51.

" Clerkus and knyghtes · welcometh kynges mynstrales,
And for love of here lordes · lithen hem at festes :
Much more, me thenketh · riche men auhte
Have beggers by-fore hem · whiche beth godes mynstrales." [1]

But his advice was not heeded, and long after his time the minstrels continued to be admitted to the castle halls. In erecting the hall the builder took into account the probable visits of musicians, and often raised a gallery for them above the entrance door, opposite to the dais, the place where the master's table was set.[2] This custom long survived the Middle Ages. At Hatfield a minstrels' gallery of the seventeenth century adorns the hall of that beautiful place, and is still, on great occasions, put to the use it was originally intended for.

PLAYING UPON
THE VIELLE.
(*From the MS.* 10
*E.IV ; English ;
early Fourteenth
Century.*)

The classic instrument of the minstrel was the *vielle*, a kind of violin or fiddle with a bow, something like ours, a drawing of which, as used in the thirteenth century, is to be found in the album of Villard de Honnecourt.[3] It was delicate to handle, and required much skill ; in proportion therefore as the profession lowered, the good performer on the *vielle* became rarer ; the common tambourine or tabor, which needed but little training, replaced the *vielle*, and true artists complained of the music and the taste of the

---

[1] " Piers Plowman," Text C, pass. viii. l. 97.

[2] See a drawing of such a gallery in a miniature reproduced by Eccleston, " Introduction to English Antiquities ; " London, 1847, p. 221. To the sound of the minstrels' music four wild men or mummers are dancing with contortions ; sticks lie on the ground, no doubt for their exercises ; a barking dog is jumping between them.

[3] " Album de Villard de Honnecourt," edited by Lassus and Darcel, 1858, plate I.

day. It was a tabor that the glee-man of Ely wore at
his neck when he had his famous dialogue with the King
of England, which proved so bewildering for the monarch:
"He came thence to London ; in a meadow he met the
king and his suite ; around his neck hung his tabor,
painted with gold and rich azure."[1]

The minstrels played yet other instruments, the harp,
the lute, the guitar, the bag-pipe, the rota (a kind of small
harp, the ancient instrument of the Celts), and others.[2]

The presents, the favour of the great, rendered enviable
the lot of the minstrels ; they multiplied accordingly,
and the competition was great, which made the trade less
profitable. In the fifteenth century, the king's minstrels,
clever and able men, protested to their master against
the increasing audacity of the false minstrels, who
deprived them of the greater part of their revenues.
"Uncultured peasants," said the king, who sided with
his own men, "and workmen of different trades in our
kingdom of England have passed themselves off as minstrels ; some have worn our livery, which we did not

---

[1] "Si vint de sà Loundres ; en un prée
    Encontra le roy e sa meisnée ;
    Entour son col porta soun tabour,
    Depeynt de or e riche azour."

"Le roi d'Angleterre et le jongleur d'Ely," edited with "La riote du
monde," by Francisque Michel, Paris, 1834, p. 28.—"*Viola.* Save thee,
friend, and thy music : Dost thou live by thy tabor ?" And the tabor
player, in "Twelfth Night" (iii. 1) is the Clown.

[2] At Exeter Cathedral may be seen many of the musical instruments
used in the fourteenth century, sculptured in the "Minstrels' Gallery,"
where angels are performing (see the plate). The instruments they use
have been identified by M. Carl Engel as being : the cittern, the bag-pipe,
the clarion, the rebec, the psaltery, the syrinx, the sackbut, the regals, the
gittern, the shalm, the timbrel, the cymbals. "Musical Instruments,"
South Kensington Museum Art Handbook, p. 113. [The duties of the
court minstrels of Edward IV are declared in the Black Book of the Orders
of that king's household (Harl. MS. 610, fol. 23), and their instruments
are enumerated ; "some vse trumpetts, some shalmes, some small pipes,
some are stringe-men." L. T. S.]

Cittern. Bagpipe. Clarion. Rebec. Psaltery. Syrinx. Sackbut. Regals. Gittern. Shalm. Timbrel. Cymbals.

THE MINSTRELS' GALLERY AT EXETER. [p. 209.

(Fourteenth Century.)

grant to them, and have even given themselves out to be our own minstrels." By means of these guilty practices, they extorted much money from the king's subjects, and although they had no understanding nor experience of the art, they went from place to place on festival days and gathered all the profits which should have enriched the true artists, those who had devoted themselves entirely to their profession, and did not exercise any low trade.

The king, to protect his men against such unlawful competition, authorized them to reconstitute and consolidate the pre-existing gild of minstrels ; no one could henceforth exercise this profession, whatever his talent, if he had not been admitted into the gild. A power of inquiry was granted to the members of the society, who had the right to have false minstrels fined, the money to be applied to candles lit in the chapel of the Holy Virgin at St. Paul's and in the " royal free chapel of St. Anthony." For a pious motive was associated then with most actions, and minstrels, so badly treated by the generality of religious writers, were in this case bound, says the king, to pray in those two chapels for him while alive and for his soul when dead, for his " dearest consort Elizabeth queen of England," and for the soul of his " dearest lord and father " ; this till the end of time. Women were, as well as men, admitted into the fraternity. [1]

Such was the will of the king ; in the same manner, and without any better success, the price of bread and the wage for a day's labour were lowered by statute, all of which had but a limited and temporary effect.

[1] Rymer's " Fœdera," April 24, 1469. See Appendix XI. On minstrels' gilds in various English cities, the Beverley one being perhaps the most famous (none, however, possessing documentary proofs of its existence so old as the French ones, the Paris gild, for example, which was reformed in 1321 and lasted till 1776), see Chambers, " Mediæval Stage," ii. 258. Having known various vicissitudes, the royal or London gild " still exists as the Corporation of the Master, Wardens and Commonalty of the Art and Science of the Musicians of London." Ibid. ii. 261.

The authorities had other reasons for watching over singers and itinerant musicians ; while they showed indulgence to the armed retainers of the great, they feared the rounds made by those glee men with no other arms than their vielle or tabor, but sowing sometimes strange disquieting doctrines under colour of songs. These were more than liberal, and went at times so far as to recommend social or political revolt. The Commons in parliament denounced by name, at the beginning of the fifteenth century, the Welsh minstrels as fomentors of trouble and causes of rebellion. Their political songs encouraged the insurgents to resistance ; and parliament, who bracketed them with ordinary vagabonds, knew well that in having them arrested on the roads, it was not simple cutpurses whom it sent to prison. " *Item* : That no westours and rimers, minstrels or vagabonds, be maintained in Wales to make kymorthas or quyllages on the common people, who by their divinations, lies, and exhortations are partly cause of the insurrection and rebellion now in Wales. *Reply* : Le roy le veut." [1]

Popular movements were the occasion for satirical songs against the great, songs composed by minstrels and soon known by heart among the crowd. It was a popular song which furnished to John Ball the text for his famous speech at Blackheath in the revolt of 1381:

> " When Adam delved and Eve span,
>   Who was then the gentleman ? "

Again, under Henry VI, when the peasants of Kent rose, and their allies the sailors took and beheaded the Duke of Suffolk at sea, a satirical song was composed, became popular and has come down to us. As before killing him they had given a mock trial to the king's favourite, so in the song they present the comedy of his funeral ;

[1] " Rolls of Parliament," iii. p. 508, A.D. 1402.

nobles and prelates are asked to come and sing their responses, and in this pretended burial service, which is in reality a hymn of joy and triumph, the minstrel calls down heavenly blessings on the murderers. At the end the Commons are represented coming in their turn to sing a sarcastic *Requiescant in pace* over all English traitors.[1]

The renown of the popular rebel, Robin Hood the outlaw, who lived in the twelfth century if he ever lived at all, went on increasing. His manly virtues were extolled ; picturesque companions were, later, invented for him : Friar Tuck, Maid Marian, Little John and all the imaginary inhabitants of Sherwood Forest ; listeners were told how this pious man, who, even in the worst danger, waited till mass was over before thinking of his safety, boldly robbed great lords and high prelates, but was merciful to the poor ;[2] which was an indirect notice to the brigands of the time that they should be careful to discern in their rounds between the tares and the wheat.

The sympathy of the minstrels for ideas of emancipation, which had made such progress in the fourteenth century, was not only evinced in these songs, but also in the remodelled romances recited by them in presence of the nobles, and which henceforth were full of high-flown declarations on the equality of men. The hearer did not take offence ; the greater poets, favourites of all that counted, the king himself in his public statements proclaimed liberal truths which it was hardly expected would be acted upon literally. Thus Chaucer

---

[1] See Appendix XII, p. 437.

[2] The songs about him were collected by J. Ritson ; " Robin Hood Ballads," London, second edition, 1832. Most of them are only of the sixteenth century, but a few are of an earlier date. Robin Hood's popularity was, however, well established in the fourteenth century, as shown by a line in " Piers Plowman," Skeat's edition, Text B, passus v., l. 79. On Robin Hood as the hero of popular songs, of many games and of plays, see Chambers, " Mediæval Stage," i. 174.

celebrates in his most eloquent verse the only true nobility
in his eyes, that which comes from the heart.[1] Thus
also King Edward I, on summoning the first true English
parliament in 1295, declared that he did so inspired by
the old maxim which prescribes that what concerns all
should be approved by all, proclaiming a principle whence
have since issued the most radical reforms of society, and
on which the American insurgents founded, centuries
later, their claim to independence.[2]

Such direct appeals from the king to his people contributed early to develop among the English the sense
of duty, of political rights and responsibilities. In days
of trouble, when parliament scarcely yet existed, the same
king thought he should explain his conduct to the people
and allow them to form an opinion : " The king about
this, and about his estate and as to his kingdom, and how
the business of the kingdom has come to naught, makes
known and wishes that all should know the truth of it ;
which ensues . . . "[3]

In France the enunciation of liberal principles was
frequent in royal edicts, but the emptiness of these fine
words and the interested motives which caused them to

1 " The Wyf of Bathes Tale " (sixty-eight lines on the equality of
men and on nobility) ; again, in the " Parson's Tale " : " Eek for to pryde
him of his gentrye is ful greet folye . . . . we ben alle of o fader and of
o moder ; and alle we been of o nature roten and corrupt, both riche and
poure " (Skeat's edition of the " Canterbury Tales," vol. iv. p. 596). Not
less striking, these lines of a French poem of the same century, quoted in
the Discourse upon the state of letters in the fourteenth century, " Histoire
Littéraire de la France," vol. xxiv. p. 236 :

"Nus qui tien face n'est vilains,
Mès de vilonie est toz plains
Hauz hom qui laide vie maine :
Nus n'est vilains s'il ne vilaine."

2 " Sicut lex justissima, provida circumspectione sacrorum principum
stabilita, hortatur et statuit ut quod omnes tangit ab omnibus approbetur,
sic.," etc. Rymer's " Fœdera," year 1295, vol. ii. p. 689.

3 " Fœdera," year 1297, vol. ii. p. 783.

be used were scarcely veiled at all. Louis X, " le Hutin,"
in his ordinance of July 2, 1315, declares that, " as according to the law of nature every one is born free," he has
resolved to enfranchise the serfs on his own estates. He
adds, however, that he will do so for money. Three days
later, fearing that his benefit is not sufficiently prized, he
supplements his first statement by a new one in which
his exalted ideas and his present needs are boldly inter-
twined : " It may be that some, ill-advised and in default
of good counsel, might misunderstand such great benefit
and favour and wish rather to remain in the baseness of
servitude than to come to free estate : wherefore we
order and commit to you that, *for the aid of the present war*,
you levy on such persons according to the amount of
their property, and the conditions of servitude of each
one, as much and sufficiently as the condition and riches
of those persons may bear and as the necessity of our
war may require." [1]

Well then might the minstrels imitate the king himself
in repeating axioms so well known, and which, according
to appearance, there was so little chance of seeing carried
out. But ideas, like the seeds of trees falling on the soil,
are not lost, and the noble who had gone to sleep to the
murmur of verses chanted by the glee-man waked up one
day to the tumult of the crowd collected before London,
with the refrain of the priest John Ball for its war-cry.
And then he had to draw his sword and show by a massacre
that the time was not yet come to apply these axioms, and
that there was nothing in them save song.

Still were the trees dropping their seeds. Poets and
popular singers had thus an influence over social movements, less through the maxims scattered throughout
their great works than by those little unpolished pieces,
struck off on the moment, which the lesser among them
composed and sang for the people, at the cross-roads in

[1] Isambert's " Recueil," vol. iii. pp. 102, 104.

times of trouble, or by the peasants' hearth in ordinary times, as a reward for hospitality.[1]

Minstrels, however, as singers of songs, propagators of thoughts, tellers of romances, were to disappear. An age was beginning when books and the art of reading spread among the people, and a more and more numerous public would read and cease to listen ; the theatres were, moreover, about to offer a spectacle much superior to that of the little troop of musicians and wandering singers, and would compete with them more powerfully than the " rude husbandmen and artificers of various crafts," against whose impertinence Edward IV was so indignant. Replaced, unwanted, the minstrels proper ceased to exist as a class, leaving however behind them a variety of men who could claim them as ancestors, street musicians, mirth mongers, or the " blind crouder with no rougher voice then rude stile," who sang for Sir Philip Sidney " the olde song of Percy and Douglas."

A FOURTEENTH-CEN-
TURY JUGGLER.
(*From MS.* 10 *E. IV.*)

In fact, the period of the Taillefers who would go to death in the fight while singing of Charlemagne was a limited one ; the lustre which the jongleurs or trouvères of the twelfth and thirteenth centuries, who confined themselves to the recitation of poetry, had shed on their profession, was effaced in proportion as they associated

[1] A not at all rare occurrence. See in the *fabliau*, " Le povre Clerc," how the itinerant verse teller is asked by the peasant who receives him to say, while the supper is cooking : " Some of those things that are in writing, either a song or a story of adventure." Bédier, " Les Fabliaux," 2nd ed., 1895, p. 391.

more closely with the mannerless bands of tumblers, 'ugglers, leaders of performing bears (*ursinarii*, the Latin documents of the time name them),[1] conjurors, and ribalds of all kinds.[2]

These bands had always existed, but the chanters of romances, tellers of knights' high deeds, and of saints' edifying examples, admitted even into the cloister, finding grace before St. Thomas Aquinas,[3] had, in the heyday of their fame stood above them, or apart from them. At all times, however, in castles and at fairs, were to be found buffoons and jugglers, whose coarseness exhilarated the spectators. The precise details which the contemporaries give as to their performances show not only that their jokes would not be tolerated among the rich of to-day, but that there are even few out of the way villages where

---

[1] Performing animals or wild ones in cages enjoyed a popularity which proved more constant than that of minstrels, since it has continued unabated from the early middle ages to the present time. *Ursinarii* frequently appear in the accounts of the Shrewsbury corporation quoted by Chambers who gives, e.g. this noteworthy entry : " In regardo dato ursinario domini Regis pro agitacione bestiarum suarum ultra denarios tunc ibidem collectos. . . ." (Mediæval Stage, ii. 251 ; year 1517). The English kings, as is well known, had their menagerie in the Tower, as the French ones had theirs in Paris. St. Louis sent, " as a great gift," in 1255, an elephant to Henry III ; " and we do not believe any had been seen before in England," wrote Matthew Paris who, good draughtsman as he was, painted the portrait of the wondrous beast. The miniature in MS. Nero D I, in the British Museum, fol. 169, is by him, according to Madden, " Historia Anglorum," Rolls, Preface.

[2] " There saugh I pleyen jugelours,
　　Magiciens and tregetours,
　　And phitonisses, charmeresses,
　　Olde wiches, sorceresses
　　That use exorsisaciouns
　　And eke thes fumygaciouns."
　　　　　　(Chaucer's " House of Fame," l. 169.)

[3] Chambers, " Mediæval Stage," i. 58, quoting, the " Summa Theologiæ " : " Sicut dictum est, ludus est necessarius ad conservationem vitæ humanæ," etc. On the distinction between the higher and lower minstrelsy, see ibid. pp. 59 ff.

peasants on a festival would accept them without disgust. The great of former days found pleasure, however, in them, and in the troop of mummers and tumblers who went about wherever mirth was wanted, there always were some who excited laughter by the ignoble means described in John of Salisbury's " Polycraticus "—" so shameful that even a cynic would blush at seeing them." [1] But people of high degree did not blush, they laughed. Two hundred years later, some sacrilegious clerks, out of hate for the Archbishop of York, made themselves guilty of the same monstrous buffooneries in his very cathedral, and the episcopal letter relating their misdeeds with the precision of a legal report, adds that they were committed *more ribaldorum*.[2] Langland, at the same epoch, shows that one of his personages is not a true minstrel, either of the higher or of the lower sort, since he is neither able to " telle faire gestes," nor to practise those welcome turpitudes.[3]

The greater was the feast, the coarser were often the deeds and songs of the mirth-mongers. In this way, in particular, were they accustomed to celebrate Christmas. Thomas Gascoigne, in the sort of theological dictionary compiled by him, beseeches his readers to abstain from hearing such Christmas songs, for they leave on the mind images and ideas which it is almost impossible afterwards to wash out. He adds as a warning the story of a man he personally knew : " I have known, I, Gascoigne, Doctor in Divinity, who am writing this book, a man who had heard at Christmas some of those repulsive songs.

[1] Lib. i. chap. viii.

[2] " Historical Papers from the Northern Registers," ed. Raine, Rolls Series, p. 398. Cf. Bodleian MS. 264, fos. 21, 51, 56, 91, etc.

[3] " Ich can nat tabre ne trompe · ne telle faire gestes,
     Farten ne fithelen · at festes, ne harpen,
     Japen ne jogelen · ne gentelliche pipe,
     Nother sailen ne sautrien · ne singe with the giterne."
          (" Piers Plowman," ed. Skeat, Text C, passus xvi. l. 205.)

It so happened that the shameful things he had heard
had made such a deep impression on his mind that he
could never in after time get rid of those remembrances
nor wipe away those images. So he fell into such a deep
melancholy that at length it proved deadly to him." [1]

The representations of the dance of Salome to be
found in mediæval stained glass or manuscripts give an
idea of the sort of tricks and games considered the fittest
to amuse people of importance while sitting in their hall
or having their dinner. It is by dancing on her hands,
head downwards, that the young woman gains the suffrages

FAVOURITE DANCES IN MEDIÆVAL ENGLAND.
(*From MS. 10 E. IV.*)

of Herod. As the idea of such a dance could not be
drawn from the Bible, it obviously arose from the customs
of the time. At Clermont-Ferrand, in the stained glass
of the cathedral (thirteenth century), Salome dances on
knives which she holds with each hand, she also having
her head downwards. In a window at the Lincoln cathedral she has no knives, but her " dance " is of the same
sort and her red-stockinged feet touch the upper line
of the glass panel. At Verona, she is represented on the

[1] " *Loci e libro veritatum* ; Passages selected from Gascoigne's Theological Dictionary" (1403–48), ed. Thorold Rogers, Oxford, 1881, p. 144.

most ancient of the bronze gates of St. Zeno (ninth century) bending backwards and touching her feet with her head. Those standing by are filled with surprise and admiration, one puts his hand to his mouth, the other to his cheek, in an involuntary gesture of amazement. She may be seen in the same posture in several manuscripts in the British Museum ; Herod is sitting at his table with his lords, while the young woman dances head downwards.[1] In another manuscript, also of the fourteenth century, minstrels are shown playing on their instruments, while a professional dancing girl belonging to their troop performs as usual head downwards, but this time, as at

FAVOURITE DANCES IN PERSIA.
(*From a pencil-case.*)

Clermont, her hands rest on two swords. The accounts of the royal exchequer of England sometimes mention sums paid to passing dancers, who, no doubt, must also have performed surprising feats, for the payments are considerable. Thus, in the third year of his reign, Richard II pays to John Katerine, a dancer of Venice, six pounds thirteen shillings and fourpence for having played and danced before him.[2]

In the East, where, in our travels, we have sometimes the surprise of finding ancient customs still living

[1] For instance, MS. Add. 29704, fol. 11. This particular illumination seems to be of the fourteenth century.
[2] Devon's "Issues of the Exchequer," p. 212.

which we can at home only study in books, the fashion
for buffoons and mimics survives, and even remains the
great distraction of princes. The Bey of Tunis, when
I was there years ago, had fools to amuse him in
the evening, who insulted and diverted him by the con-
trast between their permitted insolence and his real power.
Among the rich Moslem women of the same city, few of
whom could read, the monotony of days spent by them
till death came under the shadow of the same walls, behind
the same gratings, was broken by the tales of the female
fool, whose duty was to enliven the harem by sallies of
the strangest liberty. As for dances, they frequently
consist, in the East, in performances similar to that of
Salome, such as shown in our manuscripts. Women
dancing head downwards constantly appear in Persian
pictures ; several examples may be seen in the Victoria
and Albert Museum, and the same subject often occurs
on the valuable pencil-cases formerly made with so much
taste and art in Persia.

If our ancestors of the fourteenth century could enjoy
such pleasures, no wonder that moralists declared more
and more openly against both minstrels and mimics and
ranked them with those rogues and vagabonds denounced
as a public danger by parliament. As years pass the
discredit grows. In the sixteenth century Philip Stubbes
saw in minstrels the personification of all vices, and he
justified in bitter words his contempt for " suche drunken
sockets and bawdye parasits as range the cuntreyes, ryming
and singing of uncleane, corrupt and filthie songes in
tavernes, ale-houses, innes, and other publique assemblies."
Their life is like the shameful songs of which their heads
are full, and they are the origin of all abominations ; the
more dangerous because their number is so great:

" Every towne, citie, and countrey is full of these
minstrelles to pype up a dance to the devill : but of
dyvines, so few there be as they maye hardly be seene.

"But some of them will reply, and say, What, sir !
we have lycences from justices of peace to pype and use
our minstralsie to our best commoditie.   Cursed be those
lycences which lycence any man to get his lyving with
the destruction of many thousands !

"But have you a lycence from the archjustice of
peace, Christe Jesus ?   If you have not . . . than may
you, as rogues, extravagantes, and straglers from the
heavenlye country, be arrested of the high justice of
peace, Christ Jesus, and be punished with eternall death,
notwithstanding your pretensed licences of earthly men." [1]

Such was the state of degradation the noble profession
of the old singers had reached ; the necessity either of
obtaining a licence or of joining a gild, as prescribed by
Edward IV, had been powerless to check the decay.   With
new manners and inventions their *raison d'être* disappeared ;
the ancient reciters of poems, after having mingled with
the disreputable troops of caterers to public amusement,
saw these troops survive them, and, regular players apart,
there henceforth only remained upon the roads those
coarse buffoons, bearwards, and vulgar music makers
whom thoughtful men held as reprobates.

[1] Phillip Stubbes' "Anatomy of Abuses," ed. F. J. Furnivall, New
Shakspere Society, 1877–79, pp. 171, 172.   Stubbes' opinion was shared
by all the religious writers or moralists of the sixteenth century.

A PERFORMING BEAR.
(*From MS.* 10 *E. IV.*)

A SHAM MESSENGER.
(*From MS.* 10 *E. IV.*)

CHAPTER II

MESSENGERS, ITINERANT MERCHANTS AND PEDLARS

ALL his life long, kind, loving, merry Chaucer, a good observer, a good listener and good talker, was fond of travels and travellers, of roamers and tale-tellers, of people who came from afar, bringing home with them many stories if little money, stories in which much invention no doubt was mingled with a little truth : but what is the good of raising a protest against harmless invention ? Is not sometimes their mixture with " sooth " a pleasant one ? Thus, he said :

> " Thus saugh I fals and sothe compouned
> Togeder fle for oo (one) tydynge."

Interested in all that was human he studied ordinary types and rare ones ; he observed mine Host, and looked also for seekers of adventure, and was never tired of hearing their tales :

> " Aventure,
> That is the moder of tydynges,
> As the see is of welles and of sprynges."

No greater pleasure for him than to see :

> " Winged wondres faste fleen,
> Twenty thousand in a route,
> As Eolus hem blew aboute."

He was in this a real *connoisseur*, fully appreciating the
merit of a well-told fable and knowing how useful and
pleasant some such may be found to beguile slow-winged
time.   Long before he started from the Tabard, " faste
by the Belle," for a journey which millions of Englishmen have since performed at his heels, allured by the
music or merriment of his word, he had this same taste
for " unkouthe syghtes and tydynges," as well as for
" thinges glad."   Finding himself once in great " dis-
tresse " of mind, with a heavy heart, " disesperat of all
blys," what did he dream of to " solace " himself, but
of meeting and hearing the whole innumerable tribe of
tale-tellers, wayfarers, and adventure seekers, by fancy
assembled in an immense house, " made of twigges, salwe,
rede and green eke ? "   He wanted us to know,
and he wrote of the " House of Fame," where after
having met the bard " that bare of Thebes up the fame "
(Statius), and " gret Omere," and " Venus' clerke Ovide,"
" Englyssh Gaunfride " (of Monmouth, of Arthurian
fame), and many more, he thought that there was no
room for him, and feeling his distress as keen as ever,
dreamed of something else, willing

> " Somme newe tydyngis for to lere,
> Somme newe thinge, Y not what,
> Tydyngs other this or that,
> Of love, or suche thinges glad." [1]

---

[1] All the extracts here are from the " House of Fame," book iii.
" Complete Works," ed. Skeat, Oxford, 1894, vol. iii. pp. 33 ff.

In this he had full satisfaction ; his dream took another turn, and he was led towards the place he wanted, where things glad were to be found, a temple not of fame, but of tales and tidings, of noise and merriment :

> " And theroute come so grete a noyse,
> That had hyt stonde upon Oyse,
> Men myght hyt have herd esely
> To Rome, Y trowe sikerly."

The noise went up to the sky from innumerable apertures, for

> " This hous hath of entrees
> As feele (many) as of leves ben on trees,
> In somer whan they grene ben."

Never for one instant is the place quiet nor silent ; it is always

> " Filde ful of tydynges,
> Other loude or of whisprynges ;
> And over alle the houses angles,
> Ys ful of rounynges and of jangles,
> Of werres, of pes, of mariages,
> Of restes, of labour and of viages."

War and peace, and love and travels, all this he was to make in after-time the subject of his " Canterbury Tales," and he represents himself in this earlier poem as if coming to the well and spring of all tales, placed somewhere in the land of dreams and fancy, yet surrounded by peop'e who were neither fanciful nor dreamy creatures, but bony beings, on the contrary, with strong muscles and alert tongues, and the dust of the road to Rome or the East on their feet ; surrounded, in fact, by these very roamers we are now trying to call up one by one from the past, and who receive in the " House of Fame " such an apotheosis as befits their quaint if rather questionable character. Good Chaucer

lends a willing ear, and the ways of speech of these people
are carefully preserved in his verse for those who after
him may find interest in them. In this manner they
spoke : every person, says the poet,

> " Every wight that I saugh there
> Rouned (muttered) in eche others ere,
> A newe tydynge prevely,
> Or elles tolde alle oppenly
> Ryght thus, and seyde ; ' Nost not thou
> That ys betyd, late or now ? '
> —' No,' quod he, ' Telle me what.'
> And than he tolde hym this and that,
> And swore therto that hit was sothe ;
> ' Thus hath he sayde ' and ' Thus he dothe,'
> And ' Thus shal hit be ' and ' Thus herde Y seye.' "

And the delight is that the tale repeated by many is always
new, for it is never exactly the same ; the fib fattens as
it grows old, so that it may serve your pleasure many a
time and oft :

> " Whan oon had herde a thinge ywis,
> He come forthright to another wight,
> And gan him tellen anon ryght,
> The same thynge that him was tolde,
> Or hyt a forlonge way was olde,
> But gan sommewhat for to eche (increase)
> To this tydynge in this speche
> More than hit ever was . . .
> As fire ys wont to quyk and goo
> From a sparke sprongen amys,
> Tille alle a citee brent up ys."

That there may be no mistake about the sort of people
to whom the pleasant art of stretching a lie is so familiar,
Chaucer is careful to name them and there we find a most
every one of our friends already mentioned or hereafter
described the sea or land wayfarers :

> " And lord ! this hous in alle tymes
> Was ful of shipmen and pilgrimes,
> With scrippes (bags) bret-ful of leseyngs (lies)
> Entremedled with tydynges.

And eke allone be hemselve,
O many a thousand tymes twelve
Saugh I eke of these pardoners,
Currours, and eke of messangers
With boystes crammed ful of lyes."

What Chaucer gathered from these shipmen, pardoners, couriers, and messengers, he assures us it was not his intention to tell the world,

" For hit no nede is redely;
Folke kan hit synge bet than I."

Whether or not some doubt may have afterwards entered his mind about the great poetical faculty of " folke," certain it is that, for the delight of future ages, he did not stick to his word, as every reader of the " Canterbury Tales " well knows.

These " boystes " which Chaucer represents, carried by messengers and couriers, were filled in the way he describes only in a metaphorical sense, and this left room for more solid ware, for letters and parcels too, since in those old simple days, the messengers were the only equivalent for mail and for parcels post. They were to be found in the service of abbots, bishops, nobles, sheriffs, courts of justice,[1] and of the king. Such a costly fore-runner of the post was not, of course, available for every-body ; people did as they best could. The poor man

---

[1] " A suit respecting civil matter was commenced in this reign (Ed. I), as in earlier or subsequent reigns, by the purchase of a writ and sometimes by bill. . . . The writs were committed to messengers who had to travel into the different parts of the kingdom and deliver them to the sheriffs or other proper officers to be served on the defendants." Horwood, " Year-books of Edward I," years 30–31, p. xxv. Against the *purchase* of the writs the Commons protested, claiming (35 Ed. III, year 1351–2) that this was contrary to Magna Charta, according to which the king " ne vendra ne deleiera droit à nulli." The king refused to give up what he considered as a legitimate profit, but promised that the tariff would be lowered. " Rolls of Parliament," ii., 241.

waited till some friend was going a journey ; the rich only had express messengers, entrusted with their errands to distant places and with the carrying of their letters, generally written at dictation by a scribe on a sheet of parchment, and then sealed in wax with the master's signet.[1] The king kept twelve messengers with a fixed salary ; they followed him everywhere, in constant readiness to start ; they received threepence a day when

A PROFESSIONAL MESSENGER.
(*From the MS.* 10 E. IV.)

they were on the road, and four shillings and eightpence a year to buy shoes.[2] They were entrusted with letters

[1] See the representation of lords and ladies dictating their letters to scribes, and of messengers carrying them to their destinations in the MSS. at the British Museum, Royal 10 Ed. IV, fol. 305, 306, etc., and Add. 12228 fol. 238.

[2] "King Edward II's Household and Wardrobe Ordinances," 1323, ed. Furnivall, 1876, p. 46. The French kings had a much larger number : " Les riches personnages entretenaient des messagers de pied et des chevaucheurs : de ces derniers le roi de France en avait une centaine . . . de moindres seigneurs se contentaient de deux ou trois. Les chevaucheurs étaient payés à forfait : au XIVe siécle, 18 francs par jour (present value) pour un parcours de 55 kilomètres environ. . . . Les messagers de pied, par journée de 30 kilomètres en moyenne, touchaient 9 francs chez le Roi (1380) ; à la solde des particuliers ou des villes leur salaire variait de 5 à 10 francs. Un voyage de nuit valait le double : 20 francs ; de même les

for the kings of France and Scotland ; sent to call together the representatives of the nation for Parliament ; to order the publication of the papal sentence against Guy de Montfort ; to call to Windsor the knights of St. George ; to summon the " archbishops, earls, barons, and other lords and ladies of England and Wales " to London to be present at the funeral of the late queen (Philippa) ; to prescribe the proclamation in the counties of the statutes made in Parliament ; to command the " archbishops, bishops, abbots, priors, deans, and chapters of the cathedral churches of all the shires to pray for the soul of Anne, late Queen of England, deceased." [1]

Edward III sends messengers or heralds to foreign parts, viz., France, Germany, Brabant, Flanders, Scotland, to call the nobility of these countries to a great tournament, a sort of international match to be held on St. George's Day. The amount of the expense so incurred, which is not less than thirty-two pounds, shows that the messengers must have had long protracted journeys and must have had to visit every part of the countries allotted to each of them.[2]

Sometimes the king got into trouble with his Commons on account of expenses for messengers, which he did not always feel inclined to pay from his own purse. Such a case happened in 1378, and the Commons took this opportunity to once more assert their views about

courses périlleuses." D'Avenel, " L'évolution des moyens de transport," Paris, 1919, p. 142. Cf. Thorold Rogers, " History of Agriculture and Prices," i. 665, iv. 712.

[1] Anne of Bohemia, first wife of Richard II, born at Prague in 1366, grand-daughter of blind King John of Bohemia killed at Crécy, herself dying of the plague at Shene, 1394, leaving her husband almost crazy with grief. " Issue roll of Thomas de Brantingham," ed. F. Devon, London, 1835, pp. xxxii, xxxvii, xliv, 408 ; " Issues of the Exchequer," 1837, pp. 220, 255. Whole pages of Thomas de Brantingham's roll (e.g. pp. 154–155) are filled with payments received by messengers, which show the frequent use made of their services.

[2] 32 Ed. III, " Issues of the Exchequer," p. 169.

the French and other foreign possessions of their sovereign, Ireland being included among them. They plainly state, as they had before, that these countries and the expenses concerning them are a matter for the king, not for them ; it is a sort of kingly luxury with which they will have nothing to do. They remonstrate, therefore, that about forty-six thousand pounds sterling have been spent and entered as an item of national expense " for the safeguard of certain countries, places and fortresses, for which the Commons ought in no way to be charged. These are partly in the march of Calais and partly at Brest, Cherbourg, in Gascony, and in Ireland ; and also expenses over certain messengers to Flanders, Lombardy, Navarre, and Scotland."

The Government peremptorily refuses to accept this kind of reasoning, and returns a spirited reply : " To which it was answered that Gascony and the other forts which our lord the king has in the parts beyond, are and must be as barbicans for the kingdom of England, and if the barbicans are well kept, with the safeguard formed by the sea, the kingdom wil be secure of peace. Otherwise we shall never find rest nor peace with our enemies ; for then they would push hot war to the thresholds of our houses, which God forbid. Besides, through these barbicans our said lord the king has convenient gates and entrances towards his enemies to grieve them when he is ready and can act." Telling reasons are also given for retaining among public expenses the costs of the journeys of messengers north and south.[1] None the less did the Commons of England long continue to consider the French wars, glorious perhaps, but undoubtedly expensive, as a personal quarrel of their sovereign, and as, in fact, little more than a rivalry between two French sovereigns speaking the same language and belonging to the same family.

[1] 2 Rich. II, year 1378, " Rolls of Parliament," vol. iii. p. 36.

Besides letters, couriers and messengers had many strange parcels to carry from one place in the country to another : presents to fair ladies, commodities of all sorts for their own masters. Thus, in the year 1396, we find a servant of the Duke de Berri sent as a messenger to Scotland, and travelling all the way thither from France across England to fetch certain greyhounds of which his master was especially fond. He is accompanied by three men on horseback, to help him in taking care of the hounds, and he carries a safe-conduct from Richard II, to travel without hindrance through the English dominions with his followers and their belongings.[1]

Among the missions given by the king to his servants are some which, at the present day, would seem singularly repugnant. He might, for instance, charge one of his faithful retainers to carry the quarters of a criminal's body executed for treason to the great towns of England. In this case he did not employ simple messengers ; they were personages of trust, followed by an escort to convey the remains. Thus Edward III, in the fifty-first year of his reign, paid not less than twenty pounds to " Sir William de Faryngton, knight, for the costs and expenses he had incurred for transporting the four quarters of the body of Sir John of Mistreworth, knight, to different parts of England." [2]

Of all travellers, the messenger was the swiftest ; first, because travelling was his business ; he was a good horseman, an experienced person, clever in getting out of trouble on the road and at the inns ; then he had the right of way ; woe to whoever thought to stop him ; there were immense fines if the master were powerful, still more if the man were the king's messenger. A messenger of the queen, who had been imprisoned by

[1] Rymer's " Fœdera," April 3, 1396 (19 Rich II).
[2] " Issues of the Exchequer," p. 202.

the constable of Roxburgh Castle, did not hesitate to claim £10,000 sterling for contempt of his sovereign, and £2,000 as indemnity for himself.[1]

When, on August 7, 1316, Jacques d'Euse, cardinal-bishop of Porto, was chosen pope at Lyons, and assumed the name of John XXII, Edward II being at York learnt the news ten days afterwards through Laurence of Ireland, messenger of the house of the Bardi. And indeed we find by the accounts of the king's household that this prince paid Laurence twenty shillings on the 17th of August to reward him for his trouble. It was only on the 27th of September that, being still at York, the king received by Durand Budet, a messenger of cardinal de Pelagrua, the official letters announcing the election ; he gave five pounds to the messenger. Finally, the pope's nuncio having arrived in person shortly afterwards, bearing the same news no longer so fresh, the king made him a present, inversely proportionate to his speed, of a hundred pounds.[2]

Such was the custom, presents were made to the bringers of good news ; royal messengers had thus a chance of casually increasing their meagre pay of three-pence a day. Most fortunate were those who brought word to the king himself of happy events. Edward III gave a forty marks pension for life to the queen's messenger who came announcing the birth of the Prince of Wales, the future Black Prince ; he gave thirteen pounds three shillings and fourpence to John Cok of Cherbourg, who told him of the capture of King John at Poictiers ; he settled a pension of one hundred shillings upon Thomas of Brynchesley who brought him the good news of the capture of Charles of Blois.[3]

---

[1] " Rolls of Parliament," i. p. 48 (18 Ed. I).

[2] " Wardrobe Accounts of Edward II," Archæologia, xxvi. 321, 336.

[3] Extract from a letter to the author : " Yesterday I was reading your ' Vie Nomade,' and that portion of it which speaks of the rewards given in fourteenth and fifteenth centuries to messengers who brought good tidings

Sometimes messengers, in spite of their privileges and cleverness, were liable to find themselves in very difficult plight. In time of war they had to conceal their real function, and were in constant danger of being stopped and having their bag searched and their letters opened. People felt strongly about foreigners living in England, many of them being friars who might disclose the secrets of the realm in their private correspondence. The Commons therefore asked for very strict rules to be passed in order to remedy this possible evil, and we find them, in the year 1346, when England was at war with France, recommending the creation of something like the *cabinets noirs* of a later date.[1]

Langland in his " Visions " graphically compares the different modes of travelling of messengers and such other wayfarers as merchants going with their goods from one place to another. The one is the swiftest of all, no one would dare to stop him ; the other is retarded by his pack, his debts, his fear of robbers which prevents his travelling at dark, the impossibility for him to use short cuts across the fields, while short

to the king. It may interest you to know that a remnant of this custom still survives. The officer sent by a general after a victory to convey the despatch to the Queen, receives besides a promotion in rank (or a decoration), a pecuniary reward. The officer who brought the news of the fall of Sebastopol to the Queen received the rank of Colonel, and a present of 500 guineas.

" My brother A.D.C., Major Anson, who carried home from China the despatch announcing the fall of Pekin, was promoted Colonel, and received a present of 500 guineas.—St. James' Club, May 30, 1890.— F. Grant."

What happened, in our less ceremonious days, when the news was brought of the Marne, of Ypres, of Messines ? Doubtless it was not brought ; it came.

[1] " Item, be it prohibited everywhere that any alien send letters beyond the sea, or receive letters which come thence ; unless he shew them to the chancellor or to some other lord of the Privy Council, or at least to the chief wardens of the ports or their lieutenants, who shall further show them to the said Council." " Rolls of Parliament," vol. ii. p. 163, 20 Ed III.

cuts are freely allowed to messengers : no hayward
would disturb them ; no man in his senses, no " wys
man " would " wroth be " on account of his crops being
spoiled by a messenger ; the messenger shows his letters
and is free to go :

> " . . . Yf a marchaunt and a messager · metten to-gederes,
> And scholde wende o way · where both mosten reste . . .
> The marchante mote nede be lette (kept) · lengere then the messagere;
> The messager doth na more · bote with hus mouthe telleth
> Hus erande and hus lettere sheweth · and is a-non delyvered.
> And thauh thei wende by the wey · tho two to-gederes,
> Thauh the messager make hus wey · a-mydde the whete,
> Wole no wys man wroth be · ne hus wed (pledge) take ;
> Ys no haiwarde yhote (bidden) · hus wed for to take :
> _Necesitas non habet legem._
> Ac yf the merchaunt make hus way · overe menne corne,
> And the haywarde happe · with hym for to mete,
> Other hus hatt, other hus hode · othere elles hus gloves
> The marchaunt mot for-go · other moneye of hus porse . . .
> Yut thauh thei wenden on way · as to Wynchestre fayre,
> The marchaunt with hus marchaundise · may nat go so swithe
> As the messager may · ne with so mochel ese.
> For that on (one) bereth bote a boxe · a brevet (letter) ther-ynne,
> Ther the marchaunt ledeth a male (trunk) · with meny kynne thynges,
> And dredeth to be ded there-fore · and (if) he in derke mete
> With robbours and revers (thieves) · that riche men dispoilen ;
> Ther the messager is ay murye · hus mouthe ful of songes." [1]

Wayfarers there were in whom both characteristics
were united, the slowness of pace of the merchant and
the lightness of heart of the messenger. These were
the pedlars, a very numerous race in the Middle Ages,
one of the few sorts of wanderers that have not yet entirely
disappeared. A jovial race they seem to have been ;
they are so now, most of them, for their way to success
is through fair speech and enticing words ; and how
could they be enticing if they did not show good humour
and jollity ? ' Gaiety " mends their broken wares, and
colours the faded ones, and blinds customers to otherwise

[1] Text C, pas. xiv. ll. 33–59.

obvious defects. They have always been described thus ;
they were merry and sharp-tongued ; such was Shakespeare's Autolycus ; such is, in a novel of our time, the
jovial owner of the dog Mumps, Bob Jakin of " The
Mill on the Floss." " ' Get out wi' you, Mumps,' said
Bob, with a kick ; ' he is as quiet as a lamb, sir '—an
observation which Mumps corroborated by a low growl,
as he retreated behind his master's legs." About the
exact scrupulousness prevailing among the tribe the
opinion has perhaps not been quite so consistent, which
is the best that can be said for it.

One good point about them, however, is that in
mediæval England, whatever may have been their reputation, they entirely escaped legislation. Very possibly
they were impliedly included in statutes against vagrants
and rovers ; but they may at least argue that as a matter
of fact they are not named in any Act of Parliament, and
pass unobserved or nearly so by the Westminster legislator down to a comparatively recent date. They are
for the first time named in a statute during the reign of
Edward VI, in which, it is true, they are treated in a
contemptuous manner, being described as more " hurtful
than necessary to the common wealth." This is called
" an acte for tynkers and pedlers," and is to the following
effect : " For as muche as it is evident that tynkers,
pedlers and suche like vagrant persons are more hurtfull
than necessarie to the Common Wealth of th's realm,
Be it therefore ordeyned . . . that . . . no person or
persons commonly called pedler, tynker or pety chapman
shall wander or go from one towne to another or from
place to place out of the towne, parishe or village where
such person shall dwell, and sell pynnes, poyntes, laces,
gloves, knyves, glasses, tapes or any suche kynde of wares
whatsoever, or gather connye skynnes or suche like things
or use or exercise the trade or occupation of a tynker,"
except those that shall have a licence from two justices

of the peace ; and then they will be allowed to travel
only in the " circuyte " assigned to them.[1]

Queen Elizabeth, too, had a word for pedlars, and it
was not more complimentary than what her brother
had to say about them, although " scollers of the Universityes " joined them on her ist of disreputable roamers.
They figure in her " Acte for the punishment of
vacabondes " ; and a very curious list of wanderers is
found in it : " It ys nowe publyshed," says the queen,
" that . . . all ydle persones goinge aboute in any
countrey of the said Realme, using subtyll craftye and
unlawfull games or playes, and some of them fayninge
themselves to have knowledge in phisnomye, pa'mestrye,
. . . and all fencers, bearwardes, comon players in inter-
ludes and minstrels not belonging to any baron of this
rea'me . . . all juglers, pedlars, tynkers, and petye chapmen . . . and all scollers of the Universityes of Oxford
or Cambridge y^t goe about begginge . . . and all shipmen
pretendinge losses by sea . . . shalbee deemed roges
vacabounds and sturdy beggers intended of by this present
act." [2]   But the case of pedlars was not seriously taken
in hand before the reign of William III who put a tax
upon them and, ominously enough, bound them to certify
commissioners for transportation how they travelled and
traded.[3]

The late date of this statute of pedlars, if it may be
called so, is the more remarkable that they swarmed along
the roads in the Middle Ages, more numerous than
tinkers or any other wandering representatives of petty
trades.   There were not then as now large shops in every
village with all the necessaries of life ready provided for the
inhabitants.   The shop itself was itinerant, being nothing
else than the pack of travelling chapmen.   In the same way

[1] 5 and 6 Ed. VI, ch. 21.   Statutes, vol. iv. part i. p. 155.
[2] 14 Eliz. ch. v.   " Statutes," vol. iv. part i. pp. 590 ff
[3] 8 and 9 Will. III, ch. 25

as the literature propagated by the minstrels, as news, tales, and letters, pardons from Rome and many other commodities, so household wares were carried about the country by indefatigable wayfarers. A host of small useful things, or sometimes useless, but so pleasing ! were concealed in their unfathomable boxes. The contents of them are pretty well shown by a series of illuminations in a fourteenth-century manuscript, where a pedlar is represented asleep at the foot of a tree, while monkeys have got hold of his box and help themselves to the contents. They find in it vests, caps, gloves, musical instruments, purses, girdles, hats, cutlasses, pewter pots, and a number of other articles.[1]

As to the means by which pedlars came by their goods, a variety seem to have been used by them, and purchase was only one among several. A proverbial saying preserved for us by Langland shows how they secured furs for their country customers. The author of the " Visions " states how Repentance came once to Avarice, and examined him as to his usurious doings :

" ' Hastow pite on pore men · that mote nedes borwe ? '
' I have as moche pite of pore men · as pedlere hath of cattes,
That wolde kille hem, yf he cacche hem myghte · for coveitise of
    here skynnes.' " [2]

a practice which cannot fail to be deeply resented by all lovers of cats.

The regular merchants whom Langland and Chaucer describe, so splendid to look at that no one knew they were " in dette," adorned with Flaundrish hats and "botes clasped faire and fetisly," were a very different sort of

[1] Cf the contents of the pack of a French " porte-balle " of the eighteenth century : " . . . Un de ces merciers ambulants qu'on appelle porte-balles et qui lui crie : Monsieur le chevalier, jarretières, ceintures, cordons de montre, tabatières du dernier goût, vraies jaback, bagues, caehets de montre. . . ." Diderot, " Jacques le Fataliste." Ed. Asseline, p. 30.
[2] Text B, pas. v. l. 257.

people ; but though no mere wanderers, they were, too, great wayfarers. Many of them had had to visit the continent to find markets for their goods, and for their purchases. Through them too, and it was in fact, perhaps, the safest and most reliable among many such channels of information, ideas of what was going on in the outer world and how things were managed in France and elsewhere, points of similitude and comparison, were introduced into England and made the subject of thought and discussion.

A PEDLAR ROBBED BY MONKEYS.
(*From MS.* 10 *E. IV.*)

During the fourteenth century the foreign trade of England had greatly increased ; there was a constant intercourse with Flanders, with Bruges above all other towns, for the sale of home produce : wools especially, and woolfels, cheese, butter, tin, coal,[1] etc., with the

[1] The English coaling trade had greatly increased in the fourteenth century ; large quantities cf coal were brought by water from Newcastle and other places to London and partly consumed on the spot, partly exported. The importance of coal mines did not escape the notice of the Commons, who stated in the year 1376–7 that, " en diverses parties deinz le Roialme d'Engleterre sont diverses miners de carbons, dont les communes du dit partie ont lour sustenantz en grande partie." 51 Ed. III, " Rolls of Parliament," ii. 370. Cf Salzmann. " English Industries of the Middle Ages,"

Rhine country, with Gascony, with Spain, for the purchase of wines ;[1] with the Hanse towns, Lombardy, Venice, and the East. Unintelligent regulations constantly interfered, it is true, with this development, but so strong was the impulse that it went on steadily. One of the most persistent and most noxious of these regulations was the prohibition to export money or bullion, which governments were never tired of renewing.[2] English merchants were forbidden, when purchasing goods in foreign countries, to pay for them with money ; they had to pay in kind, with wools, cheese and other home produce, which of course might or might not be found acceptable by the vendor. It was, in other words, forbidden to use money as a means of facilitating exchange, which is its very *raison d'être*, and people had to return to the primitive practice of *troc*, or exchange in kind. It had sometimes worse effects than that of impeding transactions ; foreign merchants might, as once did the Flemings, show their appreciation of the rules imposed on their English purchasers by answering their proffer of wools and cheese with a beating and imprisonment until they would alter their laws or their minds. For

1913, ch. I, and H. Hall, "A select Bibliography for the study, sources and literature of English Political Economy," London, 1914.

[1] The trade in wines was enormous, especially with Gascony, and subjected to the most minute regulations. Not only the importation of it was the occasion of ceaseless interfering, but the retail sale in towns was perpetually regulated anew by local ordinances. Woe to the vintner who was detected meddling in any unfair way with his liquor ; he might experience the chastisement inflicted upon John Penrose, who for such an offence was sent to the pillory in 1364, was made to drink publicly there his own stuff, had what he could not drink poured over his head, and was besides sentenced to renounce his trade for ever. Riley, " Memorials of London," 1868, p. 318.

[2] Same rules in France : " Que nul billon, vaissellemente, joyaux d'or et d'argent ne soint traits hors dudit royaume par personne quelle que ce soit, si ce n'estoit vaissellemente de prélats ou de nobles ou d'autres gens d'église pour lour service." Ordinance of Jean le Bon, dated from London, 1358 ; Isambert, vol. v. p. 39.

which treatment, English merchants sent doleful complaints to Parliament. In such cases retaliation upon Flemings in England might be demanded, but no thought was entertained, even by the injured party, of repealing laws considered as an indispensable safeguard for the kingdom.[1]

Not much wiser were the rules applied to merchant shipping, made worse by constant change, a defect which was noticeable in every trade regulation of that time. Some are curious as being an attempt to establish the long lived, but more moderate rules devised by Cromwell in 1651 : " Item, to increase the navy of England which is now greatly diminished, it is assented and accorded, that none of the king's liege people do from henceforth ship any merchandize in going out or coming within the realm of England in any port, but only in ships of the king's liegeance." But the very next year this impossible statute was altered so as to practically annul it : " It is ordained and granted that the said ordinance only have place as long as ships of the said ligeance in the parts where the said merchants happen to dwell be found able and sufficient." [2] The same unsteadiness of purpose was shown in almost every branch of the yet unbaptized science of political economy.

Not less worthy of notice than this attempt at a Navigation Act is the claim made, even then, by the Commons of England to a traditional supremacy over the seas. In one of their innumerable petitions concerning the decay of the navy, which seems to have been a favourite complaint in England from the remotest period down to our own time, they state that the rash and often

[1] " Rolls of Parliament," 45 Ed. III, year 1371, vol. ii. p. 306. While this legislation was strictly enforced in England, the royal government, according to petitions of the Commons and with remarkable *naïveté*, often wrote to princes on the continent, recommending them to allow their own subjects to bring to England money, bullion, and plate.

[2] Statute 5 Rich. II st. i. ch. 3, and 6 Rich. II, year 1381–2

useless pressing of ships for the king's service had brought about a most dangerous decrease of the navy ; many mariners addicting themselves to other trades, while only " twenty years ago, *and always before*, the shipping of the Realm was in all the ports and good towns upon the sea or rivers, so noble and plenteous that all the countries held and called our said sovereign : the King of the Sea (*le Roi de la Mier*)." [1] As these were trading ships, only occasionally used for war purposes, this gives an idea of the importance to which British merchant shipping had risen in the fourteenth century and which it desired to recover.

The rules concerning foreign merchants coming to England were in the same manner constantly changed ; sometimes the hardest restrictions were put upon them, and sometimes everything was done to allure them to come. The result was the same ; trade was impeded doubtless, but it went on, and in spite of the un-steadiness of legislation, of retaliatory measures (as when, for instance, Hanse merchants were imprisoned in England and their goods seized on account of misdeeds committed by Prussians, " ceux de la seigneurie de Pruys," no reason of complicity being alleged, but only it seems one of geographical vicinity [2]), in spite of restrictions innumer-able, the intercourse steadily increased, to the great benefit of the community and the wider diffusion of ideas. In the ninth, the twenty-fifth, the twenty-seventh, and other years of his reign, King Edward III again and again stated that he took foreign merchants under his special protection : " To replenish the said realm and lands," he said on one of these occasions, " with money and

[1] " Rolls of Parliament," 46 Ed. III, year 1372, vol. ii. p. 311.
[2] Ibid., 11 Rich II, A.D. 1387, vol. iii. p. 253. The penalties are removed for the Hanse merchants but not for the Prussians, " Et en le mesne temps soient lettre du privé seal envoié al Mestre de Pruys de repaier et due redresse faire as merchantz Engleis des arestes et autres tortz et damages à eux fait deinz la seigneurie de Pruys, come reson demande."

plate, gold and silver and merchandises of other lands, and to give courage to merchants strangers to come with their wares and merchandises into the Realm and lands aforesaid, we have ordained and established that all merchants strangers which be not of our enmity, of what land or nation that they be, may safely and surely, under our protection and safe conduct, come and dwell in our said realm and lands, where they will, and from thence [freely] return," selling their goods to whom they please, being exempted from purveyance and only paying the ordinary customs.[1] If war is declared between England and their country, they will have forty days to quit the realm, during which time they shall be allowed to continue their sales, and even more delay will be allowed them in case they are ill, or are detained by bad weather. This last was, as we have seen, a very necessary proviso, for a merchant coming with his goods in the depth of winter to a broken bridge might be stopped a rather long time ; as also if, reaching the sea-coast, he found contrary winds. The statute of the twenty-fifth year provided that the liberal intentions of the king towards foreign merchants should be brought by way of proclamation to the notice of the officers and inhabitants of all the English counties, trading cities, seaports, etc.[2]

Thus protected and impeded by turns, foreign trade jogged on, and as common interest was, after all, stronger than popular prejudice and narrow regulations, it managed to thrive in England. Foreign gilds were established in London ; foreign settlements were created in several trading towns,[3] foreign fleets visited the English coasts

---

[1] Statute 27 Ed. III st. ii. ch. 2.

[2] 25 Ed. III stat. iii. ch. 2.

[3] See, for particulars about the " Gildhalda Teutonicorum " in Dowgate Ward, Thames Street, and afterwards in the Steel-house, Herbert's " Livery Companies," London, 1837, vol. i. pp. 10–16. The importance of Italian settlements of money-changers and money-lenders (whence the " Lombard streets " or " rues des Lombards " surviving in many towns) are well known.

at regular intervals, none with more important results than the fleet of the Venetian Republic. It began to call regularly at the ports of Flanders, England, and the North, in the year 1317 ; each ship had on board thirty archers for its defence, commanded by young Venetian noblemen. There was in the fourteenth century a Venetian consul at Bruges, and the commander of the galleys did not fail to put himself in communication with him. The fleet, or " galleys of Flanders," as it was called, brought to England cotton from Egypt, cloth of silk from Venice, cinnamon, pepper, cloves, saffron, camphor, musk, and other drugs or spices from the East, sugar from Egypt and Sicily, etc. The trade of Venice in the eastern Mediterranean was very extensive ; it was carried on freely, except during occasional wars with the Saracens, and the commercial interest that the Italian Republics had in the continuation of a good understanding with the infidel was one of the principal causes of the cessation of crusades. From England the Venetian galleys took back wools and woollen cloths, leather, tin, lead, sea-coal, cheese,[1] etc.

The importance of this intercourse with the continent, which fortunately the variations in the laws of the land were unable to check, gave prominence in the community to the English merchant. He is already in the fourteenth century, and has been ever since, one of the main supports of the State. While the numerous applications of Edward III to Lombard bankers for ready money are well known, it is sometimes overlooked how often he had recourse to English merchants, who supplied him with that without which his archers' bows would have remained unstrung. The advice and goodwill of the

---

[1] These and many other particulars about English trade with Venice are to be found in Rawdon Brown's " Calendars of State Papers . . . in the Archives of Venice," London, 1864 (Rolls) ; see also J. Delaville le Roulx, " La France en Orient au XIVᵉ siècle," Paris, 1886, vol. i. p. 199.

whole class of merchants could not be safely ignored ; therefore their attendance was constantly requested at Westminster to discuss money and other State matters. Some families among them rose to eminence, like the De la Poles of Hull, who became earls of Suffolk with descendants destined to die at Agincourt, to be checked by Joan of Arc at Orleans, to be made dukes, and to be impeached for high treason. It was, too, the time of " thrice Lord Mayor of London " [1] Dick, afterwards Sir Richard Whittington, who, if we trust the legend, did not entertain the same feeling as the above-mentioned pedlars for cats. Another man of the same sort a little later was the famous William Canynge, of Bristol, who made a large fortune there in trading with foreign countries. One of his ships was called the *Mary Redcliffe*, a name as well as his own since associated with the memory of the Bristol boy-poet, Thomas Chatterton.

The feeling that the king of England should be *le Roi de la Mier* goes on increasing. The " Libelle of Englyshe Polycye," a sort of consular report, written however in verse, about 1436, is quite positive :

> " Kepte (keep) than the see about in specialle,
> Whiche of England is the rounde walle ;
> As thoughe England were lykened to a cité,
> And the walle enviroun were the see.
> Kepe than the see that is the walle of Englond,
> And than is Englonde kepte by Goddes sonde (decision)." [2]

And those traditions having been continued, Montesquieu was able to write, in his " Esprit des Lois ": ' Other nations have made the interests of commerce yield to political interests. Eng and has always made her political interests yield to her commercial ones.

[1] For the first time in 1397–98. He was a liberal lender of money to Kings Henry IV and Henry V.

[2] Th. Wright, " Political Poems," Rolls Series, ii. 202 ; also edited by Herzberg and Pauli, Leipzig, 1878.

" This is the people in the wor'd that has best known how to avail itself of these three great things : religion, commerce, and liberty." [1]

Below men in such exalted situations as a Whittington (praised to the skies in the " Libelle ") or a Canynge, the bulk of the merchant community throve as best they could. One of the necessities of their avocation was constant travel'ing. They were to be met along the roads almost as much as their poorer brothers the pedlars.

A RICH MERCHANT TRAVELLING (CHAUCER'S MARCHAUNT).
(*From the Ellesmere MS.*)

They also made great use of the water-courses, and carried their goods by boat whenever possible. Hence the constant interference of the Commons with the erection of new mills, weirs, and other hindrances on rivers by the owners of the adjoining lands. The " Rolls of Parliament " are full of petitions asking for the complete suppression of all new works of this sort as being detrimental to the " common passage of ships and boats on the great rivers of England," or stating that ' the merchants who

[1] Bk. xx, chap. 7 : " Esprit de l'Angleterre sur le Commerce."

frequent the water between London and Oxford used to have free passage on the Thames from London to Oxford, with their ships to carry their goods and to serve the commonalty and the people, but now they are disturbed by weirs, locks, mills, and many other hindrances." [1] The reasons why merchants preferred such a conveyance were that the cost of carriage was less ; that, save for the occasional meeting of unexpected locks and weirs, they were more certain than on ordinary roads to find before them a clear course ; and that they were better able to protect themselves against robbers.

They could not, however, go everywhere by water, and willingly or not they had then to betake themselves to the roads, and incur all the mischances that m ght turn up on the way or at the inn. In his " Visions," Langland describes how one of his mischievous characters once rifled at the inn the boxes of travelling chapmen:

" ' Thus, ones I was herberwed,' quod he · ' with an hep of chapmen,
I roos whan thei were arest (having their rest) · and yrifled here males ' " (their trunks).

Repentance, who had just been asking if his interlocutor had never made " restitucioun," wonders at this strange statement as to how things went on at the inn :

" That was no restitucioun, quod Repentance · but a robberes thefte."

To which the careless creature retorts in a way that reminds one of Chaucer's French of Stratford-atte-Bow:

" ' I wende (believed) ryflynge were restitucioun,' quod he · ' for I lerned nevere rede on boke,
And I can no Frenche in feith · but of the ferthest end of Norfolke.' " [2]

---

[1] " Rolls of Parliament," 25 Ed. III, year 1350, and Ed. I or II *anno incerto*, vol. ii. p. 232 and vol i. p. 475.
[2] Text B, pas. v. l. 232.

Between the " male " of these chapmen and the mere pack of the pedlar the difference is not considerable ; it is not very great either if compared to the " male " of the merchant we have met before, who travels slowly on account of an encumbrance represented by the poet as the emblem of " men that ben ryche." So that these three links kept pretty close together the chain of the it nerant trading community. They all had to go about and to experience the gaieties or dangers of the road, the latter being of course better known to the richer sort than to the poor Bob Jakin of the day. The reasons for this constant travelling were numerous ; the same remark applies to merchants of the fourteenth century as to almost all other classes : there was much less journeying than to-day for mere pleasure's sake, but very much more, comparatively, out of necessity. We cannot underrate the causes of personal journeys suppressed by the post and telegraph (and telephone, unheard-of when the present work was first published), with the money and other facilities they have introduced. But besides the lack thereof, the staple and fairs were, in the fourteenth century, potent causes impelling merchants to move about.

The staple was the subject of constant regulations, complaints, new regulations and new complaints. The fundamental law concerning it is the well-known statute of 1353, the mechanism of which the following extracts will show :

" We (i.e. the king and Parliament) have ordained . . . first, that the staple of wools, leather, woolfels, and lead, growing or coming forth within our said realm and 'ands, shall be perpetually holden at the places underwritten, that is to say, for England at Newcastle-upon-Tyne, York, Lincoln, Norwich, Westminster, Canterbury, Chichester, Winchester, Exeter, and Bristow ; for Wales at Kaermerdyn ; and for Ireland at Dublin, Waterford,

Cork, and Drogheda, and not elsewhere ; and that all the said wools, as well old as new, woo fels, leather, and lead, which shall be carried out of the said realm and lands shall be first brought to the said staples, and there the said wool and lead, betwixt merchant and merchant or merchant and others, shall be lawfully weighed by the standard ; and that every sack and sarpler of the same wools so weighed be sealed under the seal of the mayor of the staple."

Any English may bring and sell wool at the staple ; but only foreign merchants are allowed to take it out of the realm. It is prohibited to stop carriages and goods going to the staple. It is ordained also " that in every town where the staple shall be holden, shall be ordained certain [streets] and places where the wools and other merchandises shall be put ; and because that the lords or guardians of the houses and places, seeing the necessity of merchants do set percase their houses at too high ferm, we have ordained that the houses which be to be leased in such manner, shall be set at a reasonable ferm," after the estimation of the local authority, assisted by four discreet men of the place.[1] It need scarcely be said that the staple was often removed from one town to another, from England to Calais and from Calais to England, etc., according to inscrutable whims and fancies, and with very detrimental results for all traders.

The fairs, the very name of which can scarcely fail to awaken ideas of merry bustle, gay clamour, and joyous agitation, were subjected to no less stringent regulations, so that the word reminded many people not merely of pleasure but also of fines, confiscations, and prison.

[1] Statute 2 of 27 Ed. III, A.D. 1353. Canterbury was made a staple town " en l'onur de Saint Thomas," " Rolls of Parliament," vol. ii. p. 253, same year. As an example of the changes affecting the staple system, see the statute 2 Ed. III, chap. 9 (A.D. 1328), by which all staples were abolished —for a time.

When the time came for a fair, no sale was permitted in the town except at the fair, under pain of the goods exhibited being seized. All the ordinary shops were to be closed. Such regulations were meant not only to insure the largest possible attendance at the fair, but also to secure for the lord of it the entirety of the tolls he had a right to.

An inquest holden at Winchester, famous for its St. Giles's fair, gives an idea of the manner in which these commercial festivities were solemnized. The fair belonged to the Bishop of Winchester. On the eve of St. Giles's Day, at early dawn, the officers of the bishop went about the town announcing the conditions of the fair, which were these : no merchant was to sell or exhibit for sale any goods in the town, or at a distance of seven leagues round it, except inside the gates of the fair. The same proclaimed the assise of bread, wine, and ale ; tasted the wine, broke the casks where they detected " insufficient " wine. They proved all weights and measures ; they destroyed false ones and fined the owners. All merchants were to reach the fair not later than a certain time (the feast of the Nativity of the Virgin Mary) ; if they came later they were not admitted except with a special licence from the bishop. The usual allowance is made in case they may have been kept back by a storm at sea, or by some mischance on land, " infortunium in terra," which in this time of bad roads, and of such determined robbers as Sir Robert de Rideware, was not infrequent. A court of " pie powder," that is, " of the dusty feet," [1] was held in the fair itself, and any suit arising from transactions or trouble there was determined

---

[1] " *Pedis pulverisati curia.* Ea est quæ in nundinis constituitur, ad nundinalium rixas litesque celerrime componendas. . . . Dictum præcipue de mercatoribus vagabundis, qui nundinas pagatim insectantes omnes discurrunt provincias, nec sistendi locum agnoscunt, sed de his etiam qui ex omni parte ad nundinas confluunt." H. Spelman, " Glossarium archaiologicum," ed. tertia, Londini, 1687, p. 455.

by this tribunal at once, and without appeal. Similar rules were in existence at the Westminster fair, and at many others.[1] The importance of these meetings is shown by the constant recurrence in the " Rolls of Parliament " of petitions concerning them, beseeching the king to grant a fair to a certain lord or to a certain town, or to suppress a neighbouring town's fair, for fear it may hurt the petitioners' own.

People from the counties and from the continent flocked to the fairs. The largest and the more widely known were those of Winchester,[2] Abingdon for cattle, Bartholomew fair [3] in Smithfield (London), Stourbridge fair, the most important of all, Weyhill, mentioned in Langland's " Visions," [4] etc. In the time of Elizabeth,

[1] These and other particulars about the way in which fairs were managed at Westminster and Winchester are to be found in a petition with an inquest of the year 1302, 30 Ed. I, in the " Rolls of Parliament," vol. i. p. 150. The Winchester Fair on St. Giles' hill, " Montem sancti Egidii," was one of the most famous English fairs. Langland mentions it, and gives a graphic account of the cheating that went on among unscrupulous merchants. " Visions," Text C, pas. vii. l. 211.

[2] See " Charter of Edward III [as to] St. Giles' Fair, Winchester," ed. G. W Kitchin, London, 1886.

[3] This fair, immortalized by Ben Jonson, disappeared only in 1855. See H. Morley's " Memoirs of Bartholomew Fair " (2nd ed. 1874).

[4] Mentioned as " Wy," text C, passus vii. l. 211. Weyhill fair, near Andover, Hampshire, " is a famous one to this day, and lasts eight days. The fair for horses and sheep is on October 10th, that for cheese, hops, and general wares, on October 11th and the six days following." W. W. Skeat, " Vision concerning Piers the Plowman," ii, 83. See a list of English fairs in Mr. Elton's Report, Market Rights Commission, 1889, vol. i. 5. There were fairs established especially for herrings and other fishing prcduce at Yarmouth, Scarborough, and other towns on the sea-coast. The rigours of Lent and the number of fasting days throughout the year gave particular importance to these articles of consumption. Hence, too, the attention paid to fisheries and the regulations to prevent the catching of small fish, the destruction of spawn and bait, etc. Great complaints are made against the use of the net called " wondyrchoun," which drags from the bottom of the sea all the bait " that used to be the food of great fish." Through means of this instrument fishermen catch " such great plenty of small fish that they do not know what to do with them, but fatten their pigs

Harrison, describing England, could not help expressing his pride in the importance and renown of English fairs, about which he writes thus : " As there are no great towns without one weekelie market at the least, so there are verie few of them that have not one or two faires or more within the compasse of the yeare, assigned unto them by the prince. And albeit that some of them are not much better than Lowse faire or the common Kirke-messes beyond the sea, yet there are diverse not inferiour to the greatest marts in Europe, as Sturbridge faire neere to Cambridge, Bristow faire, Bartholomew faire at London, Lin mart (Linne), Cold faire at Newport pond for cattell, and diverse other." In all of which people were kept merry with ales and beers of various flavour and strength known by as significant names as those of present day dances, fox-trot, mother's rest, and others, which to-morrow will, they too, need interpretation : " Such headie ale and beere in most of them, as for the mightinesse thereof . . . is commonlie called huffe cap, the mad dog, father whoresonne, angels food, dragon's milke, go by the wall, stride wide, and lift leg. . . . Neither did Romulus and Remus sucke their shee wolfe (or sheepheards wife) Lupa, with such eger and sharpe devotion, as these men hale at huf cap, till they be red as cockes and little wiser than their combs." [1]

Stourbridge fair belonged to the city and corporation of Cambridge, and was held in September, lasting three weeks. Tents and wooden booths were erected at that time on the open fields, so as to form streets ; each trade had its own street as in real cities, and as may still be seen now in the bazaars of the East. Among the principal articles sold at this fair were : " ironmongery, cloth,

---

with them." " Rolls of Parliament," 1376-7, vol. ii. p. 369. As to salmon fishing in the Thames, see ibid., vol. ii. p. 331, A.D. 1376.

[1] Harrison's " Description of England," ed. Furnivall, 1877, first published 1577, part i. book ii. chap xviii. pp. 295, 302.

wool, leather, books." The last article became in several
fairs an important one when the art of printing spread ;
there was in the North Hundred of Oxford, in the sixteenth century, a fair at which an extensive sale of books
took place, and this, as Professor Thorold Rogers has
observed, is the only way to account for the rapid diffusion
of books and pamphlets at a time when newspapers and
advertisements were practically unknown. " I have more
than once," adds the same authority, " found entries of
purchases for college libraries, with a statement that the
book was bought at St. Giles' fair." [1] No reader of
Boswell needs to be reminded how the father of Dr.
Johnson had a booth for book selling on market days
at Uttoxeter, in doing which he was merely keeping up,
as we see, a mediæval tradition of long standing. How
young Samuel refused once to accompany his father to
the market, and, in after-time, repaired on a rainy day
to the spot, and there did penance, has been alluded to
before.

Even at the present day books continue to be an
article of sale at the fairs in many French villages, and
sheets of printed matter are taken from thence to cottages,
where, under the smoky light burning in winter by the
fireside, people, not very dissimilar to their forefathers
of five hundred years ago, look at the image of mediæval
heroes and of the worthies of the world, by the side of
whom now begins to appear that of the heroes of the
Great War.

To the fairs, along with mummers, jugglers, tumblers,
beggars, and the whole of the catchpenny tribe, the pedlar
was sure to resort, in the approved Autolycus fashion.
" He haunts," says the clown in " Winter's Tale,"
" wakes, fairs, and bear-baiting." There he might exhibit
" ribands of all the colours i' the rainbow ; points, more

[1] " History of Agriculture and Prices in England," vol. iv. chap. iv.
p. 155. As to Stourbridge fair, ibid. vol. i. chap. vii. p. 141.

than all the lawyers in Bohemia can learnedly handle, though they come to him by the gross ; inkles, caddisses, cambricks, lawns. Why, he sings them over, as they were gods or goddesses ; you would think a smock were a she-angel, he so chants to the sleeve hand, and the work about the square on't." [1] So that everybody might remark, as does the honest clown to fair Perdita, " You have of these pedlars that have more in them than you'd think, sister." A favourable view, adopted, magnified, sublimated by another great poet whose Wanderer is a pedlar, but what a pedlar and what a part does he not play in the community !

> " By these Itinerants, as experienced men,
> Counsel is given ; contention they appease
> With gentle language ; in remotest wilds,
> Tears wipe away, and pleasant tidings bring ;
> Could the proud quest of chivalry do more ? " [2]

Less aspiring most of them, not unsatisfied with their lot, careless of robbers, having few wants, pedlars of the past plodded the miry roads of Plantagenet England, as they did in the time of Shakespeare, merrily singing some " Winter Tale " ditty :

> " Jog on, jog on, the foot-path way,
> And merrily hent the stile-a :
> A merry heart goes all the day,
> Your sad tires in a mile-a."

---

[1] " Winter's Tale," iv. 3. Cf. " The foure Ps," by John Heywood, London, 1545, one of the " Ps " is a pedlar, whose wares are enumerated in full.

[2] Wordsworth, " The Excursion," Bk. viii.

FOREST LIFE. WOOD-CUTTERS.
(*From the MS.* 10 *E. IV.*)

CHAPTER III

OUTLAWS, WANDERING WORKMEN, AND PEASANTS OUT OF BOND

THE mountebanks, the musicians, and their fellows have stayed us at the street corners, in the castle halls and courtyards ; the pedlars have led us to the peasants' cots, the fairs and markets. With the outlaws we must leave the highroad for the pathless woods, fens and solitudes.

England at that time was not the immense meadow, furrowed by railways, of the present day ; there still remained much of those forests spoken of by Cæsar in his Commentaries, and where the Plantagenet kings and their predecessors had so ealously maintained their rights of the chase. The woods were not so well policed as they are now ; they offered to bandits and men fleeing from justice a more extensive asylum than any six-circled sanctuary. In the popular mind the idea of the great rustling forest, and the idea of the free life that the outlaws led there, were often mingled in one and the same sentiment of sympathy.   Besides, therefore, the praise of the Arthurian heroes, is found in the poetry of the time that of the trees and bushes, that of the valiant men who, dwelling in the copse, were supposed to have struggled for the public liberties, Hereward, Fulk Fitz-Warin, Robin Hood.   Were a man pursued, if the sanctuary was too far or not to his taste, he took to the forest ; it was easier to get there he remained nearer to his kin, and was about as safe as if he had crossed over to the continent.

Robbers, bandits, poachers, knights in trouble might thus meet as comrades in the depths of the wood.   The forest is the first thought of the proscribed squire in the " Nut Brown Maid," the masterpiece of English poetry in the fifteenth century, a musical duet of love, full of the wild charm of the great forest, with a well-accented cadence, frequent rhymes and assonances charming the ear as the oft repeated rustling of the forest leaves.   On the verge of capture, the poor squire is fain to choose between a shameful death and retreat into " the grene wode." His betrothed, who is nothing less than a baron's daughter, wishes to follow him ; and then, in every couplet, her lover, in order to try her, pictures to her the terrors and dangers of the fugitive's life ; she may perhaps see him taken and die a robber's death :

" For an outlawe this is the lawe, that men hym take and binde
    Wythout pytee, hanged to bee, and waver with the wynde."

With this, a thrilling description of the life in the woods, of the brambles, snow, hail, rain; no soft bed; for roof the leaves alone :

" Yet take good hede, for ever I drede, that ye coude not sustein
    The thorney wayes, the depe valeis, the snowe, the frost, the reyn,
    The cold, the hete ; for drye or wete we must lodge on the playn ;
    And, us above, noon other roue (roof), but a brake, bussh or twayne."

No delicate food, but only such as the wood affords :

"For ye must there in your hande bere a bowe redy to drawe,
    And as a theef thus must ye lyve, ever in drede and awe."

Worse even, and the trial becomes harder ; the young
girl must cut off her lovely hair ; life in the forest does
not allow of that ornament. Lastly, to crown all : I
have already in the forest another sweetheart, whom I
love better, and who is more beautiful. But, as resigned
as Griselda, the betrothed replies : I shall go none the
less into the forest ; I will be kind to your sweetheart,
I will obey her, " for in my mynde, of all mankynde,
I love but you alone." Then the lover's joy breaks out :
" I wyl not too the grene wod goo, I am noo banysshyd
man," I am not an obscure squire, but the son of the
Earl of Westmoreland, and the hour of our wedding is
now come.[1]

All the fugitives whom the forest received into its
depths were not romantic knights, followed by baronesses
patient as Griselda and brave as Bradamante. To pass
from poetry to real facts, they were for the greater part
formidable rovers, the same against whom Edward I
and Edward III had enacted the rigorous law for suspects [2]
mentioned above. This caste was composed, first of the
organized bands of brigands whom the statute calls
Wastours, Roberdesmen, and Drawlatches, then of
thieves, sharpers, and malefactors of all kinds, of
outlaws of various sorts suffering that civil death
alluded to by the lover in the ' Nut Brown Maid.'

The sentence of outlawry was usually the starting-
point for a wandering life which by necessity became a
life of brigandage. To be declared an outlaw, a crime

    [1] "The Nut Brown Maid," in Skeat's "Specimens of English Litera-
ture," Clarendon Press, 1887, p. 96.
    [2] Statute of Winchester, 13 Edward I, chap. iv., confirmed by
Edward III. See before p. 156.

or a misdemeanor must have been committed ; a private suit of a purely civil character was not enough ; [1] but to come within sight of the gallows, no great guilt was necessary ; hence the large number of outlaws. In a criminal lawsuit of the time of Edward I [2] the judge explains from his bench that the law is this : if the thief has taken anything worth more than twelve pence, or if he has been condemned several times for little thefts, and the total may be worth twelve pence or more, he ought to be hanged : " The law wills that he shall be hanged by the neck." Still as the judge observes in the case of a woman who had stolen a carpet lying on a hedge, worth eightpence, the law is milder than in the days of Henry III, for then a theft of the value of fourpence would hang a man.[3]

The man became an outlaw, and the woman a *weyve*, that is, abandoned to the mercy of every one and unable to claim the protection of justice. The author of " Fleta " expresses with terrible force the condition of persons so punished ; they have wolves heads which may be cut off with impunity : " For she is a weyve whom no one will own, and it is equivalent to outlawry so far as penal consequences go. An outlaw and a weyve bear wolves

[1] " Item videtur nulla esse utlagaria si factum, pro quo interrogatus est, civile sit et non criminale." Bracton, Rolls Series, vol. ii. p. 330.

[2] " Year Books of Edward I." Rolls Series, years 30–31, p. 533.

[3] " Year Books of Edward I," Rolls Series, years 30–31, pp. 537–538. In the case of this woman, freedom was granted " propter parvitatem delicti," and because she had been one year in prison; and no confiscation took place, because her husband was absent in Paris, and it would have been inappropriate to, maybe, wrong that man who was, like every husband, the owner of his wife's chattels. " Et nota," beautifully adds the judge (or the reporter), " quod melius est nocentem relinquere impunitum quam innocentem punire." But the court, at the same time, fines an innocent, known to it as such, for fear of displeasing the king ; a circumstance that the recorder is bold enough to note down : " Et nota quod fecerunt hoc Justiciarii magis ad appruyamentum (profit, for the king got the money) Regis faciendum quam ad legem manutenendum, quia hoc dixerunt in terrorem." Ibid. pp. 503–507.

heads, which may be cut off by any one with impunity, for deservedly ought they to perish without law who would refuse to live according to law." [1]   The outlaw lost all his property and rights ; all the contracts to which he was a party fell void ; he was no longer bound to any one nor anybody bound to him.   His goods were forfeit : " the chattels of an outlaw shall belong to our lord the king " ; if he had lands the king kept the usufruct for a year and a day, at the end of which he restored them to the chief lord (*capitalis dominus*).[2] There were also hard legal rules on this subject ; a man accused of murder and acquitted suffered confiscation nevertheless, if he had fled, fearing justice. Listen to the magistrate :

FOREST LIFE—A SHOOTING CASUALTY.
(*From the MS.* 10 *E. IV.*)

" If a man be acquitted of manslaughter and of assent and help the justices shall thereupon ask the jury if the prisoner took to flight ; if they say No let him go quits, if Yes, the king shall have his chattels." [3]   It may be

[1] " Fleta," lib. i. chap. xxvii.
[2] " Bracton," vol. ii. pp. 340–342.
[3] " Year Books of Edward I," year 30–31, p. 515   Sometimes a man would profit by the absence of an enemy on the continent and affirm to a magistrate that he was in flight, and cause him to be declared an outlaw ; thus the priest, John Crochille, complains to parliament of having been unjustly outlawed during a journey which he had made to the Court of Rome, in 1347 (" Rolls of Parliament," vol. ii. p. 178) ; the priest, Robert of Thresk, is also declared outlaw during his absence from the kingdom, " by the malice of his accusers " (ibid., 1347, vol. ii. p. 183).   John of Gaunt orders the restitution of his goods to " nostre tenant neif, Johan Piers," whose belongings had been seized, " à cause q'il deust estre utlagé, à ce q'est dit, et ore il nous est certifié par recorde, q'il n'est pas utlagé."

readily believed that the draconian severity of such regulations was not calculated to lessen the audacity of those whom they concerned, and that the excessive rigour of these penalties would often transform the fugitive of a day, who had doubted the clear-sightedness of the judge, into a professional brigand and highway robber.

Besides people of this kind there were the rovers, who, without being threatened with outlawry, had fled the village or the farm to which they belonged. The villein who, without special licence, left his master's domain, could resume his previous life and intercourse with his kin, only by placing himself at his lord's mercy, or, which was less risky, after having passed a year and a day in a free town without leaving it and without the lord, often unaware of the place, having interrupted the prescription. In this latter case he became a free man, and the ties which bound him to the soil were broken. But if he confined himself to wandering from place to place he might be re-taken any day that he reappeared at his own door.

An example of this may be seen in a characteristic lawsuit of the time of Edward I, a report of which has come down to us :—*A* presents a writ of imprisonment against **B**. Heiham, counsel for *B*, says : It is not for us to defend ourselves, *A* is our villein, his writ cannot take effect against us. This is verified, it s found that *A* is the son of a villein of *B*, that he ran away, and several years afterwards returned home, " to his nest," where he was taken as a villein. The judge declares that this seizure was legal ; that a villein might wander about during six, seven years or more, but if at the end he were found " in his own nest and at his hearth," he might be seized as continuing to be his lord's lawful property ; the fact of his return put him into the condit on he was

Oct. 12, 1374. " John of Gaunt's Register," ed. S. Armitage Smith, document 1544.

in before his departure. On hearing this decision the delighted counsel appropriately cites the scripture, ' He fell into the pit which he hath digged." [1]

At that period a villein could still be sold as chattel, given away as a present, donated to a convent for the benefit of one's soul : " I Hugo de Ringesdon . . . gave and conceded . . . to God and B essed Mary and the Abbot and convent of Sulby, for the salvation of my soul and that of my ancestors and successors, in perpetual frank almoigne, Robert son of Juliana de Walton, with all his sequel and all his chattels, nothing remaining of any bond with me or my successors for ever." [2]

Or again : " Be it known to all, now and hereafter, that I John, son of Thomas [of Wurtham], have sold . . . to Hugo abbot of Saint Edmunds . . . Serval, son of William of Wurtham with all his sequel . . . and all the tenement which he held from me . . . for sixteen shillings of silver which the said abbot gave me." [3]

If the actual sale of a man, sold as such, was infrequent, the transfer of a tenement, tenant included,

---

[1] " Cecidit in foveam quam fecit." Psalm vii. 16 : " cecidit " should be " incidit." " Year Books," Edward I, year 21–22, p. 447. In another case, counsel delighted at a statement of the judge, exclaims in his joy : " Beatus venter qui te portavit." Ibid. p. 437. Judges sometimes indulged in familiar speech, bets and witticisms : " I will wager a cask of wine on it." " If you find it, I will give you my hood." " Year Books of Edward II," ed. G. J. Turner, Selden Society, 1914, years 1310–1311, pp. 44, 168.

[2] Late thirteenth century, in Madox, " Formulare Anglicanum," London, 1702, fol., p. 416.

[3] " Sciant presentes et futuri quod ego Johannes filius Thome vendidi et quietum clamavi de me et heredibus meis domino Hugoni abbati Sancti Edmundi et successoribus suis inprimum Servalum filium Willielmi de Wurtham cum tota sequela sua et omnibus catallis suis et cum toto tenemento quod de me tenuit in Wurtham sine ullo retenemento pro sexdecim solidis argenti quos idem abbas michi dedit. Et ut hec mea vendicio . . . firma sit . . . presentem cartam meam feci . . ." Temp. Ed. I, MS. Addit. 14850, in the British Museum fol. 59. " The existing evidence," says Vinogradoff, " entitles one to maintain that a villain could be lawfully sold, with all his family, his sequela, but that in practice such transactions were uncommon." " Villainage in England," Oxford, 1892, p. 151.

was of constant occurrence ; the man and his kin changed hands as the plot of land to which he was bound. The monastery of Meaux, near Beverley, having claimed, against the abbot of St. Mary of York, the right to fish in the Wathsand and Hornsey meres, and no satisfactory proof being available on either side, recourse was had by the two religious disputants to judicial duel. The combat was severe : " It took place at York and lasted from morning to evening, our champion," says the Meaux chronicler, " slowly succumbing." Before complete defeat, however, " the duel was interrupted by the cleverness of a certain judge, Roger de Thurkelby, a friend of ours " ; Meaux yielded the fishing rights to York, but York " granted us one toft, with a man holding that toft in villeinage, and his sequel." [1]

The change in customs made the separate sale of the man himself practically impossible in the fourteenth century,[2] but the *adscriptio glebæ* remained imperative, and every means was taken to prevent the villeins from uprooting themselves and ceasing to be, like their own trees, fixtures liable to change masters with the trees.

The villein's highest desire was of course manumission and complete independence : a dream so ambitious that most of them scarcely dared to form it, up to the time of the peasants' revolt, when it became general,

---

[1] " Chronica Monasterii de Melsa," Rolls, ii. 97 ff., the case being of the second half of the thirteenth century. The duel was, of course, one *cum fuste et scuto*, the fighters clubbing each other to their best, as in the case of the before mentioned Thomas de Bruges. Above, p. 117.

[2] The year books of Edward I show a marked tendency in the judge to interpret the laws and customs in a sense favourable to the freeing of the villein. One of the harsh theories of former days is declared by him " pejus quam falsum pur ce qe ce est heresie." " Year Books of Ed. I," years 30–31, A.D. 1302, ed. Horwood, Rolls, p. 167. See also, in the vol. for the years 34–35, the suit p. 13. But the judge could act thus only in doubtful cases : a man having acknowledged, in the presence of his master, that he was a villein, the judge says to the master : " Prenez le par le cou, comme votre vilain, lui et sa descendance à toujours." Vol. for the years 30–31, p. 201.

and was realized—for a day.   Second to that he wanted
the commutation for a cash payment of the harassing
personal labour due by him to his lord, a change which
went on increasingly in the course of the fourteenth
century.[1]   When neither was possible and the burden
became unbearable, he would, happen what may, try
to escape and live elsewhere unknown and masterless.[2]

The villein, when in this mood, had two great temp-
tations, the cities with their franchise, which even his
master did not dare infringe,[3] and the forest, where he was
out of reach.   Noblemen sometimes allowed their villeins
to become merchants and go from city to city.   They were
very near freedom, but not quite free ; they had to pay
" chevage " to their master as a sign of subjection,
and if these serfs ceased to pay, the mere fact made them
runaways, " just like domestic *cerfs* (red deer)," says
Bracton, indulging in an, even then, antiquated pun.
They can be run after and captured like any domestic
animal.[4]

---

[1] See an example of such commutation, with a tariff established, " ex
antiqua et usitata consuetudine," for various services according to the season,
for oats to be supplied to the lord (the abbot of Bury), etc., in MS. Addit.
14850, British Museum, fol. 143 ; year 1438.

[2] This was a last resort, more and more frequently adopted however,
especially after the plague.   As Mr. Oman has justly observed, by natural
disposition the villeins " were reluctant to abscond and throw up their
share of the manorial acres, for only in extremity will the peasant, who has
once got a grip on the soil, consent to let it go."   " The Great Revolt of
1381," Oxford 1906, p. 9.

[3] " A . . . n. Sr le Roi et Seigneurs de Parlement monstrent les chivalers
des countees en ycest present Parlement, que come les Seigneurs parmy
le Roialme d'Engleterre eient plusours vileins queux s'enfuont de lour
Seigneurs et de lour terres en diverses citees et burghs enfranchisez, de jour
en autre, et la demuront tout lour vies, par cause desqueux franchises les
ditz Seigneurs ne pount aprocher lour ditz vileins. . . ."   They want to be
enabled to forcibly take them back.   Their petition is rejected : " Le Roi
s'advisera."   15 Rich. II, " Rolls of Parliament," iii. p. 296.

[4] " Ad similitudinem cervorum domesticorum."—" Henrici de Bracton, De Legibus et Consuetudinibus Angliæ Libri V," ed. Travers Twiss,
London, 1878, i. p. 48.

Scarcely less tempting was the forest. Escaped peasants provided the wandering class with its most numerous recruits. In England several causes, the chief of which was the great plague of 1349,[1] had in the fourteenth century upset the relations of the working classes with the rich, and the proportions between the rate of wages and the cost of necessaries. Confronted with a longing for emancipation which arose on all sides, parliament—the House of Commons as willingly as the king—passed stern laws for the maintenance of the *statu quo ante pestem*. Thence came among the various sorts of peasants, both the villeins bound to their plot of land ("theirs" with the understanding they should perform the customary services due to the lord), and the landless labourers free to hire themselves out for wages, an immense desire to move about and see other parts. In their own hamlet, they found, nothing was to be got but the same obligations and the same wages as before the plague ; but in such another county, they heard or supposed, there were better pay and less exacting masters[2] ; besides, why not mingle with the class of free labourers ? It was numerous and increased un-

---

[1] According to Seebohm ("The Black Death and its place in English History," two articles in the *Fortnightly Review* in 1865), more than half of the population died during the epidemic which had begun in July 1348 and lasted till the end of 1349. Three archbishops of Canterbury died in one year. Knyghton, a contemporary, gives a striking picture of the plague at Leicester. "There were scarcely any who took heed of riches or cared for anything. . . . And sheep and oxen wandered through the fields and among the crops ; there was no one to go after and collect them ; but there perished an untold number in out of the way ditches and under hedges." In the autumn the price of labour was so exorbitant that a large part of the crops were left on the ground ('Twysden's "Decem Scriptores," col. 2599). "Through this pestilence," say the Commons in Parliament, "cities, boroughs and other towns and hamlets throughout the land have decayed, and from day to day are decaying and several are entirely depopulated." 25 Ed. III, A.D. 1351, "Rolls of Parliament," vol. ii. p. 227.

[2] See a concrete example of such reports being brought from the north to the south by pilgrims, further, p. 279.

ceasingly, in spite of the law. All did not succeed in concealing their past ; and when the danger of being " put into stocks " and sent back to their masters became great, they fled again, changed county and became roamers. Others, discontented with or without cause, only quitted their place to become straightway homeless vagabonds of the most dangerous kind. Thus in the precincts of Westminster, the chapter house of the Abbey where the Commons sat, resounded with ever new complaints against the increasing lawlessness of peasants and labourers of all sorts. The Commons, who, generally speaking, represented the landowners of the country, and a trading bourgeoisie [1] with somewhat aristocratic tendencies, rose with force against the wishes for freedom of a class of workers whom they in no way represented. They were for the re-establishment of all the old laws and customs, and the strict rejection of new demands. But the current was too strong, and it swept by the laws, ever renewed and ever inefficient.

The plague was still raging, Parliament could not meet ; the thinning of the ranks of the workers by death, and the excessive wage demands, or refusals to work at all, of the survivors, who preferred to live on alms, created such a dangerous state of confusion that the king issued, on his own authority and that of his council in June 1349, an ordinance which formed the basis of the famous Statute of Labourers of 1351 [2] and of all the subsequent ones.

---

[1] As shown by the surnames of the members, at that period ; in numerous cases, a mere indication of profession : Johannes le Baker, Galfridus le Fisshere, Johannes le Carpenter, Robertus Chaundeler, Ricardus Orfevre, Radulphus le Taverner, etc. " Return of the names of every member returned to serve in every Parliament," London, 1878, a blue book, pp. 18, 31, 146 and *passim* ; on p. 229, duly appears, as a knight of the shire, for Kent, " Galfridus Chauceres."

[2] Both documents, the first in Latin, the second in French, in " Statutes of the Realm " ; a text, revised on the originals, is in the Appendix to Miss Bertha H. Putnam's " Enforcement of the Statutes of Labourers during the first Decade after the Black Death," New York, 1908, pp. 8* and 12*.

The most striking of its dispositions aimed at an or conscription of labour, something like what we seen of late, under the pressure of necessity, occasion of what has been for the world an even g calamity :

" Any man or woman, in our realm of England, of whatever condition, either free or servile, sound in body and under the age of sixty years, living not by merchandise nor practising a definite craft, nor having personally wherewith to live, nor possessing land which he would cultivate, nor being somebody else's servant, if he is requested to serve in a service congruent to his status, shall be bound to serve the one that shall thus request him." He is moreover forbidden to receive any wages or compensations different from those of the twentieth year of the King's reign, that is those which were barely sufficient before the plague and were entirely inadequate now. Later in the year, a new ordinance forbade any one to leave the desolated realm, " unless he were a merchant, a notary or an undoubted messenger." [1]

The Commons could not imagine that, for mere villeins, there might be such a thing as necessity, and they uniformly attributed the new requests to the "malice of servants," who exacted both higher wages and other terms of engagement than before. They would not work " without taking hire that was too outrageous." [2]

---

[1] The taking of money out of the realm was especially feared : " Quamplures ejusdem regni nostri cum pecunia quam in eodem regno habere poterunt, ad partes exteras in dies se transferunt et transferre proponunt." Dec. 1, 1349, Rymer's " Fœdera," vol. v. p. 668.

[2] " Rolls of Parliament, vol. ii. p. 233. Compare the French ordinances ; that of John the Good, January 30, 1350 (Isambert, " Recueil général des anciennes lois françaises," iv. p. 576), orders the idle people of Paris, picturesquely described as " gens oiseux ou joueurs de dez ou enchanteurs (singers) es rues ou truandans ou mandians, de quelque estat ou condition qu'ils soient, ayans mestier ou non, soient hommes ou femmes," to either work or go away, which was less radical and still less to the point than the English rules. Another order of the same king (Nov. 1354, ibid. p. 700)

Formerly they hired themselves for a year ; now they wanted to remain their own masters and to hire themselves by the day : the statute forbids them to do so.

Three years later the complaints are renewed ; [1] the value of corn is very low and labourers refuse to receive it as payment ; they persist also in desiring day hire ; all these doings are condemned once more. The quarrel continues and grows embittered. In the thirty-fourth year of his reign Edward III threatens to have the guilty branded on the forehead with an F, as a sign of " fauxine " (falsehood).[2] In 1372, Parliament declares that " labourers and servants flee from one county to another, some go to the great towns and become artificers, some into strange districts to work, on account of the excessive wages, none remaining for certain in any place, whereby the statute cannot be put in execution against them." [3]

The Commons of the Good Parliament of 1376 secured the confirmation of all the previous statutes. Prohibitions were renewed against any going out of their " own district " (*pays propre*), whether they were villeins proper, or " labourers and artificers and other servants." The economic changes that had taken place had rendered possible, however, what was not so formerly ; labourers were wanted and it was not rare to find landowners who employed them in spite of the laws, even by the day, and at other wages than those of the tariff. The parliamentary petitions declare that " they are so willingly

was directed against the workmen who since the plague were exacting exorbitant wages, and, in addition to that, " wine, meat and other unwonted things." If denied, they preferred to do nothing but would go to taverns and there had been heard to say that, " owing to the great price they are accustomed to take, they will work only two days a week," a kind of difficulty which, dating back six centuries, is not entirely of the past.

1 " Rolls of Parliament," vol. ii. p. 261, parliament of 1354.
2 Statute 34 Ed. III, chap. 10, A.D. 1360-1.
3 " Rolls of Parliament," ii. p. 312.

REAPING TIME.

(From the MS. 2 B. vii. Fourteenth Century.)

[*p. 267.*]

" We haue the payne and traveyle, rayne and wynd in the feldes."   (John Ball's speech in Berner's Froissart.)

received in strange places suddenly into service, that this reception gives example and comfort to all servants, as soon as they are displeased with anything, to run from master to master into strange places as is aforesaid." And this would not go on, observe the Commons, if when they offered their services in this fashion they were " taken and put in the stocks.' True, indeed, but the landowners who needed help, and whose crops were waiting on the ground, were too happy to meet with " servantz corores " (runaway), whoever they might be ; and instead of taking them " to the nearest gaol," to pay and use them. The labourers knew it, and their traditional masters had to show less severity. For on some unreasonable demand or over-strong reprimand, instead of submitting as formerly, or venturing a protest, the workman said nothing but, " par grande malice," went away : " As soon as their masters challenge them with bad service or offer to pay them for their service according to the form of the said statutes, they flee and run away suddenly out of their service and out of their own district, from county to county, from hundred to hundred, from town to town, in strange places unknown to their said masters." [1]

Worse still, and inevitable, many among them, unable or unwilling to work, took up begging or robbing as a profession. These " wandering labourers become mere beggars in order to lead an idle life, and betake themselves out of their district commonly to the cities, boroughs, and other good towns to beg, and they are able-bodied and might well ease the community if they would serve."

[1] " Rolls of Parliament," ii. p. 340, A.D. 1376. To have them outlawed brings no relief to their masters, for they manage not to be caught and carefully avoid the places where they are known : " Et si les ditz servantz corores soient utlagez à la sute de la partie, il n'est profit al sutour, ne damage ne chastiement al servant futyf, par cause q'ils ne poont estre trovez ne jà ne pensent repeirir en pays là où ils ont ensi servi." Same petition.

So much for the beggars ; [1] now for the robbers :
" And the greater part of the said wandering servants
commonly become strong robbers, and their robberies
and felonies increase from one day to another on all sides,"
acting in small bands of " two, three or four together,"
and plundering " simple villages." Energetic measures
must be taken ; let it be prohibited to give alms to this
sort of people, and " let their bodies be put in the stocks
or taken to the next gao'," to be sent afterwards to where
they belong. Edward III had already condemned to
prison, by his ordinance of 1349, those who, under colour
of charity " sub colore pietatis vel elemosine," came to
the aid of sturdy beggars, those vagabonds who went
through the country " giving themselves to idleness and
vice, and sometimes to theft and other abominations."
The same complaints recur in the time of Richard II.
Hardly is he on the throne than they are repeated from
year to year : 1377, 1378, 1379, revealing to us the
existence of early unions and federations of villeins and
labourers who, advised by men better informed than themselves, " lours counseillours, meyntenours et abettours,"
defend their assumed freedom, sometimes by force—
" menassent les ministres de lours seignurs de vie et de
membre "—sometimes by law, invoking written texts
and " exemplifications " whose value they have learnt,
and swear to remain " confederated " and to help each
other at all cost against their masters.[2]

---

[1] Langland shows, in the same way, the shameless beggar who goes,
bag on shoulder, asking from door to door, who may very well if he pleases
gain his bread and beer by work ; he knows a trade, but he prefers not to
exercise it :

> " And can som manere craft · in cas he wolde hit use,
> Thorgh whiche craft he couthe · come to bred and to ale."

" Piers Plowman," Text C, pass. x. l. 155 ; see also ibid., pass. i. l. 40.

[2] " . . . Par colour de certains exemplificacions faitz hors de livre
de Domesday des manoirs et villes deinz queux ils sont demurantz, et par
vertue d'icelles exemplificacions et lour male interpretacion d'icelles, ils

Statutes multiplied to no purpose ; the king had to recognize in his ordinance of 1383 that the "fe.tors (id.ers) and vagrants" overran the country "more abundantly than they were formerly accustomed."[1] In 1388 he renewed all the orders of his predecessors, re-enacting for rustics rules similar to those of the *Inscription maritime* still applied to-day in France, for what concerns seafaring, to the seaside population : any one who reached the age of twelve without having done anything else than "working at the plough and cart or other labor or service of husbandry," will have to continue in this state his life long, "without being allowed to learn a trade or handicraft," and if one is found to be a party to a contract of apprenticeship the contract shall be void.

The king reminds, at the same time, the mayors, bailiffs, stewards, and constables of their duties, and asks them in particular to repair their stocks and keep them always ready for wanderers to cease in them their wanderings.[2]

No vain threats nor light penalties. The prisons of those days little resembled the well-washed buildings now to be seen in most English towns, at York for instance, where the guilty ones are apt to find more cleanliness and comfort than they ever knew before. They were mostly fetid dungeons, where the damp of the walls and the stationary position compelled by the irons corrupted the blood and engendered hideous maladies.

Many a wandering workman, accustomed to an active life and the open air, came thus, thanks to the incessant

---

s'aferment (affirm) d'estre quites et outrement deschargez de tout manere de servage due sibien de lour corps come de lour tenures. . . . Et qe plus est, ils se coillient ensembles à grantz routes et s'entrelient par tiel confederacie qe chescun aidra autre à contester lours seignurs à fort mayn." Rich. II, chap 6, year 1377 ; "Rolls of Parliament," vol. iii. pp. 17, 46, 65.

[1] Statute 7 Rich. II, cap. 5.
[2] Statute 12 Rich. II, cap. 3.

ordinances of king and Parliament, to repent in the dark
for his boldness, and during days and nights all alike,
to regret his liberty, his family, and his "nest." The
effect of such a treatment on the physical constitution
of the victims may be guessed or imagined, but without
any imagining the reports of justice show it only too
clearly. A roll of the time of Henry III reads, for instance, as follows :

"Assizes held at Ludinglond. The jury present that
William le Sauvage took two men, aliens, and one woman,
and imprisoned them at Thorlestan, and detained them
in prison until one of them died in prison and the other
lost one foot, and the woman lost either foot by putre-

IN THE STOCKS.
(*From the MS.* 10 *E. IV.*)

faction. Afterwards he took them to the Court of the
lord the king at Ludinglond to try them by the same
Court. And when the Court saw them, it was loth to
try them, because they were not attached for any robbery
or misdeed for which they could suffer judgment And
so they were permitted to depart." [1]

How in such a condition the poor creatures could
"depart" and what became of them, the Assize Rolls do
not say. Certain it is that no sort of indemnity was given

[1] "Gleanings from the Public Records," by Mr. H. Hewlett, in the
"Antiquary," March, 1882, vol. v. p. 99. Concerning ill-treatment
inflicted on prisoners, see a petition of the Commons, 1 Ed. III, A.D.
1326–7, "Rolls of Parliament," vol. ii. pp. 9, 12.

to help them out of trouble in their horrible condition. The justice of our fathers did not stop at trifles.

The stocks, which according to the laws of Richard II were always to be kept in good condition ready for use, consisted of two beams placed one on the other. At proper intervals round holes were cut ; the upper beam was raised, and the legs of the prisoners were passed through the holes ; sometimes there was a third beam, in the openings of which the wrists of the wretches were also caught ; the body sometimes rested on a stool, some-times on the ground. In certain places the stocks were pretty high ; the sufferer's legs were placed in them and he remained thus, his body stretched on the ground in the damp, his head lower than his feet ; but this refine-ment of cruelty was not habitual.[1]

Stocks are still to be seen in many places in England ; for instance, in the picturesque village of Abinger, where they stand on the green, near the churchyard. Others in a very good state of preservation are in existence at Shalford, near Guildford. They have not long ceased to be used in England ; vagabonds and drunkards were seen in them within the memory of men who were not old when the present book was written. According to their remembrance people when released felt so benumbed that they were scarcely able to stand, and experienced great difficulty in getting away.

But the threat of prisons so unhealthy and of stocks so unpleasant did not hold back the labourers more and more weary of being tied to the soil. Every pretext for leaving their place was welcome ; they even dared to use that of a devotional journey. They set out, staff in hand, " under colour of going far on a pilgrimage," and

[1] See, besides the plates here, representations of these instruments of punishment in, e.g. Foxe's " Actes and Monuments." London, 1563, ol. pp. 390, 1272, etc., and in Butler's " Hudibras, adorned with cutts esigned and engraved by Mr. Hogarth," London 1761 ; at p. 140, the night and his squire, " check by joul," says the poet, in the stocks.

never returned. But a new restraint was to be applied
to tame this turbulent spirit, the obligation for every
one to furnish himself with a kind of letter of travel or
passport, in order to move from one county to another.
None might leave his village if he did not carry a " letter
patent stating the cause of his going and the date of his
return, if he were to return." In other words, even with
the right to go and settle definitively elsewhere, a permit

THE STOCKS AT SHALFORD, GUILDFORD.
(*Present state.*)

for moving had to be procured. These letters would
be sealed by a " good man " (*prod homme*), assigned in
each hundred, city, or borough, by the justices of the
peace, and special seals were to be expressly made,
said the statute, bearing the king's arms in the centre,
the name of the county around, and that of the hundred,
city, or borough across. Even the case of fabricating
false letters was foreseen, which shows how well was
realized the ardent desire of many men of this class to

leave the place where they were tied. Every individual
surprised without regular papers would be sent to jail.

Beggars were treated as "servants" who had no
"testimonial letters." [1] What was wanted was to impose
immobility upon as many people as possible, and thus
hinder the disquieting peregrinations of so many rovers.
As for beggars incapable of work, they must nevertheless cease frequenting the highroads, and must end
their days in the cities where they chance to be at the
time of the proclamation, or at most in some town near

A CRIPPLE AND OTHER BEGGARS.
(*From the MS.* 10 E. IV.)

ne spot where they were born; they shall be taken there
ithin forty days, to stay "for the rest of their lives."

What is stranger, and lacking other proofs, would
now to what class students then belonged, is that they
e included in the same category ; they were accustomed,
1 returning to their homes, or on making pilgrimages,
going to the university, to hold out a hand for the
arity of passers-by and to knock at the door of possible
vers. They were ranked with the beggars, and put
irons if they lacked the regulation letter ; this docu-
ent was to be given them by the Chancellor, and that

[1] 12 Rich. II, cap. 7.

was the only difference : " And that the scholars of the universities that go so begging have letters testimonial of their Chancellor upon the same pain." [1]

Again, in the following year (1389), a new statute reproves the custom of " artificers, labourers, servants," etc., who keep for their own use harriers and other dogs, and on " feast days, when good Christians are at church hearing Divine service," get into the parks and warrens of the nobility and destroy the game. Much more, they avail themselves of these occasions when they meet together armed, without fear of being disturbed, to " hold their assemblies, conversations, and conspiracies, to rise against and disobey their allegience." The thickets of the seignorial forests must have sheltered many a meeting of this kind during church services on the eve of the great revolt of 1381 ; [2] in such retreats no doubt were brought forth some of the living and stirring ideas which, transported from place to place by the wanderers, made the people of different counties understand that they were the same people, suffering from a variety of abuses longing for relief.

In a revolt like this, the part played by the wandering class is considerable, and the historian should not neglect it. If we do not take this element into account it is hard to explain the extent and importance of movement which came near having consequences comparable to those of the French Revolution. " I had lost my heritage and the kingdom of England," said Richard I

---

[1] 12 Rich. II, cap. 7. Cf. above, p. 236.
[2] On which see, e.g. André Réville and Ch. Petit-Dutaillis, " Le sou vement des travailleurs d'Angleterre en 1381," Paris, 1898 ; G. M. Trev yan, " England in the age of Wycliffe," chapters vi and vii ; " T Peasants' rising and the Lollards, a collection of unpublished document edited by E. Powell and G. M. Trevelyan, London 1899, with data r only on the great rising, but on some later troubles (1392, 1398) of les magnitude, but important as signs ; C. Oman, " The Great Revolt 1381," Oxford, 1906.

on the evening of the day when his presence of mind had saved him, and he was right. Why was the French Jacquerie a commonplace, powerless rising compared to the English revolt ? The reasons are manifold, but one of the chief was the absence of a class of wayfarers as strong, active, and numerous as that of England. This class served to unite all the people : by its means those of the South learnt the ideas of those of the North, what each suffered and desired ; the sufferings and wishes were not always identical, but it was enough to know that all had reforms to demand. Thus, when the news came that the revolt had begun, the people rose on all sides, and while it was apparent that the desires of each were not absolutely similar, yet the basis of the contention being the same, and all wishing for more independence, they went forth together without being otherwise acquainted than by the intermediary of the wayfarers. The kings of England, indeed, had perceived the danger, and on different occasions had promulgated statutes bearing especially on the talk indulged in by these wanderers about the nobles, prelates, judges, and all the depositaries of public power. Edward I had said in one of his laws :

" Forasmuch as there have been oftentimes found in the country devisors of tales, whereby discord, or occasion of discord, hath many times arisen between the king and his people, or great men of this realm ; for the damage that hath and may thereof ensue, it is commanded, that from henceforth none be so hardy to tell or publish any false news or tales, whereby discord, or occasion of discord, or slander may grow between the king and his people, or the great men of the realm ; and he that doth so, shall be taken and kept in prison, until he hath brought him into the court who was the first author of the tale." [1]

The danger of such speeches, which touched the acts

[1] Statute 3 Ed. I, stat. 1, cap. 34, A.D. 1275.

and even the thoughts of the great men of the kingdom, became menacing anew under Richard II, and in the first years of his reign the following statute was enacted, reinforcing that of 1275 :

" Item, Of devisors of false news and reporters of horrible and false lyes, concerning prelates, dukes, earls, barons, and other nobles and great men of the realm, and also concerning the chancellor, treasurer, clerk of the privy seal, steward of the king's house, justices of the one bench or of the other, and of other great officers of the realm about things which by the said prelates, lords, nobles, and officers aforesaid were never spoken, done, nor thought . . . whereby debates and discords might arise betwixt the said lords or between the Lords and the Commons, which God forbid, and whereof great peril and mischief might come to all the realm, and quick subversion and destruction of the said realm, if due remedy be not provided : it is straitly defended upon grievous pain, for to eschew the said damages and perils, that from henceforth none be so hardy to devise, speak, or to tell any false news, lyes, or other such false things, of pre-lates, lords, and of other aforesaid, whereof discord or any slander might rise within the same realm ; and he that doth the same shall incur and have the pain another time ordained thereof by the statute of Westminster the first." [1]   In vain : two years later broke out the revolt of the peasants, and the depositions of the rebels when brought before the judge leave no doubt as to the part played by wayfarers in the carrying of political news from one county to another.

The mason John Cole, of Lose, in the parish of Maid-stone, Kent, turns informer, betrays twenty-seven of his companions, giving their names (some proved innocent), and saving his own head.   Their plan was to make the otherwise unpopular John of Gaunt, king of England,

[1] Statute 2 Rich. II, chap. 5.

on the mere report that he had freed his " natives." The rebels had decided to send to him in order to ascertain, and if the news proved true, to depose his nephew young Richard II. The report had been brought to the city of Canterbury by pilgrims, *peregrini*, arriving from the North, obviously to worship at the shrine of St. Thomas.[1]

In mediæval France during the endless wars, and the brief intervals between them, the roads were held by plundering brigands : labourers or knights by birth. Soldiers, the dregs of the lowest or highest classes, considered the rest of society as their devoted prey, the highway resounded with the noise of arms, the peasant fled. Troops originally equipped for the defence of the land attacked without scruple all whom they thought less strong than themselves and worth robbing. Such people " turned French," as Froissart puts it, and " turned English " according to the interest of the moment.

The vagrants threatened with the stocks by the English law were of another kind, and whatever the number of brigands among them these were not the majority ; the peasants mostly sympathized with, instead of fearing, them. Thus the English revolt was not a desperate enterprise ; it was conducted with extraordinary coolness and practical sense. The insurgents showed a calm

[1] Document published (but only in an English translation) by W. E. Flaherty : " Sequel to the great rebellion in Kent, of 1381," " Archæologia Cantiana," vol. iv. pp. 67 ff. The author interprets *peregrini*, at one place by strangers, at another by pilgrims ; the latter is the real meaning.

Some traces of kindness to his tenants, on the part of John of Gaunt are found in his Registers. He orders wood and charcoal to be carried to the castle of Tutbury where his wife was to spend the winter, and insists that the work be done in summer, so that his tenants and bondmen be not grieved by the carrying thereof in the bad season..." Si voullons et vous mandons que vous faces faire et carier à nostre dit chastel ccc quarters de carbons, et aussint vous faces carier tout la boys abatuz par vent que vous bonement pourrez en nostre dit chastel pur fuaille, et que ce soit fait toute voies en ceste saison d'estée, issint que noz tenantz et bondes ne soient pas chariez ne grevez ove la cariage d'ycelle en temps de yver." " John of Gaunt's Register," ed. S. A. Smith, 1911, vol. ii. p. 203, year 1373.

consciousness of their strength which strikes us, and struck much more the anxious knights in London ; they went with their eyes open, and, if they destroyed much, they wished also to reform. It was possible to treat and come to an understanding with them ; truth to say, the word and pledge given them will be broken, and the prison, the rope and the block will quickly put an end to the revolt ; but whatever the Lords and Commons sitting at Westminster may say,[1] the new bonds will not have the tenacity of the old ones, and a great step towards freedom, one with which the continent has nothing comparable, will have been made.

In France, the beast of burden, ill-nourished, ill-treated, fretted by the harness, trudged wearily along with shaking head, wan eye and a halting gait ; his sudden bolts only caused new loads to be added to his fardel, and that was all ; centuries were to pass before the day of accounting came and, in blood too, the account would be settled.

[1] And they said it in the most peremptory language, highly approving of the king's breaking his word and revoking the sweeping manumissions (" manumisimus universos ligeos et singulos subditos nostros," Walsingham, ii. 467, Rolls) he had granted out of fear ; the lords and the commons answer : " à une voice qe cele repele fuist ben faite, adjoustant que tiele manumission ou franchise des neifs ne poast estre fait sanz lour assent q'ont le greindre interesse : a quoy ils n'assentèrent unques de lour bone grée, n'autrement, ne jamais ne ferroient pur vivre et murrir touz en un jour." " Rolls of Parliament," iii. p. 100 ; year 1381. So they would rather die, all of them in a day, than assent to a freedom granted " without the assent of those most interested " : and it never occurred to them that those most interested could possibly be the villeins themselves and not the villeins' masters.

PART III

RELIGIOUS WAYFARERS

A FRIAR ON A JOURNEY (CHAUCER'S " FRERE ").
(*From the Ellesmere MS.*)

CHAPTER I

WANDERING PREACHERS AND FRIARS

WHILE the inward consciousness of common
wants and longings for better days spread
everywhere, by means of that crowd of work-
people whom we find in England ceaselessly on the move
in spite of statutes, the guiding ideas were sown broad-
cast by another kind of roamer, the preachers. Sprung
also from the people, they had studied ; as we have seen
it was not necessary to be rich in order to go through
the course at Oxford ; the villeins even sent their children
there, and the Commons, of scant liberalism as we know,
protested against this emancipation of another kind, this
advancement by means of learning, " avancement par
clergie." Preventive measures, they thought, were indispensable to save " the honour " of the freemen of the
realm, by which they meant privilege ; ideas of honour
have changed. But, even then, it was going too far,
and the king, who had after all learnt a lesson in 1381,
rebuked the Commons with a " le roi s'avisera " which

was then, and is to-day, the form of royal refusal.[1] These
clerks knew what was the condition of the people ; they
knew the miseries of the poor, which were those of their
father and mother and of themselves ; the intellectual
culture they had received enabled them to transform
into precise conceptions the general aspirations of the
tillers of the soil. The former are not less necessary
than the latter to every important social movement ; if
both are indispensable to the making of the tool, handle
and blade, it is these definite views which form the blade.

The roaming preachers knew how to sharpen it, and
they were numerous. Those whom Wyclif sent to
popularize his doctrines,[2] his " simple priests," or " poor
priests," did just what others had done before them ;
they imitated their forerunners, and no more confined
themselves to expounding the difficult and not always
democratic theories of their master than the mendicant
friars, or monks, or secular priests, friends of the revolution, strictly kept to the precepts of the gospel. Their
sympathies were with the people, and they showed it in
their discourses. Wyclif contributed to the increase
of these wanderers ; his people came from the same
stock as the others ; if it was easy for him to find clerks
ready to act as his missionaries, the reason was that many
in the kingdom were already prepared for such a task,
and only awaited their opportunity.[3] The revolutionary

[1] " Item priont les communes . . . de ordeiner et commander que
null neif ou vileyn mette ses enfantz de cy en avant à Escoles pur eux avancer
par clergie, et ce en maintenance et salvation de l'honour de toutz Franks
du Roialme." " Rolls of Parliament," vol. iii. p. 294, 15 Rich. II, 1391.

[2] Beginning at an uncertain date : before the papal schism, i.e. 1378,
according to Shirley, Introduction to " Fasciculi Zizaniorum," 1858,
Rolls series ; " several months before the revolt of 1381 broke out,"
according to Oman, " The Great Revolt," 1906, p. 19.

[3] Their activity as wandering preachers is well shown by "The tenor of
the complaint made to the Kinge and his councell against John Fox, Maior
of Northampton, and others exhibited in French by Richard Stermers
worthe, a wolman," year 1392–3. According to the deponent the Mayor

leader John Ball was a secular priest, and so was the well-known Lollard, William Thorpe.

All, in fact, did the same kind of work. For different motives and with different aims, they led to the same results : the belief that the State, the Church, the Government, the Court, the rule of the masters, whether spiritual or temporal, were not what they should be, and that a change *must* come. Doubts and discontents always help each other ; whoever strikes at the tree shakes the tree. Wyclif's theory, " both before and after the rising, was that temporal lords had a right to their property, but that churchmen had no right to theirs." [1]   His teachings helped, however, to spread doubts as to the legitimacy of both. Though it had nothing to do with Lollard tenets, the diffusion thereof was facilitated by the papal schism of 1378 : another great tree that was shaken.

Men able to address a crowd scoured the country, drawing together the poor and attracting them by harangues filled with what people who suffer always like to hear. The statute passed just after the revolt clearly shows how much the influence of the wandering preachers was feared. Their dress even and manner of speech are described ; these malcontents have an austere aspect, they go " from county to county, and from town to town in certain habits under dissimulation of great holiness." They dispense of course with the ecclesiastical papers which regular preachers ought to carry ; they are " without the licence of our Holy Father the Pope, or of the Ordinaries of the

who welcomes every " errant Lollard," has caused "the whole towne in manner to become Lollardes. . . . All ribauds infected with Lollardry, that come to the said towne are all courteously received and maintayned as yf they were prophetts before all others." The day after Christmas, the Mayor "brought with him . . . an errant Lollard to preach within All Saints Church." He did the same later, bringing the " parson of the church of Wynkpole, an errant Lollarde, to preach." Powell and Trevelyan, "The Peasants' risings and the Lollards," London, 1899, pp. 45 ff.

[1] G. M. Trevelyan, " England in the age of Wycliffe," 1899, p. 199.

places, or other sufficient authority." They make themselves heard, and their successors to this day have never
ceased to follow suit, " not only in churches and church-
yards, but also in markets, fairs, and other open places
where a great congregation of people is." Their real
subject is not dogma, but the social question ; on their
lips the religious sermon becomes a political harangue.
" Which persons," the statute says, " do also preach
divers matters of slander, to engender discord and dis-
sension betwixt divers estates of the said realm as well
spiritual as temporal, in exciting of the people, to the
great peril of all the realm." They are cited to appear
before the ecclesiastic authority, the ordinaries, but refuse
to " obey to their summons and commandments." Let
the sheriffs and others of the king's officers henceforth
watch with care these wandering orators and send to prison
those unable to show proper certificates.[1]

We may gain an idea of their speeches by recalling
the celebrated harangue of the priest John Ball,[2] the
most stirring of these travelling orators. Certainly, in
the Latin phrase of the " Chronicle of England," his
thoughts are given too solemn and too correct a form,
but all that we know of the circumstances matches so
well his undoubted purports, that his actual speech cannot
have differed, in its trend at least, from what the chronicler
has transmitted to us. The popular saying quoted before
serves as his text, and he develops it in this manner :

" At the beginning we were all created equal ; it is
the tyranny of perverse men which has caused servitude
to arise, in spite of God's law ; if God had willed that
there should be serfs He would have said at the beginning

---

[1] Statute 5 Rich. II, 2, cap 5.
[2] He has often been considered as an adherent of Wyclif, for no reason
save that both, at the same time, wanted radical reforms, not a few however of a different kind. Ball had some religious ideas peculiar to himself ;
thus, according to him, natural children could not go to heaven.

"WHEN ADAM DELVED AND EVE SPAN." [*p.* 287.

(*The motto of John Ball's speech illustrated from the MS.* 2 B. vii. *Fourteenth Century*).

of the world who should be serf and who should be lord." [1]

What made Ball powerful was that he found his best weapons in the Bible ; quoting it he appealed to the good sentiments of the lowly, to their virtue, their reason ; he showed that the Divine Word accorded with their interest ; they would be " like the good father of a family who cultivates his field and plucks up the weeds." The same ideas are attributed o him by almost all the chroniclers. Froissart uses to describe his doings almost the same words as the statute already quoted. He represents him when he found a congregation of people, especially on Sundays, after mass, preaching in the open air sermons similar to that in the " Chronicon Angliæ " : " This preest," says Froissart, " used often tymes on the sondayes after masse, whanne the people were goynge out of the mynster, to go into the cloyster and preche, and made the people to assemble about hym, and wolde say thus : A ye good people, the maters gothe nat well to passe in Englande, nor shall nat do tyll every thyng be common, and that there be no villayns nor gentylmen. . . . What have we deserved or why shulde we be kept thus in servage ? we be all come fro one father and one mother, Adam and Eve : whereby can they say or shewe that they be gretter lordes than we be, savynge by that they cause us to wyn and labour for that they dispende . . . They dwell in fayre houses, and we have the payne and traveyle, rayne and wynde in the feldes ; and by that that cometh of our labours they kepe and maynteyne their estates. . . . Lette us go to the kyng, he is yonge, and shewn hym what servage we be in. . . . Thus Johan sayd on sondayes whan the people issued out of the churches in the vyllages . . . and so they wolde murmure one with another in the feldes and in the wayes as

[1] " Chronicon Angliæ," 1328–1388, ed. E. Maunde Thompson, 1874, Rolls Series, p. 321.

they went togyder, affermyng howe Johan Ball sayd
trouthe." [1]

So the enthusiastic multitude promised to make him
archbishop and chancellor of that kingdom in which he
dreamed there should be " equal liberty, equal .rank,
equal power " for all ; but he was taken, drawn, hanged,
beheaded, and quartered,[2] and his dream remained a dream.

Meanwhile, politics apart, there might yet be found
in the fourteenth century some of God's elect who,
alarmed by the crimes of the world and the state of sin
in which men lived, left their cells or the paternal roof
to go about among villages and towns and preach conversion. There remained some, but they were rare.
Contrary to others, these did not speak of public affairs,
but of eternal interests ; they had not always received
sacred orders ; they acted as volunteers to the celestial
army. Of this sort was the before mentioned Richard
Rolle, of Hampole, whose life was partly that of a hermit,
partly of a wandering preacher. He was neither monk,
nor doctor, nor priest ; when young, he had abandoned
his father's house to go and lead a contemplative life in
solitude. There he meditated, prayed, and mortified
himself ; crowds came to his cell to listen to his exhortations ; he had ecstatic trances ; his friends took off
his ragged cloak, mended it, and put it back on his shoulders
without his perceiving it. He later left his retreat, and
for a long time travelled over the north of England,
becoming a wanderer, " changing place continually,"
preaching to lead men to salvation. He finally settled
at Hampole, where he ended his life in seclusion, writing
incessantly, and edifying the neighbourhood by his devotion ; he died the year of the great plague, 1349. Scarcely
was he dead than his tomb attracted pilgrims, pious people
brought offerings there, miracles were performed. In the

---

[1] Lord Berners' " Froissart," cap. ccclxxxi.
[2] " Chronicon Angliae," 1328–1388, Thompson's edition, 1874, p. 322.

nuns' convent at Hampole, which drew from the vicinity
of his tomb great honour and profit, an "Office of St.
Richard, the hermit," was composed, as we have seen,
to be sung when he should be canonized. But the office
of the old hermit and itinerant preacher has never had
occasion to be sung down to the present day.[1]

The wandering preachers met with in the villages
were not always Lollards sent by Wyclif, nor inspired
men who, like Rolle of Hampole, held their mission
from their conscience and from God ; they were often
members of an immense and powerful caste sub-divided
into several orders, that of the mendicant friars. The
two principal branches were the Dominicans, Preachers, or
Black friars, and the Franciscans, Friars minor or Grey
friars, both established in England in the thirteenth century,[2] the " men of this [world] that most wide walken,"
said Langland.[3]

The immortal satires of Chaucer should not blind
us to the initial merit of these orders, nor cause us
to see in the members thereof, at all times, nothing
but impudent and idle vagabonds, at once impious,
superstitious, and greedy—

> "A Frere ther was, a wantoun and a merye;
> *   *   *   *   *
> Ful wel biloved, and famulier was he

---

[1] " English Prose Treatises of Richard Rolle of Hampole," edited
by Rev George Perry, 1866, Early English Text Society, Preface, pp.
ix, xv–xix. See before, p. 141.
[2] The Dominicans in 1221 ; the Franciscans in 1224. See Dr.
Jessopp, " The Coming of the Friars," London, 1888, pp. 32–34, a work
in which shine the ample knowledge and wide sympathies of the late rector
of East Dereham, the " Arcady for better for worse " where he spent so
many years. When Taine made his last visit to England I wanted, if I
may be permitted to recall a personal souvenir, to give him a lunch where
each of those invited would be a representative Englishman. Robert
Browning represented poetry ; Augustus Jessopp, who deeply impressed
the chief guest, the country clergy.
[3] " Vision," Text C, pas. xi. l. 14.

With frankeleyns overal in his cuntre,
And eek with worthi wommen of the toun;

   *   *   *   *   *

Ful sweetly herde he confessioun,
And plesaunt was his absolucioun.
He was an esy man to yeve penance,
Ther as he wiste to han a good pitance;
For unto a povre ordre for to geve
Is signe that a man is wel i-shreve.

   *   *   *   *   *

He knew wel the tavernes in every toun,
And every ostiller or gay tapstere." [1]

A WORLDLY ECCLESIASTIC.
(*From the MS.* 10 E. *IV.*)

In Chaucer's days, such friars were many, but some
better ones could also be met ; not only those, rare indeed
in the fourteenth century, who continued the traditions
of their founder, living among the poor, poor as they,
and withal wise, devout, and compassionate : Chaucer's
friar was of a different sort ; he avoided acquaintance
with " a lazer or a beggere," unwilling to deal " with
such poraile." But even among those who lived careless
of the rule, some were at work whose thoughts, dangerous

[1] Prologue to " Canterbury Tales."

as they might be, were not so base, those friars namely
who, when the moment came, could be confounded with
the simple priests of their enemy Wyclif, and who were
certainly comprised along with them in the statute of
1382. Certain it is that many friars, in their roaming
career, preached in the market place, just like John Ball,
the new doctrines of emancipation. Hence they alone
among the clergy, at the hour of the great revolt, still
preserved a certain popularity among the lowly ; and the
monastic chroniclers, their natural enemies, complacently
paraded in their narratives this new grievance against these
detested orders.[1] Langland, who cursed the revolt, cursed
also the friars for having a share of responsibility in it.
Envy has whispered into their ears and said : study logic,
law, and the hollow dreams of philosophers, and go from
village to village proving that all property ought to be
in common—the very teaching of John Ball :

> " and proven hit by Seneca
> That alle thyng under hevene · ouhte to beo in comune." [2]

Always armed with good sense, Langland plainly
declares that the author of these subversive theories lies ;
the Bible says, " Thou shalt not covet thy neighbour's
goods." Formerly the life of the friars was exemplary,
Charity dwelt among them ; this was in the days of
the great saint of Assisi, the friend of men, the friend of
birds, the friend of all that had been created and could
suffer.[3]

[1] Jack Straw, according to the confession which his contemporary the
monk Thomas Walsingham relates of him, would have liked to keep no
other ecclesiastics on earth but the mendicant friars : " Soli mendicantes
vixissent super terram qui suffecissent pro sacris celebrandis aut conferendis
universæ terræ." " Historia Anglicana," vol. ii. p. 10, Rolls Series.

[2] " Piers Plowman," Skeat's edition, Text C, pass. xxiii. l. 274.

[3]   " Ac it is ferre agoo · in seynt Fraunceys tyme."
Text B, pass. xv. l. 226.

And, indeed, what a holy mission their founder had given them ! Coarsely dressed, barefoot, getting only such food as was freely offered them, they were to go into the towns and visit the poorest, most densely popu- lated and unhealthiest suburbs, to seek out the lost.

" And all the brothers," said Francis, in his rule, " are to be clad in mean habits, and may blessedly mend them with sacks and other pieces ; whom I admonish and exhort, that they do not despise or censure such men as they see clad in curious and gay garments and using delicate meats and drinks, but rather let every one judge and despise himself." They must never quarrel, but be " meek, peacable, modest, mild and humble. . . . And they are not to ride unless some manifest necessity or infirmity oblige them. Whatsoever house they go into, they shall first say, ' Peace be unto this house,' and, accord- ing to the Gospel, it shall be lawful for them to eat of all meats that are set before them." They must beg in order to get the necessaries of life, but they must receive them in kind, never in money. " The brothers shall not make anything their own, neither house nor place, nor any other thing ; and they shall go confidently to beg alms like pilgrims and strangers in this world, serving our Lord in poverty and humility." [1]

All the miseries, all the hideous blemishes of humanity, every kind of outcasts, the physical or moral lepers, were to have their sympathy ; and the lower classes in return would love and venerate them, and grow morally better, owing to their word and example. Eccleston relates that a friar minor once put on his sandals without permission to go to matins. He dreamt afterwards that he was arrested by robbers, who cried out, " Kill him ! Kill him ! "

" But I am a friar minor," said he, sure of being respected.

[1] " The Rule and Life of the Friars Minors," in Dugdale's " Monas- ticon Anglicanum," London, 1817, vol. vi. p. 1504.

"Thou liest, for thou art not barefoot." [1]

The first of their duties was to remain poor, in order to be able, having nothing to lose, fearlessly to use firm language to the rich and powerful of the world. When on his death-bed, in 1253, wise and courageous Robert Grosseteste, Bishop of Lincoln, a great friend of theirs, and because a friend of theirs, reminded them of their rule, appropriately quoting a line of Juvenal's .

"Cantabit vacuus coram latrone viator."

The friars were to be like the traveller without money, whose peace of mind is never disturbed by meeting robbers.[2]

St. Francis had not wished his friars to be men of learning and study ; he was afraid especially of those subtle theological and metaphysical researches which uselessly absorbed the life of so many great clerics. Others enough, he thought, would devote themselves to such speculations ; he wanted to fill a gap and in this line there was no gap. His rule was so strict that the famous Roger Bacon, who belonged to his order, had to apply to the pope to be permitted to use ink and parchment [3] What the saint desired was to send throughout the world an army of missionaries who would devote themselves materially and morally to the welfare, body and soul, of all the weary, the derelict, the dregs of humanity. Thus practised, with no room left for the pride of knowledge, disinterestedness was the more absolute, servitude the

---

[1] "Liber de adventu Minorum in Angliam," in "Monumenta Franciscana," ed. Brewer, Rolls Series, 1858, p. 28. The author, Thomas of Eccleston, himself a Franciscan, saw the most flourishing period of the mendicant orders ; his book, of extreme naïveté, abounds in visions and tales of wonders.

[2] Matthew Paris, "Historia Anglorum," London, 1866, vol. iii. p. 145, Rolls Series.

[3] "Monumenta Franciscana," Rolls, p. xxix.

more voluntary, and the effect on the masses the greater.
The subtlety of teachers was not necessary for the ful-
filling of this task ; and the striking example of the
poverty of the consoler, heedless of his own troubles, was the
best of consolations.   Above all, the vanity of the apostle
must be killed, the greatness of his merit must be apparent
to God only.   With a heart so purified he would neces-
sarily have a sufficient comprehension of the problems
of life and of the high moral aims accessible even to
the lowest to be naturally eloquent ; the study of the
" Summæ," in repute, was useless.

But too many dangers surrounded the sublime foundation, and the first was knowledge itself.   " The Emperor
Charles, Roland and Oliver," once said the Saint, " and
all the paladins and all strong men, have pursued the
infidel in battle till death, and with great pains and
labour have won their memorable victories.   The holy
martyrs died struggling for the faith of Christ.   But in
our days there are people who seek glory and honour
among men simply by the narration of the deeds of heroes.
In like manner there are some among you who take more
pleasure in writing and preaching on the merits of the
saints than in imitating their works."   This reply St.
Francis made to a novice who wished to have a psalter.
He humorously added, " When you have a psalter you
will wish to have a breviary, and when you have a breviary
you will sit in a chair like a great prelate, and will say to
your brother, ' Brother, fetch me my breviary.' " [1]

The popularity of the friars had soon become immense,[2]

[1] " Speculum Vitæ B. Francisi et sociorum ejus, opera fratris Guil.
Spoelberch," Antwerp, 1620, part i. cap. 4.

[2] Thirty-two years after the friars had appeared in England, they
already possessed forty-nine convents (" Monumenta Franciscana," ed.
Brewer, 1858, p. 10).   In Matthew Paris will be found a good description
of the behaviour of the friars minor in England on their arrival, of the poor,
humble, and useful life that they first led.   " Historia Anglorum," ed.
Madden, 1866, vol. ii. p. 109.

and it was found that they had monopolized in England everything that concerned religion.[1] By a quite human contradiction—let Brutus be Cæsar—their poverty had invited riches, and their self-denial power ; the hovels where they lodged at first had become sumptuous monasteries with chapels as large as cathedrals ; the rich wanted to be buried there, in tombs chiselled with the latest refinements of the florid Gothic. Their apologists of the fifteenth century relate with admiration that in their fine library at London, for in spite of the rule they had a fine library, there was a tomb adorned with four cherubims ; [2] that their church, begun in 1306, was three hundred feet long, ninety-five wide, and sixty-four feet high, with the columns all of marble as well as the pavement. Kings and princes had enriched the building ; some had given the altars, others the stalls ; Edward III, " for the repose of the soul of the most illustrious Queen Isabella, buried in the choir " (who had ended her immoral life in the habit of the Santa Clara nuns), repaired the great middle window, blown down by the wind. In the same church was preserved the heart of Queen Eleanor, mother of Edward I. Relating that it was there, Rishanger, a monk of Saint Albans and a contemporary, made thereupon a remark, which Walsingham, also a monk of St. Albans, gleefully reproduced in his " Historia Anglicana ": " Her body was buried in the monastery of Ambresbury, but her heart in London, in the church of the Minorites, who, like all friars of every order, claim for themselves something of the bodies of any powerful persons dying ; after the manner of the dogs assembling

---

[1] See " Defensionem curatorum contra eos qui privilegiatos se dicunt " (4to, undated), a speech made in 1357, by Richard Fitz-Ralph, Archbishop of Armagh, in which are denounced the successive encroachments of the mendicant friars to the detriment of the secular clergy.

[2] " Monumenta Franciscana," ut supra, pp. 514, etc. This library had been founded by the celebrated Richard Whittington, who was Mayor of London in 1397–98, 1406–07, and 1419–20.

round corpses, where each one greedily awaits his portion
to devour." [1] Gilbert de Clare, Earl of Gloucester, had
given for the same building twenty trees from his forest
of Tunbridge. Rich merchants, the mayor, the aldermen,
followed suit. The names of the donors were inscribed
on the windows, and Langland was indignant, and recalled
the precept, " Let not thy left hand know what thy right
hand doeth." We learn thus that the third window on
the west had been given by Walter Mordon, " stoke-
fyschmonger," and Mayor of London. The second
window on the south was due to John of Charlton, knight,
and his wife, whose arms figured in it ; the fourth to
Walter de Gorst, fellmonger of London ; the fifth to the
Earl of Lancaster ; the fourth on the west to " various
collections, and thus it does not bear a name." One of
the donors is styled the special father and friend of the
friars minor.

It could be but a delight for the Wyclifites to reproach
the friars with all these mundane splendours ; Wyclif
revels in it :

" Freris bylden mony grete chirchis and costily waste
housis, and cloystris as hit were castels, and that with-
oute nede. . . . Grete housis make not men holy, and
onely by holynesse is God wel served." Those convents
are " Caymes Castelis." [2]

Interminable lists, too, of cardinals, bishops, and
kings who have belonged to the order are drawn up, not
forgetting even " certain persons of importance in the
world,"—the very antithesis of their founder's intent.
Finally, they enumerate the dead who at the last moment
assumed the habit of the friars : " Brother Sir Roger

---

[1] " More canum cadaveribus assistentium, ubi quisque suam parti-
culam avide consumendam expectat."   Rolls Series, vol. i. 38 ; *sub anno*
1291–92.

[2] Wyclif's " Select English Works," ed. Thos. Arnold, 1869, vol. iii.
pp. 348, 380.

PSALM SINGING.   THE INTERIOR OF A FRIAR'S CHURCH.   [*p.* 299.
(*From the MS. Domit. A.* xvii. *in the British Museum.*)

Bourne, knight, buried at Norwich in the friars' habit, 1334."[1]

The pride and riches of the Dominicans are just as great. The author of " Pierce the Ploughman's Crede," towards the end of the fourteenth century, accurately describes one of their monasteries, the splendid columns to be seen there, the sculptures, paintings, and gildings that adorn the chapter house, so beautiful that it obviously reminds the author of the one at Westminster, or of the painted chamber, " la chambre peinte," where at times Parliament sat :

" As a Parlement-hous · y-peynted aboute,"

the magnificent stained glass windows ornamented with the arms of the nobles or the mark of the merchants who have given them (" merkes of marchauntes "), and " lovely ladies," their bronze figures lying on the slabs, " in many gay garmentes," the imposing tombs of knights heightened with gold.[2]

The proportions are reversed ; as great as the modesty required by the holy founder was now the pride. The faults Chaucer reproaches them with creep in among them ; they become interested, greedy, coarse men of the world. The necessity for them to live among the laity had been one of their chief dangers ; they were to save the laity, but were instead corrupted by it ; they caught the plague that they were to cure. Before even the middle of the

[1] " Monumenta Franciscana," p. 541. Hence the reproaches of the satirists :

" Of these frer mynours me thenkes moch wonder,
   That waxen are thus hauteyn, that som tyme weren under."

Thomas Wright's " Political Poems and Songs," 1859, vol. i. p. 268, Rolls Series.

[2] " Pierce the Ploughman's Crede," ed. Skeat, 1867, Early English Text Society, pp. 7–9 ; written about 1394 ; author unknown, the same possibly who composed " The Plowman's Tale," e.g. in Wright's " Political Poems," both works strongly influenced by Langland's " Visions."

thirteenth century, one of them had had a revelation that ' Demons celebrated every year a council against the order, and had found three means (to pervert it), that is, intercourse with women, the receiving of useless persons, and the handling of money." [1]

Mendicity is now their trade, which some practice well, others better ; miracles of self-denial were demanded of them, and behold, on the contrary, prodigies of selfishness. It is no longer religion, it is their order which must be promoted ; they preach not on behalf of Christ, but on behalf of their convent ; the reversal is complete. All borrow largely from the treasure of good works amassed by their first apostles and spend it madly. The respect of the multitude lessens, their renown for holiness declines ; they cast into the other scale of the balance so many faults and disorders that it overweighs. And what remains henceforth ? Superstition replaces devotion ; some, in spite of the rule, have studied metaphysics and sciences, the *trivium*, the *quadrivium* [2] ; for a larger number, however, it is not learning but a gross materialism that veils the superhuman ideal of Francis of Assisi. Contact with their habit is equivalent to a good deed ; if the dress is assumed on the death bed the demons will take flight. Numberless visions have revealed to them these articles of a new faith : " Thei techen lordis and namely ladies," says Wyclif, " that if they dyen in Fraunceys habite, thei schul nevere cum in helle for vertu thereof." [3]

[1] " Liber de adventu Minorum," in " Monumenta Franciscana," p. 52.
[2] Grammar, logic, rhetoric—Arithmetic, geometry, music, astronomy.
[3] " Select English Works," vol. iii. p. 382. A satire of the fourteenth century states in the same way :

> " Isti fratres prædicant per villas et forum
> Quod si mortem gustet quis in habitu minorum
> Non intrabit postea locum tormentorum,
> Sed statim perducitur ad regna cœlorum."

But if burial is requested for a pauper in one of their privileged churches, " the keeper is absent," is the answer, and admittance is refused :

And so it came to pass that, not only poets like
Chaucer and Langland, not only reformers like Wyclif,
but also the universities [1] and the monks of the old-
established orders, waged open war against the friars.
To which the monks were moved partly, it is true, by
jealousy, when they saw these newly created brotherhoods
rising in importance, in numbers and in wealth, but partly,
also, by the sight of undeniable abuses and worldliness.
In such an authoritative work as the " English History,"
written in St. Albans Abbey by Chaucer's contemporary,
Thomas Walsingham, the present state and behaviour of
the friars is thus described : " The friars, unmindful of
their profession, have even forgotten to what end their
orders were instituted ; for the holy men their law-givers
desired them to be poor and free of all kind of temporal
possessions, that they should not have anything which
they might fear to lose on account of saying the truth.
But now they are envious of possessors, approve the
crimes of the great, induce the commonalty into error,
and praise the sins of both ; and with the intent of acquiring possessions, they who had renounced possessions,
with the intent of gathering money, they who had sworn
to persevere in poverty, call good evil and evil good,
leading astray princes by adulation, the people by lies,
and drawing both with themselves out of the straight

" Gardianus absens est, statim respondetur
Et sic satis breviter pauper excludetur."

Wright's " Political Poems," Rolls Series, vol. i. pp. 256–57.

[1] The complaints of the University of Oxford against the friars, stating
how they wrongfully attracted with fruit and drink mere children, and
taught them how to beg and to ingratiate themselves with the great, were
among the severest : " Nam pomis et potu, ut populus fabulatur, puerulos
ad religionem attrahunt et instigant, quos professos non instruunt sicut
exigit ætas illa, sed mendicationis discursibus permittunt intendere ; atque
tempus, quo possint addiscere, captandis favoribus amicorum, dominarum
et dominorum, sinunt consumere, in offensam parentium, puerorum periculum et ordinis detrimentum." Year 1358, " Munimenta Academica,"
Rolls Series, i. p. 207.

path." Walsingham adds that a familiar proverb in his time was, "He is a friar, therefore a liar." [1]

The sanctity of the institution and the unworthiness of many of its members caused it to be at once venerated and detested ; however contemptible be the man, what if, after all, the keys of heaven were in his hand ? Respect mingled with fear in the feeling for him. Thus poets laughed at the friars, popular story-tellers scouted them ; distrust, doubt, contempt spread, extending from the lowly friar to the reverend bishop himself ; churchmen

SPRINKLING DINERS WITH HOLY WATER.
(*From the MS.* 10 E. IV.)

were caricatured on the very stalls upon which they sat ; Master Reynard was represented delivering a sermon while wearing episcopal insignia, and neither the miniaturist, charged with illuminating an imposing volume of Decretals, nor those who had entrusted him with the work, found anything improper in his satirising on the margin the whole ecclesiastical hierarchy, from bishops to monks or clerks. One of the latter is shown forgetting in the kitchen his sprinkler and bucket of holy water ;

[1] " Hic est frater, ergo mendax." " Historia Anglicana," 1867–69, vol. ii. p. 13, Rolls Series.

then remembering what he has come for and going to sprinkle the masters at table, then returning to the kitchen maid.[1] In the same ironical spirit the author of a popular song of the fourteenth century wrote :

> " Preste ne monke ne yit chanoun,
> Ne no man of religioun,
> Gyfen hem so to devocioun
>   As done thes holy frers.
> For summe gyven ham to chyvalry,
> Somme to riote and ribaudery ;
> Bot ffrers gyven ham to grete study,
>   And to grete prayers."

Several stanzas follow which cannot be quoted.[2]

The people, therefore, fitfully saw in the friars their protectors and allies in case of revolt, while at other times they pursued them in the streets with stones, struck them and lacerated their garments : angels or else devils ? they were not sure. " At the same time the preaching friars took to flight because they feared to be maltreated and ruined, because the commonalty bore with them very reluctantly, on account of their proud behaviour, for they did not behave as friars ought."[3]

" Know ye," says the king, " that we have understood, that some persons of our kingdom of England, by the instigation of the evil spirit, . . . do and daily strive to do harm and scandal to our beloved in Christ, the religious men, friars of the order of minors, . . . openly and secretly stirring up our people against them to destroy the houses of the said friars, tearing their habits from them, striking some, and ill-treating them, against our peace."[4]

From another point of view, that of public safety, the

---

[1] Brit. Mus. MS. Roy. 10 E. IV, fol. 100, ff. See also in MS. 17 C. xv. in the British Museum a satirical picture of a "ffryer."
[2] Wright's " Political Poems," vol. i. p. 263.
[3] 20 Ed. II., " Croniques de London," ed. Aungier, Camden Society, p. 54.
[4] Proclamation of Richard II, year 1385 ; Rymer's " Foedera," ed. 1704, vol. vii. p. 458.

Commons were indignant at the number of foreigners among the friars, whom they considered a permanent danger to the State. They requested "that all the alien friars, of whatever habit they might be, should void the realm before the Feast of St. Michael, and if they remained beyond the said feast they should be held as out of the common law," that is, outlawed.[1]

The friars kept their assurance, they were blessed in the days of their good deeds ; now they speak loud and make themselves feared ; to the Pope alone they are amenable ; they carry their heads high, their power is independent, they have become a church within the Church. Along with the priest who preaches and confesses in his parish is to be seen the wandering friar, who preaches and confesses everywhere ; his universal presence and power are sources of conflict ; the parish priest finds himself abandoned ; the religious wayfarer brings the unknown, the extraordinary, and everybody runs to him. He lays down his staff and wallet and begins to talk ; his language is that of the people, the whole parish is present ; he busies himself with their eternal welfare, and also with their earthly interests, for lay life is familiar to him, and he can give appropriate advice. But his teaching is sometimes suspicious. "These false prophets," says not Wyclif, but the Council of Saltzburg in 1386, "by their sermons full of fables often lead astray the souls of their hearers" ; they make game of the authority of the parish priests.[2]

To stop their progress proved impossible. The tide rose and swept away the embankments ; the excellent had become the worst, *corruptio optimi pessima*, and the old adage was verified to the letter. In spite of grievances, protests, derisive songs and stories, they were met everywhere, in the hut and in the castle, begging from the rich

[1] "Rolls of Parliament," 20 E. III, vol. ii. p. 162, A.D. 1346.
[2] Labbe, "Sacrosancta Concilia," Florence, vol. xxvi. col. 729.

and knocking also at the door of the poor. They sat at the board of the noble, who treated them with consideration ; with him they played the part of the fashionable man of religion ; they interested, they pleased. Wyclif shows them creeping into familiarity with the great, liking " to speke bifore lordis and sitte at tho mete with hom, . . . also to be confessoures of lordis and ladyes." [1] Langland, in " Piers Plowman," is equally severe on " frere Flaterere." In a Wyclifite treatise of the same period we read, " Thei geten hem worldly offis in lordis courtis, and summe to ben conseilours and reuleris of werris, and also to ben chamberleyns to lordes and ladies." [2]

Courting popularity among all people, they were different men and acted differently in the villages where they made their rounds ; to their wallet they added store of thread, needles, ointments, with which they traded :

" Thei becomen pedleris, berynge knyves, pursis, pynnys and girdlis and spices and sylk and precious pellure and forrouris for wymmen, and therto smale gentil hondis (dogs), to gete love of hem. ' [3]

They were more and more the subject of song and cause of mirth, but they did not mind, being the better advertised thereby :

> " Thai wandren here and there,
> And dele with dyvers marcerye,
>   Right as thai pedlers were.
> Thai dele with purses, pynnes, and knyves,
> With gyrdles, gloves, for whenches and wyves." [4]

---

[1] " Select English Works," vol. iii. p. 396.
[2] " The English Works of Wyclif, hitherto unprinted," edited by F. D. Matthew, Early English Text Society, 1880, p. 13. Most of the pieces in this collection are only attributed to Wyclif, this one among them. See also Gower's " Vox Clamantis," Roxburghe Club, 1850, p. 228.
[3] " English Works of Wyclif hitherto unprinted," p. 12.
[4] So also in Chaucer's " Prologue " :

> " His typet was ay farsud ful of knyfes
> And pynnes, for to yive faire wyfes."

The anonymous author, a contemporary of Chaucer,
adds :

> " I was a frere ful many a day,
> Therefor the sothe I wate (know).
> But when I sawe that thair lyvyng
> Acordyd not to thair preching,
> Of I cast my frer clothing,
> And wyghtly went my gate " (my way).[1]

Between the scepticism of the century and blind
credulity, superstition flourished. The friars pretended
they could sell the merits of their order at retail. They
were so numerous and prayed so devoutly, that they had
a surp.us of piyers in store. Why not distribute this
superfluous wealth to men of faith and good will ? They
did so, for cash of course ; it was an exchange of wealth ;
like will to ike. The friars went about the country dis-
counting these invisible riches, and sel ing to pious souls,
under the name of *letters of fraternity*, drafts upon heaven.
What is the use of these parchments ? they were asked.
They give a share in the merits of the whole order of St.
Francis.—What are they good for ? Wyclif was asked.
" Bi siche resouns thinken many men tha: thes lettris
mai do good for to covere mostard pottis." [2]

Discredited as they were at the end of the century,
the friars had not, however, lost all hold over the people.
Henry IV usurped the throne, and soon found that he
must reckon with the friars. A good many among them
were indignant at his enterprise, and some preached here
and there, during the first years of his reign, that Richard II
was still living and was the true king, and this was one
more case, and a very important one, of political ideas
vulgarised by wayfarers throughout the country. Henry IV
sent them to gaol. One who was brought before him

[1] Wright's " Political Poems and Songs," 1859, vol. i. pp. 264 and 268.
[2] " Select English Works," vol. i. p. 381. See also Wright's " Political
Poems and Songs," 1859, vol. i. p. 257.

reproached him violently for the deposition of Richard :
"But I have not usurped the crown, I have been elected,"
said the king.—"The election is null if the legitimate
king is living ; if he is dead he is dead by thy means ;
if he was killed by thee, thou canst have any title to the
throne."—"By my head," cried the prince, "I will have
thine cut off ! "

The accused were advised to throw themselves on the
king's mercy ; they refused, and requested to be regularly tried by a jury. Neither in the city nor in Holborn
could any one be found to sit on that jury ; inhabitants
of Highgate and Islington had to be fetched for the purpose. These men declared the friars guilty ; the poor
wretches were drawn to Tyburn, hanged, then beheaded,
and their heads were placed on London Bridge (1402).
The convent was permitted to gather their remains, and
bury them in holy ground. The Islington and Highgate jurors came weeping to the Franciscans to implore
their pardon for a verdict of which they repented.

For several years, in spite of these punishments, friars
continued to preach about the country in favour of
Richard II, maintaining that he still lived, although
Henry IV had taken care to have a public exhibition in
London of the corpse of his assassinated predecessor.[1]

In the fifteenth century the reputation of the friars
only grew worse. The abuses of which they were the
living personification were among those which best served

---

[1] "Eulogium historiarum," ed. Haydon, Rolls Series, London, 1858,
vol. iii. p. 392. What the condemned friars were accused of was thus
explained to them : "Similiter vos in hypocrisi, adulatione et falsa vita
audivistis falsas confessiones in quibus injunxistis populo pro pœnitentia
ut quærerent regem Ricardum in Wallia. Vos etiam in hypocrisi, adulatione et falsa vita collegistis magnam summam pecuniæ mendicando et misistis
ad Audeonum (Owen) Glendour proditorem, ut veniat et destruat totam
linguam Anglicanam," a language which Henry prided himself in speaking
and which he had used in parliament to claim the crown. "Rolls of Parliament," iii. 422.

to draw later adherents to Luther. If there remained in
their ranks men who knew how to die, like that unfortunate
friar Forest, who was hung alive by chains above a wood
fire and slowly roasted, while Bishop Latimer, himself to
be burnt later, addressed the dying man " with pious
exhortations " to repentance,[1] the mass of them remained
the object of universal contempt. This was one of the
few points on which it sometimes happened that Catholics
and Protestants agreed. Sir Thomas More, beheaded
for the Catholic faith, spoke of the friars in the same strain
as his adversary Tyndal, strangled for the Protestant
faith. In his eyes they were but dangerous vagabonds.
He relates, in his " Utopia," the dispute between a friar
and a fool, on the question of pauperism. " ' You will
never,' said the friar, ' get rid of beggars, unless you also
make an edict against us friars.' ' Well,' said the fool,
' it is already made, the cardinal passed a very good law
against you when he decreed that all vagabonds should
be seized and made to work, for you are the greatest
vagabonds that can be.' When this was said, and all
eyes being turned on the cardinal, they saw he did not
disown it ; every one, not unwillingly, began to smile,
except the friar." [2]

A class, as historians have observed, which no longer
justifies its privileges by its services, is in imminent danger ;
if it reforms in time, it may be saved ; if it does not, it
is doomed. In England, the friars were doomed. But
nothing is ever entirely lost, and while, for centuries,
Chaucer's merriment made people merry at the expense
of the begging orders, it is only fair, before parting with
them, to recall such an unprejudiced testimony as that of

---

[1] Year 1533, Holinshed, " Chronicles," London, 1587, vol. iii. p. 945.
Friar Forest had refused the oath of supremacy.

[2] " Libellus vere aureus . . . de optimo reipublicæ statu deque noua
Insula Vtopia . . . cura P. Ægidii . . . nunc primum . . . editus,"
Louvain, 1516, lib. i.

Bacon, in his essay " Of Love ":   " There is in man's nature a secret inclination and motion towards love of others, which, if it be not spent upon some one or a few, doth naturally spread itself towards many, and maketh men become humane and charitable ; as it is seen sometime in friars."

A GAME OF FOX AND GEESE.
(*From the MS.* 10 *E. IV.*)

CHAPTER II

THE PARDONERS

"INDULGENCE" was at first simply a commutation of penance. The punishments inflicted for sins were of long duration ; fasting and mortification had to be carried on for months and years. The faithful were permitted to transform these interminable chastisements into shorter expiation. Thus a clerk might exchange a year of penance against three hundred lashes, reciting a psalm at each hundred.[1] Tables of such exchanges were drawn up by competent prelates. The learned and autocratic Theodore, born at Tarsus, Cilicia, an encyclopædic mind and a strong disciplinarian, archbishop of Canterbury from 669 to 690, who left on the British church a permanent mark, had published a tariff allowing people to be excused of a month's penance on bread and water if they sang instead twelve hundred psalms with bended knees ; for a year's penance the singing was increased, and each course of psalter singing was accompanied with three hundred strokes in the palm of the hand (*palmatæ*). But it was possible to compensate

[1] Hardy, " Registrum palatinum Dunelmense," vol. iii. p. cxxxiv.

a year's penance and escape at the same time the psalms, fasts and strokes by paying a hundred shillings in alms.[1] In another such table, drawn up in the ninth century by Halitgarius, bishop of Cambrai, is found this additional facility, that if the sinner, sentenced to a month's penance on bread and water, chooses rather the singing of psalms he may be allowed not to kneel while he sings, but then instead of twelve hundred he will have to sing fifteen hundred and eighty psalms. He may in the same manner be excused of more than one month, up to twelve, in which last case, if he chooses not to kneel, he will have to sing no less than twenty thousand one hundred and sixty psalms.[2]

Laymen, who had their choice, frequently preferred a payment in money, the rich having to pay more than the poor, and the sums thus obtained were usually well employed. We have seen them serve for the support of roads and bridges ; they were also applied in reconstructing churches, in helping the sick of a hospital, and in covering the expenses of numerous public enterprises. The entirety of punishments was taken off by a plenary indulgence ; thus the French pope, Urban II, at the Council of Clermont, in 1095, granted one to all those who, through pure devotion and not to acquire booty or glory, should go to Jerusalem to fight the infidel ; and this was the first crusade.

Little by little the idea of an actual commutation vanished, and was replaced by a different system, known as the theory of the " Treasury." It had indeed become obvious as the use of indulgences spread, and they were more and more easily gained, that they could no longer be justified as offering to the sinner only his choice between

[1] " Theodori archiepiscopi Cantuariensis pœnitentiale," in Migne's " Patrologia," vol. xcix. col. 938 and 940.
[2] " Halitgarii episcopi Cameracensis liber pœnitentialis," in Migne's " Patrologia," vol. cv. col. 706.

several sorts of even penances. They were something else. A short, well selected prayer, a small gift in money, would now exempt devout people from the greatest penalties and from numberless years of a possible purgatory ; the one could scarcely be considered as the equivalent of the other ; how was the equilibrium established between the two scales ? The answer was that the deficiency was made up by the application to the sinner of merits, not indeed his own, but of Christ, the Virgin, and the sain s, of which there was an inexhaustible " treasury," the dispensation of which rested with the Pope and the clergy.

This theory was acted upon long before being put forth in express words ; it does not appear to have been more than vaguely alluded to before the fourteenth century, when Pope Clement VI, the " Doctor Doctorum," gave a perfectly clear definition and exposition of the " treasury " system. In a bull of the year 1350, he explains that the merits of Christ are infinite, and those of the Virgin and the saints, superabundant. This excess of unemployed merit has been constituted into a treasury, " not one that is deposited in a strong room, or concealed in a field, but which is to be usefully distributed to the faithful, through the blessed Peter, keeper of heaven's gate, and his successors." However largely employed, there ought to be " no fear of an absorption or a diminution of this treasury, first on account of the infinite merits of Christ, as has been said before, then because the more numerous are the people reclaimed through the use of its contents, the more it is augmented by the addition of their merits." [1] The treasury had therefore no chance of ever being found empty, since the more was drawn from it the more it grew. Such is in all its simplicity the theory of the " treasury," which has ever since been maintained, with no change in the theory but much in the practice.

[1] See Appendix XIII, p. 438.

With so much to distribute among the faithful, the Church had recourse, for insuring its repartition, to certain people who went about, supplied with official letters, and who offered to good Christians a particle of the heavenly wealth placed at the disposal of the successors of Peter. They expected in return some portion of the earthly riches their hearers might be possessed of, and which could be applied to more tangible uses than the " treasury." The men entrusted with this mission were called sometimes *questors*, on account of what they asked, and sometimes *pardoners*, on account of what they gave.[1]

Many a man lives in our remembrance owing to his portrait. If his image had not been preserved by an artist of genius his memory would have been abolished. Who would remember, but for her tomb at Lucca, lovely Ilaria del Carretto ? Many among us would not suspect that the long vanished pardoner ever existed if the master-painter, Chaucer, had not drawn, from life, his unlovely portrait. " Lordyngs," says the one in the " Canterbury Tales ":

> " Lordyngs, quod he, in chirches whan I preche,
> I peyne me to have an hauteyn speche,
> And ryng it out, as lowd as doth a belle,
> For I can al by rote which that I telle.
> My teeme is alway oon, and ever was ;
> *Radix omnium malorum est cupiditas.*"

In the pulpit he leans to the right, to the left, he gesticulates, wanders in his talk ; his arms move as much as his tongue ; it is a wonder to see and hear him:

> " I stonde lik a clerk in my pulpit,
> And whan the lewed people is doun i-set,
> I preche so as ye have herd before,
> And telle hem an hondred japes more.

---

[1] The two words were used as interchangeable. Du Cange quotes a text of 1389, reading : " Come il fust venu en la ville de Necie près Faloise un questeur ou porteur de pardons." *Sub verbo* " Perdonantia."

Than peyne I me to strecche forth my necke
And est and west upon the people I bekke,
As doth a dowfe (pigeon), syttyng on a berne;
Myn hondes and my tonge goon so yerne,
That it is joye to se my businesse.

*   *   *   *   *

I preche no thyng but of coveityse.
Therefor my teem is yit, and ever was,
Radix omnium malorum est cupiditas."

The description may seem to-day improbable and
exaggerated, but it is not. A verifying from authentic
sources and a search for documents only shows once
more Chaucer's marvellous exactness ; not a trait in his
picture that may not be justified by letters from papal
or episcopal chanceries.

These *quæstores,* or *quæstiarii,* as they were officially
called, were, says Boniface IX, speaking at the very
time that the poet wrote his tales, sometimes secular
clerics and sometimes friars, most of them extremely
impudent. They dispensed with ecclesiastic licences,
and went from place to place delivering speeches, showing
their relics and selling their pardons. It was a lucrative
trade and the competition was great ; the success of
authorized pardoners had caused a crowd of self-appointed
ones to issue from the school or the priory, or from
mere nothingness, greedy, with glittering eyes, as in the
" Canterbury Tales " : " suche glaryng eyghen hadde he
as an hare " ; true vagabonds, infesters of the highroads, who having, as they thought, nothing to fear,
boldly carried on their impostor's traffic. They over-
awed their listeners, spoke loud, and unbound upon
earth without scruple all that might be bound in heaven.
Much profit arose therefrom ; Chaucer's pardoner got
a hundred marks a year, which was easy enough for him,
since, having received no authority from any one, to no
one did he render any accounts, but kept all the gains for

himself. In his measured language the Pope tells us as much as the poet, and it seems as though he would dupli- cate, line by line, the portrait drawn by the story-teller, his contemporary.

First, says the pontifical letter, these pardoners swear that they were sent by the Court of Rome. " Certain religious, who even belong to one or the other of the mendicant orders, and some secular clerks, even endowed with privileged benefices, affirm that they are sent by us or by the legates or the nuncios of the apostolic see, and that they have received a mission to treat of certain affairs, . . . to receive money for us and the Roman Church, and they go about the country under these pretexts."

From Rome also comes Chaucer's personage ; he moves about the country, and in exchange for his pardons tirelessly asks for goods and money, which certainly will not go to Rome :

> " a gentil pardoner . . .
> That streyt was comen from the court of Rome . . .
> His walet lay byforn him in his lappe,
> Bret-ful of pardoun come from Rome al hoot."

*　　*　　*　　*　　*

> " What ! trowe ye, whiles that I may preche
> And wynne gold and silver for I teche,
> That I wil lyve in povert wilfully ?

*　　*　　*　　*　　*

> For I wol preche and begge in sondry londes,
> I wil not do no labour with myn hondes . . .
> I wol noon of thapostles counterfete,
> I wol have money, wolle, chese, and whete."

" Thus," continues the Pope, " they proclaim to the faithful and simple people (" the lewed people," says Chaucer's man) the real or pretended authorizations which they have received ; and irreverently abusing those which are real, in pursuit of infamous and hateful gain, they carry further their impudence by mendaciously attributing to themselves false and pretended authorizations of this kind."

What does the poet say ? That the charlatan has ever fine things to show, that he knows how to dazzle the simple, that he has his bag full of parchments with awe-inspiring seals, maybe genuine, maybe not ; [1] that the people look on and admire, and the parson gets angry but holds his tongue :

> " First I pronounce whennes that I come,
> And thanne my bulles schewe I alle and some ;
> Oure liege lordes seal upon my patent
> That schewe I first, my body to warent,
> That no man be so hardy, prest ne clerk,
> Me to destourbe of Cristes holy werk.
> And after that than tel I forth my tales.
> Bulles of popes and of cardynales,
> Of patriarkes, and of bisshops, I schewe,
> And in Latyn speke I wordes fewe
> To savore with my predicacioun,
> And for to stere men to devocioun."

As for that " turpem et infamem quæstum " branded by the Pontiff, it is the ever-recurring burden of the unholy discourse :

> " Now good men, God foryeve yow your trespas,
> And ware yow fro the synne of avarice.
> Myn holy pardoun may you alle warice (redeem),
> So that ye offren noblis or starlinges,
> Or elles silver spones, broches, or rynges.
> Bowith your hedes under this holy bulle."

---

[1] In England as elsewhere forgers were busy. One is captured at great expense in the year 51 Ed. III : " To John Compton, one of the king's archers of his crown. In money paid to him for the expenses of himself and other archers in his retinue, coming from Gloucester to London, to conduct and deliver up Thomas Pardoner and Reginald Clerc, forgers of the seal of the Lord the Pope . . . also for hire of horses for the same Thomas and Reginald and for divers other costs occurred in their safe conduct, £6." Devon, " Issues of the Exchequer," 1837, p. 203.

READING IN CANTERBURY CATHEDRAL OF A FABRICATED PAPAL BULL, A.D. 1399. [*p.* 319.

(*From the MS. Harl.* 1319.)

The effect of solemn parchments and large seals displayed from the pulpit rarely failed upon the crowd, and in some circumstances of more importance than the retail selling of the merits of saints in heaven, recourse was had to such exhibitions. When Henry of Lancaster came to turn his cousin Richard II out of the English throne, the first thing he did, according to Créton, was to have a pretended papal bull, granting a plenary indulgence, read from the pulpit of Canterbury cathedral and commented by Archbishop Arundel (whose brother, the earl, King Richard had caused to be summarily executed). As Créton was not present when this scene, which he describes only on hearsay, took place, the speech he gives is the more interesting, for it may be considered an average speech, such a one as was usual and likely to have been pronounced on the occasion.

" My good people," the Archbishop is supposed to have said, " hearken all of you here : you well know how the king most wrongfully and without reason has banished your lord Henry ; I have therefore obtained of the holy father who is our patron, that those who shall forthwith bring aid this day, shall every one of them have remission of all sins whereby from the hour of their baptism they have been defiled. Behold the sealed bull that the Pope of renowned Rome hath sent me, my good friends, in behalf of you all. Agree then to help him to subdue his enemies, and you shall for this be placed after death with those who are in Paradise."

" Then," continues the narrator, describing the effect of the speech, " might you have beheld young and old, the feeble and the strong, make a clamour, and regarding neither right or wrong, stir themselves up with one accord, thinking that what was told them was true, for such as they have little sense or knowledge. The archbishop invented this device . . ." [1]

---

[1] " Archæologia," vol. xx. p. 53, John Webb's translation. See Appendix XIV, p. 439.

The burst of eloquence of Chaucer's pardoner is a caricature, but not an unrecognizable one, of the grave discourses of this sort.

The Pope has still more to say : " For some insignificant sum of money, they extend the veil of a lying absolution not over penitents, but over men of a hardened conscience who persist in their iniquity, remitting, to use their own words, horrible crimes without there having been any contrition nor fulfilment of any of the prescribed forms." It almost seems as if the Pope himself had listened in disguise, on the road to Canterbury, to Chaucer's man saying :

> " I yow assoile by myn heyh power,
> If ye woln offre, as clene and eek as cler
> As ye were born.
>
> * * * * *
>
> I rede that oure hoste schal bygynne,
> For he is most enveliped in synne.
> Come forth, sire ost, and offer first anoon,
> And thou schalt kisse the reliquis everichoon,
> Ye for a grote ; unbocle anone thi purse."[1]

Boccaccio, in one of the tales which he represents himself as telling under the name of Dioneo, pictures, he too, an ecclesiastic of great resemblance, moral and physical, to Chaucer's man. He was called Frà Cipolla, and was accustomed to visit Certaldo, Boccaccio's village on the hill top, still very much now as it was then, with the writer's house conspicuous in the main street. " This Frà Cipolla was little of person, red-haired (Chaucer's pardoner had " heer as yelwe as wex ") and merry of countenance, the jolliest rascal in the world, and to boot, for all he was no scholar, he was so fine a talker and so ready of wit that those who knew him not would not only have esteemed him a great rhetorician, but had

[1] Prologue to the " Canterbury Tales," and Prologue to the " Pardoner's Tale."

avouched him to be Tully himself, or maybe, Quintilian; and he was gossip, or friend, or well-wisher, to well-nigh every one in the country." If his hearers gave him a little money or corn or anything, he would show them the most wonderful relics ; and besides they would enjoy the special protection of the patron saint of his order, St. Anthony : " Gentlemen and ladies, it is, as you know, your usance to send every year to the poor of our lord Baron St. Anthony of your corn and of your oats, this little and that much, according to his means and his devoutness, to the intent that the blessed St. Anthony may keep watch over your beeves and asses and swine and sheep ; and, beside this, you use to pay, especially such of you as are inscribed into our company, that small due which is payable once a year." [1]

Such people had few scruples and knew how to profit by those of others. They released their customers from all possible vows, and remitted any penance, for money ; they were a living encouragement to sin, making it so easy to atone for. The more prohibitions, obstacles, or penances were imposed, the more their affairs prospered ; they passed their lives undoing what the real clergy did, the richer for it, and the clergy the poorer. The Pope again tells us : " For a small compensation they remit vows of chastity, of abstinence, of pilgrimage beyond the sea to Sts. Peter and Paul of Rome, or to St. James of Compostela, and any other vows." They allow heretics to re-enter the bosom of the Church, illegitimate children to receive the sacred orders, they remove excommunications and interdicts ; in short, as their power comes from themselves alone, they see no reason to restrain it and they use it to the full and without stint. Lastly, they affirm that " it is in the name of the apostolic chamber that they take all this money, and yet they are never known

[1] " The Decameron of Giovanni Boccaccio " . . . done into English . . . by John Payne, London, 1886, vol. ii. p. 278, tenth Tale, sixth Day.

to give an account of it to any one : ' Horret et merito indignatur animus talia reminisci.' " [1]

They went yet further ; they had formed regular associations for systematically speculating on public credulity ; thus Boniface IX orders in 1390, that bishops should make an inquiry into everything that concerns these " religious or secular clerics, their people, their accomplices, and their associations "; that they should imprison them without other form of law, " de plano ac sine strepitu et figura judicii " ; should make them render accounts, confiscate their receipts, and if their papers be not in order hold them under good keeping, and refer the matter to the sovereign pontiff.

There were indeed authorized pardoners who paid the produce of their receipts into the treasury of the Roman Court. The learned Richard d'Angerville, otherwise de Bury, Bishop of Durham, called by Petrarch, whom he had met at Avignon in 1330, "vir ardentis ingenii," speaks, in a circular of December 8, 1340, of apostolic or diocesan letters, subject to a rigorous visa, with which the regular pardoners had to be furnished.[2] But many did without them, and the bishop notices one by one the same abuses as the Pope and as Chaucer. " Strong complaints have come to our ears that the questors of this kind, not without great and rash boldness, of their own authority, and to the great danger of the souls who are confided to us, openly setting at nought our jurisdiction, distribute indulgences to the people, dispense with the execution of vows, absolve the perjured, homicides, usurers, and other sinners who confess to them ; and, for a little money paid, grant remission for ill-atoned crimes, and are given to a multitude of other abuses." Henceforward all curates, vicars and chaplains must refuse to admit these pardoners to preach or to bestow indulgences,

1 See Appendix, XV p. 440   2 Same Appendix.

whether in the churches or anywhere else, " if they be not provided with letters or a special licence " from the bishop himself. And this was a most proper injunction, for with these bulls brought from far-off lands, adorned with unknown seals " of popes and of cardynales, of patriarkes and of bisshops," it was easy to make people believe that all was in order. Meanwhile let all those who are now wandering round the country be stripped of what they have taken, and let " the money and *any other articles* collected by them or on their behalf," be seized : the common people not being always possessed of actual cash, Chaucer's pardoner contented himself with " silver spones, broches, or rynges." One more allusion is to be noticed in this text to those associations of pardoners which must have been so harmful.

They employed, in fact, inferior agents ; the general credulity and the widespread wish to get rid of religious trammels which men had imposed on themselves, in the shape of vows or otherwise, or which had been imposed on them on account of their sins, were a mine for the perverse band, the veins of which they carefully worked. By means of these subordinate representatives of their fanciful power, they easily extended the field of their operations, and the complicated threads of their webs covered the whole kingdom, sometimes too strong to be broken, sometimes too fine to be perceived.

Occasionally, too, the bad example came from very high quarters ; all had not the Bishop of Durham's virtue. Walsingham relates with indignation the behaviour of a cardinal who made a stay in England when the marriage between Richard II and the emperor's sister, Anne of Bohemia, was being negotiated. For money this prelate, just like the common pardoners, removed excommunications, dispensed people of pilgrimages to St. Peter, St. James, or Jerusalem, and had the sum that would have been spent on the journey duly computed and given to him ; [1] and it is much to be regretted from every point of view that the curious tariff of the expenses of a journey thus estimated has not come down to us.

The list of the misdeeds of pardoners was in truth enormous, and it is found even larger on exploring the authentic ecclesiastical documents than in the work of Chaucer himself. Thus in a bull of Pope Urban V, dated 1369, mention is made of practices apparently untried by the otherwise experienced " gentil pardoner of Rouncival." These doings were customary with those employed by the Hospitallers of St. John of Jerusalem in England. Helped by the connivance of the " very priors " of the order, they pretended to be " privileged " and exempted from the formality of showing apostolic letters before they were allowed to proceed with their preachings and to offer to the people their " negotia quæstuaria." The parish rectors and curates naturally enough objected to such pretensions, but their complaints were ill received, and the pardoners, to get rid of them, sued them before some distant authority for contempt of their cloth and privileges. While the suit was being determined they remained free to act as they liked. Sometimes they were so lucky as to secure sentence against the priest who had tried to do his duty, and even succeeded in having him excommunicated : which could of course but be a cause of great merriment among the unholy tribe.

" Very often, also," adds Pope Urban, " when they mean to hurt a rector or his curate, they go to his church on some feast-day, especially at such time as the people are accustomed to come and make their offerings. They

---

[1] " Excommunicatis gratiam absolutionis impendit. Vota peregrinationis ad apostolorum limina, ad Terram Sanctam, ad Sanctum Jacobum non prius remisit quam tantam pecuniam recepisset, quantam, juxta veram æstimationem, in eisdem peregrinationibus expendere debuissent, et ut cuncta concludam brevibus, nihil omnino petendum erat, quod non censuit, intercedente pecunia, concedendum." " Historia Anglicana "; Rolls Series, vol. i. p. 452.

begin then to make their own collections or to read the
name of their brotherhood or fraternity, and continue
until such an hour as it is not possible to celebrate mass
conveniently that day. Thus they manage perversely to
deprive these rectors and vicars of the offerings which
accrue to them at such masses." They have, on the
other hand, Divine service performed " in polluted or
interdicted places, and there also bury the dead ; they
use, as helps to their trade, simple and almost illiterate
subordinates, who spread errors and fables among people
as ignorant as themselves."

Such abuses and many others, constantly pointed out
by councils, popes, and bishops, moved the University
of Oxford to recommend, in the year 1414, the entire
suppression of pardoners, as being men of loose life and
lying speeches, spending their profits " with the prodigal
son," remitting to sinners their sins as well as their
penances, encouraging vice by the ease of their abso-
lutions, and drawing the souls of uneducated people
" to Tartarus." But this request was not listened to,
and pardoners continued to prosper for the moment.[1]

At the same time that they sold indulgences, the
pardoners showed relics. They had been on pilgrimage
and had brought back pieces of bone and fragments of
all kinds, of holy origin, they said. But although the
credulous were not lacking among the multitude, the
disabused among the better sort were numerous and they
scoffed without mercy. The pardoners of Chaucer and
Boccaccio, and in the sixteenth century of Heywood and
Lyndsay,[2] exhibited the most unexpected trophies. The
Chaucerian one, who possessed a piece of the sail of St.

[1] See Appendix XV, p. 444.
[2] Lyndsay, "Ane Satyre of the Thrie Estaits" performed at Linli hgow,
1540; Early English Text Society, 1869; John Heywood, "The Pardoner
and the Frere, the Curate and Neybour Pratte," 1533; "The foure Ps,"
1545.

Peter's boat is surpassed by Frate Cipolla, who had
brought back much better from Jerusalem. "I will,
as an especial favour, show you," said he, "a very holy
and goodly relic, which I myself brought aforetime from
the Holy Lands beyond seas, and that is one of the
Angel Gabriel's feathers, which remained in the Virgin
Mary's chamber, whenas he came to announce to
her in Nazareth!"[1] The feather, which was from the
tail of a parrot, through some joke played upon him
was replaced in the holy man's box by a few coals;
when he perceived the metamorphosis he showed
no embarrassment, but began the narrative of his long
voyages, and explained how, instead of the feather, the
coals on which St. Lawrence was grilled would be seen
in his coffer. He had received them from "My Lord
Blamemenot Anitpleaseyou," the worthy patriarch of
Jerusalem, who also showed him "a finger of the Holy
Ghost as whole and sound as ever it was, . . . and one
of the nails of the cherubim, . . . divers rays of the
star that appeared to the three Wise Men in the East,
and a vial of the sweat of St. Michael whenas he fought
with the devil"; he possessed also "somewhat of the
sound of the bells of Solomon's Temple in a vial."

Poets' jests; but less exaggerated than might be
thought. Was there not shown to the pilgrims at Exeter
a bit "of the candle which the angel of the Lord lit in
Christ's tomb"? This was one of the relics brought
together in the venerable cathedral by Athelstan, "the
most glorious and victorious king," who had sent emis-
saries at great expense on to the Continent to gather these
precious spoils. The list of their treasure-troves, which
has been preserved in a missal of the eleventh century,
comprises also a little of "the bush in which the Lord
spoke to Moses," and a lot of other curiosities.[2] Some

[1] Payne's "Boccaccio," vol. ii. pp. 280, 287.
[2] "The Leofric Missal" (1050-1072), edited by F. E. Warren, 1883,
Clarendon Press, pp. lxi, 3, 4.

of the Virgin's milk was, as all know, venerated at Walsingham and in various other places.

Matthew Paris relates that, in his time, the friar preachers gave to Henry III a piece of white marble on which there was the trace of a human foot ; nothing less, according to the testimony of the inhabitants of the Holy Land, than the mark of one of the Saviour's feet, left by Him as a souvenir to His apostles after His Ascension. " Our lord the king had this marble placed in the church of Westminster, to which he had already lately offered some of the blood of Christ." [1]

In the fourteenth century kings continued to set the example to the common people, and to collect relics of undemonstrable authenticity. In the accounts of the expenses of Edward III, in the thirty-sixth year of his reign, a hundred shillings are put down for a messenger who had brought him a vest of St. Peter's.[2] In France, at the same period, King Charles V " le sage " had one day the curiosity to visit the cupboard at the Sainte Chapelle, where the relics of the passion were kept. He found there a phial with a Latin and Greek inscription indicating that it contained some of the blood of Jesus Christ. " Then," relates Christine de Pisan, " that wise king, because some doctors have said that, on the day that our Lord rose, nothing was left on earth of His worthy body that was not all returned into Him, would hereupon know and inquire by learned men, natural philosophers, and theologians, whether it could be true that upon earth there were some of the real pure blood of Jesus Christ. Examination was made by the said learned men assembled about this matter ; the said phial was seen and visited with great reverence and solemnity of lights, in which when it was hung or lowered could

[1] " Historia Anglorum " (Historia minor), ed. Sir F. Madden, London, 1866 ; vol. iii. p. 60, Rolls Series.
[2] Devon's " Issues of the Exchequer," 1837, p. 176.

be clearly seen the fluid of the red blood flow as freshly
as though it had been shed but three or four days since :
which thing is no small marvel, considering the passion
was so long ago. And these things I know for certain
by the relation of my father who was present at that
examination, as philosophic officer and counsellor of the
said prince."

After this examination made by great "solemnity of
lights," the doctors declared themselves for the authenticity of the miracle ;[1] which was not in reality more
surprising than that at the cathedral at Naples, where the
blood of the patron saint of the town may still be seen to
liquify several times a year, and for several days each time.

In every country of Europe the pardoners enjoyed,
not to say endured, the same reputation and acted in the
same manner. Be it France, Germany, Italy, or Spain,
they were found living, so long as there remained any,
as Chaucer's pardoner did. In France, Rabelais has
the cheaters cheated by his beloved Panurge. The clever
vaurien used to place his penny in their plate so skilfully
that it seemed to be a silver piece : for which he made
bold to take change, leaving only a farthing. " ' And I
did the same,' said he, ' in all the churches where we
have been.'—' Yea, but,' said I, ' you . . . are a thief,
and commit sacrilege.'—' True,' said he, ' as it seems to
you ; but it does not seem so to me. For the pardoners
give it me as a gift when they say, in offering me the relics
to kiss : *Centuplum accipies*—that is, that for one penny
I take a hundred ; for *accipies* is spoken by them according to the manner of the Hebrews, who use the future
tense instead of the imperative, as you have in the book,
Diliges Dominum, id est, dilige.' "[2]

---

[1] " Le livre des fais et bonnes mœurs du sage roy Charles," by Christine
de Pisan, chap. xxxiii. vol. i. p. 633 ; " Nouvelle Collection de Mémoires,"
ed. Michaud and Poujoulat, Paris, 1836.

[2] " Pantagruel," book ii. chap. xvii., " Comment Panurge gagnoit
les pardons."

Pardoners, of course, never appear on the boards of the old French theatre, but to be derided :

" *Pardoner* : I mean to show you the comb of the cock that crowed at Pilate's, and half a plank of Noah's great ark. . . . Look, gentlemen, here is a feather of one of the seraphs near God. Don't think it is a joke ; here it is for you to see.

" *Triacleur* : Gogsblood ! 'tis the quill from a goose he has eaten at his dinner ! " and so on.[1]

The same in Spain. Lazarillo de Tormes, the page of many masters, happens, at one time, to be in the service of a pardoner : the very same individual Chaucer had described two hundred years before. He, too, knows how to use Latin when profitable : " Hee woulde alwayes bee informed before he came, which were learned and which not. When he came to those which he understood were learned, he woulde be sure never to speake worde of Latin, for feare of stumbling : but used in suche places a gentle kind of Castilian Spanish, his tong always at libertie. And contrariwise whensoever hee was informed of the reverend *Domines* (I meane such as are made priestes more for money than for learning and good behaviour), to hear him speake amongs suche men you would saye it were St. Thomas : for hee woulde then two houres together talke Latin, at lest which seemed to bee, though it was not." [2]   A trick which, as is well known, Sganarelle, many years after, did not disdain to use when put upon his last shifts as the " Médecin malgré lui."

Pardoners lived merrily ; certain it is that after a busy day they must have been cheerful companions at the inn. The thought of the multitude of sins they had pardoned, of excommunications they had removed,

---

[1] " Farce d'un pardonneur, d'un triacleur et d'une tavernière," Viollet le Duc, " Ancien théâtre français," Paris, 1854–57, vol. ii. p. 50.

[2] "The Pleasaunt Historie of Lazarillo de Tormes, . . . drawen out of Spanish by David Rouland, of Angelsey." London, 1586, Sig. G. iii.

of penalties they had remitted—themselves mere vagabonds threatened with the jail or gallows—the knowledge
of their impunity, the strangeness of their existence, the
triumphant success of the mad harangues in which they
attributed to themselves the keys of heaven, must have
made their hearts swell with uncontrollable merriment.
Their heads were filled with anecdotes, sacred or profane ;
native coarseness and assumed devotion, the real and the
artificial man, jostled each other to the sound of jugs and
vessels clattering on the table. See in the margin of an
old psalter the lean figure of Master Reynard [1] : a crozier
between his paws, a mitre on his head, he is preaching
a sermon to the wondering crowd of ducks and geese of
the poultry yard. The gesture is full of unction, but
the eye shaded by the tawny hair has a cruel glitter, which
ought to give warning of the peroration. But no, the
poultry yard clucks devoutly and fears nothing ; woe to
the ducks when the mitre has fallen : " And Thou, Lord,
shalt laugh at them," says the psalmist on the same page.

A singular knowledge of the human heart those individuals must have had, going through such strange
experiences day by day. Never were more unworthy
beings supposedly clothed with greater supernatural powers.
The deformed monster squatting on the apse of the cathedral laughs and grimaces hideously on his airy pedestal.
And up to the clouds rise the fretted spires ; the
chiselled pinnacles detach themselves like lace upon the
sky ; the saints pray their eternal prayer under the porch ;
the bells send forth their peals into space, and souls are
seized with a thrill, with that mysterious awe caused by
the sublime. The monster laughs ; hearts believe themselves purified, but he has seen their ugly sores, a sinister
hand will touch them and prevent their cure ; the edge

[1] A favourite subject among miniaturists, and to be found in several
manuscripts (2 B. vii ; 10 E. IV) in the British Museum. See the head-
piece of the present chapter.

of the roof reaches the clouds ; but his look goes
through the dormer window, he detects a cracking beam,
worm-eaten boards giving way, and a host of obscure
creatures slowly pursuing under the wooden shafts their
secular labour of destruction : he laughs and grimaces
hideously.

On the tavern bench the pardoner is still seated.
There come Chaucer, the knight, the squire, the friar,
the host—old acquaintances. We are by ourselves, no
one need be afraid to speak, the foaming ale renders
hearts expansive ; and the unseen coils of that tortuous
soul unfold to view, he gives the summary of a whole
life, the theory of his existence, the key to his secrets.
What matters his frankness ? he knows that it cannot
hurt him ; time and again has the bishop brought his
practices to light, but the crowd always troops around
him. And who knows if his companions—who knows
if his more enlightened companions, to whom he shows
the concealed springs of the automaton—will, to-morrow,
believe it lifeless ? their memory, their reason will tell
them so, yet still their heart will doubt. If custom is
the half of belief, theirs is well-rooted ; how much more
that of the multitude ! And the pardoner himself, do
you suppose that he always sees clearly what he is, do
you think that his scepticism is absolute ? he for whom
nothing is holy, whose very existence is a perpetual
mockery of sacred things, he also has his hours of doubt
and terror, he trembles before that formidable power
which he said he held in his hands, and of which he has
made a toy ; he does not possess it, but others may, and he
stands aghast ; the monster looks upon himself and is
afraid.

Very easy it was to lead the popular belief into the
channel of the marvellous. Decrees had been deemed
necessary to prevent the conjuring up of spectres or ghosts
in those long watches passed with the dead ; disobedience

was attempted, people believed they succeeded. In presence of the horrible a strange reaction of the heart would take place, a wind of madness passed predisposing men to see and believe anything, a nervous and demoniacal merriment seized upon all, and dances and lascivious games were started. Dancing went on in the cemeteries during the solemn vigils of religious feasts, there was dancing also during the watch for the dead. The Council of London, in 1342, prohibited " the superstitious customs which cause prayer to be neglected, and unlawful and indecent meetings " held in such places.[1] The Council of York, in 1367, also forbade " those guilty games and follies, and all those perverse customs . . . which transform a house of tears and prayers, into a house of laughing and excess." The palmers' gild of Ludlow allowed its members to go to night-watches of the dead, provided that they abstained from raising apparitions and from indecent games.[2] As to professional sorcerers, the belief in them was so profound that they were sent to the stake, as happened to Petronilla of Meath, convicted of having manufactured powders with " spiders and black worms like scorpions, mingling with them a certain herb called milfoil, and other detestable herbs and worms." [3] She had also made such incantations that " the faces of certain women seemed horned like the heads of goats "; there-

[1] Labbe, " Sacrosancta concilia," Florence edition, vol. xxv. col. 1177, and vol. xxvi. col. 462. In 1419, Henry Chicheley, Archbishop of Canterbury, ordered public prayers, litanies, and processions, to protect the King of England and his army against the wicked operations of magicians. Wilkins, " Concilia Magnæ Britanniæ," vol. iii. p. 392.

[2] " Si vero masculus quisquam voluerit, ut est moris, ejusdem defuncti vel defuncte nocturnis vigiliis interesse, hoc fieri permittatur, dumtamen nec monstra larvarum inducere, nec corporis vel fame sue ludibria, nec ludos alios inhonestos, presumat aliqualiter attemptare." Toulmin Smith, " English Gilds," p. 194.

[3] " Araneis et aliis vermibus nigris ad modum scorpionum, cum quadam herba quæ dicitur millefolium et aliis herbis et vermibus detestabilibus." Thos. Wright, " Proceedings against Dame Alice Kyteler, 1324," Camden Society, 1843, p. 32.

fore she had her due punishment and " was burnt before
an immense multitude of people with all the accustomed
ceremonial." Such facts explain the existence of the
pardoner.

Let us add that the search for the philosopher's stone
was the constant occupation of many renowned doctors ;
every one had not that clear good sense, good humour
and penetrating spirit which permitted Chaucer to smil-
ingly unravel before us the mysteries of the alchemist,
shaking the alembics and retorts, and in the odd-shaped
apparatus which frightened the imagination, showing not
the newly created ingot of pure metal, but the mixture
prepared beforehand by the impostor.[1] Not a plant or
a stone without supernatural virtues ; the vain beliefs
inherited from the ancients had been rejuvenated and
expanded. People thirsted for such pretended learning.
Gower thinks he does well to insert in a love poem all
he believes he knows on the constitution of the world
and the virtues of things ; [2] even with professionally
learned men the mass of fabulous statements fills volumes.
Bartholomew the Englishman, whose work is an encyclopædia of scientific knowledge in the thirteenth century,
is positive that the diamond destroys the effect of venom
and of magic incantations, and that it reveals its wearer's
fear ; that the topaz prevents sudden death, etc.[3]

A pleasure it is, and like a whiff of fresh air when
emerging from a damp cellar, to remember that in an
age not totally exempt from these weaknesses no one
condemned them with more eloquence than our Molière :
" Without speaking of other things," said he, " I have

[1] " The Canons Yeomans Tale."
[2] The whole of book vii of his " Confessio Amantis " is devoted
to the exposition of a system of the world and to the description of the inner
nature of beings and substances. The " Roman de la Rose " is not less
explicit on these matters (confession of Nature to Genius).
[3] " De Proprietatibus Rerum," lib. xvi, a work of immense repute,
translated into English by Trevisa in 1398, into French, Spanish, Dutch.

never been able to conceive how even the smallest pecu-
liarities of the fortune of the least man could be found
written in the skies. What relation, what intercourse,
what correspondence can there be between us and worlds
separated from our earth by so frightful a distance ? and
whence can this fine science have come to men ? What
god has revealed it ? or what experience can have shaped
it from the observation of that great number of stars which
have not been seen twice in the same arrangement ? "

A PARDONER (CHAUCER'S PARDONER).
(*From the Ellesmere MS.*)

Trouble and eloquence lost ; there will always be a
Timocles to observe with a wise air : " I am incredulous
enough as to a great many things, but for astrology, there
is nothing more certain and more constant than the success
of the horoscopes which it draws." [1]

So vanished into smoke the tempests which Chaucer,
Langland, and Wyclif raised against the hypocritical
pardoners of their day. They lingered on till the six-

[1] " Les Amants magnifiques."

teenth century, and then were entirely suppressed in the twenty-first session of the œcumenical council of Trent, July 16, 1562, Pius IV being Pope. It is stated in the ninth chapter of the " Decree of Reform," published in that session, that since " no further hope can be entertained of amending the questors of alms " (*eleemosynarum quæstores*), otherwise pardoners, " the use of them and their name are entirely abolished henceforth in all Christendom : "[1] the first of old-time wayfarers to entirely disappear.

[1] " Conciliorum generalium Ecclesiæ Catholicæ," vol. iv. p. 261, " Pauli V. Pont. max. auctoritate editus," Rome, 1623. See Appendix XV, p. 444.

A PILGRIMAGE TOWN, ROCAMADOUR, IN GUYENNE.
(*Present state.*)

CHAPTER III

PILGRIMS AND PILGRIMAGES

I

IN spite of the merits of physicians, soothsayers, and sorcerers, maladies sometimes resisted the best remedies, and the patient would then vow to go on a pilgrimage, ride, walk, or have himself carried there, and pray for his cure. He went to our Lady of Walsingham, for example, or to St. Thomas of Canterbury, whose medical powers were considered, beyond comparison, the best of all : " Optimus egrorum, medicus fit Thomas bonorum," was the motto stamped on some of the pewter ampullæ, with miraculous water in them, which pilgrims brought back as a souvenir from Canterbury : " For good people that are sick, Thomas is the best of physicians." And surely praying at his shrine, after an open-air journey on foot or horseback, was a better way of preserving one's health than swallowing the black beetles and fat bats of John of Gaddesden, the court physician.

Pilgrimages were incessant ; they were made to
fulfil a vow as in cases of illness or of great peril, or in
expiation of sins. Confessors frequently gave the going
on a pilgrimage as penance, and sometimes ordered that
the traveller should go barefoot or in his shirt. " Commune penaunce," says Chaucer's parson in his great
sermon, speaking of atonement which must be public,
" commune," because the sin has been public too, " is
that prestes enjoynen men comunly in certeyn caas, as
for to goon, peradventure, naked in pilgrimage or barfot,"
that is to say, naked in their shirts. In accordance with
a vow made during a tempest, Æneas Sylvius Piccolomini,
later Pope Pius II, walked ten miles barefoot on the frozen
ground, to White Kirk, near North Berwick, and had, on
his return, " to be born, rather than led by his servants." [1]

Another motive for pilgrimages, and, more than any
other, characteristic of the times, was to annoy the king.
Thus in the fourteenth century English people flocked
to the tomb of the selfish, narrow-minded and vengeful
Thomas, Earl of Lancaster, of whom popular prejudice
had made a saint.[2] The crowd hastened through a spirit
of opposition to Pontefract, where the rebel had been
decapitated, by order of his relative, King Edward II, and
the pilgrims became every year more numerous, to the
great scandal of the sovereign and of the Archbishop of
York. A letter of this prelate shows the uselessness of the

[1] Winter of 1435 ; he was coming on a mission to James I of Scotland.
" Romance of a King's Life," pp. 52, 97.
[2] First cousin to Edward II, executed in 1322. Froissart had no doubt
as to the authenticity of his miracles. " Thomas erle of Lancastre, who
was a noble and a wyse holy knyght, and hath done syth many fayre myracles
in Pomfret, where he was beheeded " (vol. i. chap. vi. in Lord Berners'
translation). The body of Charles de Blois, killed at the battle of Auray
in 1364, but this one an undoubtedly pious warrior, also worked miracles,
and Froissart imagined that Urban V had canonized him : " His body [was]
after sanctifyed by the grace of God and called Saynt Charles, and canonized
by Pope Urban the V ; for he dyde, and yet dothe many fayre miracles
dayly." Vol. i. cap. 226 of Lord Berners' translation.

prohibitions : the idea of a semblance of persecution of believers devised by an archbishop only excited zeal and devotion ; men hoped to please the martyr by al owing themselves to be slightly martyred. Thus, while awaiting a canonization that never came, though insisted upon by the next king, crowds collected near the tomb, so numerous and tumultuous that there happened " homicides and mortal wounds, . . . and that greater dangers yet and doubtless most imminent are to be feared." [1]

All this began the very year after the execution of the " saint." The official was enjoined to hinder these meetings by any means, and to disperse them until the Pope should pronounce. But the gatherings continued, and Henry of Lancaster wrote in 1327 to the Archbishop of York asking him to refer the matter to the Sovereign Pontiff, and " bear witness to the fame of the miracles which God works by our very dear lord and brother." [2] The same year the Commons took the question in hand and petitioned for the canonization of the same Thomas, which was scarcely parliamentary business.[3] In 1338, a London pepperer had for sale a mazer bowl ornamented with an " image of St. Thomas of Lancester." [4] Humphry de Bohun, Earl of Hereford and Essex, who died in 1361, bequeathed money for pious men to make a variety of pilgrimages on his behalf, and he specially recommended that " a good man and true ' should be

[1] " Non absque homicidiis aliisque lætalibus verberibus . . . et de majoribus periculis verisimiliter imminentibus multipliciter formidatur . . ." A.D. 1323, " Historical Papers from the Northern Registers," ed. Raine, 1873, p. 324, Rolls Series.

[2] The archbishop did write to this effect to the Pope (John XXII) on February 24, 1327, asking him to make inquiry with a view to canonization. " Historical Papers from the Northern Registers," p. 340.

[3] Petition to Parliament, 1 Ed. III, 1326–7. " Rolls of Parliament," vol. ii. p. 7.

[4] " Memorials of London," Riley, 1868, p. 203. The miracles worked by the same are also noted in the contemporary " Croniques de London " (Camden Society, ed G. J. Aungier, p. 46), and by many others.

hired and charged to go to " Pountfreyt and to offer there, at the tomb of Thomas, late earl of Lancaster, 40s." [1]

To make a saint of a rebel was the most energetic means of protesting against the king, and the people would not miss this opportunity under some of their sovereigns. Henry III, in 1266, had been obliged to forbid Simon de Montfort being considered as a saint, although Simon having died under excommunication, as was represented to the king by the bishops and barons, authors of the petitions comprised in the " Dictum de Kenilworth," [2] had little chance of ever being canonized. Latin hymns were nevertheless composed in his honour, as for a saint. [3]

The rebel was hardly dead than popular feeling, often unfavourable to him during his life, forthwith recognized in him nothing else than the hero who had fought against a tyrant and, through sympathy for the man, or antipathy for the king, assigned therefore to him a place in heaven. The active revolt, rudely interrupted

[1] J. Nichol's " Wills of the Kings and Queens of England," 1780, p. 54. A chapel had been built on the hill where the earl had been beheaded. The offerings brought there by the pilgrims were, in 1334, the subject of a curious debate between the prior and the convent of Pontefract on the one hand, and the Lord of Wake on the other ; this lord had " taken possession of the said chapel and the offerings brought there, and had taken the keys with him." The prior and the convent in a petition to Parliament requested to have the " administration of these offerings," as " spiritual things within their parish and belonging to their church," " Rolls of Parliament," vol. ii. p. 84.

[2] " Ne . . . pro sancto vel justo reputetur, cum in excommunicatione sit defunctus, sicut sancta tenet Ecclesia." " Dictum de Kenilworth," § viii., in " Select Charters," ed. Stubbs, 1870, p. 410.

[3] Salve Symon Montis Fortis
    tocius flos militie,
    Duras penas passus mortis,
    protector gentis Angliæ.

" Ora pro nobis, beate Symon, ut digni efficiamur promissionibus Christi." Hymn composed shortly after the death of Simon ; Warton, " History of English Poetry," ed. Hazlitt, 1871, vol. ii. p. 48.

by punishment, continued thus in the latent state, and every one came to see God Himself take the part of the oppressed, and proclaim the injustice of the ruler by working miracles at the tomb of his victim. The sovereign defended himself as he could ; he dispersed the rabble and prohibited the miracles.

De par le Roi, défense à Dieu
De faire miracle en ce lieu,

read an ironical distich written in France in the " Diacre Paris " days. Similarly disposed, Edward II, on October 2, 1323, wrote "to his faithful John de Stonore and John de Bousser," ordering an inquiry which would be followed by graver measures. He recalled to them that " a little time ago Henry de Montfort and Henry de Wylynton, our enemies and rebels, on the advice of the royal Court, were drawn and hanged at Bristol, and it had been decided that their bodies should remain attached to the gibbet, so that others might abstain from similar crimes and misdeeds against us." But on the contrary, the people made relics of these bloody and mutilated remains, and surrounded them with respect. Reginald de Montfort, William de Clyf, William Curteys, and John his brother, and some others, in order to render the king odious to the people, had organized false miracles at the gibbet where the corpses of these rebels were still hanging, which was nothing short of " idolatry."

Severe measures were required in several places at the same time ; while these bodies were venerated at Bristol, a mere image of Thomas of Lancaster, in the Cathedral of London, was attracting pilgrims and working miracles. In this same year, 1323, on June 28th, Edward II is found writing with great irritation to the Bishop of London :

" It has come to our ears—and it is very displeasing to us—that many among the people of God, confided to your charge, victims of a diabolical trickery, crowd round

a panel placed in your church of St. Paul's, where are
to be seen statues, sculptures, or images, and among
others that of Thomas, late Earl of Lancaster, a rebel,
our enemy. Silly visitors, without any authorization
from the Roman Church, venerate and worship this
image as a holy thing, and affirm that it there works
miracles : this is a disgrace for the whole Church, a shame
for us and for you, a manifest danger for the souls of
the aforesaid people, and a dangerous example to others." [1]

The bishop knows it, continues the king, and secretly
encourages these practices without any other motive
than that of profiting by the offerings, thus making
" shameful gains. . . . By which," adds Edward II, " we
are deeply afflicted." The usual prohibitions follow.[2]

These were occasional pilgrimages. Others were in
favour for a much longer time owing to the reputation
of the departed for sanctity, and not to political motives.
For many years crowds came, as we have seen, to visit
the tomb of Richard Rolle, the hermit of Hampole.
Even in this, fashion ruled ; some relics or tombs of hermits or of saints enjoyed for a period universal favour ;
then all of a sudden, through some great miracle, another
saint rose to pre-eminence, and the others, by degrees,
sank into obscurity.

Convents, which had neither relics nor bodies of
illustrious saints to attract pilgrims, nor a marvellous thorn-
tree like that of Glastonbury, would have sometimes a pious
artist to fabricate an image fit to draw visitors ; it would
be inaugurated with solemnity, work miracles, it was hoped,
and enjoy a more or less wide fame. Thomas of Burton,
Abbot of Meaux, near Beverley, relates in the chronicle
of his rich monastery, written by himself at the end of
the fourteenth century, one of the most remarkable facts
of this kind. Abbot Hugh of Leven, one of his prede-

[1] Rymer's " Fœdera," edit. 1704, vol. iv. p. 20.
[2] Ibid., vol. iii. p. 1033. Cf. Knox and Leslie, " The Miracles of
Henry VI," 1924.

cessors, had in the first half of the century ordered a new
crucifix for the choir of the chapel : " And the artist
never worked at any fine and important part, except on
Fridays, fasting on bread and water. And he had all
the time a naked man under his eyes, and he laboured
to give to his crucifix the beauty of the model. By the
means of this crucifix, the Almighty worked open miracles
continually. It was then thought that if access to this
crucifix were allowed to women, the common devotion
would be increased and great advantages would result
from it for our monastery. Upon which the Abbot of
Citeaux, by our request, granted us leave to let men and
honest women approach the said crucifix, provided,
however, that the women did not enter the cloister, the
dormitory, and other parts of the monastery. . . . But
profiting by this license, to our misfortune, women began
to come in increasing numbers to the said crucifix, while
in them devotion is cool, and all they want is to see the
church, and they increase our expenses by our having
to receive them." [1]

This naïve complaint is interesting from several points
of view ; it plainly shows what was done to bring such
or such a sanctuary into favour with the pilgrims ; [2] in
the present case the effort did not succeed, the prodigies
do not seem to have long responded to the expectation,

[1] See Appendix XVI, p. 445.
[2] On the *advertising* of certain pilgrimages by means, sometimes, of the
most famous of mediæval romances, see the capital work of Joseph Bédier,
" Les Légendes épiques, Recherches sur la formation des Chansons de Geste,"
Paris, 1908, 4 vols. On the especial veneration of saints who had been
road and bridge builders, see III, p. 72, where, speaking of the immense
popularity of the pilgrimage to Saint James of Compostela in the eleventh
century, Bédier says : " Ce fut l'époque héroïque du pèlerinage. C'est alors
que la route romaine commence à se peupler d'asiles pour les voyageurs ;
c'est alors qu'exercent leur activité les saints que l'Eglise vénère parce qu'ils
furent de bons ingénieurs, réparant les chaussées, desséchant les marécages,
jetant des ponts sur les rivières et les torrents, saint Dominique de la Calzada,
et ce Français, saint Aleaume de Burgos, ancien moine de la Chaise-Dieu."

and people came only from curiosity to visit the church and the fine crucifix of the monastery. From the artistic point of view the fact is still more important, for this is the most ancient example of sculpture from the nude living model to be found in mediæval England ; and this anonymous sculptor ought to be remembered, which he is not, as one of the precursors of the Renaissance in his country.

Another attempt to make a chapel popular had been tried in the parochial church of Foston ; but the Archbishop of York, William Grenefeld, was scandalized, and by a letter full of good sense put an end to the " great concourse of simple people who came to visit a certain image of the Holy Virgin recently placed in the church, as if this image had something more divine than any other images of the sort." [1]

The fact was, as may be noticed even in our days, that, with or without the co-operation of the clergy, some statues had a far better reputation than others ; wonders were expected of them, and they were worshipped accordingly ; the same vicissitudes were observable for images as for relics and tombs of saints. This statue had healed sick people without number, and that one was known to have moved, to have made a sign, to have spoken a word. Pictures of miracles worked by statues constantly recur in manuscripts ; one, for instance, is to be found in several English books of the fourteenth century.[2] It shows how a poor painter, being busy colouring and gilding

[1] " Sane nuper ad aures nostras pervenit quod ad quandam imaginem beatæ Virginis in ecclesia parochiali de Foston noviter collocatam magnus simplicium est concursus, acsi in eadem plus quam in aliis similibus imaginibus aliquid numinis appareret." Year 1313, Wilkins' " Concilia," vol. ii. p. 423.

[2] See e.g. MS. 2 B. vii. in the British Museum, fol. 211, and 10 E. IV., fol. 209. The story of this miracle has been told by numberless authors in the Middle Ages ; the text of one version of the tale, with references to the others, will be found in G. F. Warner, " Miracles de Nostre Dame," Roxburghe Club, 1885, pp. xxxiv and 63.

a statue of the Virgin, with a most ugly devil under her feet, the Evil One, angry at such an unflattering portrait, came and broke the ladder on which the artist was standing ; but as he was falling and about to be killed, the stone Virgin bent towards him, and extending her arm held him safe until help came.

Statues did not always act so graciously, but were guided by circumstances, as was seen in the church of St. Paul-extra-muros at Rome. A visitor, according to the relation of the learned Thomas Gascoigne, chancellor of Oxford, had insulted the image of the saint, saying : " ' Why hast thou got a sword, I mean to have thy sword,' and he was trying to take it out of the hands of the statue. But through God's doing, the statue raised its sword on the impious man, and clove his head to the chin ; and then death followed. This happened at the time when Eugene IV was Pope of Rome, and a witness of the scene reported it to me ; this witness was a beadel of the said Pope, called Master Erasmus Fullar, a priest of the kingdom of Hungary." [1]

II

Apart from pilgrimages, in fashion but for a time, English people usually went to Durham to visit the tomb of the holy Confessor Cuthbert, and the place where was kept his ever-victorious banner ; to the shrine of King Edward the Confessor in Westminster ; to St. Albans, St. Edmund's Bury, St. David's, on account of the saints after whom these towns are named ; to Chichester, to worship the body of St. Richard the Bishop ; to Glastonbury, with its holy thorn-tree, and its church founded

[1] " *Loci e libro veritatum,* passages selected from Gascoigne's Theological Dictionary " (1403–1458), edit. Thorold Rogers, Oxford, 1881, p. 206. This Fullar is known to have come to England, where he saw Gascoigne. Eugene IV was Pope during the second quarter of the fifteenth century.

by St. Joseph of Arimathea ; to Waltham, where a cross of black marble had been miraculously found in the time of King Knut. Lincoln, York, Peterborough, Hayles with its Holy Blood, Winchester (for St. Swithin, who, among other merits, had had that of being a bridge builder), Holywell, Beverley with its St. John, and a number of other places,[1] shrines and miraculous and wishing wells had also attractions for the pilgrim ; but none could stand comparison with Walsingham and Canterbury.

At Walsingham there were a church and a chapel, now destroyed, the latter with a miraculous bejewelled statue of the Virgin, and some of her milk, the chapel being exactly similar, it was said, to the Santa Casa of Loretto, which was a wonder in itself, for the English copy had been built in the eleventh century, long before the Casa was heard of. Owing to innumerable gifts the place was resplendent with gold and precious stones. Visiting Cologne and the famous shrine of the wise men of the East, Roger Ascham writes : " The three kings be not so rich, I believe, as was the Lady of Walsingham."[2] People came in crowds ; many among the British kings came too ;[3] the road leading to Walsingham was called the palmers' way, and chapels were built along its line. The town was full of inns, hospitals, and religious buildings, as was usually the case with the more famous of these places.

The milk and the image, as most of the pilgrimage statues, were destroyed at the Reformation, some of the wooden ones being burnt like the heretics, or with them at Smithfield, as happened when Friar Forest died at

[1] " No fewer than thirty-eight of these pilgrims' Meccas in the County of Norfolk alone." Sidney Heath, " Pilgrim Life in the Middle Ages," London, 1911, p. 30.
[2] To Edw. Raven, Jan. 20, 1551. " Whole Works," Giles, 1865, p. 252.
[3] " Henry III, Edward I, Edward III, David Bruce, Q. Catherine after Flodden, Henry VII and Henry VIII visited the famous shrine." Walcott, " English Minsters," 1879, II, 229.

the stake.[1] The gold and silver ones were turned to more practical uses. " I have pullyd down," Dr. London, one of the Visitors of religious houses, writes to Thomas Cromwell, " the image of our Lady at Caversham, wherunto wasse great pilgremage. The image ys platyd over with sylver, and I have putte yt in a cheste fast lackyd (locked) and naylyd uppe, and by the next bardge that commyth from Redyng to London yt shall be browght to your Lordeschippe. I have also pullyd down the place she stode in with all other ceremonyes, as lights, schrds (shrouds), crowchys (crosses), and imagies of wex hangyng about the chapel, and have defacyed the same thorowly in exchuyng of any farther resortt thedyr. . . . At Caversham ys a propre lodginge wher the chanon lay, with a fayer garden and an orchard mete to be bestowed upon som frynde of your lordeschip's in thees parties." [2]

In especially large numbers people hired horses at Southwark, with relays at Rochester, and set out for St. Thomas of Canterbury. This was the highroad to the continent ; a regular service of hired horses had been established along it. Twelvepence was paid from Southwark to Rochester, twelvepence from Rochester to Canterbury, sixpence from Canterbury to Dover. The horses were branded in a prominent manner, so that unscrupulous travellers should not be tempted to quit the road and appropriate their steeds.[3] The sanctuary of St. Thomas had, indeed, a world-wide reputation.

We can scarcely realize now the thrill of horror that went throughout Christendom, as far as the Levant, as far as Iceland, when the news came that Archbishop

---

[1] The " Image of Darvell Gathern," greatly venerated by the Welsh, was burnt with him. Ellis, " Original Letters," 1st series, II, 82 ff.

[2] Ellis, *ibid.*, pp. 79, 80, Sept. 1537 (?).

[3] Patent of 19 Richard II in the appendix to Mr. Karkeek's essay, " Chaucer's Schipman and his Barge, ' The Maudelayne,' " Chaucer Society " Essays," 1884.

Thomas Becket,[1] Legate of the Pope, former chancellor of England, had been massacred in his cathedral of Canterbury by four knights of Henry II, on the evening of Tuesday, December 29, 1170, his brain and blood splashing the pavement. Everything combined to increase the enormity of the crime ; the holiness of the place, which should have afforded sanctuary, even to a murderer, the rank of the victim in the hierarchy of the Church, the dying man's brave and pious words, the presence of the cross born at his side by his assistant, Edward Grim, himself severely wounded, and, above all, the fame and character of the prelate, an archbishop Turpin of real life, who, like the companion of Roland, and while already engaged in holy orders, had proved a plucky military leader, unimpeachable, moreover, from the moral point of view, and fearless throughout his life. Like the Archbishop of Reims of the " Song of Roland," whose brain had flowed down his face,[2] he had died at the hands of barbarians, who had not, however, the excuse of being infidels.

Rarely did a single act cause such universal indignation. Public opinion proclaimed Thomas a saint even before the Pope could take action, which he did, however, with a promptitude rare in such cases, canonization being proclaimed in February, 1173. The body was scarcely buried in the crypt of the cathedral,[3] than pilgrims came to it, their numbers ceaselessly increasing. The life of the archbishop was the subject of numberless miniatures,[4]

[1] Becquet or Becchet, of Norman blood, both on his father's side, who was from Thierceville, as on his mother's, who was from Caen.

[2]   Desuz le frunt li bullit la cervelle.

A real Turpin, but who long survived the event, was Archbishop of Reims at the time of the Roncevaux disaster.

[3] Moved in July, 1220 to Trinity Chapel, behind the high altar.

[4] A beautifully illustrated fragment of a life of the saint, in French verse of the thirteenth century, has been published with facsimiles by Paul Meyer : " Fragments d'une vie de saint Thomas de Cantorbéry," Paris, 1885. A

sculptures,[1] painted windows. Some of the latter, dating back to the thirteenth century, still remain at Canterbury, Sens, Chartres, and other places. Matthew Paris wrote and illuminated with his own hand, Walsingham tells us, a biography of the archbishop ; churches dedicated to him multiplied in England and out of England : " On the heights of Fourvières," wrote Dean Stanley, " overlooking the city of Lyons, is a chapel dedicated to Saint Thomas of Canterbury. Four years before his death, it is said, he was walking on the terraced bank of the river underneath, and being asked to whom the chapel should be dedicated, he replied, ' To the next martyr,' on which his companion remarked, ' Perhaps, then, to you.' " [2]

The prophecy was fulfilled. Entirely renovated, and forming now part of the pilgrimage church at Fourvières, such a chapel still exists, still dedicated to St. Thomas ; it has been allotted to the fraternity of " Notre Dame de Compassion " for their exercises, which consist chiefly in praying for the conversion of England. On the threshold are engraved four riming Latin lines : " Happy the place, happy the church where Thomas's memory survives ; happy the land which gave birth to the prelate, happy that which received him, an exile." [3]

Churches dedicated to him were especially numerous in Normandy, from which his family came, a chapel at

remarkable thirteenth-century picture of the murder, with obvious attention to historical exactitude, is in one of the MSS. of the Yates Thompson Collection, reproduced in the Catalogue of the sale (March 23, 1920), lot xxxiv.

[1] Something yet remains of the bas relief representing his life above the portal of the southern transept of the cathedral at Bayeux.

[2] " Historical Memorials of Canterbury," chap. iv.

[3] Felix locus, felix ecclesia,
In qua Thomæ vivit memoria,
Felix terra quæ dedit præsulem,
Felix illa quæ fovit exulem.

Caen bearing the grim name of " Saint Thomas l'Abattu "
(the stricken down). His life was told in verse and
prose, in Latin, French, Icelandic, the most noteworthy
of those lives being that in French verse by Garnier de
Pont-Sainte-Maxence, as remarkable for its literary as
for its historical value, the author, a contemporary, having
taken as much pains to ascertain the truth as would the
most conscientious of the historians of to-day.[1] He had
begun writing two years after the event, and had
remodelled several times his poem because new documents,
of which several are versified into his text, or new facts
had come to his knowledge. He established himself at
" Chantorbire," where every man, every stone had been
a witness, and he appealed, in order to learn the truth,
to the friends, the servants, the sister of Saint Thomas.
His work was thereby delayed, but he preferred that :

> A Chantorbire alai ; la vérité oï ;
> Des amis saint Thoma la vérité cuilli,
> Et de cels ki l'aveient dès l'enfance servi,
> D'oster et de remettre le travail en suffri.

Proud of the trouble he had taken, he was proud also of
the good French he spoke, far better, of course, than that
of ordinary Anglo-Norman writers : " My language is
good, for I was born in France." He thereupon submits
to the custom, not yet quite obsolete, of abusing those
who write on the same subject. Don't forget, he says
to his readers in the first lines of his poem, that " all
physicians are not good healers ; and it is not all clerks
who know how to well sing and well read. . . . Some
claim to be the best, and are in reality the worst." He,
however, claims to be the best ; and though his boast
may incline us to be the more critical, yet we must needs
grant that it is not groundless, considering his accuracy,

[1] " La vie de Saint Thomas le Martyr, par Garnier de Pont-Sainte-
Maxence," ed. C. Hippeau, Paris, 1859 ; new ed. by E. Walberg, Lund, 1922.

the excellence of his French, the lifelike vividness of his
scenes and dialogues, the interest of the views and sentiments, at times very liberal, expressed by him : " God
loves the humble and the poor, who live by their work,
whose every day is a hard one . . . and who lead clean
lives ; God will exalt them."

To the mass of pilgrims who from the earliest moment
had begun to visit Canterbury, Garnier, " standing by
the tomb, a number of times read his sermon about Saint
Thomas the martyr and his passion. And they heard
nothing but truth absolute." [1]

Great and small, by land and by sea, from every part
of Christendom, " men of foreign countries, of a variety
of languages," says Garnier, flocked henceforth to the
place in such numbers, that the road, followed by pilgrims
from the West of England, or by foreigners from abroad,
landing at Southampton, to reach Canterbury by way of
Winchester, was, and is still, called " The Pilgrims' Way." [2]

Kings and emperors came with the rest ; first of all,
the cause of the tragedy, Henry II, who, to avoid excommunication, after a first penance at Avranches, in the course
of which he had promised to go on a pilgrimage, at the
Pope's choice, to Rome, Jerusalem, or St. James's,
appeared for a severer test at the shrine of his dead enemy,
on July 12, 1174. Walking the streets barefoot, dressed
in haircloth and a woollen shirt, looking a " mendif "
(beggar), having fasted for days on bread and water, the
bells in the minster tolling a funeral knell, he kissed the

[1] Epilogue, p. 205.
[2] On which see, e.g. " The Old Road," by H. Belloc, London, 1904 ;
Sidney Heath, " Pilgrim Life in the Middle Ages," London, 1911, chap.
viii. A characteristic decree of the Venetian Senate, showing the popularity
of this pilgrimage abroad, authorizes on Aug. 3, 1402, Lorenzo Contarini,
captain of the Venetian galleys setting sail for Flanders, to visit St. Thomas's
shrine, in accomplishment of a vow, to go thither and return in one day while
the galleys would be at Sandwich, but not to sleep away from his vessel.
" Calendar of Venetian State papers relating to English Affairs," ed. Rawdon
Brown, Rolls series, 1864, I, 42.

pavement of the cathedral at the place where Thomas
had fallen. Led, then, to the crypt, the proud Plantagenet,
the ruler of England and of half of France, conqueror of
Ireland, suzerain of Scotland, was flogged on his bare
shoulders by the prelates present, beginning with Gilbert
Foliot, Bishop of London :

"Li evesques de Lundres tint el puing le balai."

Thus, "beaten and punished," he spent the night,
on the cold pavement, "in psalms and orisons," before
the tomb, and gave to the sister of the saint a mill, well
worth ten marks of revenue—

"Bien valt dis mars par an la rente qu'ele en a." [1]

Henry's rival and suzerain, the King of France, the
former crusader, brave, pious and inefficient Louis VII,
came shortly after ; a prodigious and unparalleled event,
the first time a king of France had ever set foot on British
soil. Feeling that for him death was near, and having
had, although three times married, only one son, he decided
in 1179 to have the young prince crowned at once, but
before the ceremony, Philip, aged fourteen, while boar
hunting, lost his way in the forest of Compiègne, and,
separated from his companions, endured for days such
hardships before a charcoal-burner found him and led
him out of the maze that his life was despaired of. The
king, in his anguish, had at night a vision of St. Thomas
Becket, whom he had well known, promising life for his
son if he himself went to Canterbury as a pilgrim. Louis's
advisers recommended not to risk a journey which would
place him at the mercy of his enemy, the Plantagenet
king. But again, and yet again, St. Thomas appeared
at night, now threatening disaster. Louis started then
with a brilliant retinue, and no untoward event marred
the journey. Henry II, on the contrary, very meek

[1] Garnier, ibid. pp. 210 ff.

now when his former chancellor was in question, came to meet the French monarch at Dover ; both went together to Canterbury ; Louis remained two days in prayer, and offered the monks a gold cup and a magnificent gem shown henceforth to pilgrims as the " regale of France." By a special charter he granted them, besides, one hundred casks of wine to be taken yearly for ever, at vintage time, from his cellars of Poissy-sur-Seine.

He returned to find his son on the way to recovery ; and, having had him crowned, died within a year. The son, one of whose first acts was to confirm his father's hundred casks' charter, was that famous Philip August whose victory at Bouvines, in 1214, settled the fate of France and made it certain that she would be a great nation.[1]

It became henceforth a sort of tradition for British kings to make this pilgrimage. Back from Palestine and his Austrian prison, Richard Cœur-de-Lion went, on his return, to Canterbury out of gratitude for his recovered freedom. When king in his turn, his brother, John, went too ; so did Henry III, Edward I, and nearly all English monarchs ; so did the French king, John the Good, when a prisoner in England[2] ; so did, in

---

[1] The original charter of Louis VII has disappeared, but the confirmation by his son still exists. It reads : " Noverint igitur universi, presentes pariter et futuri, quod intuitu beati martiris quondam Cantuariensis Archiepiscopi, ad cujus tumulum pro salute anime et sanitate corporis impetranda, pater noster in multa devotione fuerat profectus, conventui monachorum Sancte Trinitatis ibidem Deo servientium centum modios vini, ad mensuram Parisiensem, singulis annis tempore vendemiarum, in castellaria Pissiaci accipiendos, in elemosynam concessit . . . quod factum patris nostri ne aliqua possit oblivione deleri et aliqua malignantium invidia violari, manu nostre confirmationis apposita, precipimus immutabiliter custodiri." Given at Nantes, year 1180. Text, facsimile and comment in " Archæologia Cantiana," vol. IV, 1861, p. 127.

" Muids " (modii) were of a different sort, according to places ; those " of the Paris measurement " contained 270 of our litres and were therefore quite goodly casks.

[2] Berners' Froissart, ed. Ker, I, p. 393.

December 1400, Manuel II, Palæologus, emperor of Constantinople [1] ; so did, in 1416, Emperor Sigismund, grandson of the blind King Jean de Luxembourg, who had been killed at Crécy, himself then the dominant figure in Europe, a quick-witted and, for the time, liberal-minded sovereign, who, present one day in the Paris Parliament, when justice was being rendered, and seeing a plebeian about to lose his suit simply because he was a plebeian, rose from his seat, and, to the wonder of the assembly, touching him with his sword, made him a knight. A remarkable man was that Canterbury pilgrim, as a man as well as an emperor.

Accompanied by another emperor, Charles V, King Henry VIII came too, but having changed his mind later about a great many matters, he ordered every shrine to be destroyed, showing especial vindictiveness towards all that recalled Thomas Becket. If alive, he thought, the archbishop would have probably been, just as the recently beheaded More and Fisher, opposed to the new dogma of the royal supremacy : most probably, indeed. No mercy should therefore be shown to his bones and to that shrine, where Henry must have seen in former days a silver image of his own father bequeathed to be placed as near the tomb as it could possibly be. The monument was razed with particular care, and the long venerated bones scattered. Having appointed himself Head of the Church, Henry considered that he was free to undo what another Head of the Church, a Pope of long ago, had done, and, if it so pleased him, to un-canonize a saint. While, therefore, allowing many other British saints to remain on the calendar, he issued in 1539 " certain injunctions," in which, after having informed his

[1] On the extraordinary voyage of the " basileus and autocrator " and his stay of four years away from his besieged capital, see Schlumberger, " Un Empereur de Byzance à Paris et à Londres," " Revue des Deux Mondes," Dec. 15, 1915.

priests that if they continued to marry he would send
them to jail, he reviewed the life of Becket, showed to his
own satisfaction that he was no saint, but rather " a
rebel and a traitor to his prince," that " he gave appro-
brious names to the gentlemen which then counselled him
to leave his stubornness," that a scuffle ensued with these
" gentlemen," and so " in the throng Becket was slain."

The King, therefore, commands English people to
cease calling the most famous of all the saints they had a
saint, " and that his images, and pictures, through the
whole realm . . . be plucked down . . . to the intent
his grace's loving subjects shall be no longer blindly
lead and abused to commit idolatry " ; if they persist,
they will go to jail, " at his grace's pleasure." [1] In the
same way had they been recommended shortly before
not to call this one, or that one, of their loving sovereign's
daughters legitimate, so long as he himself chose to call
them bastards ; there was a gradation in the penalties,
and in the case of the daughters it was death.

Equally inimical dispositions were shown during
the next reign by Archbishop Cranmer towards his
predecessor, and one of the articles of his " Visitation
to be had within the diocese of Canterbury " had for its
object to ascertain " whether they have put out of their
church books this word *Papa* and the name and service
of Thomas Becket." [2]

Times had changed.   But,

" Whan that Aprille, with his showres swoote,"

had long before, in the year 1388, caused spring flowers

---

[1] Wilkins, " Concilia Magnæ Britanniæ," vol. iii, 1737, p. 847.   On
the discovery in 1888 of bones supposed to be those of the archbishop, see
Canon A. J. Mason's " What became of the Bones of St. Thomas ? A contribution to his fifteenth Jubilee," London, 1920.

[2] 2 Ed. VI, " Miscellaneous Writings of Thomas Cranmer," Parker
Society, Cambridge, 1846, p. 147.

to bloom, matters were different, and, as all know who
can read English,

> "from every schires end
> Of England, to Canterbury they wende,
> The holy blissful martir for to seeke,
> That hem hath holpen whan that they were seeke."

III

In those holy journeys, as in Chaucer's book, all
ranks of society were mingled together. The majority
of these pilgrims were sincere and in good faith ; they
had made a vow and came to fulfil it. With such dispositions, the knight who found a pilgrim like himself
upon the road would not be inclined to keep haughtily
aloof ; besides, if the distances were great between class
and class at this period, familiarity was still greater. The
distance has indeed diminished at the present day, and
familiarity also, as though in compensation. The noble
felt himself sufficiently raised above the common people
not to be afraid of using a kind of jovial intimacy with
them on occasion ; at the present time, when superiority
of rank is of less importance, many are more attentive
and take care not to overstep a limit which is not now so
patent as before.

Arrived at the end of the journey, all prayed ; prayed
with fervour in the humblest posture. The soul was
filled with religious emotion when from the end of the
majestic alley formed by the great pillars of the church,
through the coloured twilight of the nave, the heart
divined, rather than the eye saw, the mysterious object
of veneration for which such a distance had been traversed
at the cost of such fatigue. Though the practical man
galloping up to bargain with the saint for the favour of
God, though the emissary sent to make offering in the
name of his master might keep a dry and clear eye, tears

coursed down the cheeks of the poor and simple in heart ;
he tasted fully of the pious emotion he had come to seek,
the peace of heaven descended into his bosom, and he
went away consoled.

Such was the happy lot of humble devout souls. Pilgrims, however, were undoubtedly a very mixed race ;
no reader of Chaucer needs to be reminded that the talk
on the way was not limited to edifying subjects, and
that pilgrims themselves, even allowing the greater number
to have been sincere, were not all of them vessels of
election. Some went like gypsies to a fair and tried to
gather money by begging ; some went for the pleasures
of the journey and the merriments of the road and of
the inn ; so that satirists, paying more attention to the
abuse than to the less visible good that came along with
it, began to raise a cry which grew louder and louder
until, at the time of the Reformation, it was something
like a storm. Whom did Langland see on Palmers'
way, near Walsingham ? Those same false hermits we
have already met by the highroads and at the corner of
bridges, and in what objectionable company !

> " Eremytes on an hep · with hokede staves,
>   Wenten to Walsyngham · and hure (their) wenches after :
>   Grete lobies and longe · that loth were to swynke,
>   Clothede hem in copis · to be knowe fro othere,
>   And made hem-selve eremytes · hure eise to have." [1]

Wyclif denounced pilgrimages most persistently, so
much so that, when later some of his followers had to
renounce their heresies, belief in the usefulness and sanctity
of pilgrimages was one of the articles they had to subscribe.
Thus, in his vow of abjuration, the Lollard William
Dynet of Nottingham, on December 1, 1395, swears in
these words : " Fro this day forthwarde I shall worshipe
ymages, with praying and offering unto hem, in the

[1] " Piers Plowman," ed. Skeat, Text C, pass. 1, l. 51.

worschepe of the seintes that they be made after ; and also I shal nevermore despyse pylgremage." [1]

But other Lollards refused to recant. Questioned by Archbishop Arundel the irreconcilable enemy of his sect, William Thorpe confesses in 1407 having preached against that passion " to seek and visit the bones or images . . . of this saint and of that," so uncontrollable that, "ofttimes divers men and women of these runners thus madly hither and thither into pilgrimage, borrow hereto other men's goods (yea, and sometimes they steal men's goods hereto), and they pay them never again." [2]

For " divers men and women " those journeys being chiefly pleasure trips, nothing, Thorpe continues, is forgotten that may make them more pleasurable, "and finding out one pilgrimage, they will ordain beforehand to have with them both men and women that can well sing wanton songs ; and some other pilgrims will have with them bagpipes : so that every town they come through, what with the noise of their singing, and with the sound of their piping, and with the jangling of their Canterbury bells, and with the barking out of dogs after them, they make more noise than if the king came there away, with all his clarions and many other minstrels."

Chaucer's pilgrims had not, perhaps, quite so magnificent a record, and when they crossed Dartford or Rochester did not outnoise the king himself ; they had, in any case, no women singers ; but their miller was provided with a sonorous bagpipe :

> " A baggepype wel coude he blowe and sowne,
> And ther-with-al he broghte us out of towne."

Their monk's bridle was heard jingling " as loude as

[1] Printed in " The Academy," Nov. 17, 1883, p. 331.
[2] " The Examination of Master William Thorpe," 1407, Arbers' " Engl. Garner," vi, 84. Cf. " Anecdotes . . . tirées . . . d'Etienne de Bourbon, XIIIe siècle," ed. Lecoy de la Marche, " Sextus titulus, De Peregrinatione."

dooth the chapel-belle " ; they talked boisterously, wrangled,
and made merry,

> " For trewely, confort ne mirthe is noon
>   To ryde by the weye doumb as a stoon,"

and dogs, of course, did not remain " doumb " for them
any more than for the king.

One more objection of Thorpe's to those journeys
was that, " if these men and women be a month out in
their pilgrimage, many of them shall be, a half-year after,
great janglers, tale-tellers, and liars." Chaucer's pilgrims
were certainly, in their way, and no one nowadays objects,
great " tale-tellers."

Archbishop Arundel, who seems at times to be the
one interrogated (but we must not forget that we have
only Thorpe's version, unrevised by the other party),
makes a more picturesque than telling answer : " Lewd
losell ! thou seest not far enough in this matter ! for
thou considerest not the great travail of pilgrims. . . .
I say to thee that it is right well done, that pilgrims have
with them both singers and also pipers : that when one
of them that goeth barefoot striketh his toe upon a stone,
and hurteth him sore and maketh him to bleed, it is well
done that he or his fellow begin then a song or else take
out of his bosom a bagpipe to drive away with such mirth
the hurt of his fellow."

Lay writers of a reforming mind objected to pilgrimages, not so much on account of the worship of images,
but because they thought these travels an encouragement
to laziness and idle living. We know the opinion of
Langland. The same views are expressed by an author
of a quite different turn of mind, the one who wrote the
"Roman de Renart," and who has a special chapter to inform
us " of the pilgrimage of Reynard and how he went to
Rome." Reynard cannot but consider that he has greatly

and many a time sinned, and feeling some anxiety about
his misdeeds, goes to a hermit and confesses himself.
Such are the faults he has to declare that the holy man
does not dare absolve him, but advises him to go to Rome
and ask the absolution of the Pope. Reynard accordingly
" takes his scrip and burdon [that is, his wallet and staff,
as did all pilgrims], and begins to move on, and takes
his way ; he looks quite like a pilgrim, his scrip fits his
neck beautifully." But travelling alone is not pleasant ;
he meets Belin the Sheep, and persuades him to come
with him, and a little farther " Bernart the arch-priest,"
a donkey, who was eating thistles in a ditch ; he also
secures this new companion.

As night is coming, the three, finding themselves near
the house of Primaut the Wolf, enter without ceremony
and make themselves at home, while the owner of the
place is away. They find there " salted meat, cheese,
and eggs . . . and good ale. Belin drinks so much
that he loses his head, and then begins to sing, and the
arch-priest to organ-bray, and Master Reynard sings in
falsetto." But their merriment is soon at an end. The
alarm has been given ; Ysengrin, Hersent, and a number
of other wolves, relations, friends, compeers of Primaut,
who all of them owe grudges to Reynard, come round
and besiege the pilgrims. They escape with great
difficulty. Ill-pleased with these grievous adventures,
they agree not to go to Rome at all, and Reynard, to
whom, rather against likelihood, the author here lends
his own thoughts, winds up the enterprise with a speech :
" ' My lords,' says he, ' by my head, this wandering is
loathsome and tiring. There is in the world many a
good man that has never been to Rome ; such an one
has come back from the Seven Saints who is worse than
he ever was. I mean to take my way home, and I shall
live by my labour and seek honest earnings ; I shall be
charitable to poor people.' Then they cried, ' Be it so,

be it so,' and they betook themselves homewards," converts to better lives, for a time.[1]

The same mode of reasoning was used later on, at the time of the Renaissance, by no less a man than Erasmus, who has described in his most satirical vein the vanities of pilgrims and pilgrimages. He supposes a meeting of two friends, Menedemus and Ogygyus, the latter just back from Compostela, and, what is more interesting for us, from Walsingham, " the most holy name in all England. . . . The towne is almost susteynyd by the resort of pylgrymes." The faithful believer Ogygyus goes on describing the wonders of the place, the gold and silver and precious stones offered to the miraculous statue of our Lady, the marvels worked at the holy wells, the miracle of the knight towards whom the portal of the church stretched out, the beautiful relics, and especially the crystal phial containing the Virgin's milk. " Whan ye sexten sawe us, he dyd runne to the aultre, and put apon hym his surplese and his stole about his nekke, knelyd downe relygyously and worshipyd it, and streght-forthe dyd offre the mylke to us to kysse." The same ceremony with surplice and kneeling, though it has disappeared at Walsingham with the phial itself, may still be seen elsewhere any day, in Milan, for example, at the tomb of San Carlo Borromeo.

Ogygyus and his friends make their offerings, not without remarking that some unscrupulous visitors, by a clever trick, pick money out of the plate instead of leaving in it any of their own : a trick which, as we have seen, was used by Panurge on a certain day when he was somewhat " escorné et taciturne " for lack of pence.

Erasmus ends his dialogue in the same strain as the author of " Reynard ":

[1] See Appendix XVII, p. 446.   On Reynard, the date, composition and sources of this work, see Léon Foulet, " Le Roman de Renard," Paris, 1914.

"I have enough to do," says sceptical Menedemus,
"with my statyons of Rome.

"*Ogygyus.* Of Rome, that dyd never see Rome?

"*Menedemus.* I wyll tell you, thus I go my statyons
at home. I go in to the parler, and I se unto the chast
lyvynge of my doughters ; agayne frome thense I go
in to my shope, I beholde what my servauntes, bothe
men and women, be doynge. From thense into the
kytchyn, lokynge abowt, if ther nede any of my cownsell ;
frome thense hyther and thyther, observynge howe my
chylderne be occupyed, what my wyffe dothe, beynge
carefull that every thynge be in ordre : these be statyons
of Rome.

"*Ogygyus.* But these thynges saynt James wold dow
for yow.

"*Menedemus.* That I shuld se unto these thynges
holy Scripture commaundethe ; that I shuld commyt
the charge to sayntes I dyd rede yt never commaunded." [1]

Thus far Menedemus, whose task in life seems to
have consisted in seeing to it that others fulfilled theirs.
The friend of Erasmus, Sir Thomas More, took the
opposite view, and wrote a dialogue in defence of images,
relics, and pilgrimages, but in vain.[2] The time of the
Reformation had come ; doubt was becoming general,
and from peasant to baron all the people assimilated
arguments like those of Latimer :

"What thinke ye of these images that are had more
then their felowes in reputation ? that are gone unto
with such labour and werines of the body, frequented

[1] "A Dialoge or communication of two persons, deuysyd and set forthe
in the laten tonge, by the noble and famose clarke, Desiderius Erasmus,
intituled ye pylgremage of pure deuotyon. Newly translatyd into Englishe."
London (1540 ?), 16°.

[2] "A Dyaloge of syr Thomas More knyghte . . . wherin be treatyd
dyuers maters, as of the veneration and worshyp of ymagys and relyques,
praying to sayntys, and goyng on pylgrymage, wyth many othere thyngys
touchyng the pestylent sect of Luther and Tyndale." London, 1529, 4°

with such our cost, sought out and visited with such confidence ? what say ye by these images, that are so famous, so noble, so noted, beying of them so many and so divers in England. Do you thinke that this preferryng of picture to picture, image to image, is the right use, and not rather the abuse of images ? " [1]

These times were yet to be. In the Middle Ages pilgrims came to offer their prayers, and also money, each one according to his means. When the king, in his perpetual goings and comings, turned aside to visit a revered shrine, he usually gave seven shillings, as shown by the ordinances of Edward II for his household. [2]

Before going away the pilgrims, who had admired, besides the shrine and its jewels, the stained glass of the church, the monumental curiosities of the place and some-times its fortifications, [3] bought, just as now, medals or signs as remembrances of their journey. [4] The author of the supplement to the " Canterbury Tales " at the beginning of the fifteenth century, shows the pilgrims purchasing in the town various sorts of *sygnys* or *brochis*, so

[1] "The sermon . . . made . . . to the conuocation of the clergy " (28 Henry VIII), in " Frutefvll sermons preached by the rt. rev. father and constant martyr of Jesus Christ, M. Hugh Latymer," 1571, p. 10.

[2] Ordinance for the state of the wardrobe and the account of the house-hold, June, 1323. " King Edward II's Household and Wardrobe Ordin-ances," ed. Furnivall, Chaucer Society, 1876, p. 62.

[3] In the continuation of Chaucer's tales, the Knight is represented inter-preting to his son the strong and weak points in the continuous wall at Canter-bury, and discussing whether it was proof against gunshot :

" And a-poyntid to his sone the perell and the dout,
Ffor shot of arbalast and of bowe, and eke for shot of gonne."

" The Tale of Beryn," ed. Furnivall and Stone, E.E.T.S., 1909, p. 9.

[4] C. Roach Smith has described a number of them in his " Collectanea Antiqua," London, 1848, vol. i. p. 81, and vol. ii. p. 43. He has given drawings of many which had been " discovered chiefly in the bed of the Thames, and in making the approaches to new London Bridge." See also " Guide to mediæval room, British Museum," 10 7, p. 69; Heath, " Pilgrim Life," 1911, ch. VI.; Forgeais, " Plombs historiés trouvés dans la Seine," 2d. ser. " Enseignes de Pélerinages," 1863. See below, p. 418.

that people who saw them might know where they had been :

> " Then, as manere and custom is, signes there they boughte,
>   Ffor men of contre shulde know whom they hadde [s]oughte." [1]

They were of lead or pewter, and perforated to be more easily sewn on the breast or cap, like those sold at the present day at St. Anne d'Auray in Brittany, but larger. At Canterbury they represented St. Thomas, or were in the shape of an ampulla or tiny flask, containing water from the miraculous well ; at St. James's they represented shells ; at Amiens the head of St. John the Baptist : " Ecce signum faciei beati Johannis Baptiste " ; at Rome the holy sudary, called the vernicle ; [2] at Rocamadour the Holy Virgin.[3] The right of selling these signs was a source of profit, and it sometimes belonged exclusively to a convent or to a private family.   At Rocamadour this

---

[1] " Tale of Beryn," *ibid.* p. 7.

[2] Among the ornaments worn by Chaucer's pardoner was a " vernicle " on his cap, as may be seen above in the plate, p. 336.   Sir Thomas More, in his " Dialogue," describes as follows the vernicle represented on pilgrims' medals : How, says he, can it be maintained that Christ blames images, " where he lykyd to leve the holy vernacle, thexpresse ymage also of hys blessid vysage, as a token to remain in honour among such as lovyd hym from ye tyme of hys bytter passyon hytherto, whych as it was by the myracle of hys blessid holy hand expressed and lefte in ye sudari : so hath yt bene by lyke myracle in that thyn corruptyble cloth kepte and preservyd uncorrupted thys xv. C. yere freshe and well perceyved, to ye inwarde cumforte, spyrytuall reioysyng and grete encreace of fervoure and devocyon in the harts of good crysten people " (Sig. B. iii.).

[3] Most of them mentioned by Garnier in his " Vie de Saint Thomas," where, after stating that men of all sorts flocked to Canterbury, he adds (ed. Hippeau, p. 205) :

> " Et anpules raportent en signe del veiage,
>   Mès de Jerusalem en est la croix portée,
>   Et de Rochemadur Marie en plum getée,
>   De Saint Jame la scale, qui en plum est muée ;
>   Or à Deus saint Thomas cele ampule donée,
>   Qui est par tut le mund chérie et honorée."

right had been conceded in return, it seems, for military services, to the De Valon family, lords of Thegra.[1] They and the Bishop of Tulle appointed a deputy to superintend the sale, and the product was divided by halves between them and the bishop. Such were the benefits derived from these sales that clandestine manufactories of pewter medals were established by the inhabitants, who sold numbers of them, to the great detriment of the authorized shop and in defiance of ever-recurring prohibitions. Once, however, in 1425, free sale was allowed to all the people of the place ; the country had been reduced to such poverty that the bishop renounced his privilege for two years, out of charity and for the benefit of his flock.

Pilgrims when going home were careful to wear prominently sewn on their garments these testimonials of their holy travels. In the above-quoted dialogue of Erasmus, the sceptical Menedemus wonders at the appearance of his friend : " I pray you, what araye is this that you be in ; me thynke that you be clothyd with cockle schelles, and be laden on every side with bruches of lead and tynne. And you be pretely garnyshed with wrethes of strawe, and your arme is full of snakes eggs," thus uncivilly designating the beads of his chaplet. The French king Louis XI, of grim memory, was never without some such pewter medals and brooches, and wore them on his hat. " And truly," writes his contemporary, Claude de Seyssel, " his devotion seemed more superstitious than religious. For to whatever image or church of God and the saints or of Our Lady that he heard the people were devoted, or where miracles were worked, he went there to make offerings, or sent a man there expressly. He had, besides, his hat quite full of images, mostly of lead or pewter, which he kissed on all occasions when any good or bad news arrived, or that his fancy prompted him ; casting himself upon his knees so

[1] " Guide du pélerin à Rocamadour," by M. le Chanoine Laporte, Rocamadour, 1862, chap. viii.

suddenly at times, in whatever place he might be, that he seemed more like one wounded in his understanding than a rational man." [1]

Professional pilgrims outshone in this respect all the others. For, beside the occasional pilgrim who came to make an offering to such or such a shrine in accomplishment of a vow and afterwards returned to take up again the course of his ordinary life, there was the pilgrim by calling or by penance (for such a life-long penance was sometimes inflicted), whose whole existence was spent travelling from one sanctuary to another, always on the road, and always begging. With the professional pardoner, the professional palmer, back from many countries, adorned with many tokens, the witness of many wonders, the hero of many adventures, was the most curious type of the religious wayfaring race, with hardly any equivalent in our days. Like the pardoner and the friar, the palmer could not but have a great experience of men and things ; he had seen much, and he invented more. He too had to edify the multitude to whom he held out his hand for alms, and the fine stories, in which he rarely missed giving himself a part to play, were his livelihood ; failing this, his daily bread failed too. By dint of repeating his tales, he came to almost believing them, then quite ; and his voice henceforth took that accent of certitude which alone begets conviction in audiences. Besides, he came from so far that he might indeed have seen marvels ; around us, of course, life flows on without prodigies, almost without events in its flat monotony ; but it is common knowledge that in distant parts things are quite different. And the best proof is that none of those who have undertaken the journey comes back disappointed, quite the contrary ; the

[1] " Les louenges du roy Louys xij^e. de ce nom, nouvellement composées par maistre Claude de Seyssel, docteur en tous droits." Paris, 1508, sign. f. iii.

pleasure of believing them is moreover innocent enough,
why should we deprive ourselves of an enjoyment
exhilarating for the mind and good for the soul ?

Clever people, poets, men of the world, deprived
themselves of this pleasure, and made up for the loss by
laughing at pilgrims and story-telling travellers. So did
Chaucer, as we have already seen, who held up to ridicule
in his " House of Fame," shipmen and pilgrims, with their
bags " brimful of lies." To the same effect but in graver
mood, Langland wrote in his "Visions":

> " Pylgrimis and palmers · plyghten hem to-gederes,
> To seche saint Iame · and seyntys of rome,
> Wenten forth in hure (their) way · with meny un-wyse tales,
> And haven leve to lye · al hure lyf-tyme." [1]

The crowd felt otherwise ; they listened, laughed perhaps sometimes, but more often recollected themselves
and remained attentive. The pilgrim was so interesting !
he was a play in himself, a living story, he had on his feet
the dust of Rome and of Jerusalem, and brought news
of the " worshippers " of Mahomet. He was a picture
too, with his bag hung at his side, not for lies, but for
provisions, and his staff, at the top of which was a knob
and sometimes a piece of metal with an appropriate motto
like the device on a bronze ring found at Hitchin, a cross
with these words, " Hæc in tute dirigat iter " (" May
this safely guide thee on thy way "). [2] The staff had at the
other end an iron point, like an alpenstock of the

[1] Skeat's edition, Text C, pass. i. l. 47.

[2] See the drawing of this ring in vol. viii. of the " Archæological Journal,"
p. 360. The long stick, or pilgrim's staff, and the bag or " scrip " were the
characteristic signs of pilgrims. In the romance of King Horn, the hero
meets on his road a *palmer*, and to disguise himself changes clothes with him ;
in this transformation the author only points out the chief particulars, that is
to say, the staff and the bag. " Horn took burdon and scrippe." (" King
Horn, with fragments of Floris and Blauncheflur," ed. by J. H. Lumby,
Early English Text Society, 1866.) We have seen above, p. 362, that
Reynard on his way to Rome took just the same implements.

present day ; as may be seen in numerous drawings in mediæval manuscripts.

The whole race of wanderers was, however, as we know, looked at askance by the king's officers ; these goings and comings disquieted the sheriff. We have already met labourers who, weary of their lord, left him under pretext of distant pilgrimages, and laid down without scruple the pilgrim's staff at the door of a new master who would pay them better. False pilgrims were not less numerous than false pardoners and false hermits ;

AN ENGLISH PILGRIM.
(*From the MS.* 17 C. xxxviii.)

they were condemned to repose, under pain of imprisonment, by the same statutes as the beggars and wandering workmen. Henceforward, orders Richard II in 1388, they too must have permits with a special seal affixed by certain worthy men.[1] Those without a permit should be forthwith arrested, unless infirm and incapable of work, for their good faith is then evident, and it is not for the love of vagabondage that they painfully go and visit " optimum ægrorum medicum," Saint Thomas. Even greater severity was shown when it was a matter of

[1] Statute 12 Rich. II, cap 7.

crossing the sea ; would-be pilgrims must be furnished with regular passports ; and the law applied to " all manner of people, as well clerks as other," under pain of confiscation of all their goods. The exceptions made by the king show besides that it is wanderers of doubtful status and motives whom he has in view, for there are dispensations for the " lords and other great persons of the realm," for the " true and notable merchants," and lastly, for the " king's soldiers." [1]

This passport or " licence," this " special leave of the king," could only be available at certain ports, namely, London, Sandwich, Dover, Southampton, Plymouth, Dartmouth, Bristol, Yarmouth, Boston, Kingston-upon-Hull, Newcastle-upon-Tyne, and the ports of the coast facing Ireland. Heavy penalties were laid on all port wardens, inspectors, ship captains, etc., who were neglectful, or so bold as to show favour to roamers. In the year 1389, the king restrained pilgrims from embarking anywhere else than at Dover or Plymouth. To put to sea elsewhere, an " especial licence from the king himself " was necessary.[2] A number of such licences, as will be seen further, are still in existence.

IV

But the attraction of distant pilgrimages was great,[3] especially the three without equal : Rome, Jerusalem, and St. James's of Galicia, held so sacred that, while most

[1] Statute 5 Rich. II, st. 1, c. 2. Restrictions on pilgrimage-making existed also in France. See an ordinance of Charles VI, February 27, 1399, prohibiting pilgrimages to Rome. " Recueil d'Isambert," vol. vi. p. 843.

[2] " Rolls of Parliament," 13 Rich. II, vol. iii. p. 275, and statute 1, cap. 20 of 13 Rich. II.

[3] As to the number of pilgrimages, their origin, and history, see the " Dictionnaire géographique, historique, descriptif, archéologique des pélerinages anciens et modernes," by L. de Sivry and M. de Champagnac, Paris, 1850, 2 vols. 8vo, forming vols. xliii. and xliv. of Migne's " Encyclopédie théologique."

of the vows taken by the benefactors of the great bridge at Avignon could be remitted on account of their gifts to this useful structure, exception was made if the question was of a pilgrimage to be performed to one of those three places.[1] With or without letters men crossed the Channel, for which they paid sixpence, or if they had a horse, two shillings.[2] They arrived at Calais, stopping there some time in a " Maison-Dieu," or hospital, which had been built and endowed by pious souls with revenues " for the sustenance of the pilgrims and other poor folks repairing to the said town to rest and refresh them." [3]

Setting out again, they went to Boulogne to pray to a miraculous virgin, whose hand still exists enclosed in a reliquary. The statue itself was thrown into a well by the Protestants in 1567, replaced on the altar in 1630, pulled down again at the Revolution and burnt, but one of the faithful saved the hand, which the church of Notre Dame preserves to this day. Chaucer's travelled gossip, the Wife of Bath, had among other pilgrimages, made this one to Boulogne.[4] People also went to Amiens to venerate the head, or rather one of the heads, of St. John the Baptist.[5] Great was their wonder when, con-

[1] Ripert-Monclar, " Bullaire du Pont d'Avignon," 1912.

[2] Statute 4 Ed. III, c. 8.

[3] Petition of the Calais burgesses, " Rolls of Parliament," vol. iii. p. 500, 4 Henry IV, A.D. 1402. In Dover too, on the opposite shore, there was such a house, the inventory of which has been printed : Walcott, " Inventories of St. Mary's Hospital or Maison-Dieu, Dover," London, 1869. In the diary of his travels, during the sixteenth century, the Greek Nicander Nucius observes that the town of Dover seemed to be made almost entirely of inns and hotels. " The Travels of Nicander Nucius of Corcyra," Camden Society, 1841.

[4] See Prof. J. W. Hales' letter to *The Academy* of April 22, 1882, p. 287. A view of the old church, of which very little now remains, could be seen, Mr. Enlart writes me, in a picture by Van der Meulen, but it was destroyed by the Germans in one of their air raids during the late Great War, when they shelled the Museum.

[5] This relic so greatly attracted the English that they had founded in the cathedral a chapel of " Notre Dame Englesque " (Sancta Maria Anglica),

tinuing their journey, they fell in with another at Constantinople. Perhaps, let us hope, they were content with remarking as " Mandeville " does : Which is the true one ? " I wot nere, but God knowethe ; but in what wyse than men worschipen it, the blessed seynt John holt him a-payd." [1] Then also people went to the shrine of the three kings at Cologne, to Paris where innumerable relics were kept, to Chartres, where, besides a famous statue of the Virgin, was shown the tunic she wore on the day of the Annunciation (preserved in the cathedral since 861),[2] to Vezelay, Tours, Le Puy, and to many other places in France, among which the celebrated and to the present day most frequented church of Our Lady of Rocamadour in Guyenne. The fame of this pilgrimage among Englishmen is attested by Langland, when he advises people belonging to the religious orders to cease pilgrimage-making, and rather practice virtue at home :

" Right so, if thow be religious· renne thou never ferther
To Rome ne to Rochemadore." [3]

It was a shrine of great renown. Roland, according to a legend, went there before starting for the ill-fated expedition in which he met his death, and a large piece of rusted iron is still shown in the old church as part of the famous Durandal. Henry II of England came there, too, as a pilgrim, as did many other illustrious travellers, Simon de Montfort among them.[4] The place was fortified ; it had a part to play in the Hundred Years' War,

and the leopards of England, writes Prof. Enlart, are still to be seen in the stained glass.

[1] Halliwell's edition, 1866, p. 108.
[2] See the remarkable articles by Emile Male, on " L'Art du Moyen Age et les Pélerinages," in the " Revue de Paris," 1920 ; in the number of Feb. 15, an article on " Les Routes de France et d'Espagne."
[3] Text B, p. xii. l. 37.
[4] A. B. Caillau, " Histoire critique et religieuse de Notre Dame de Roc-Amadour," Paris, 1834, pp. 73 ff

FORTIFIED ENTRANCE TO THE SANCTUARIES OF ROCAMADOUR. [*p.* 373

(*Restored.*)

and Froissart has told us " howe Sir Robert Carrol and Sir John Chandos . . . toke Guaches, Rochemador, and diuers other townes, the which wer newly turned frenche." [1]

Then there were Spanish pilgrimages, and especially the world-famous one at Compostela, where English travellers went in large numbers, most of them direct by sea, though some preferred the lengthy, picturesque land road, dotted with famous shrines good for the soul, and where all sorts of adventures might be expected.[2] Licences authorizing the owners and the captain of such or such a ship to carry to St. James's a fixed number of pilgrims fill pages in Rymer's "Fœdera." They were granted pursuant to the before-mentioned statute of Richard II, and are all drawn after one or two models, the text in Latin, with the name of the ship in French, like the one here translated, of the year 1394 :

" The king, to all and each of his Admirals, etc., greeting.

" Know you that we have given licence to Oto Chambernoun, William Gilbert, and Richard Gilbert, to receive and embark in the harbour of Dartmouth a hundred pilgrims in a certain ship belonging to the same Oto, William, and Richard, called la Charité de Paynton, of which Peter Cok is captain ; and to take them to Saint James's, there to fulfil their vows, and from thence to bring them back to England, freely and without hindrance, notwithstanding any ordinances to the contrary." [3]

[1] Berners' Froissart, vol. i. ch. cclviii.

[2] William Wey, in the fifteenth century, notices the large number of English ships at " Grwne " (Coruña), the usual port of landing for Compostela : " In porto Grwne erant de Anglicis, Wallicis, Hibernicis, Normannis, Francis, Britonnibus· et aliis LXXX^{ta} naves cum topcastellis et quatuor sine topcastellis ; numerus navium Anglicarum erat XXX^{ij}." He notes the words and music of a song sung by little Spanish boys, dancing before pilgrims and offering good wishes, in exchange for which they hoped to get some small coin. " Itineraries," Roxburghe Club, 1857, pp. 154, 156.

[3] " Fœdera," ed. 1704, vol. vii. p. 468, 17 Rich. II.

A few provisos are added, the keeping of which the pilgrims should swear to before leaving England ; they must upon their oath bind themselves to do nothing contrary to the obedience and fealty they owe the king ; they must not take out of the realm gold or silver in money or bullion beyond what is necessary to their journey, and they must not, it is sometimes added, reveal the secrets of the kingdom.

During the following century these licences became innumerable, or maybe they have been preserved in larger numbers. They show that, in fact, fleets loaded with English pilgrims plied towards St. James's. We find that " Le Petre de Darthmouth " is allowed to carry sixty pilgrims ; " La Marie de Southampton," a hundred ; " La Sainte Marie de Blakney," sixty ; " Le Garlond de Crowemere," sixty ; " La Trinité de Wells," forty ; " Le Thomas de Saltash," sixty ; and so on. Numbers usually vary from thirty to one hundred.[1]

It must not be thought that these ships, carrying as much as a hundred passengers besides their crew on this rather long journey, were great, well-appointed vessels. They very much resembled the pilgrim-ships of the present day, which carry every year to Jeddah, on the Red Sea, crowds of Arabs on their way to Mecca. The travellers were huddled together in most uncomfortable fashion, and had ample opportunities to do penance and offer their sufferings to the saint. This is no surmise, for one of those English pilgrims duly allowed to go to Galicia, provided they did not reveal the secrets of the realm, has rimed an account of his experiences, so we know what they were. Do not think of laughing, says he, when you go by sea to St. James's ; there is sea-sickness ; the sailors push you about under pretext that you hinder the working of the ship ; the smell is not pleasant :

[1] " Fœdera," 12 Hen. VI, 1434, vol. x. pp. 567–569.

TRAVELLING BY SEA IN THE FOURTEENTH CENTURY.

(*From the MS. Harl.* 1319.)

" Men may leve alle gamys
    That saylen to Seynt Jamys !
    Ffor many a man hit gramys (vexes)
        When they begin to sayle.

Ffor when they have take the see,
    At Sandwych or at Wynchylsee,
    At Bristow, or where that hit bee,
        Theyr hertes begyn to fayle."

The mocking remarks of the seamen are painful to bear.
Says the captain :

" Some ar lyke to cowgh and grone
    Or hit be full mydnyght ; "

and then turning to his men :

" ' Hale the bowelyne ! now, vere the shete !
    Cooke, make redy anoon our mete,
    Our pylgryms have no lust to ete,
        I pray God yeve hem rest ! '

' Go to the helm ! what, howe ! no nere ?
    Steward, felow ! A pot of bere ! '—
        ' Ye shalle have sir, with good chere,
            Anon alle of the best.' "

Sick pilgrims could not eat, and were jeered at, they
found the time long ; some, with a book on their knees,
tried to read, but then they felt as if their head would
burst :

" Som layde theyr bookys on theyr kne,
    And rad so long they myght nat se ;—
    ' Allas ! myne hede wolle cleve on thre ! ' "

When at their worst, comes a facetious sailor to bawl
out in their ears : Cheer up, in a moment we shall be
in a storm !

> " Then cometh oone and seyth : ' Be mery ;
> Ye shall have a storme or a pery ' (a squall)
>
> *   *   *   *   *
>
> Thys mene whyle the pylgryms ly
> And have theyr bowlys (basins) fast theym by,
> And cry after hot malvesy."

In short, they were very unhappy, and as the narrator said at first, little inclined to games and laughter.[1]

Votive offerings plentifully adorned venerated sanctuaries ; if, by striking a wax statuette while making appropriate incantations an enemy might do you great harm, on the other hand, by placing your image in the chapel of a saint, great favours might be gained for you, especially in cases of sickness.[2] Thus were to be seen prisoners' irons, warriors' swords, cripples' crutches, jewels and precious stones, sculpted or painted images representing devotees or actual miracles performed for them, tablets and offerings of all sorts.[3] At Rocamadour tresses of women's hair were shown as a threat as well as an admonition. " They were," relates the knight of La Tour Landry, those of " ladies and gentille women that had be[en] wasshe in wyne, and in other thinges for to make the here of colour otherwise thanne God made

[1] " The Stacions of Rome and the Pilgrim's Sea Voyage," ed. Furnivall, Early English Text Society, 1867, p. 47.   This complaint on the Compostela pilgrimage is of the fifteenth century.   On the Compostela sanctuary and on the propagation of certain artistic notions through the influx of pilgrims, see the before quoted article by E. Male, " Revue de Paris," Feb. 1920.

[2] " The Paston Letters," ed. Jas. Gairdner, vol. i. p. 48.   Letter of Margaret Paston of September 28, 1443.

[3] Especially noteworthy in this respect at the present day is the Church of Santa Maria delle Grazie, near Mantua (in which the famous author of the " Cortegiano," Baldassare Castiglione, is buried), where life-size, realistic wax figures, wearing real garments or armour, form a continuous series above the arches on both sides of the nave.   Each scene commemorates a miraculous intervention of the Virgin : innocents saved at the moment of their execution, the halter breaking, the axe stopped, etc.   The " custode " also directs attention to a stuffed animal, dangling from the roof, and which he describes as a " crocodilo " which used to desolate the country.

THE SOUTHERN ENTRANCE TO SAINT JAMES OF COMPOSTELA.
Twelfth Century.   [*p.* 381.

it, the whiche ladies and gentille women that aught
(owned) the tresses were comynge thedirward on pilgrimage,
but they may never have powere to come withinne the
chirche dore unto the tyme that thei hadde cutte of the
tresses of her here," [1] which, says he, were still there in
his day.

Another story to the same effect is told by Miélot,
who reports how a very fair lady, who had led an ill life,
lost her sight as a punishment, through the will of Heaven.
She went on a pilgrimage to Rocamadour, prayed to the
Virgin, and was healed, but could not, however, enter the
sanctuaries. She then confessed on the spot to a priest,
who, " looking at her fair face," said : " Dear friend, I
well know that with these fair tresses of your hair you
have done great hurt to those to whom you have shown
them. I decide that they must be cut off in honour of
God and of our Lady." This was done ; " the tresses
were cut, and the priest had them carried inside the
church on a pole, on which were placed the tresses of
women who would be saved." Then the lady was able
to enter the church, and she praised the Virgin. But as
she was going away she could not help thinking " of her
fair hair that she had left," and she exclaimed : " Holy
Mary, my heart is sorrowful for my hair that I leave
you, and I cannot well make up my mind to it." She
had scarcely spoken when the tresses were at once restored
to her " as fair as they were before ; " but the blindness
came back too, and blind she remained for ever, which is
a good example, " ung bel exemplaire," for ladies that
" seek false pleasures in their fine waists and faces." [2]

Indulgences were an immense attraction ; they had

[1] " The Book of the Knight of La Tour Landry," translated from the
French, ed. Thomas Wright, Early English Text Society, 1868, p. 70. The
original French is of the fourteenth century.

[2] " Miracles de Nostre Dame," collected by Jean Miélot, ed. G. F.
Warner, Roxburghe Club, 1885, p. 58. This version of the tale is of the
fifteenth century, but the story itself is much older.

been freely granted on a large scale to every important shrine, and popular imagination still further magnified them. The pilgrim from Rome, back in his village, exaggerated as willingly their amount as that of the marvels which he had seen, or thought he had seen. One such pilgrim, an Englishman of the fourteenth century, dazzled by his recollections, has rimed his impressions of a journey taken by him to Italy. As a poet he does not rank high, but he does not pretend to, and his only aim is to supply precise figures and definite information. His strong narrow devotion allowed him to pay attention to nothing except thousands of bodies of martyrs that he never tires of enumerating. By thousands also are reckoned the years of indulgence which he flashes in the eyes of his stay-at-home countrymen :

> " Gif men wuste (knew), grete and smale,
> The pardoun that is at grete Rome,
> Thei wolde tellen in heore dome (in their opinion),
> Hit were no neod to mon in cristiante
> To passe in to the holy lond over the see
> To Jerusalem, ne to Kateryne." [1]

His readers will have first a brief and simplified history of Rome ; it is a city to which came long ago the Duchess of Troy with her two sons, Romulus and Romulon, who afterwards founded the town. The duchess thus seems to have chosen to settle in a city which did not yet exist, but Rome is a land of wonders. It was pagan, until Peter and Paul (and then the very facts inject their eloquence into our traveller's lines) :

> " Hit hedde i-bought,
> With gold ne selver, ne with no goode,
> Bot with heore flesch and with heore blode."

The enumeration of the churches thereupon begins, and for each of them are invariably told the amount of

[1] i.e. St. Catherine of Mount Sinai.

indulgences attached to it and of relics kept there. The benefits are proportioned to the merits ; thus when a man sees the *vernicle*, that is, the holy sudary which received the image of the Saviour, he gets three thousand years of pardon if he dwells in Rome, nine thousand if he comes from a neighbouring country,

> "And thou that passest over the see,
>   Twelve thousend yer is graunted to the."

When you enter Sts. Vitus and Modestus, the third of your sins are remitted. Then, you descend into the catacombs :

> "But thou most take candel liht,
>   Elles thou gost merk (dark) as niht,
>   For under the eorthe most thou wende,
>   Thou maight not see bifore ne bihynde,
>   For thider fledde mony men
>   For drede of deth to saven hem,
>   And suffrede peynes harde and sore,
>   In hevene to dwelle for ever more."

The bodies of martyrs are countless ; [1] four thousand of them at Saint Prudence, thirteen hundred at Saint Prassede, seven thousand at Sts. Vitus and Modestus. From time to time a famous name brings up an historic glimpse, such as the account of the foundation of Rome, or an abridged life of Constantine ; at first a pagan and a leper,

> "In Mahoun was al his thouht."

---

[1] William Wey, in the fifteenth century, thus mentions the catacombs : "Item ibi est una spelunca nuncupata Sancti Kalixti cimiterium, et qui eam pertransit cum devocione, illi indulgentur omnia sua peccata. Et ibi multa corpora sanctorum sunt, que nullus hominum numerare nequit nisi solus Deus." "The Itineraries of William Wey," Roxburghe Club, 1857, p. 146. Wey, like the author of the poem, sometimes mentions prodigious numbers of bodies of martyrs ; at the church called Scala Celi, " sunt ossa sanctorum decem millia militum ; " in one single part of St. Peter's at Rome, are " Petronella et xiii millia sanctorum martyrum."

But according to our author's information, he was converted and cured by Pope Sylvester. The church of St. Mary the Round formerly bore another name :

> "Agrippa dude hit make
> For Sibyl and Neptanes sake. . . .
> He gaf hit name Panteon."

He placed there a magnificent golden idol sitting, of a peculiar form :

> " Hit looked forth as a cat,
> He called it Neptan."

This idol had a cap or cover of brass which was one day blown off by the wind, and carried to the church of St. Peter. Then Pope Boniface asked the Emperor Julian to give him the Pantheon, to which that prince consented ; and one year, on November 1st, the hatless cat having been removed, the sovereign pontiff consecrated the building, and baptized it St. Mary the Round.

As for relics, there are few objects mentioned in Holy Writ which have not been recovered, and may not be venerated at Rome.[1] The table of the Last Supper is there, as well as Aaron's rod, fragments of the multiplied loaves and fishes, hay from the stall at Bethlehem, a swaddling-cloth of the infant Jesus, and several other things, some of which are strange enough. Part of these relics are still in the same churches, for instance, at Santa Maria Maggiore,[2] " Seinte Marie the Maiour," the portrait

---

[1] William Wey said of the church of the Holy Cross : " Item, ibi sunt duo ciphi, unus plenus sanguine Ihesu Cristi, et alter plenus lacte beate Marie Virginis," " Itineraries," p. 146. Those who drink at the three fountains which gushed out at the death of St. Paul are cured of all maladies ; those who visit the church of St. Mary of the Annunciation will never be struck by lightning; at the church of St. Vivian there is " herba crescens quam ipsa plantavit et valet contra caducum morbum." At the church of St. Sebastian is shown a foot-print of Jesus ; and it is, in fact, still to be seen there at the present day. Ibid. pp. 143–148.

[2] In the Borghese chapel.

of the Virgin painted by St. Luke. This is not, however, according to our pilgrim, a picture really made by St. Luke ; he was going to do it, and had prepared his colours, when he suddenly found the portrait before him, finished by the hands of angels :

> " Seint Luik while he lived in londe,
> Wolde have peynted hit with his honde,
> And whon he hedde ordeyned so
> Alle colours that schulde ther to,
> He fond an ymage al a-pert,
> Non such ther was middelert,
> Mad with angel hond and not with his
> As men in Rome witnesseth this." [1]

More complete and conscientious in his descriptions, an educated Englishman of the following century, a voracious reader, and active writer, of books, no other than the chronicler and theologian, John Capgrave, prior of King's Lynn, having gone to Rome on a pilgrimage, about the year 1450, composed, on his return, a " Solace of Pilgrimes," wanting to imitate, he said, Pythagoras, Plato, St. Jerome, Marco Polo, and him whom he considered as his compatriot, the then unmasked Mandeville, who, all of them, having travelled, wrote of their journeys :

[1] " The Stacions of Rome," fourteenth century, ed. F. J. Furnivall, Early English Text Society, 1867. Another version of the " Stacions," with variants, was printed by the same in " Political, Religious, and Love Poems," Early English Text Society, 1866, p. 113. See in this last volume notes by W. M. Rossetti on the " Stacions," pp. xxi-xlviii, paralleling the information furnished by the English author with that given by the Italian Francino, who wrote on the same subject in 1600, and whose numbers are much less exaggerated. Mr. Rossetti states also what is still shown at Rome of the relics named in the " Stacions."

The Saint Luke legend appears in a somewhat different form in William Wey, according to whom the saint was about to paint when he fell asleep, and the angels made the picture for him, " Itineraries," p. 143. A similar legend is attached to the great wooden crucifix of Byzantine workmanship, called in the middle ages the " Saint Vou " (the Holy Face, *vultus*), at Lucca, begun by Nicodemus after the Ascension, and miraculously finished during his sleep. Bédier, " Légendes épiques," 1908, II; 210.

" Also there was a man of Venys whech they called Marcus
Paulus ; he laboured all the Soudane's londe and descryved
on to us the nature of the cuntre, the condiciones of the
men and the stately aray of the great Cane (khan) houshold.
Eke Jon Maundevyle Knyth of Yngland, aftir his laboure,
made a book ful solacious on to his nacyoun. After all
these grete cryeris of many wonderfull thingis I wyl folow
with a smal pypyng of such straunge sitis (sights) as I
have seyn and swech straunge thingis as I have herd." [1]

This justice must be rendered him that, while his
book is full of " straunge thingis," he never adds any
of his own invention ; when he says, this I have seen, it
can, if not afterwards destroyed, still be seen to-day ;
when he copies an inscription, his copy, as can be easily
verified, is accurate. But, fond of books, he believed
in them ; who ever failed to believe in what he loved ?
The " Mirabilia Romæ " are the guide of this guide-book
maker ; [2] so that to the enumeration of the holy places
with their relics and indulgences, and his description of
the ancient, now vanished, church of St. Peter, and all
the famous sanctuaries of the papal city, he adds the
wonders of fabulous Rome, with the temple on Capitol
hill, and in it, " a mervelous craft, that of every region
of the world stood an ymage made all of tre and in his
hand a lytil belle ; as often as ony of these regiones was
in purpos to rebelle a geyn the grete mageste of Rome,
a non this ymage that was assigned to that regioun schulde
knylle his bell." This device, so celebrated in the middle
ages, was due to that great enchanter " Virgil," the magic
of whose lines had been appreciated for different motives
in Roman days.

[1] " Ye Solace of Pilgrimes, a description of Rome *circa* A.D. 1450, by
John Capgrave," ed. Mills and Bannister, Oxford, 1911, 4°.
[2] As well as that of the author of the poem. This immensely popular
work of unknown date was in existence anyhow in the XIIth century. See
" Mirabilia Urbis Romæ, the Marvels of Rome," with notes by F. M.
Nichols, London, 1889.

The attractions of Rome were, for the pilgrim, without peer in Italy, but other cities could almost rival it ; Venice especially was full of wonders, and was admired and visited accordingly, witness, for example, the travelling notes of a troop of French pilgrims in the year 1395. In this "most excellent, noble, great and fine town all seated in the sea," may be seen, they aver, the arm of "our Lord St. George," the burdon (staff) of St. Nicholas, one of the water-pots of Cana, one ear of St. Paul, some of the "roasted flesh of St. Lawrence turned to powder," three of the stones thrown at St. Stephen, the body of St. Mark, "which is a very fine and noble thing." There is, besides, "in the Maison-Dieu of Venice one of the molar teeth of a giant that was called Goliath, which giant David killed, and know you that this tooth is more than half a foot long and weighs twelve pounds." [1]

Thus did returning travellers relate their recollections, to the delighted wonderment of their countrymen. The wish to set out in their turn was awakened in them, and those who remained in their village associated themselves to the pious journey by their prayers and some small gift of money. All along his road the pilgrim found similar dispositions ; to receive and help him was to share in his merits, and thus it was that people in the humblest ranks, assisted from place to place,[2] could accomplish distant pilgrimages. The rules of several gilds provided for the case of a member setting out to fulfil a vow. In order to participate in his good work, all the "bretheren and sisteren" accompanied him out of the town, and on bidding him farewell offered him their gift.

[1] " Le Saint Voyage de Jhérusalem du Seigneur d'Anglure," ed. Bonnardot and Longnon, " Societé des Anciens Textes Français," 1878, pp. 3, 4.

[2] On the normal cost of such journeys (from Rouen to St. James of Compostela, in 1377, 343 fr. of our present money), see d'Avenel, " Histoire économique," vi. 621.

They watched their friend go off with his deliberate step, beginning a journey across many countries, to last many months, sometimes several years. They returned to the town, and the elders, who knew the world, no doubt told what strange things their friend was like to see in those distant lands, and what subjects for edification he would meet with on his way.

The gild of the Resurrection at Lincoln, founded in 1374, had among its rules, " If any brother or sister wishes to make pilgrimage to Rome, St. James of Galicia, or the Holy Land, he shall forewarn the gild ; and all the bretheren and sisteren shall go with him to the city gate, and each shall give him a half-penny at least." The same rule was observed by the Fullers' gild of Lincoln, founded in 1297 ; the pilgrim going to Rome was accompanied as far as Queen's Cross, outside the town, if he left on a Sunday or a feast-day ; and if he could let them know of his return, and it were not a working day, all went to meet him at the same place and accompanied him to the monastery. The tailors of the same city also gave a half-penny to him among them who was going to Rome or St. James, and a penny to him who went to the Holy Land. The ordinances of the Gild of the Virgin, founded at Hull in 1357, had : " If any brother or sister of the gild wishes, at any time, to make a pilgrimage to the Holy Land, then, in order that all the gild may share in his pilgrimage, he shall be fully released from his yearly payment until his return."

Some gilds kept open house for pilgrims, always with the same object of having a part thereby in the merits of the traveller. Thus the gild-merchant of Coventry, founded in 1340, maintained " a common lodging-house of thirteen beds," to receive poor travellers who cross the country going on pilgrimage or from any other pious motive. This hostelry was managed by a governor, aided by a woman who washed the feet of the guests and took care of them. The annual expenditure on this foundation was ten pounds sterling.[1]

When one of the king's servants had a pilgrimage to make, the prince, in consideration of his motive, willingly authorized him to depart, and even helped him with money. Edward III gave to William Clerk, one of his messengers, one pound six shillings and eightpence, to help him in his expenses during the pilgrimage undertaken by him to Jerusalem and Mount Sinai.[2] If the man were of great importance, and especially if he intended to fight the unbelievers, public prayers were offered for his journey, his "triumphal fighting," and his safe return, as was done when Henry of Lancaster, cousin to Edward III, went "to the parts beyond sea with certain great and noble men of this realm" to attack the enemies of the cross, in this case, the pagans of Prussia. The prayers were prescribed for Sundays and fête days, when there would be "the greatest multitude of people in the churches."[3]

All this in spite of the fourteenth century's not being, as we have seen, an age of deep and true devotion. The Popes lived at Avignon, their prestige was declining, particularly in England; even bishops showed at times scant respect for the Roman Court. Nowhere can be found, not even in Wyclif, more daring accusations and more scandalous anecdotes concerning the Pope than in the chronicle written by Thomas of Burton, Abbot of Meaux, near Beverley. He even speaks with a t nge of irony of indulgences. As a special favour to the faithful who died during a pilgrimage to Rome, Clement VI "ordered the angels of Paradise," writes the abbot, "to lead their souls straight to the gates of heaven without

[1] Toulmin Smith, " English Gilds," pp. 157, 177, 180, 182, 231.
[2] Devon's " Issues of the Exchequer," 1837, p. 159.
[3] Mandate from the Archbishop of York, Feb. 1, 1351–2, in Raine, " Historical Papers from the Northern Registers," p. 402

making them pass through purgatory." The same Pope granted what the pilgrim of the " Stacions " seems to have ignored, that those who looked upon the holy sudary should return to the state they were in before baptism. Lastly, " he confirmed all the indulgences granted by two hundred sovereign pontiffs his predecessors, which are innumerable." [1] Clement was, indeed, the two hundredth.

At the period when monastic chroniclers did not scruple to record anecdotes on the Roman Court like those in Thomas of Burton's, general devotion was not merely lessened, it was disorganized, unbalanced. The chroniclers show, indeed, that excesses of impiety co-existed with excesses of fervour ; the false pardoner, retailer of the merits of the saints, fell in upon the highway with the bleeding flagellant.[2] The papacy might show commendable good sense by its condemnations of both ; [3] its decrees did not suffice to restore the equilibrium of

---

[1] " Chronica monasterii de Melsa," ed. E. A. Bond, 1868, vol. iii. p. 88, Rolls Series. The Abbot declares that Clement VI replied to the reproaches of his confessor as to his bad life : " Quod facimus modo facimus consilio medicorum." About his theory of the " treasury," see *supra*, p. 314. The Pontiff, Pierre Rogier, a Frenchman, of great learning and extraordinary memory, of knightly manners, fond of festivities and amusements, had been an opponent of Edward III in the matter of benefices, which may have still increased the Abbot's animosity. His decision as to the angels was inserted in his bull on jubilees, which were to recur every fifty years instead of every century ; it concerns pilgrims coming to the jubilee.

[2] " In which year (1350) there came into England certain penitents, noblemen and foreigners, who beat their bare bodies very sharply, to the effusion of blood, now weeping, now singing ; yet, as was said, they did this too unadvisedly, being without licence from the apostolic see." Walsingham, " Historia Anglicana," Rolls Series, vol. i. p. 275. See also Robert de Avesbury, " Hist. Edwardi Tertii," ed. Hearne, Oxford, 1720, p. 179. The flagellants whipped themselves with knotted cords furnished with nails, they prostrated themselves to the ground singing, with their arms extended cross-wise.

[3] The flagellants were condemned by Clement VI in 1349 ; he ordered the archbishops, bishops, &c., to have them imprisoned. Labbe, " Sacro-sancta Concilia," Florence ed., vol. xxv. col. 1153.

men's minds, and the bounds of reason were continually being passed ; in ardent piety as in impious revolt men went to the verge of madness. The account of the repulsive sacrileges committed in York Cathedral by the partisans of the Bishop of Durham seems unbelievable, yet the facts cannot be doubted, being reported by the archbishop himself.[1] Faith weakened or went astray ; men became at once sceptical and intolerant. It was not in them the modern, serenely cold and imperturbable scepticism, but a violent movement of the entire being, impelled to burn what it adores. The man acts by fits ; he doubts his doubt, his burst of laughter dazes him ; he has had his revel and his orgy, and when the white light of morning comes he will be the prey of despair, shed tears, be racked with anguish, proclaim his conversion and vow maybe to go on a pilgrimage. Walsingham sees one of the causes of the peasants' revolt in the incredulity of the barons : " Some among them believe, it is said, that there is no God, they deny the sacrament of the altar and resurrection after death, and consider that as is the end of the beast of burden, so is the end of man himself." [2]

Such incredulity did not exclude superstitious practices. To go straight forward was the privilege of the happy few ; the many, instead of opening the gates of heaven with their own hands, imagined they could have it done by that of others ; they had Paradise gained for them by the neighbouring monastery, as they had their

---

[1] Letter of the Archbishop of York to his official, " Historical Papers from the Northern Registers," ed. Raine, pp. 397–399. The guilty were not worthless vagabonds ; one has the title of *magister*, another is professor of civil law.

[2] " Nam quidam illorum credebant, ut asseritur, nullum Deum esse, nihil esse sacramentum altaris, nullam post mortem resurrectionem, sed ut jumentum moritur, ita et hominem finire." " Historia Anglicana," vol. ii. p. 12. Langland also complains of the scepticism of the nobles, who question the mysteries, and make these grave matters the subject of light conversation after meals. " Piers Plowman," Text C, pass. xii. l. 35.

lands tilled for them by their tenants ; eternal welfare had become a matter of commerce and could be bought with the letters of fraternity of the mendicant friars and the lying indulgences of false pardoners. Men lived at their ease, and when the sad hour came, made pious donations in their wills, as if they could, according to the strong words of the French historian, Claude de Seyssel, " corrupt and win over by gifts God and the saints, whom we ought to appease by good works and by penitence for our sins." [1] Very instructive reading is that of the last wills and testaments of the rich lords of the fourteenth century. Pages are filled with devotional bequests ; gifts are left to shrines, convents, chapels, and hermits ; testators who had abstained from going in their lifetime, made pilgrimages by proxy after their death, paying the proxy. The same Humphrey Bohun who sent " a good man and true " to the tomb of Thomas of Lancaster, also ordered that after his demise a priest should be sent to Jerusalem, " chiefly," said he, " for my lady mother, and for my lord father, and for ourselves," with the obligation to say masses at all the chapels which he might meet on his way.[2] Elizabeth de Burgh, Lady Clare, ordered by her will, that five men-at-arms should fight in her name in case there should be a " comune vyage," otherwise a crusade, within seven years following her death. They would receive one hundred marks each, and the merit of their fights would accrue to their employer, and not to themselves, their own recompense being of this world, and consisting in the hundred marks.[3]

[1] " Les louenges du roy Louys xij.," by Claude de Seyssel, Paris, 1508.
[2] " A Collection of the Wills of the Kings and Queens of England," &c., printed by J. Nichols, London, 1780. Will of Humphrey Bohun, Earl of Hereford and Essex, who died 1361, p. 54.
[3] She died November 4, 1360. Nichols, ibid. p. 29.

V

Most difficult and holiest of all, the pilgrimage to Jerusalem remained, in spite of so many indulgences attached by the Popes to the churches in Rome, the one without peer, as well as it was the oldest established ; it dated back, indeed, from, at least, the days of Constantine. Settled in Palestine during the fourth century, St. Jerome writes to Paulinus : " From all the world people are flocking here. The whole of mankind fills the city." [1]

This is confirmed by his friend the enthusiastic Paula, in whose veins flowed the ardent blood of the Scipios and the Gracchi, and who trying to persuade her beloved Marcella, a rich and pious Roman matron, to join them there, tells her that all the greatest and best, those from Gaul, those from Britain, " divisus ab orbe nostro Britannus " (for she, too, knows those classics whom Jerome constantly quotes), without speaking of the Persians, the Armenians, and all the East, are to be met in the Holy Land : " A variety of languages, but one only religion." There are " so many places of prayer that one cannot visit them all in one day." And such places ! " What sentences, what words would be appropriate to tell you of the cave of our Saviour ? and of that stable where, as a babe, He cried : a spot to be honoured rather by silence than by inadequate words. Where are the vast porticoes, the gilt canopies ? . . . In this poor earthly place the Maker of heaven was born ; here He was wrapped in swadling clothes, here seen by the shepherds, here revealed by a star, here adored by the Magi." Come, Oh come ! " Will not the moment arrive when a breathless traveller shall announce to us that our Marcella has reached Palestine . . . Will not the day come when we can visit together the Saviour's grotto,

[1] From Bethleem, last quarter of the fourth century. Migne, " Patrologiæ Latinæ tomus XXII," col. 582.

weep at His tomb, kiss the wood of the cross, and be raised in our minds with the rising Lord on the Mount of Olives ? " [1]

But even then, thoughtful, level-headed St. Jerome feared that enthusiasm might be carried too far, and everyday duties neglected for the excitement of the Palestine journey. It was, of course, in itself a pious and laudable thing, if one could properly do so, to come and venerate " the places where the feet of our Lord had stood, and the almost recent traces left of His nativity and His passion." But this should not be considered a Christian's chief duty : " Do not think that something is lacking in your faith because you have not seen Jerusalem. I do not consider myself any better because I live here." To lead a good life is the chief thing : " What is praiseworthy is not to have been at Jerusalem, but to have lived righteously there. . . . The places where the cross was and the Resurrection occurred, benefit those who bear their cross and who, with Christ, rise again every day. . . . The palace of heaven is just as accessible from Britain as from Jerusalem." To thousands who have never seen the holy city " the gate of paradise is wide open. . . . A grand thing it is to be a Christian, not to seem one." [2]

The movement, however, once started never stopped. On the contrary, it gathered strength ; hospices for pilgrims going to Jerusalem dotted the roads leading to their usual places of embarkation (chiefly Marseilles and Venice), several being built at the principal crossings of the Alps, the Great and the Little Saint Bernard, the St. Gothard, Mount Cenis, etc. A " Confrérie des Pélerins

---

[1] " Epistola XLVI Paulæ et Eustochii (one of her daughters) ad Marcellam, De Sanctis Locis." Migne, ibid., col. 483 ff. From Bethleem, same period.

[2] From Bethleem, same period. Migne, ibid. To Paulinus col. 580 ff. ; to Desiderius, col. 493 ff.

de la Terre Sainte " had been founded in Paris for them by Louis, first Duke of Bourbon, who, greatly interested, like his grand father Saint Louis, in the freeing of the Holy Sepulchre, and bearing for a time the empty title of King of Thessalonica, had been chosen as leader of one of those numerous crusades that never took place.[1]

During a period of two hundred years pilgrimages to Jerusalem had had, indeed, for their object a conquest and not simply an inspection of the holy places. All nations had taken part, from the first of those prodigious attempts, the crusades, in 1096, to the last one in 1270, in which St. Louis died before the walls of Tunis, while his companion, young Edward of England, loth to give up, had sworn not to go home without having struck a blow at the Saracens in Holy Land, and returned as King Edward I, wounded, but having occupied Acre and kept his word.

The crusade, after those great expeditions, eight in number, continued to be talked about as much as ever ; mere talk, it is true, in most cases. In the midst of their wars the kings of France and of England berated each other for being the only hindrance to the departure of the Christians, for neither would go, leaving his rival behind, free to act in his absence. Philip VI of Valois and Edward III both protest that, but for the other, they would go and fight the Saracen. " It is the fault of the English," writes Philip, " that the holy journey beyond sea has been hindered." It is the doing of the King of

---

[1] He and numerous companions had received the Cross at the hands of the Patriarch of Jerusalem in 1316, and the plan seemed for a time so near realization that nobles and villeins sold their lands and houses, to take part in the crusade. A plan thereof and a draft of the contract with the Marseilles shipowners has been published with excellent notes, by A. de Boislisle, " Annuaire-Bulletin de la Société de l'histoire de France," 1872, pp. 230 and 246. The latest date suitable for the start is stated to be the middle of April. Full details are given as to the supplies of every sort, to be provided for the galleys, food and the rest : " panis biscoctus," i.e. biscuit.

France, solemnly proclaims Edward III to the world,
which has turned him from the " sancto passagio trans-
marino." [1]

The utmost that was usually attempted,[2] now consisted
in small, ineffectual expeditions, so ill-conceived at times
as to cause the wonderment and even the merriment of
the infidel : such as the Franco-Anglo-Genoese crusade
of 1390, with Louis, third Duke of Bourbon, as
commander-in-chief, and which, on the recommendation
of the Genoese, who suffered more than any from the
inroads of the Barbaresques, went to lay siege, of all places,
to the city of Mahdia, the " Aufrike " of Froissart,[3] on
the east coast of Tunisia. The French were apparently
the most numerous, but, says Froissart, " Also the Duke
of Lancastre had a bastarde sonne called Henry of Lancastre : he had devocion to go in the same voyage, and
he provided him of good knightes and squiers of
Englande that accompanyed him in that voyage." The
comte de Foix had also, ready at hand, a " bastarde sonne "
of his own, whom he sent with a large retinue. The
English prince was not, however, the future Henry IV,
who was no bastard, but his half-brother, John Beaufort,
who being an adulterine son well answered to the description. Henry had intended to go, hence Froissart's mistake, but he went instead to fight the pagans in Prussia
and Lithuania, and, being fond of pilgrimages and
shrines, performed, as a pilgrim, the journeys to Rome
and Jerusalem, before he assumed the crown and had,
in spite of his religious dispositions, his cousin Richard
assassinated.

[1] Robert of Avesbury, " Historia Edwardi Tertii," ed. Hearne, Oxford,
1720, pp. 63, 115.
[2] The single and last attempt on a grand scale was the ill-starred campaign
against Sultan Bajazet which ended in the disaster and massacre of Nicopolis,
September, 1396 ; on which and on all those latter-day attempts, see Delaville
le Roulx, " La France en Orient au XIVe Siècle," Pari', 1886, 2 vols.
[3] Built on Cape Africa, hence her name in the chronicles of the time.

The start from Genoa for the new Tunisian expedition was splendid to see ; so the starts usually were : " Great pleasure it was," says Froissart, " to beholde their departynge, and to se their standardes, getornes (banners) and penons, wavynge in the wynde, shynynge against the sonne, and to here the trompettes and claryons sowning in the ayre with other mynstrelsy," so that the whole sea rang with the music.[1]

The Saracens were dumbfounded at this visit : what had they done, and what could be the object ? That the Genoese had grudges against them was natural enough ; but what ailed the others ? Ready for the stoutest defence of their walled Mahdia, they were, however, curious to ascertain the reason, and they sent one of their number, who spoke Italian, to explain " howe we have in nothynge trespassed them ; of a trouthe, afore this tyme, there hath been warre bytwene us and the Genovoys," but that does not concern Christians from " farre countreys." The Genoese " are our neighbours, they take of us and we of them ; we have been auncyente enemyes and shall be, excepte whan treucc is betwene us." But why are the others interfering ?

The leaders of the army agreed that a reply should be sent ; they held council, twelve of them, " in the duke of Burbons tent," and gave an answer to the effect that the reason why they made this war " was bycause the Sonne of God, called Jesu Chryst . . . by their lyne and generacyon, was put to deth and crucyfyed," and also because the Saracens did not believe in baptism, nor " in the Virgyn Mary, Mother to Jhesu Cryst. . . ."

" At this aunswere the Sarazyns dyd nothinge but laugh and sayd howe that aunswere was nothynge reason-

[1] Berners' Froissart (Ker, v. 361), where, however, the following passage does not appear : " Et autres ménestrels faire leur mestier de pipes et de chalemelles et de naquaires, tant que du son et de la voix qui en yssoient la mer en retentissoit toute."

able, for it was the Jewes that put Chryst to dethe and not they. Thus the siege still endured." [1]

The usual ally of the infidel did not fail him : sickness, fevers, and epidemics worked havoc among the besiegers, who had, of all months, selected July for their attempt. They tried to storm the city, but were repulsed with great loss, and after some eight weeks of fruitless labour, brilliant combats, and many deaths, accepted a patched-up treaty granting the Genoese some slight advantage ; raised the siege, and returned home, with probably less " trompettes and claryons sowning in the ayre " than when they had started.

The acceptance of a discussion with the infidel during this abortive crusade was characteristic of the time. More prone than before to examine inherited beliefs, a good many men were found in the fourteenth century to question the very principle of the crusade. We crush the infidel, why not convert him ? Is it not wiser, more reasonable, and even more conformable to the religion of Christ ? Were the apostles whom He sent to us Gentiles covered with armour and provided with swords ? Reflections like these occur in the works, not only of reforming minds like Wyclif or Langland,[2] but of pious well-meaning conservative thinkers like Gower, who says in his " Confessio Amantis " :

> " To sleen and fighten they us bidde
> Hem whom they shuld, as the boke saith,

---

[1] Berners' Froissart, ed. Ker, 1902, vol. v, chap. 165, 167, 170. Cf. Delaville le Roulx, " La France en Orient au XIVe Siècle," Paris, 1886, chap. iv. At p. 14, vol. ii, a list of all the chief participants in this crusade.

[2] Langland speaks of the Saracens without cursing them ; they might be saved, but for Mahomet who deceived them in anger at not being made pope ; Christians ought to convert them ; the pope makes indeed bishops of Nazareth, Nineveh, etc., but they take care never to visit their indocile flocks ; let us not forget that " Jews, Gentiles and Saracens " are sincere in their beliefs. " Piers Plowman," Text C, pass. xviii. ll. 123 ff.

Converten unto Cristes feith.
But herof have I great merveile
How they wol bidde me traveile ;
A Saracen if I slee shall,
I slee the soule forth withall,
And that was never Cristes lore."

Failing crusades, then, just as before those great
military undertakings had begun, small troops of pilgrims,
privately formed, started on the road to Jerusalem, still
in their eyes, in spite of all St. Jerome might have said,
the best road to heaven. They were, however, many of
them, inspired by mixed motives, for this was also the
road to adventure, and there, again, were very apparent
the chivalric and restless instincts of the period.

A good number of such caravans came from England ;
the English were already, and had been even before, and
continue to this day, great travellers. They were to be met
everywhere, and their knowledge of French stood them in
good stead in most of the countries they went through.
This was, as " Mandeville " states, the common language
of the upper classes everywhere ; [1] it was also that spoken
in the East by the European, the " Frank." Trevisa,
finding that the English were forgetting that language,
deplores it ; how will they do if they go abroad ? " That
is harme for hem and they schulle passe the see and
travaille in straunge landes and in many other places." [2]
They tried to acquire notions of it before setting out on
their travels, and employed competent persons to compose
manuals of conversation for them to learn, in the words

[1] In his book is written (in French) : " And know you that I would have
put this little book into Latin for brevity, but because many understand
Romance better than Latin, I have put it into Romance, that it be understood,
and that the lords and knights and other noblemen who do not know Latin,
or but little, and who have been beyond seas, may know and understand
whether I speak truth or not." Sloane MS. 1464, fol. 3, at the British
Museum, a French MS. of the beginning of the fifteenth century.

[2] In his translation of Ralph Higden's " Polychronicon," ed. C. Babington,
vol. ii. p. 161, Rolls Series.

of the author of one such work, an Englishman of the fourteenth century, " how to speak and pronounce well, and to write correctly sweet French, which is the finest and most graceful language, the noblest to speak of any in the world after Latin of the schools, and is better prized and loved than any other by all men ; for God made it so sweet and lovable chiefly to IIis own praise and honour. And therefore it may well compare with the language of the angels in heaven, on account of its great sweetness and beauty." So spoke this teacher of what he had to teach.[1]

The English went much abroad ; every author who draws their portrait lays stress on their taste for moving about, and their love of distant travel ; the moon is considered, in consequence, as their planet. According to Gower, the moon's influence is the cause why they visit so many far-off countries :

> " Bot what man under his [*i.e.*, the moon's] pouer
> Is bore, he schall his place change
> And seche manye londes strange ;
> And as of this condicion
> The Mones disposicion
> Upon the lond of Alemaigne
> Is set, and ek upon Bretaigne,
> Which nou is cleped Engelond,
> For thei travaile in every lond." [2]

Wyclif places them under the patronage of the same planet, but draws different conclusions therefrom ; [3]

    1 " La Manière de Langage," ed. Paul Meyer, " Revue Critique," vol. x., 1870, pp. 373, 382 ; dedication dated May 29, 1396.
    2 " Confessio Amantis," " Complete Works," ed. G. C. Macaulay, Oxford, 1899, ff. four vols., vol. iii. p. 253.
    3 According to him, the English, who, as history shows, have certainly improved, are wanting in perseverance, " Et hinc secundum astronomos lunam habent planetam propriam, quæ in motu et lumine est magis instabilis." " Fasciculi Zizaniorum," ed. Shirley, p. 270, Rolls Series. Caxton later also considers the moon as *par excellence* the planet of the English : " For we englysshe men ben born under the domynacion of the mone, whiche is

Ralph Higden the chronicler expresses himself in these terms, most of which seem prophetic, they have proved so exact : " That people are curious enough that they may know and tell the wonders that they have seen ; they cultivate other regions, and succeed still better in distant countries than in their own, . . . wherefore it is that they are spread so wide through the earth, considering every other land that they inhabit as their own country. They are a race able for every industry." [1]

A number of those adventure seekers were established in Italy, where they had become *condottieri*, and went fighting up and down the peninsula according to the will of whomsoever paid them. Such were John Hawkwood, whose tomb still adorns the cathedral at Florence,[2] William Gold, and several others. Fierce folk they were, with ardent passions, ready sometimes, as in Homeric days, to do and sacrifice as much to recover a fugitive girl as to take a town. One letter of William Gold may give an idea of the temper of these bellicose wanderers. On August 9, 1378, he wrote to Louis Gonzaga, lord of Mantua, concerning the girl Jeannette, of France :

" . . . Let her be detained at my suit, for if you should have a thousand golden florins spent for her, I will pay them without delay ; for if I should have to follow her to Avignon I will obtain this woman. Now, my lord, should I be asking a trifle contrary to law, yet ought you not to cross me in this, for some day I shall do more for you than a thousand united French women could effect ;

---

never stedfaste but ever waverynge." Prologue to his " Boke of Eneydos compyled by Vyrgyle," 1490.

[1] " Polychronicon Ranulphi Higden," edited by C. Babington, 1869, vol. ii. pp. 166, 168, Rolls Series.

[2] He appears in John of Gaunt's accounts : " Item à Esmon de Wyght esquier à monsire Johan de Haukewode, de nostre doun, lxvj s. viij." " John of Gaunt's Register," ed. Armitage Smith, 1911, vol. ii. p. 299 ; no date, but of 1372, or shortly after.

and if there be need of me in a matter of greater import,
you shall have for the asking a thousand spears at my
back. Therefore, in conclusion, again and again, I
entreat that this Janet may be put in a safe place unknown
to anybody, and there kept until I send some servant of
mine for her with a letter from myself, for I would do
more for you in greater matters. And I pray you, thwart
me not about putting her in a safe place, for you alone,
and no one else are lord in Mantua.

"*The Camp under Verona, August* 9, 1378.

"P.S.—I beseech by all means that [the] said Janet
may not quit Mantua, but be in safe custody, and so you
will have obliged me for ever."

No less determined as a warrior than as a lover, and
accustomed, as it seems, in both cases, to put people to
flight, William Gold was made a citizen of Venice in
recognition of his services on April 27, 1380, and in
July of the same year received from the Doge Andrea
Contarini a pension of 500 gold ducats for life.[1]

Thinking less of the Jeannettes to be met on the way,
troops of pilgrims sailed from England, beginning their
long journey towards the Holy Land, usually provided
with letters from their sovereign, to serve both as passports and as recommendations in case of need. The
tenor of these documents, written in French or in Latin,
was usually similar to that of the following letter granted
by Edward III in 1354 to one who, it is true, was more
of a fighter than a pilgrim : "Know all men that the
noble Jean le Meingre, knight, otherwise Bussigand
[Boucicaut], our prisoner, is about to set forth, duly
licensed by us, with twelve knights to St. James, and thence
to march against the enemies of Christ in the Holy Land ;
and that we have taken him and his twelve companions,

[1] Rawdon Brown, "Calendar of State Papers relating to English Affairs
. . . at Venice," London, 1864, vol. i. pp. 24, 29 ; original in Latin.

their servants, horses, and harnesses under our protection and safe conduct." [1]

Such travellers were well received by the French King of Cyprus, of the famous Lusignan family ; they brought him news of the outer world, with them came variety and hope ; they also were sometimes able to actually assist him in his difficulties, which were ceaseless, and the king showed his pleasure in his letters. Thus James I of Lusignan, " King of Jerusalem and Cyprus," writes from Nicosia, in 1393, to Richard II, that a knight has no need of a personal recommendation to be welcome in the island ; his subjects always are. It was for him an honour and delight to be visited by " your noble relative the lord Henry Percy." [2] In the same manner the troop of French pilgrims, to which belonged the lord of Anglure, was welcomed in Cyprus, by the same king, in 1396. They reached the island on their way home, after a fearful storm, in which they nearly lost their lives.[3] As soon as James heard of their having landed he sent to them

[1] Rymer's " Fœdera," vol. v. p. 777 ; in Latin. As to Boucicaut and his more famous son, both marshals of France, see Delaville le Roulx, " La France en Orient, au XIVᵉ Siècle," Paris, 1886, vol. i. pp. 160 ff. Such letters being delivered pretty frequently, were drawn up after a common form like our passports. See the one given by Rymer in vol. vii. p. 337, A.D. 1381. In November, 1392, the Earl of Derby, future Henry IV, was at Venice, and set out thence to go to the Holy Land. He had letters for the Republic from Albert IV, Duke of Austria, and the Great Council lent him a galley for his voyage. Thomas Mowbray, Duke of Norfolk, also set out from Venice for Palestine, in February, 1398-9. He was the bearer of a letter from Richard II to the Venetian Senate. " Calendar of State Papers . . . at Venice," ed. Rawdon Brown, p. lxxxi.

[2] " Historical Papers from the Northern Registers," ed. Raine, Rolls Series, p. 425.

[3] " En celle malle fortune perdy nostre nasve l'un de ses tymons dont elle estoit gouvernée en partie, et fut renversée nostre voille par plusieurs fois en la marine, malgré tous les mariniers." The darkness was complete, and they thought their end had come; but they were saved, reaching Cyprus where they had not intended to go. " Le Saint Voyage de Jérusalem du Seigneur d'Anglure," ed. Bonnardot and Longnon, " Société des Anciens Textes Français," Paris, 1878.

provisions in plenty : a hundred chickens, twenty sheep, two oxen, much good red wine and good white bread. Then he asked them to his Court, where they were delight-fully entertained by him, by the queen, and their four sons and five daughters. Being himself a great huntsman, James asked them to go hunting with him, a pleasant offer after so many trials, and one not to be refused.

Combats, hunts, storms, encounters of all sorts, in a word, adventure, were thus associated with the idea of the voyage, the holiness of which sometimes disappeared in the midst of so many profane incidents. Well may one wonder whether Saint James was the real attraction, for a De Werchin, Seneschal de Hainaut, who, about to start on a pilgrimage to the shrine of this saint, in 1402, would make it publicly known that, " in the name of God, of our Lord St. George, and of his own lady," he would accept during his whole journey the friendly combat of arms with any knight for whom he should not have to turn from his road more than 20 leagues. He announced his itinerary beforehand, so that any one might make ready.[1]

The strange man, Jean de Bourgogne by name, who chose to sign his book of travels " Jean de Mandeville," [2]

---

[1] " Chronique de Monstrelet," bk. i. chap. viii.

[2] The voyages called " Mandeville's Voiage and Travaile " were assuredly written in the fourteenth century in French, then were translated e.g. into Latin and English. Only the portion relating to Egypt, Palestine, and Syria, *may* have been founded on a real journey. The article " Mandeville," by Mr. E. B. Nicholson and Colonel Yule in " The Encyclopædia Britannica "; a paper, " Untersuchungen über Johann von Mandeville und die Quelle seiner Reiseschreibung," Berlin, 1888 (printed in " Zeitschrift der Gesellschaft für Erdkunde," bd. xxiii. p. 177), and Mr. G. F. Warner's " The Buke of John Maundevil," being the travels of Sir John Mandeville, Kt. 1322–56," Roxb. Club, 1889, fol., with the French and English texts ; the notice by the same on Mandeville in the " Dictionary of National Biography," notices by H. Cordier in his " Bibliotheca Sinica " and in " Revue Critique," Oct. 26, 1891, represent the actual state of the question. English text in modern spelling, ed. Pollard, London, 1900. Earliest dated MS., a French one in the National Library, Paris, A.D. 1371 ;

gives somewhat similar reasons to explain why he under-
took his journey to the East in 1322 through perilous
seas and countries—or rather, according to modern discoveries—through the books of his library. He started,
or, anyhow, he studied and wrote, partly, says he, to
sanctify himself, partly to know the world and its wonders,
and to be able to speak of them ; for many persons, he
observes, are much pleased with hearing the marvels of
distant regions described. The reason he publishes
his impressions is, first, because numbers of people like
stories of the Holy Land, and find great consolation and
comfort in them ; and, secondly, to make a guide, in
order that small companies or caravans, like that of
Boucicaut and others, may profit by his knowledge.

His ideas as to the road to be followed are not unreasonable. Thus, " to go the direct way " from England to
Palestine, he advises the following itinerary : France,
Burgundy, Lombardy, Venice, Famagusta in Cyprus,
Jaffa, Jerusalem. Very often people went to Jerusalem
by way of Egypt. It was a tradition of long standing
that the greater part of the difficulties concerning the
Holy Land had their root in Egypt ; many tombs of
saints also attracted the pilgrims there, so that crusaders,
or mere pilgrims, often took that road to Jerusalem.
" Mandeville " says he himself followed this itinerary.
In 1422 Gilbert de Lannoy wrote, " at the behest of
King Henry of England, heir and Regent of France,"
that is, Henry V, a description in French of the places
through which a crusade might be led against the infidels,
for this prince, like his predecessors, continued dreaming
of a crusade. Lannoy, a practical soldier and diplomat,
who speaks only of what he has seen, gives a detailed
account of all towns, stating which are protected by walls,

the identification of Mandeville with Jean de Bourgogne, *alias* " à la Barbe,"
or " ad Barbam," a physician of Liège, who died there in 1372, seems
certain.

towers and ditches ; he notices the Venetians' warehouses for cotton at Acre, and the presence at Beirut of a great number of Christian merchants, Venetians, Genoese, Greeks, and others. He carefully mentions what sorts of provisions in wood, water, etc., may be found in each part of the country, in what plains an army can be easily arrayed, in what ports a fleet shall be safe. He pays the greatest attention to Egypt, and describes its several cities : " Item. There is Cairo, the chief town of Egypt, on the river Nile which comes from Paradise." [1] But the crusade, in anticipation of which he wrote, never took place, and the next military expedition to reach Syria through Egypt was destined to be a French one, headed by that extraordinary pilgrim, Bonaparte.

Besides his account of a journey to Egypt, Palestine, Syria, Central Asia, and China, " Mandeville " gives a description of a number of countries peopled by imaginary monsters. This fantastic part of his work, where he anticipated no less famous a traveller than Gulliver himself, did not diminish its success, quite the contrary ; it was translated into several languages, and above three hundred MSS. of it now remain. But we, less confiding than our fathers, are loth to accept the excuse he gives as a guarantee of, at least, his good faith : " Things that are long past away from sight fall into oblivion, and the memory of man cannot all retain and comprehend." [2]

Many books, beginning with that of Lannoy, came after his, more practical, less fantastic, and, of course, less famous.[3] While the renewal of the crusades became

---

[1] " A Survey of Egypt and Syria undertaken in the year 1422, by Sir Gilbert de Lannoy, Kt., translated from a MS. in the Bodleian Library," " Archæologia," vol. xxi. pp. 281, 319, giving also the French original. Born in 1386, employed by the Duke of Burgundy, then by the King of England, Lannoy died in 1462.

[2] Sloane MS. 1464, fo. 3, British Museum.

[3] And a very large quantity, beginning as early as the fourth century (to

less and less probable, the number of individual pilgrimages was on the increase. The word of the priest which could no longer uproot and set on the move entire nations, still detached here and there little groups of pious men or adventure seekers, who went to visit the holy places under favour of the Saracen's tolerant and practical spirit. For the mass of them no longer set out to fight the infidel, but to ask his permission to see Jerusalem, which was the more readily granted that it had to be paid for.

From the fourteenth century onwards, a regular service of transports existed at Venice for the use of pilgrims : " It is the rule," says a traveller of the fourteenth century, " that the Venetians send every year five galleys to the Holy Land. They all reach Beirut, which is the port for Damascus in Syria ; thence two of them bring the pilgrims to Jaffa, which is the port for Jerusalem." [1]

Many particulars about this service of transports, the purchases to make before starting, and the provisions to take, are found in a book written in the following century by William Wey, Fellow of Eton College, an experienced pilgrim with a passion for such journeys. He recommended that the price of the passage be carefully settled before starting, and that a bed with its pillows, sheets, etc., be procured. This was bought at Venice, near St. Mark's, and cost three ducats ; after the journey the whole could be sold back to the vendor for a ducat

which century belongs the " Itinerarium Burdigala Hierosolymam "), had preceded those.   See, among others, " Itinera Hierosolymitana et Descriptiones Terræ Sancta," ed. Tobler and Molinier, 1879, ff. ; " Itinéraires à Jérusalem, rédigés en français aux XIe, XIIe et XIIIe Siècles," ed. Michelant and Raynaud, 1882, both works forming part of the publications of the " Société de l'Orient Latin."   One of the best among the older guide-books was due to the French monk Bernard in the year 870.   The monk, who went by way of Egypt, is brief, accurate, matter of fact, as little emotional as possible, discards all wonders, and is often careful to add : " asseritur," " dicitur."

[1] " Le Saint Voyage de Jérusalem du Seigneur d'Anglure," ed. Bonnardot and Longnon, 1878, p. 99.

and a half : " Also when ye com to Venyse ye schal
by a bedde by seynt Markys cherche ; ye schal have a
fedyr bedde, a matres, too pylwys, too peyre schetis and
a qwylt, and ye schal pay iij dokettis ; and when ye com
ayen, bryng the same bedde to the man that ye bowt hit
of and ye schal have a doket and halfe ayen, thow hyt be
broke and worne." [1] Such settled customs and fixed
prices show better than anything else the frequency of
the intercourse.

William Wey is as obliging for his traveller as are
modern guide-book makers ; he devises mnemonics of
names to remember, a vocabulary of the Greek words
most important to know, and ready-made questions which
our manuals still repeat in more correct language :

" Good morrow.	*Calomare.*
Welcome.	*Calosertys.*
Tel me the way.	*Dixiximo strata.*
Gyff me that.	*Doys me tutt.*
Woman, haue ye goyd wyne ?	*Geneca esse calocrasse ?*
Howe moche ?	*Posso ?* "

He does not omit a sentence which must have been, and
still is, of especially frequent use : " I understond the
not—*Apopon kystys.*" Wey also gives a table of the rate
of exchange for moneys from England to Venice, Crete,
Rhodes, Cyprus, and Syria ; and a programme for the
employment of time, as now very parsimoniously distri-
buted ; he only allows " thirteen or fourteen days " to see

[1] " The Itineraries of William Wey, Fellow of Eton College, to Jerusalem, A.D. 1458 and A.D. 1462, and to Saint James of Compostela, A.D.
1456." London, 1857, Roxburghe Club, pp. 5, 6. In his first journey to
Palestine, duly " consecratus ad modum peregrinorum," Wey started from
Venice with a band of 197 pilgrims embarked on two galleys. Born about
1407, a graduate of Oxford, Wey became after the last of his journeys an
Augustinian monk at Edington, Wiltshire, and died there in 1476. He
wrote his Itineraries " rogatus a devotis viris " (p. 56) ; the text in Latin,
the " prevysyoun " for travellers in English.

everything and start back again, specifying what should be seen each day. Lastly, he gives a complete list of the towns to be traversed, with the distance from one to the other, a map of the Holy Land with all the remarkable places duly inscribed thereon,[1] a considerable catalogue of the indulgences to be gained, and full details as to what is sacred or curious in Palestine, or on the way thither, not forgetting the dogs at Rhodes, who keep watch at night outside the castle, know perfectly how to distinguish a Turk from a Christian, and who, if one of their number " sleeps instead of taking his watch at night outside the castle, kill him themselves," [2] so great is their detestation of a *slacker*.

Wey foresaw all the disagreeables to which the boorish-ness of the captain of the galley might subject you ; he recommends engaging a berth in the highest part of the boat, " for in the lawyst [stage] under hyt is ryght smolderyng hote and stynkynge." [3] You must not pay more than forty ducats from Venice to Jaffa, food included, and should stipulate that the captain stop at certain ports to take in fresh provisions. He is bound to give you hot meat at dinner and supper, good wine, pure water, and biscuit ; but it is well besides to take provisions for private use, for even at the captain's table there is great risk of having bad bread and wine. " For thow ye schal

---

[1] Pages 102–116. Such a map is exhibited in one of the glass cases of the Bodleian Library at Oxford. It is probable, but not quite sure, that this is really the map of William Wey, the one he calls " mappa mea " in his book. It has been reproduced in *fac-simile* : " Map of the Holy Land, illustrating the Itineraries of W. Wey, Roxburghe Club, 1867." It is seven feet in length and sixteen and a half inches in breadth. See also : " De passagiis in Terram Sanctam," edit. G. M. Thomas, Venice, 1879, folio, " Société de l'Orient Latin." This work contains extracts from a " Chronologia magna," compiled in the thirteenth and fourteenth centuries, with maps and plans, one especially of Jerusalem and adjoining places.

[2] P. 95.

[3] " A good preuysyoun," " Itineraries," p. 4.

be at the tabyl wyth yowre patrone, notwythstondynge, ye schal oft tyme have nede to yowre vytelys, bred, chese, eggys, frute, and bakyn, wyne, and other, to make yowre collasyun ; for sum tyme ye schal have febyl bred, wyne and stynkyng water, meny tymes ye schal be ful fayne to ete of yowre owne." It would even be prudent to take some poultry : " Also by yow a cage for half a dozen of hennys or chekyn to have with yow in the galey ; " half a bushel of seed to feed them must not be forgotten, nor what you will want to fry your own bacon and drink your wine : " Also take with you a lytyl cawdren and fryyng pan, dysches, platerrys, sawserys of tre (wood), cuppys of glas, a grater for brede and such nessaryes." You must also have remedies, " confortatyvys, laxatyvys, restoratyvys," saffron, pepper, spices.[1]

On arrival at a port it is well to leap ashore one of the first, in order to get served before others, and not to have the leavings ; this counsel of practical selfishness often recurs. On land heed must be taken as to the fruits : " beware of dyverse frutys, for they be not acordyng to youre complexioun, and they gender a blody fluxe (dysentery), and yf an Englyschman have that sykenes hyt ys a marvel and scape hyt but he dye thereof."

Once in Palestine, one must be careful about robbers ; beware of Saracens coming to talk familiarly with you : " Also take goyd hede of yowre knyves and other smal thynges that ye ber apon yow, for the Sarsenes wyl go talkyng wyth yow and make goyd chere, but they wyl stele fro yow that ye have and they may." At Jaffa you must bestir yourself and be quick, in order to have the best donkey, " Also when ye schal take yowre asse at port Jaffe, be not to longe behynde yowre felowys ; for and ye com by tyme ye may chese the beste mule, other asse, for ye schal pay no more fore the best then for the worst. And ye must yeve youre asman curtesy

[1] " A good preuysyoun," " Itineraries," pp. 5, 6

a grot." [1] This last recommendation shows the high
antiquity of " pourboires," one of the best preserved of
mediæval traditions. At last the caravan leaves the
seaside and proceeds towards the Holy City ; and then
it is prudent not to straggle too far from your companions
for fear of evildoers.

Worthy of notice is the fact that these visits to the
Holy Land were in great part performed on donkeys ;
knights themselves did not disdain mounting these modest
animals : " At this said inn did we dismount from our
asses," says the narrator of the travels of the lord of
Anglure, who, as we have seen, visited Jerusalem at the
end of the fourteenth century ; which tends to show that
if there was, as there still is, some danger of attacks by
robbers, it was not very serious. If there had been any
chance of real fight knights would hardly have ventured
getting into it on donkey-back. In fact, many of those
reports of travels in the Holy Land give the impression
of mere tourists' excursions, and what comes out most
clearly from them is the before-mentioned spirit of toler-
ance, coupled with the spirit of profit, displayed by the
Saracen. He did not forbid the entry into Palestine of
all these pilgrims, who often came as spies and enemies,
and he let their troops do very much as they liked, provided
they did not forget to pay.[2] The companions of the lord

[1] Ibid. The same scramble for asses is going on even now in Palestine
and Egypt, and modern " Saracens " are careful to ingratiate themselves
with the traveller by addressing to him a few words in the language of his
supposed nationality ; one such at the foot of the Pyramids some years ago,
would keep repeating to us, as a sesame for our purses, these three magic
words : " Bonaparte, quarante siècles." We had not, however, to deplore
the disappearance of any " knyves and other smal thynges."

[2] William Wey and his companions pay to the " Saracen lords " fifteen
ducats : " Et sic in Terra Sancta fuimus xiij diebus, pro quibus solvimus
pro conductu nostro dominis Saracenis xv ducatus." But there were two
rival sultans at war with each other, each claiming the Holy Land ; and just
as the pilgrims were about to leave, the one of those potentates whom they
had not paid got the upper hand, and they had to give fifty ducats to his new

of Anglure, and half a century later of William Wey, go where they will ; returning when it is convenient, and making plans of excursions beforehand as they would do at present. They admire the beauty of the "muscas" or mosques, the quaint appearance of the vaulted streets with light coming from apertures at the top of the vault, and with shops for Saracen merchants on both sides, in other words, the bazaar ; they are led by and receive explanations from their " drugemens ; " at certain places they meet officers entrusted with the permit of the " Soudan," as to all affairs concerning foreigners : these officers are called " consulles." They find European merchants established and doing much trade in the ports of the infidel ; they have, in fact, nothing to fear seriously but local wars (about which they were pretty sure to get timely information), or possibly calamitous encounters at sea. William Wey and his companions learn with much uneasiness on their return that a Turkish fleet with dubious purpose is ready to quit Constantinople, but happily they do not meet it.

A comparison between the experiences of both troops of pilgrims, the French and the English, is instructive, precisely because they are, in so many cases, similar. The lord of Anglure [1] had no trouble in reaching Jerusalem, being provided with the proper authorization : " Shortly after, we started thence on foot, and with the license of the lieutenant of the Sultan we entered the holy city of

governor of Jerusalem. " Itineraries," p. 99. The second Boucicaut going around the holy places for the second time within a few months in 1389, is made by the Saracens to pay again. Delaville le Roulx, " La France en Orient," i. 165.

[1] Ogier VIII, lord of Anglure, part of whose castle on the Aube river still remains, died about 1402. One of his companions held the pen for the troop during the journey and wrote the account of it entitled, in the MS. at the National Library, Paris : " Cy après s'ensuit le contenu du saint voyage de Jherusalem et le chemin pour aller à Saincte Catherine du Mont Synay et ainsi à Saint Anthoine et Saint Pol ès loingtains desers de Egipte," 1395 ; best ed. the above quoted one by Bonnardot and Longnon.

Jerusalem at the hour of vespers, and were all received and lodged in the hospital where it is customary now for pilgrims to stay." Having bought tents, they travel by land without difficulty from Palestine to Egypt, crossing the desert, noticing the places where Moses performed his miracles, visiting Cairo, which deeply impresses them by its beauty, its greatness, its gardens and monuments, and the immense number of Saracens living there. They go partly by water, partly on camels, observing on their way " two great black-feathered ostriches trotting along," to the places where St. Anthony had lived with his " porcellet," and where churches and abbeys prosper under the rule of the unmeddling Saracen. They navigate the Nile, a large river which " comes from Paradise," and where " live several serpents called cokatrices," otherwise crocodiles, of which they see one " very great and hideous " that dived into the water when they came near. There only they have a rather narrow escape, being attacked in their boat by " Arab robbers," and some of their troop are wounded with arrows, but none is killed.

Needless to say that, if Rome was full of relics, there was no want of them in Jerusalem. All the places named in the Gospel, and some others, had been identified with precision : " Item, continuing to go up towards this mountain on the right hand side, there is a house where the sweet Virgin Mary learnt at school." Near the church of the Holy Sepulchre is a large square " with two big stones on the one of which our Lord used to sit when He preached to His disciples, and our Lady sat opposite on the other." The place is shown " where St. John the Evangelist sang mass every day in the presence of our Lady after the Ascension of our Lord." You may see, too, the spot where was roasted the paschal lamb ; " even here was warmed the water with which our Lord washed the feet of His apostles." There is also a cave or well " where King Herod had the Innocents

thrown, out of spite." At Bethlehem is a church of
St. Nicholas, "in which place the sweet Virgin Mary
hid herself to draw her milk from her worthy breasts
when she would fly to Egypt. In this same church is
a marble column against which she leaned when she drew
her worthy milk, and this pillar continues moist since
the time she leaned against it, and when it is wiped, at
once it sweats again ; and in all places where her worthy
milk fell, the earth is still soft and white and has the
appearance of curded milk, and whoever likes takes of
it, out of devotion."—Hence the milk at Walsingham ?

In Egypt, too, the wonders are numerous, but many
are of a different order. Besides the churches and
hermitages there are the "granaries of Pharaoh," namely
the pyramids, which seem to the lord of Anglure and
his companions "the most marvellous thing they had
yet seen in all their travels." They are cut "in the shape
of a fine diamond," but inside they are full of animals,
who stink horribly. Mandeville, who had seen them
some years before, gives them the same origin, and utterly
discards the belief that they might have been tombs of
high personages. He mentions the hieroglyphics, about
the only thing in all his book that he does not try to
explain ; he also has a word for the grim inhabitants of
the pyramids : " Thei ben alle fulle of serpentes. And
aboven the gernerers with outen ben many scriptures
of dyverse languages. And sum men seyn that they
ben sepultures of grete Lordes, that weren somtyme ;
but that is not trewe ; for all the comoun rymour and
speche is of alle the peple there, bothe far and nere, that
thei ben the garneres of Joseph. And so fynden thei
in here scriptures and in here cronycles. On that other
partie, yif thei werein sepultures, thei scholden not ben
voyd with inne. For yee may well knowe that tombes
and sepultures ne ben not made of suche gretnesse ne of
suche highnesse. Wherfore it is not to beleve that thei

ben tombes or sepultures."[1] This powerful mode of reasoning did not, however, convince such sceptics as Mariette and Maspéro.

Besides the pyramids, the companions of the Lord of Anglure notice and greatly praise the houses with their terraces, the mosques and their " fine lamps," these same ornamented glass lamps which, after having been admired by our pilgrims in 1395 when they were fresh and new, can be seen now without going so far, in the Victoria and Albert Museum. The Egyptian animals, too, are noted by our travellers as being very striking ; besides the crocodiles there are the long-necked giraffes, so tall that " they could well take their provender on the highest lances that it is the custom now to use," and then the elephants. A very strange beast an elephant : " It could never bend to the ground to get its food on account of its great height, but it has in its snout something like a bowel, put at the further end of its snout," and this bowel " hangs down almost to the ground," and with it the beast " takes its food and carries it to its mouth." He uses it also to drink, and " when he blows air through it the noise is greater than that of any buccina," and the sound " is terrible to those unaccustomed."

At last the time came when our pilgrims had seen everything, and they had to wend their way homewards. Twice did William Wey undertake the great journey, happy to have seen, fain to see again. When he came back to England for the last time he bequeathed to a chapel, built on the model of the Holy Sepulchre, the souvenirs which he had brought back, that is to say, a stone from Calvary, another from the Sepulchre itself, one from Mount Tabor, one from the place where the cross stood, and other relics. As for the French troop of pilgrims who had left Anglure-sur-Aube on July 16,

[1] " Voiage and Travaile of Sir John Maundeville," ed. Halliwell, 1866, p. 52.

1395, they came back in the following year, complete in their numbers but for Simon de Sarrebruck, who had died of fever in Cyprus during the journey home, and lies interred in a church there. "And on Thursday, the twenty-second day of June, and the day before the eve of the feast of St. John the Baptist, in the year of grace of our Lord, 1396, we found ourselves again dining in Anglure."

A PILGRIM'S "SIGN," OUR LADY OF WALSINGHAM.
(*Original in the British Museum.*)

A BLIND BEGGAR CHEATED OF HIS DRINK BY HIS BOY.
(*From MS.* 10 *E. IV.*)

CONCLUSION

WE have followed the race of roamers in many places : on the road, at the hostelry, in woods, in taverns, in churches ; we have seen them exercising a host of different trades, a motley crew, minstrels, buffoons, quacks, messengers, pedlars, pilgrims, wandering preachers, beggars, friars, vagabonds of all sorts, labourers broken loose from the soil, pardoners, knights in search of adventure. We have accompanied them here and there over the highroads of England, and followed them to Rome itself, and the Holy Land ; there we shall leave them. To the wandering class also belong the representatives of many other professions, such as scribes, tinkers, cobblers, masons, showers of animals or bearwards, like those whom Villard de Honnecourt visited one day in order to draw " al vif," a lion. But the more important members are those above described.

The current of life represented by the multiplicity of these wayfarers is powerful ; notice has been taken of the great though not very apparent part they played in the State. The labourer breaks the bonds which for centuries have attached him to the manor, and henceforward means

to be the master of his own person and of his service, to
hire himself by the day if he chooses, and for a salary
corresponding to the rise in prices and to the demand
there may be for his work.   The reform is an inevitable
one, which will be realized by degrees, in spite of the laws
and of the will of the authorities.   There is none more
important, and its how and wherefore are to be studied
not only in the castle, but on the road and by-ways, in
the brushwood, where armed bands meet together during
church service, and on those unfrequented paths where
the false pilgrim throws down his staff to take up his tools
and look for work out of the reach of his hereditary master.
These people promote by their example and success the
emancipation which the wandering preachers justify in
their discourses, showing it to be not simply desirable,
but rightful.

The great questions of the age, social and religious,
move towards their solution, partly on the road, through
the influence of the wanderers, a direct influence from
the sincere ones, indirect from the others.   Begging friars
go from door to door, pardoners grow rich, pilgrims live
by alms and by the recital of their adventures, always on
the way, always at work.   What is this work ?   By constantly addressing the crowd, they in the end make themselves known for what they are, and cause their listeners
to pass sentence upon them ; by disabusing them they
render reform inevitable.   Thereby, too, will the rust and
superstition of the middle ages drop away, and another
step be made towards modern civilization.

Each of these strange types has, moreover, the advantage
of showing, very apparent in his own person, some characteristic side of the tastes, the beliefs, and the aspirations
of his time.   Each of those groups corresponds to a need,
an eccentricity, a vice, or a merit of the nation ; through
them we may examine, as it were, and reconstitute piece-
meal the souls of the men of long ago, and have those

men stand before us, mind and body, complete, just as the nature of the soil may be guessed from the flora of a country.

The general impression is that the English people then underwent one of those profound transformations which present themselves to the historian's view like the turning of a highway. Coming out from gorges and mountains the road suddenly leads to an opening, and the rich, sunny, fertile plain is perceived in the distance. It has not yet been reached, many hardships are still to be endured ; it will disappear again from sight at intervals, but the traveller has seen it, and knows at least in what direction to tread in order to attain it. During the age which was then beginning the emancipated peasant was to enrich himself in spite of fierce wars especially deadly for the nobility, and the Commons were to be possessed of an instrument of control over the royal power, which would be used, according to the period, more or less well, but which is the best one invented up to our day. The Parliament sitting at Westminster now is in its essential elements identical with the one that, under the Plantagenets, drew up the statutes of the kingdom. In the fourteenth century, despite ultra severe judgments from some thinkers of fame (an age, says Stubbs, " of heartless selfishness and moral degradation "), mankind did not recede, witness the host of truly modern ideas which gained a hold on the mass of the people ; among the upper classes under the influence of higher education and wider inter-course with foreign countries, which weakened the notion of the immutability of custom ; among the lower classes through the effects of abuses long experienced by men who, though patient, were no weaklings ; ideas made popular and rendered practical by the wayfarers, illiterate workmen, single-hearted preachers. All those mad freaks, all the extravagance of the religious spirit, those incessant revolts and follies which have been noticed, were sure to cause a reaction, and a longing for something nearer that reign of reason which mankind, though less remote from the goal, still continues to look for in the far distance.

On a number of questions, whether as the promoter or the object of reform, as working man or as pardoner, whether an unconscious instrument or not, wanderers will always have much to teach whoever will question them. For good or evil it may be said that they acted in mediæval history as " microbes," a numerous, scarcely visible, but powerful host. They will perhaps reveal the secret of almost incomprehensible transformations, which might have seemed to necessitate a total overturn, like the one that took place in France at the end of the eighteenth century, a new or rather a first *contrat social*. England, for many reasons, has not required this ; one among those reasons is the action of the roamers which, exerting itself on a population temperamentally steadier than many others, more persistently resolute, and less constantly troubled by wars on its territory, united the people and, thanks to that union which made it strong, allowed it to snatch in time the necessary concessions. And as, however, the calmest changes cannot take place without some disturbance, as also among the English there have been, in the course of centuries, more than one bloody fray, the nomad may perhaps end by answering his interrogator in the words of a common proverb of certain, yet unhackneyed wisdom, which should prevent pessimism and lack of hope : " Le bois tortu fait le feu droit "— Crooked log maketh straight fire.

APPENDIX

APPENDIX

I

(p. 44)

PATENT OF KING JOHN ENTRUSTING A FRENCHMAN WITH THE COMPLETION OF LONDON BRIDGE (1201)

" Literæ patentes, etc. de edificatione et sustentatione pontis Londinensis. Patent Roll 3° Iohannis, m. 2, no. 9.

" Iohannes Dei gratia rex, etc. dilectis et fidelibus suis majori et civibus Londinensibus salutem. Attendentes qualiter circa pontem Xanctonensem et pontem de Rupella Deus a modico tempore sit operatus per sollicitudinem fidelis clerici nostri Isenberti, magistri scolarum Xanctonensium, viri utique literati et honesti, ipsum de consilio venerabilis patris in Christo H. Cantuariensis Archiepiscopi [1] et aliorum, rogavimus et monuimus et etiam coegimus ut pro vestra et multorum utilitate, de ponte vestro faciendo curam habeat diligentem. Confidimus enim in Domino, quod idem pons tam necessarius vobis et omnibus transeuntibus, ut scitis, per ejus industriam, faciente Domino, poterit in proximo consumari. Et ideo volumus et concedimus quod salvo jure nostro et conservata indempnitate civitatis Londinensis, census edificiorum quæ super pontem prædictum idem magister scolarum faciet fieri sint imperpetuum ad eundem pontem reficiendum et operiendum et sustentandum. Quia igitur idem pons tam necessarius sine vestro et aliorum auxilio perfici non poterit, mandamus vobis, exhortantes quatinus memoratum Isenbertum et suos pro vestra utilitate pariter et honore sicut

---

[1] The famous Hubert Walter (or Walter Hubert) who had accompanied King Richard to Palestine and crowned King John ; archbishop from 1193 to 1205 ; for a number of years, as much the ruler of England as those kings themselves. His tomb in Canterbury Cathedral has been identified in our days.

decuerit benigne recipiatis et honoretis in hiis quæ dicta sunt, consilium et auxilium vestrum eidem unanimiter impendentes. Quicquid enim boni et honoris eidem Isenberto feceritis, nobis factum reputare debetis. Si quis vero eidem Isenberto vel suis in aliquo foris fecerit, quod non credimus, vos illud eisdem faciatis, quam citius ad vos pertinet emendari. Teste meipso, apud Molinellum, xviii. die Aprilis.

"Sub eadem forma scribitur omnibus fidelibus per regnum Angliæ constitutis."

Hearne, at the end of "Liber niger Scaccarii," London, 1771, vol. i. p. 470*; Thomas Duffus Hardy, "Rotuli Literarum Patentium in Turri Londinensi asservati," London, 1835, fol. p. 9.

II

(p. 53)

PETITION CONCERNING AN OLD BRIDGE, WHOSE ARCHES WERE TOO LOW AND TOO NARROW TO PERMIT BOATS TO PASS

"Unto the ryght wise and discrete comons of this present Parlement ; besecheth mekely the comons off the countees of York, Lincoln, Notyngham, and Derby ; That whereas ther is, and of longe tyme hath been, an usuall and a commune passage fro dyvers and many parties of the seid countees unto the citees of York, Hull, Hedon, Holdernes, Beverley, Barton, and Grymesby, and so forth, by the hie see, by the costes, unto London and elles where, with all maner of shippes charged with wolle, leed, stone, tymbre, vitaille, fewaille, and many other marchandises, by a streme called the Dike, in the counte of York, that daiely ebbith and floweth : over whiche streem ys made a brigge of tymbre called Turnbrigg, in the parisshe of Snayth in the same counte, so lowe, so ner the streem, so narrowe and so strayte in the archees, that ther is, and of long tyme hath been a right perilous passage, and ofte tymes perishinge of dyvers shippes ; and atte every tyme of creteyne [1] and abundaunce of water, ther may no shippes passe under the seid brigge, by the space of half a yere or more, and also a grete partie of the countees to the seid ryver ajonyng, is yerely by the space of xx[ti] myles and more surrownded, by cause of the lowenes and straitenes of the said brigge, to the grete hurt and damage as well to the kyng in his customes

---

[1] *Creteyne*, increase, rising flood ; in French, *crue*.

and subsidys, that shuld growe to him of the seid marchaundises, chargeable with suche diverse, as to the seid shires, countres, cites and burghes, and the inhabitants of theim. . . .

"Please hit unto your right wise discretions, consideryng the premisses, to pray and beseche the kyng our soverayn lord to graunte . . . that hit shall be lefulle to what sum ever person or persons of the seid shires, that will atte theire owne costages take away the seid brigge, and ther with and profites therof, and in othir wise, newe edifie and bilde anothir brigge there, lengere in lengthe by the quantite of v. yerdes called the kynges standard, and in hieght a yerd and a half by the same yerd heigher then the seid brigge that stondes ther nowe, aswell for passage of all maner shippes comyng therto, and voidaunce of water under the seid brigg as for passage of man, best and carriage over the seid newe brigge so to be made, with a draght lef [1] contenyng the space of iiij fete called Paules fete in brede, for the voidying thorugh of the mastes of the shippes passinge under the seid new brigg ; and that every shipmen that wol passe under the seid brigge with their shippes, may laufully lifte up and close the seid lef att their pleser ; and that the mayster of every shippe paie for every liftyng of the seid lef 1d. to the lord of the soille for the tyme beyng . . . for the lofe of Godd and in waye of charite. . . .

" *Responsio.* Le roy de l'advys et assent de lez seignurs espirituelx et temporalx et lez communes esteantz en cest present parlement, ad graunté tout le contenue en icell petition en toutz pointz."

" Rolls of Parliament," vol. v. p. 43 ; 20 Henry VI, A.D. 1442.

III

(p. 62)

LONDON BRIDGE AND ITS MAINTENANCE

At the end of his edition of the " Liber niger Scaccarii," London, 1771, vol. i. pp. 470*–478*, Hearne printed a series of curious Letters Patent relating to London Bridge. That of John, commending Isembert to the city, is given above (Appendix I.). There follow, an order of John applying the tax paid by foreign merchants established in London to the support of the bridge (Close Roll, 15 John, m. 3) ; a patent of Henry III addressed " to the brothers and chaplains of the chapel of St. Thomas on London Bridge, and to the other

---

[1] A " movable " part, just for the passage of masts.

persons living on the same bridge," to inform them that the convent of St. Catherine's Hospital, near the Tower, would receive the revenues and would take charge of the repairs of the bridge for five years (Patent 50 Hen. III m. 43, No. 129); grant of the same revenues and charge to the queen for six years (54 Hen. III m. 4, No. 11); patent of Edward I (January, 1281), ordering a general collection throughout the kingdom to ward off the danger resulting from the bad condition of the edifice (9 Ed. I m. 27); patent of the same king ordering the levy of an extraordinary tax on account of the catastrophe which, after all, had happened.

"Rex majori suo London' salutem. Propter subitam ruinam pontis London' vobis mandamus quod associatis vobis duobus vel tribus de discretioribus et legalioribus civibus civitatis prædictæ, capiatis usque ad parliamentum nostrum post Pasch' prox' futur', in subsidium reparationis pontis predicti, consuetudinem subscriptam, videlicet, de quolibet homine transeunte aquam Thamisiæ ex transverso ex utraque parte pontis London' de London' usque Suthwerk et de Suthwerk usque London', occasione defectus reparationis pontis predicti, unum quadrantem, de quolibet equo sic transeunte ibidem unum denarium, et de quolibet summagio sic ibidem transeunte unum obolum. Set volumus quod aliquid ibidem hac occasione interim capiatur nisi in subsidium reparationis pontis supra dicti. In cujus, etc. Teste rege apud Cirencestr', iiij° die Februarij" (10 E. I m. 18).

The same year, on 6th July, the king prolonged the term during which this exceptional tax should be levied to three years (p. 476*); he also, "understanding that it would hurt neither himself nor the city," granted to the mayor and commonalty of London three empty spaces, one near the wall of the churchyard "de Wolchurch," the two others near the wall of St. Paul's churchyard, for them to build thereon and let the buildings for the benefit of the bridge (10 Ed. I m. 11). Then, in the thirty-fourth year of his reign, Edward I established a detailed tariff of the tolls which all merchandise passing under or over the bridge should pay during the next three years (34 Ed. I m. 25). Even this was not enough, as we find Edward II asking all the archbishops, bishops, rectors and other ecclesiastical authorities of the kingdom to well receive the wardens of London Bridge or their delegates and allow them to piously persuade the people to make offerings for the repair of the bridge : "Eos populum ibidem piis suasionibus excitare et suarum elemosinarum subsidia ad reparationem Pontis predicti caritative invocare permittatis." (14 Ed. II pt. i. m. 19, p. 477*).

IV

(p. 65)

INQUESTS RELATING TO THE MAINTENANCE OF BRIDGES

A great many examples of these inquests may be found in the collection published by the Record Commission, " Placitorum in domo capitulari Westmonasteriensi asservatorum abbreviatio," London, 1811, fol.   Here are references to some of the more interesting ones :

Case where an abbot is explicitly obliged, as one of the conditions of his tenure, to repair a bridge, p. 205 ; 11 and 12 Ed. I.

Agreement between the abbot of Croyland and the prior of Spalding for the construction of several bridges, p. 205 ; 12 Ed. I.

Discussion as to the building of a bridge at Chester, p. 209 ; 13 Ed. I.

Refusal by the abbot of Coggeshall to repair a bridge : " Per juratores, Abbas de Coggeshale non tenetur reparare pontem de Stratford inter Branketre et Coggeshale, eo quod de tempore memorie non fuit ibidem alius pons quam quedam planchea de borde super quam omnes transeuntes salvo et secure transire potuerunt," p. 303 ; 1 Ed. II.

Measures taken to constrain the inhabitants of two towns to repair the bridges of a highway in their neighbourhood : " Distringantur villate de Aswardeby et Skredington ad reparandum pontes in pupplica strata inter Lafford et ecclesiam de Stowe juxta inquisicionem inde captam anno lvi. Henrici iij. coram Gilberto de Preston et sociis suis in comitatu Lincolniensi itinerantibus, per breve ejusdem regis," p. 305 ; 2 Ed. II.

Finding out of the person who is to repair Chesford bridge, p. 314 ; 6 Ed. II.

Refusal of the abbot of Fountains to repair Bradeley bridge, p. 318 ; 7 Ed. II.

Hamo de Morston's case, p. 328 ; 11 Ed. II, referred to above, p. 64.

Repair of the bridges of Exhorne, Hedecrone, and Hekinby, in the county of Kent, p. 339 ; 15 Ed. II.

Inquest as to Claypole bridge.   It is found that the inhabitants of Claypole are bound to repair it : " Ideo preceptum est vicecomiti Lincolniensi quod distringat homines predicte ville de Claypole ad reparandum et sustentandum pontem predictum in forma predicta," p. 350 ; 18 Ed. II, etc.

V

(p. 92)

THE KING'S JOURNEYS—PETITIONS AND STATUTES CONCERNING THE ROYAL PURVEYORS

"Nullus vicecomes vel ballivus noster vel aliquis alius capiat equos vel carettas alicujus pro cariagio faciendo, nisi reddat liberationem antiquitus statutam ; scilicet pro caretta ad duos equos decem denarios per diem, et pro caretta ad tres equos quatuordecim denarios perdiem." Magna Charta, first confirmation by Henry III, art. 23, A.D. 1216. "Statutes of the Realm," 1810, vol. i. p. 15. This article is found in successive confirmations of the great charter ; the germ of it was contained in John's original text, of 1215, art. 30.

"Item pur ceo qe le poeple ad esté moult grevé de ceo qe les bledz, feyns, bestaill, et autre manère de vitailles et biens des gentz de mesme le poeple, ont esté pris, einz ces houres . . . dont nul paiement ad esté fait, . . ." etc. Preamble to the statute 4 Ed. III, ch. iii. "Statutes of the Realm," A.D. 1330. See also statute 36 Ed. III, ch. ii.

Petition of the Commons, 25 Ed. III, 1351–52 ("Rolls of Parliament," vol. ii. p. 242) : "Item prie la commune qe là où avant ces heures les botillers nostre seigneur le roi et lour deputez soleient prendre moult plus de vyns à l'oeps le roi qe mestier ne fust ; desqueux ils mettont les plus febles à l'oeps le roi et les meliours à lour celers demesnes à vendre, et le remenant relessont à eux desqueux ils les pristerent, pur grantz fyns à eux faire pur chescun tonel, à grant damage et empoverissement des marchantz. . . ."

The inhabitants of the counties of Dorset and Somerset complain in the same way that the sheriff of these counties had taken of them "cynk centz quarters de furment et trois centz bacouns, à l'oeps le roi, come il dist, et il ne voillast pur sa graunt meistrie et seigneurie allower pur vintz quarteres fors qe pur sesse quarters, et c'est assaver bussell de dit blee fors que dis deniers, là où il vendist après pur xv deniers. Par quey vos liges gentz sount grauntement endamagé et vous, chier seigneur, n'estes servy des blées et des bacounes avauntditz. . . ." 4 Ed. III, 1331, "Rolls of Parliament," vol. ii. p. 40.

Petition of the Commons to the Good Parliament of 1376 :

"Item prie la commune qe come le roi de temps passé et ses progenitours, nobles princes, soleient avoir lour cariage, c'est assaver chivalx, charietz et charettes pur servir leur hostiel : et ore les purveours de l'hostel nostre dit seigneur le roi pur défaut de sa propre cariage et de bone governance prenont chivalx, charietz et charettes des povres communes, la environ par x leukes où le roi tient son hostel, si bien des gentz de loigne pays par xxiiii leukes ou lx passantz par la chymyne come des gentz demurrantz en mesme le pays, en grande arrerissement et poverisement des dites communes. . . ."
"Rolls of Parliament," vol. ii. p. 351.

Complaint of the clergy at being subjected to the exactions of the purveyors (1376) : "Item provisores et ministri regis pro provisionibus regiis faciendis feodum et loca ecclesiastica, invitis viris ecclesiasticis seu eorum custodibus non intrent, nec animalia aliaque res et bona inde auferant, prout fecerint et faciunt nunc indies, contra ecclesiasticam libertatem et constitutiones sanctorum patrum et statuta regni edita in hac parte. Nec in via extra feoda et loca predicta predictorum virorum cariagium carectasve capiant vel arrestent.

"Resp. Le roi le voet."
"Rolls of Parliament," vol. ii. p. 358

VI

(p. 112)

THE RECURRENCE OF LEET-DAYS AND VISITS OF JUSTICES

The Commons petition as follows the Good Parliament of 1376 : "Item où de ancien temps ad esté custume qe les presentours dussent presenter les articles du lete et de vewe de frank plegg tan soulement deux foitz par an, ... les baillifs avaunt ditz fount les povres gentz et les husbandes de pais, qeux dussent travailer en leur labours et husbandriez et pur le commune profit, venir de trois semaignes en trois à lour wapentachez et hundredez, par colour de presentement avoir, et rettent leur labours et leur husbanderiez au terre, sinoun q'ils leur veullent doner tiels ransons et fyns q'ils ne purront sustener ne endurer. . . .

"Resp. Il y ad estatutz suffisamment."
"Rolls of Parliament," 50 Ed. III, vol. ii. p. 357.
Again, the Commons having pointed out that the visits of the

justices in eyre are a very great cause of trouble and expense to the people in time of war, the king suppresses the visits of those magistrates while the war lasts, except when any "horrible" case may occur.

"Item prient les communes au roi leur seigneur q'il ne grante en nulle partie de roialme eire ne trailbaston durante la guerre, par queux les communes purront estre troblez ne empoveres, fors qe en horible cas.

"*Resp.* Le roi le voet."

"Rolls of Parliament," vol. ii. p. 305, 45 Ed. III, 1371.

VII

(p. 115)

THE DRESS OF THE WORLDLY MONK

According to the Council of London (1342) : ". . . Militari potius quam clericali habitu induti superiori, scilicet brevi seu stricto, notabiliter tamen et excessive latis, vel longis manicis, cubitos non tegentibus [tangentibus in Labbe] sed pendulis, *crinibus cum* [two words not in Labbe] furrura vel sandalo revolutis, et ut vulgariter dicitur, reversatis, et caputiis cum tipettis miræ longitudinis, barbisque prolixis incedere, et suis digitis annulos indifferenter portare publice, ac zonis stipatis pretiosis miræ magnitudinis supercingi, et bursis cum imaginibus variis sculptis, amellatis [annellatis, L.] et deauratis, ad ipsas patenter cum cultellis, ad modum gladiorum pendentibus, caligis etiam rubeis, scaccatis et viridibus, sotularibusque rostratis et incisis multimode, ac croperiis [propriis, L.] ad sellas, et cornibus ad colla pendentibus, epitogiis aut *clocis* [this word not in L.] furratis, uti patenter ad oram, contra sanctiones canonicas temere non verentur, adeo quod a laicis vix aut nulla patet distinctio clericorum." Wilkins' "Concilia Magnæ Britanniæ," London, 1737, vol. ii. p. 703 ; also in Labbe, "Sacrosancta Concilia," year 1342, vol. xxv. col. 1170.

According to the Council of York (1367) : "Nonnulli . . . vestes publice deferre præsumpserunt deformiter decurtatas, medium tibiarum suarum, seu genua nullatenus attingentes . . . ad jactantiam et suorum corporum ostentationem." Labbe, ibid. vol. xxvi. col. 467-8.

VIII

(p. 120)

EXACTIONS OF CERTAIN NOBLEMEN WHEN TRAVELLING

Petitions of the Commons, " Rolls of Parliament," vol. i. p. 290 (8 Ed II), A.D. 1314 : " Item par là où asquns grantz seignurs de la terre passent parmi le pays, ils entrent en maners et lieus de Seint Eglise et des autres, et pernent saunz congé le seignur et les baillifs gardeyns de meisme les leus, et encontre lour volunté, ceo q'il voillent saunz rien paer encontre la lei et les ordenaunces, non pas eaunz regard à l'escomenge (excommunication) doné encontre tutz tels. Et si homme les devi rien, debrisent les eus par force, et pernent et emportent ceo qe beal lour est, et batent les ministres et destruent les biens, plus qe il ne covendreit, et autres grevouses depiz ultrages fount.

" Item il prenent charettes et chivaux de fair lour cariages à lour voluntez saunz rien paer et des queux nientefoitz james n'est faite restoraunce à ceux qi les devient ; ne il n'osent suire ne pleindre pur le poair de diz seignur qar s'il le facent ils sont honiz ou en corps ou en chateux ; par quoi ladite comuneauté prie qe remedie soit fait en tels ultrages."

IX

(p. 130)

PASSAGE OF THE HUMBER IN A FERRY

" Ad peticionem hominum de Estriding petenc' remedium super nimia solucione exacta ad passagium de Humbr' ultra solitum modum." The king directs the opening of an inquest, with power to the commissioners to re-establish things in their prestine condition. " Rolls of Parliament," i. p. 202, 35 Ed. I, 1306.

Another petition under Edward II : " A nostre seigneur le [roi] et à son consail se pleint la comunauté de sa terre qe par là où homme soleit passer Humbre entre Hesel et Barton, homme à chival pour dener, homme à pée pur une maele, qe ore sunt il, par extorsion, mis à duble ; et de ceo priunt remedi pur Dieu." The king, in reply, orders that the masters of the ferry shall not take more than formerly : " vel quod significent causam quare id facere noluerint." Ibid., p. 291 ; 8 Ed. II, 1314-5.

X

(pp. 165 and 171)

THE RIGHT OF SANCTUARY

Examples of entries in the Durham sanctuary register : " Memorandum quod vj die mensis octobris, A° D^i M. CCCC LXX VII° Willielmus Rome et Willielmus Nicholson parochiæ de Forsate, convolarunt ad ecclesiam cath. Sancti Cuthberti Dunelm., ubi inter cætera pro feloniâ per eosdem commissâ et publice confessatâ, in, de, et pro occisione Willielmi Aliand, per eosdem antea occisi, pecierunt a venerabilibus et religiosis viris dominis Thomâ Haughton sacristâ ipsius ecclesiæ et Willielmo Cuthbert magistro Galileæ ibidem, fratribus et commonachis ejusdem ecclesiæ, immunitatem ecclesiæ, juxta libertates et privilegia gloriosissimo confessori Sancto Cuthberto antiquitus concessa, favorabiliter eis concedi, et per pulsacionem unius campanæ, ut est moris, favorabiliter obtinuerunt. Ibidem præsentibus, videntibus et audientibus, discretis viris Willielmo Heghyngton, Thomâ Hudson, Johanne Wrangham, et Thomâ Strynger, testibus ad præmissa vocatis specialiter et requisitis." "Sanctuarium Dunelmense," ed. J. Raine, Surtees Society ; London, 1827, No. v.

On the question of sanctuaries the councils are explicit : "Firmiter prohibemus ne quis fugientes ad ecclesiam, quos ecclesia debet tueri, inde violenter abstrahat, aut ipsos circa ecclesiam obsideat, vel eisdem substrahat victualia." Concilium provinciale Scoticanum, A.D. 1225, in Wilkins' "Concilia Magnæ Britanniæ," London, 1737, vol. i. p. 616.

As shown by the reports of cases in the Year Books, good care was to be taken by the refugee to flee to a church duly " dedicated by a bishop." Here is a case of the time of Edward I :—

" Quid[a]m captus fuit pro latrocinio, et ductus coram justiciariis et inculpatus, dixit : Domine, ego fui in ecclesia de N. et dehinc vi abstractus, unde imprimis peto juris beneficium quod mittar retro unde ibi fui vi abstractus.—*Justiciarius.* Nos dicimus quod ecclesia illa nunquam fuit dedicata per episcopum.—*Priso.* Sic, domine.—*Justiciarius.* Inquiratur per duodecim :—Qui dixerunt quod illa ecclesia nunquam fuit dedicata per episcopum.—*Justiciarius.* Modo oportet te respondere.—*Priso.* Sum bonus et fidelis : ideo de bono et malo pono, etc. (formula of submission to the decision of a jury, *patria*).—Duodecim nominati exiverunt ad deliberandos (*sic*)." "Year Books," edited by A. Horwood, 1863, vol. i. p. 541, Rolls Series. The final result is not given. The Year Books not infrequently give accounts of cases where the right of sanctuary is invoked by mere thieves as ready as any to avail themselves of the privilege.

The abuses resulting from the right of sanctuary, especially with reference to St. Martin's le Grand in London, are described as follows in one of the Commons' petitions : "Item prient les communes, coment diverses persones des diverses estatz, et auxi apprentices et servantz des plusours gentz, si bien demurrantz en la citée de Loundres et en les suburbes d'icell, come autres gentz du roialme al dite citée repairantz, ascuns en absence de lour meistres, de jour en autre s'enfuyent ove les biens et chatelx de lour ditz mestres à le collège de Seint Martyn le Grant en Loundres, à l'entent de et sur mesmes les biens et chateux illeoqes vivre à lour voluntée saunz duresse ou exécution du ley temporale sur eux illeoqes ent estre faite, et là sont ils resceux et herbergéez, et mesmes les biens et chateux par les ministres du dit collège al foitz seiséez et pris come forffaitz à le dit collège. Et auxi diverses dettours as plusours marchantz, si bien du dite citée, come d'autres vaillantz du roialme, s'enfuyent de jour en autre al dit collège ove lour avoir à y demurrer à l'entent avaunt dit. Et ensement plusours persones au dit collège fuéez et là demurrantz, pur lour faux lucre, forgent, fount et escrivent obligations, endentures, acquitances, et autres munimentz fauxes, et illeoqes les enseallent es nouns si bien de plusours marchantz et gentz en en la dite citée demurantz, come d'autres du dit roialme à lour disheriteson et final destruction. . . . Et en quelle collège de temps en temps sount receptz murdres, traitours, come tonsours du monoye del coigne le Roy, larons, robbours et autres diverses felouns malfaisours et destourbours de la pées nostre seignur le roy, par jour tapisantz et de noet issantz pur faire lour murdres, tresons, larcines, robbories et félonies. . . . Et après tieuz murdres, tresons, etc., faitz, al dit collège repairent." "Rolls of Parliament," vol. iii. p. 503, A.D. 1402.

XI

(p. 211)

A MONOPOLY OF MINSTRELSY FOR THE KING'S (EDWARD IV) OWN MINSTRELS

" *Pro Fraternitate Ministrallorum Regis* " (Rymer, " Fœdera," 24, 1469). "Rex (etc.) . . . Sciatis quod ex querelosa insinuatione dilectorum nobis Walteri Haliday, marescalli, Johannis Cliff (and six others) ministrallorum nostrorum accepimus qualiter nonnulli, rudes agricolæ et artifices diversarum misterarum Regni nostri Angliæ, finxerunt se fore ministrallos, quorum aliqui liberatam nostram eis minime datam portarent, seipsos etiam fingentes esse ministrallos nostros proprios, cujus quidem liberatæ ac dictæ artis sive occupationis ministrallorum colore, in diversis partibus regni nostri prædicti, grandes pecuniarum exactiones de ligeis nostris deceptive colligunt et recipiunt, et licet ipsi in arte vel sive occupatione illa minime intelligentes sive experti existant, et in diversis artibus et operationibus diebus ferialibus sive profestis utuntur et victum suum inde sufficienter percipiant, de loco tamen ad locum, in diebus festivalibus, discurrunt, et proficua illa totaliter percipiunt, e quibus ministralli nostri prædicti, et cæteri ministralli nostri pro tempore existentes, in arte sive occupatione prædicta sufficienter eruditi et instructi, nullisque aliis laboribus, occupationibus sive misteris utentes, vivere deberent."

For which cause, permission has been granted : " Ministrallis nostris quod ipsi, ad laudem et honorem Dei et ut specialius exorare teneantur pro salubri statu nostro et præcarissimæ consortis nostræ Elizabethæ reginæ Angliæ, dum agimus in humanis et pro animabus nostris cum ab hac luce migraverimus, necnon pro anima carissimi domini et patris nostri . . . tam in capella Beatæ Mariæ Virginis infra ecclesiam cathedralem sancti Pauli Londoniæ, quam in libera capella nostra regia sancti Anthonii, in eadem civitate nostra Londoniæ, quandam fraternitatem sive gildam (quam ut accepimus fratres et sorores fraternitatis ministrallorum regni nostri prædicti, retroactis temporibus inierunt . . .) stabilire, continuare et augmentare ac quascumque personas, tam homines quam mulieres eis grato animo adhærentes, in fratres et sorores fraternitatis sive gildæ prædictæ recipere . . . possint et valeant."

And for the good of the reconstituted gild, " volumus . . . quod nullus ministrallus regni nostri prædicti, quamvis in hujusmodi arte sive occupatione sufficienter eruditus existat, eadem arte . . . de cætero, nisi de fraternitate sive gilda prædicta sit et ad eandam admissus fuerit et cum cæteris confratribus ejusdem contribuerit aliquo modo utatur."

The beneficiaries of his monopoly will have a right to inquire throughout the realm, " de omnibus et singulis hujusmodi personis fingentibus se fore ministrallos," and to impose fines to be used " pro continua et perpetua sustentatione certarum candelarum cerearum vulgariter nuncupatarum *tapers*," in the before-mentioned chapels.

XII

(p. 213)

POPULAR ENGLISH SONGS OF THE MIDDLE AGES

The following collections may be consulted :

" Ancient Songs and Ballads from the reign of Henry II to the Revolution," collected by John Ritson, revised edition by W. C. Hazlitt, London, 1877.

" Political Songs of England from the reign of John to that of Edward II," edited by Thomas Wright ; Camden Society, London, 1839.

" Specimens of Lyric Poetry composed in England in the reign of Edward I," ed. Th. Wright, Percy Society, 1842.

" Reliquiæ antiquæ, scraps from ancient MSS. illustrating chiefly early English literature," ed. Th. Wright and J. O. Halliwell, 2 vols.

" Songs and Carols now first printed from a MS. of the xvth Century," edited by Thomas Wright ; Percy Society, London, 1847.

" Political Poems and Songs, from Edward III to Richard III," edited by Thomas Wright ; Rolls Series, London, 1859, 1861.

" Political, Religious, and Love Poems," edited by F. J. Furnivall; Early English Text Society, London, 1866.

" Catalogue of MS. Romances in the British Museum," by Henry L. D. Ward, vol. i., London, 1887. See as to Robin Hood ballads, pp. 516-23.

" Bishop Percy's folio MS.—Ballads and Romances," edited by J. W. Hales and F. J. Furnivall, Ballad Society, London, 1867.

" The English and Scottish popular Ballads," edited by Prof. F. J. Child, Boston, U.S.A., 1882, ff.

Many satirical songs are to be found in those collections on the vices of the times, the exaggerations of fashion, the ill government of the king, the Lollards, the friars, the women, with some songs in a higher key urging the king to defend the national honour and to make war. See for example Dr. Furnivall's collection, p. 4. In this work is printed the song referred to in our text on the death of the Duke of Suffolk (pp. 6-11) :

*Here folowythe a Dyrge made by the comons of Kent in the tyme
of ther rysynge, when Jake Cade was theyr cappitayn :*

*   *   *   *   *

Who shall execute yᵉ fest of solempnite ?
Bysshoppis and lords, as gret reson is.
Monkes, chanons, and prestis, withall yᵉ clergy,
Prayeth for hym that he may com to blys.

And that nevar such anothar come aftar this
His intersectures, blessid mot they be,
And graunt them to reygne with aungellis !
For Jake Napys sowle, placebo and dirige.

" Placebo," begyneth the bisshop of Hereforthe ;
" Dilexi," quod yᵉ bisshop of Chester.

XIII

(p. 314)

INDULGENCES AND THE THEORY OF THE "TREASURY" ACCORDING TO POPE CLEMENT VI

" Quantum ergo exinde ut nec supervacua, inanis aut superflua tantæ effusionis miseratio redderetur, thesaurum militanti Ecclesiæ acquisivit, volens suis thesaurizare filiis pius pater, ut sic sit infinitus thesaurus hominibus, quo qui usi sunt, Dei amicitiæ participes sunt effecti.   Quem quidem thesaurum non in ærario repositum, non in agro absconditum, sed per beatum Petrum cœli clavigerum, ejusque successores, suos in terris vicarios commisit fidelibus salubriter dispensandum, et propriis et rationabilibus causis, nunc pro totali, nunc pro partiali remissione pœnæ temporalis pro peccatis debitæ tam generaliter quam specialiter (prout cum Deo expedire cognoscerent) vere pœnitentibus et confessis misericorditer applicandum. Ad cujus quidem thesauri cumulum, beatæ Dei genetricis, omnium electorum a primo justo usque ad ultimum merita adminiculum præstare noscuntur, de cujus consumptione, seu minutione non est aliquatenus formidandum, tam propter infinita Christi (ut prædictum est) merita, quam pro eo quod quanto plures ex ejus applicatione trahuntur ad justitiam, tanto magis accrescit ipsorum cumulus meritorum."

" Dictionnaire dogmatique, historique, ascétique et pratique des indulgences," by Abbé P. Jouhanneaud, Paris, 1852, pp. 123-4, being vol. xxvii. of Migne's " Nouvelle encyclopédie théologique."

XIV

(p. 321)

SERMON ACCOMPANYING THE DISPLAY OF A PAPAL BULL (ON THE OCCASION OF THE COMING OF HENRY OF LANCASTER)

" ' Mes bonnes gens, entendez tous ici.
Vous savez bien coment le roy banny
A, à grant tort, vostre seigneur Henry,
    Et sans raison ;
Et pource j'ay fait impetracion
Au saint père, qui est nostre patron,
Que trestous ceulx auront rémission
    De leurs péchiez
De quoy oncques ilz furent entachiez,
De puis l'eure qu'ilz furent baptisiez,
Qui leur aideront tous certains en suez
    Celle journée ;
Et vesenci la bulle seellée,
Que le pappe de romme la louée
M'a envoié, et pour vous tous donnée,
    Mes bons amis.
Vueilliez lui donc aidier ses ennemis
A conquerre, et vous en serez mis
Avecques ceux qui sont en paradis
    Après la mort.'
Lors veissiez jeune, viel, feble, et fort
Murmure faire, et par commun accort,
Sans regarder ni le droit ni le tort,
    Eulx émouvoir,
Cuidant que ce c'on leur fist assavoir
Feust vérité, tous le courent de voir ;
Car de sens n'ont guères ne de savoir,
    De telz y a.
L'arcevesque ce conseil cy trouva."

" French metrical history of the deposition of King Richard II," by Créton, edited and translated into English by Rev. J. Webb. " Archæologia," t. xx. p. 310.
This speech is attributed by the chronicler to Thomas Arundel,

Archbishop of Canterbury, and is supposed to have been delivered at the time of the landing of Henry of Lancaster in 1399 (Henry IV).

XV

(pp. 324, 327, 337)

ECCLESIASTICAL DOCUMENTS CONCERNING CHIEFLY ENGLISH PARDONERS

Richard de Bury on the Pardoners, A.D. 1340 :

"Cum sit statutum in canone ne qui eleemosynarum quæstores ad prædicandum aut indulgentias clero et populo insinuandum sine literis dioecesanis aut apostolicis admittantur, literæque apostolicæ quæstoribus hujusmodi concessæ ante admissionem eorum per diocesanos examinari debeant diligenter : ex gravi tamen multorum querela ad nostrum pervenit auditum, quod nonnulli ex hujusmodi quæstoribus, non sine multa temeritatis audacia, motu suo proprio, in animarum subditorum nostrorum periculum et jurisdictionis nostræ elusionem manifestam, indulgentias populo concedunt, super votis dispensant, et perjuriis, homicidiis, usuris et peccatis aliis, sibi confitentes absolvunt, et male ablata, data sibi aliqua pecuniæ quantitate, remittunt, ac alias abusiones quamplurimas faciunt et exponunt, vobis in virtute obedientiæ, firmiter inhibemus et per vos omnibus rectoribus, vicariis et capellariis parochialibus, vestri archidiaconatus, inhiberi volumus et mandamus, ne aliqui quæstores hujusmodi, cujuscumque extiterint conditionis, ad prædicandum aut indulgentias aliquas insinuandum clero et populo in ecclesiis parochialibus ac locis aliis vestri archidiaconatus memorati, absque literis nostris et licentia speciali de cætero admittantur ; pecuniam etiam et res quascumque, per hujusmodi quæstores, aut ad eorum instantiam collectas . . . indilate faciatis sequestrari. . . . Datum in manerio nostro de la Welehall' octavo die mensis Decembris, A° D^i m°ccc°xl° et consecrationis nostræ vii^{mo}."

"Registrum Palatinum Dunelmense," edited by T. D. Hardy, vol. iii. p. 325.

Provincial Synod of Dublin, 1348 :

"Cap. xxii. *De quæstoribus.* Item, quia eleemosynarum quæstores nonnullas abusiones in suis prædicationibus proponunt, ut decipiant simplices tantum, et nonnulla alia bona subtili vel fallaci

potius ingenio extorqueant, nonnulla etiam mala in deceptionem
animarum multiplicem perpetrentur ; statuimus et ordinamus, quod
nullus amodo quæstor sine literis archiepiscopi vel dioec. admittatur
quovismodo. . . . Sacerdotes vero qui alio modo quam supra dicto,
quæstores ad prædicandum voluntarie et scienter admittunt, per
annum a celebratione divinorum ipso facto sint suspensi ; et ipsi
quæstores, si contra præmissa aliquid attentaverint, ipso facto sint
excommunicati. Et si per quadraginta dies perseveraverint, ad
significationem episcoporum capiantur et incarcerentur, quousque de
talibus aliud fuerit per loci dioecesanum dispositum. Quascunque
literas hujusmodi quæstoribus hactenus concessas revocamus, præ-
missarum sententiarum relaxatione sine absolutione loci dioecesani
reservata. Et capellani pecuniam ea occasione receptam ecclesiis
cathedralibus restituant triplicatam."

Wilkins, " Concilia," 1737, vol. ii. p. 750.

Bull of Pope Urban V, " contra quæstores hospitalis Jerusalem
in Anglia," 1369 :

" Urbanus . . . archiepiscopo Cant. ejusque suffraganeis, salutem. . . . Nuper dilectis filiis Johanne Sancti Dunstani West.,
Ricardo B. Mariæ Wolnoth, rectoribus, et Philippo de Braunton,
ac Willelmo de Eya, perpetuis vicariis parochialibus ecclesiarum
London. Exon. et Norwicen. dioec. ac nonnullis aliis rectoribus
. . . nobis referentibus percepimus, quod quæstores priorum,
præceptorum et confratrum domorum hospitalis S. Johannis Jeru-
salemitani in Anglia, de voluntate, conniventia, ratihabitione, seu
mandato dictorum priorum . . . in pluribus contra juris et rationis
metas impudenter excedunt. . . . nonnulli tamen quæstores priorum
et confratrum prædictorum, gratia quæstus hujusmodi . . . ad
rectorum et vicariorum hujusmodi ecclesias accedentes, et se ad
prædicandum seu exponendum populo hujusmodi negotia quæstuaria
offerentes, licet congrue et legitime requisiti, literas sedis apostolicæ
vel dioecesani loci eisdem rectoribus seu vicariis sic requirentibus,
ostendere seu exhibere penitus non curarunt neque curant ; quin
verius de voluntate, conniventia seu mandato de quibus prædicitur,
denegarunt expresse contra constitutiones canonicas . . . præten-
dentes ipsos priores et fratres pro se et eorum quæstoribus in ea parte
fore notorie privilegiatos, licet hoc neque notorium fuerit neque
verum ; et ut quadam astutia colorata ipsos rectores, et vicarios
exhibitionem literarum hujusmodi sic petentes, acrius fatigent laboribus
et expensis, ipsos eo quod exhibitionem literarum hujusmodi sic

deposcebant et deposcunt, tanquam injuriatores contra eorum privilegia manifestos, et quæstuum suorum impeditores proclamarunt et proclamant, ipsosque ea occasione coram eorum conservatoribus seu subconservatoribus ad loca diversa et quandoque valde remota fecerunt et faciunt ad judicium evocari, et per conservatores sive subconservatores hujusmodi contra eosdem processus indebitos fieri, eosque nonnunquam excommunicari, aggravari et denunciari licet de facto, ac alia eis gravamina quamplura inferri procurarunt et procurant, in ipsorum rectorum et vicariorum grave præjudicium et scandalum plurimorum : et insuper quæstores prædicti frequenter et potissime, quando satagunt alicui rectori seu vicario nocere, ad ipsius rectoris seu vicarii ecclesiam in aliquo die festo, præcipue quando populus solitus est offerre, accedunt, et ibidem quæstuare, seu nomina fratriæ seu fraternitatis suæ legere incipiunt et continuant usque ad talem illius diei festi horam, qua missa ibidem pro illo die convenienter non potest celebrari ; sicque rectores et vicarios hujusmodi suis faciunt oblationibus, quæ eis in missis hujusmodi obveniunt, nequiter defraudari.   Insuper in ecclesiis et locis ad eos seu dictum hospitale nullatenus pertinentibus, licet publice interdictis seu pollutis divina faciant etiam publice celebrari, et in eis pro eorum libito per se et alios sepeliunt corpora defunctorum ; officium quoque seu negotium quæstuandi personis simplicibus et quasi illiteratis committunt, qui simplices aliis simplicibus erroneum præstantes ducatum, generaliter, ut de spiritualibus taceamus, in populo diffundunt errores."

Wilkins, " Concilia," London, 1737, vol. iii. p. 83.

Letter of Simon Sudbury, Archbishop of Canterbury, A.D. 1378 :

" Simon, etc., dilecto filio commissario nostro Cantuar. generali, salutem, etc.   Ad nostrum audientiam est perlatum, quod licet eleemosynarum quæstores, nisi apostolicas vel dioecesani episcopi literas exhibuerint, admitti non debeant, vel permitti indulgentias sibi concessas insinuare, et populo prædicare ; nonnulli tamen quæstores, qui non sine multa temeritatis audacia, et deceptione multiplici animarum, ac elusione populi christiani, indulgentias remissionesque falsas et frivolas, et alia erronea . . . prædicant abusive, tam per vos, quam per official. archidiaconi nostri Cantuar. de diebus in dies indifferenter illicite admittuntur, nos, abusus hujusmodi omnimodo abolere volentes, vobis . . . inhibemus et per vos dicto officiali ac omnibus aliis nobis subditis . . . inhiberi volumus et mandamus ne quæstores hujusmodi absque nostris literis sufficientibus in hac parte, ac vobis et ipsis liquere possit literas apostolicas quæstorum hujusmodi si quas habent, per nos examinatas primitus extitisse, admittatis ibidem de cætero vel admittant."

Wilkins, " Concilia," vol. iii. p. 131.

Bull of Pope Boniface IX, A.D. 1390 :

" Ad audientiam nostram, non sine magna mentis displicentia fidedignorum quamplurimum relatio perduxit quod quidam religiosi diversorum etiam mendicantium ordinum et nonnulli clerici sæculares etiam in dignitatibus constituti, asserentes se a nobis aut a diversis legatis seu nuntiis sedis apostolicæ missos, et ad plura peragenda negotia diversas facultates habere per partes, in quibus es pro nobis et Ecclesia Romana thesaurarius deputatus, discurrunt, et veras vel prætensas, quas se habere dicunt, facultates fideli et simplici populo nunciant et irreverenter veris hujusmodi facultatibus abutentes, suas fimbrias, ut vel sic turpem et infamem quæstum faciant, impudenter dilatant, et non veras et prætensas facultates hujusmodi mendaciter simulant, cum etiam pro qualibet parva pecuniarum summula, non pœnitentes, sed mala conscientia satagentes iniquitati suæ, quoddam mentitæ absolutionis velamen prætendere, ab atrocibus delictis, nulla vera contritione, nullaque debita præcedenti forma (ut verbis illorum utamur) absolvant ; male ablata, certa et incerta, nulla satisfactione prævia (quod omnibus sæculis absurdissimum est) remittant ; castitatis, abstinentiæ, peregrinationis ultramarinæ, seu beatorum Petri et Pauli de urbe aut Jacobi in Compostella apostolorum, et alia quævis vota, levi compensatione commutent ; de hæresi vel schismate nominatim aut incidenter condemnatos, absque eo quod in debita forma abjurent et quantum possunt debite satisfaciant, non tantum absolvant, sed in integrum restituant ; cum illegitime genitis, ut ad ordines et beneficia promoveri possint, et intra gradus prohibitos copulatis aut copulandis dispensent, et eis qui ad partes infidelium absque sedis prædictæ licentia transfretarunt, vel merces prohibitas detulerunt, et etiam qui Romanæ aut aliarum ecclesiarum possessiones, jura, et bona occuparunt, excommunicationis et alias sententias et pœnas, et quævis interdicta relaxent, et indulgentiam quam felicis recordationis Urbanus Papa VI prædecessor noster, christifidelibus certas basilicas et ecclesias dictæ urbis instanti anno visitantibus concessit, et quæ in subsidium Terræ Sanctæ accedentibus conceduntur, quibusvis elargiri pro nihilo ducant, . . . et quæstum, quem exinde percipiunt, nomine cameræ apostolicæ se percipere asserant, et nullam de illo nihilominus rationem velle reddere videantur : Horret et merito indignatur animus, talia reminisci. . . .

" Attendentes igitur quod nostra interest super tot tantisque malis
de opportunis remediis salubriter providere, fraternitati tuæ de qua
in iis et aliis specialem in domino fiduciam obtinemus, per apostolica
scripta committimus et mandamus, quatenus religiosis et clericis
sæcularibus hujusmodi, ac eorum familiaribus, complicibus, et collegiis,
et aliis, vocatis qui fuerint evocandi, summarie, simpliciter, et de
plano, ac sine strepitu et figura judicii, etiam ex officio super præmissis,
auctoritate nostra, inquiras diligentius veritatem, et eos ad reddendum
tibi computum de receptis et reliqua consignandum, remota appella-
tione, compellas, et quos per inquisitionem hujusmodi excessisse, vel
non verum aut non sufficiens seu ad id non habuisse mandatum
inveneris, capias et tandiu sub fida custodia teneas carceribus manci-
patos, donec id nobis intimaveris."

Baronius' " Annales ecclesiastici " ; continuation by Raynaldus,
ed. 1752, vol. vii. p. 525.

Opinion of the University of Oxford on Pardoners, A.D. 1414 :

" *Articulus tricesimus nonus ; contra falsas prædicationes quæstorum.*—Quia inverecundi quæstores turpissimos suos quæstus ad
firmam emunt cum Simone, indulgentias vendunt cum Gyesi, et
adquisita consumunt cum filio prodigo inhoneste, sed quod magis
est detestabile, cum non sint in sacris ordinibus constituti, publice
prædicant, ac false prætendunt quod absolvendi a pœna et a culpa
tam superstites quam defunctos plenam habeant potestatem, cum
aliis blasphemiis, quibus populum spoliant ac seducunt, et verisimiliter
ad tartara secum trahunt, præstantes spem frivolam et audaciam ad
peccandum.   Abusus igitur hujusmodi sectæ pestiferæ ab ecclesiæ
limitibus deleantur."

*Articuli concernentes reformationem universalis ecclesiæ, editi per
universitatem Oxon.*   Wilkins, " Concilia," vol. iii. p. 365.

Suppression of pardoners by the Council of Trent, A.D. 1562 :

" Cum multa a diversis antea conciliis, tam Lateranensi ac
Lugdunensi, quam Viennensi, adversus pravos eleemosynarum
quæstorum abusus remedia tunc adhibita, posterioribus temporibus
reddita fuerint inutilia, potiusque eorum malitia ita quotidie magno
fidelium omnium scandalo et querela excrescere deprehendatur, ut
de eorum emendatione nulla spes amplius relicta videatur, statuit
ut posthac in quibuscumque christianæ religionis locis eorum nomen
atque usus penitus aboleatur, nec ad officium hujusmodi exercendum

ullatenus admittantur ; non obstantibus privilegiis, ecclesiis, monasteriis, hospitalibus, piis locis et quibusvis cujuscumque gradus, status et dignitatis personis, concessis, aut consuetudinibus etiam immemorabilibus. Indulgentias vero aut alias spirituales gratias, quibus non ideo christifideles decet privari, deinceps per ordinarios locorum, adhibitis duobus de capitulo, debitis temporibus populo publicandas esse decernit. Quibus etiam eleemosynas, atque oblata sibi charitatis subsidia, nulla prorsus mercede accepta, fideliter colligendi facultas datur, ut tamdem cœlestes hos Ecclesiæ thesauros, non ad quæstum sed ad pietatem exerceri, omnes vere intelligant."

"Conciliorum generalium Ecclesiæ catholicæ, Pauli V Pont. Max. auctoritate editus." Tomus iv, Rome, 1628, second paging, p. 261.

XVI

(p. 344)

THE FIRST RECORDED CRUCIFIX IN ENGLAND SCULPTURED FROM LIFE

Thomas of Burton, Abbot of Meaux, near Beverley, writes : " Dictus autem Hugo abbas xv^{us} crucifixum novum in choro conversorum fecit fabricari. Cujus quidem operarius nullam ejus formosam et notabilem proprietatem sculpebat nisi in feria sexta, in qua pane et aqua tantum jejunavit. Et hominem nudum coram se stantem prospexit, secundum cujus formosam imaginem crucifixum ipsum aptius decoraret. Per quem etiam crucifixum Omnipotens manifesta miracula fecerat incessanter. Unde tunc etiam putabatur quod, si mulieres ad dictum crucifixum accessum haberent, augmentaretur communis devotio, et in quam plurimum commodum nostri monasterii, redundaret. Super quo abbas Cistercii a nobis requisitus, suam licentiam nobis impertivit ut homines et mulieres honestæ accedere possent ad dictum crucifixum, dum tamen mulieres per claustrum et dormitorium seu alia officina intrare non permittantur. . . . Cujus quidem licentiæ prætextu, malo nostro, feminæ sæpius aggrediuntur dictum crucifixum, præcipue cum in eis frigescat devotio, dum illuc ut ecclesiam tantum introspiciant accesserint, et sumptus nostros augeant in hospitatione earundem." "Chronica monasterii de Melsa," edited by E. A. Bond, 1866–68, vol. iii. p. 35, Rolls Series.

XVII

(p. 141, 362)

THE PILGRIMAGE OF REYNARD

Tired of his sins, duly shriven, ordered by the hermit to go to Rome, and there receive absolution, Reynard,

> " Escrepe et bordon prent, si muet,
> Si est entres en son chemin,
> Molt resemble bien pélerin,
> Et bien li sist l'escrepe au col."

He does not care to travel alone and, like most pilgrims, prefers company :

> " Mes de ce se tint il por fol
> Qu'il est meüz sans compaignie,
> Le grant chemin n'ira il mie,
> Ançois l'avoit laissié à destre,
> Une sente torne à senestre,"

and leads him to a place where he finds

> " dan Belin
> Le moton qui se reposoit,"

and whom he persuades to go with him, thus avoiding, he suggests, being eaten by his owners. A third member, the donkey, is soon added to their party :

> " En lor chemin en sont entrè,
> Mes il n'orent guères erré,
> Qant trovent Bernart l'archeprestre
> En un fossé les cardons pestre,"

and he is easily persuaded to follow. They enter the forest. Night comes. Where shall they find shelter ? Why should we, Reynard remarks, look for any other " ostel " than the fine grass under this tree ?

> " Et nos queil ostel querrion
> Fors la bele erbe soz cest arbre ?
> Meus l'eim que un paleis de marbre."

Appealing as must have been the fine grass to him, Belin objects, the wood being so dangerous. So they continue their journey until they reach the " ostel Primaut," that is the house of Primaut the Wolf, who was away. There they find

> " Char salée, formache et oes . . .
> Si i trovent bone cervoise.
> Tant boit Belins que il s'envoise ;
>   Si a commencié à chanter
> Et l'archeprestre à orguaner,
> Et dan Renart chante en fauset."

Concluding speech of Reynard, after the siege of the house by the wolves, and the miscarriage of the pilgrimage :

> " Segnor, dist Renart, par mon chef,
> Cest eires est pesant et gref ;
> Il a el siécle meint prodome
> Qu' onques encor ne fu à Rome :
> Tiex est revenuz de sept seinz
> Qui est pires qu'il ne fu einz.
> Je me voil metre en mon retor,
> Et si vivrai de mon labor
> Et gaaignerai léelment,
> Si ferai bien à povre gent.
> Lors ont crié : outrée, outrée !
> Si ont fete la retornée."

" Le roman de Renart," ed. Ernest Martin, Strasbourg and Paris, 1882 ff, 7 vols. ; i. pp. 269 ff.

INDEX

Printed in Great Britain by
UNWIN BROTHERS, LIMITED, LONDON AND WOKING